THE FLOWER
AND THE CASTLE

THE FLOWER
AND THE CASTLE

An Introduction to Modern Drama

MAURICE VALENCY

The Universal Library
Grosset & Dunlap
NEW YORK

We gratefully acknowledge permission to quote excerpts from Michael Meyer's translation of "The Master Builder," "The Lady from the Sea," "John Gabriel Borkman," and "When We Dead Awaken," from *When We Dead Awaken and Three Other Plays*, published by Doubleday and Company, Inc., and by Rupert Hart-Davis; and excerpts from Arvid Paulson's translation of *Letters of Strindberg to Harriet Bosse* published by Grosset and Dunlap, Inc.

A Note to the Present Edition

At THE time of its initial publication it seemed both apt and pleasant to begin what purported to be *An Introduction to Modern Drama* with a discussion of the work of Ibsen and Strindberg, and also to end it there. But time belittles all things, and it has now become apparent that without some further effort to round out the subject, the title must be considered unduly compendious. I have, accordingly, attempted to advance my discussion somewhat further with an essay on the plays of Chekhov, whose influence on the modern theatre can be considered second in importance only to that of the Scandinavian masters. This second volume of what threatens to take on the look of a series will appear almost concurrently with the present edition of *The Flower and the Castle* which in some sense it supplements. I have called it, for reasons that will be obvious, *The Breaking String*.

It must be admitted that now that this process of amplification has been initiated, it will very likely require more firmness of character to halt it than I appear at present to have at my disposal.

There is no doubt in my mind that *The Breaking String* implies yet another volume on the drama, and perhaps, before I can conveniently say *nunc dimittis*, there will be a fourth. I must confess that I am alarmed not only by the relentless logic of this process, but also by the formidable dimensions which this introduction insists on assuming; but, in the circumstances, there seems to be nothing for it save to continue, with God's help, in the pious hope that this vastly extended work will serve some useful purpose.

15 May 1966   M. J. V.

Foreword

$\mathbb{S}$AVE for my reluctance to lengthen what is already "a successive title long and dark," I should have put Ibsen and Strindberg on the title page of this book. It chiefly concerns them.

An introduction to the study of modern drama might well be expected to deal with the dozen or so major figures from Ibsen to Brecht. But to examine in detail the work of so many is manifestly impossible in a book of manageable proportions, and there is certainly no present need to go over this material yet again in summary fashion. I have contented myself, therefore, with concentrating on the plays of the two great Scandinavians, considering that of all those who have had a hand in shaping the drama of the last half-century, these are the least dispensable, and that anyone who understands what concerns their art will have gone a long way toward comprehending the rest. The better part of this book relates, accordingly, to the ways in which Ibsen and Strindberg received and transmitted the traditions which are chiefly influential in the modern theatre.

To this end, I thought it might be of some use to sketch briefly the evolution of the dramatic genres to the point where Ibsen first made his mark in the theatre; but these chapters are in no sense intended to serve as a history of the drama, and the thoughtful reader will note that I have been scrupulous to omit whatever seemed irrelevant to the end in view, regardless of its importance in other respects. The selection of material in a discussion of this sort must, of course, in the last analysis remain a matter of opinion. If, in my effort to clarify Ibsen, I have devoted a good deal of space to Scribe and Dumas, and little or none to Shakespeare and Schiller, I have done so wholly without prejudice to the taste of those who may consider that the matter would be handled properly the other way on. The subject is spacious; there is surely room in it for more than one approach, and I have advanced my viewpoint as informative, but by no means exclusive. Something of the sort might be said also with regard to the view I have taken with regard to the relative importance of Ibsen's early plays. One might well begin the study of Ibsen with *Catiline* or *The Pretenders* or *Love's Comedy*. I have begun with *Brand*.

In presenting this material, I have tried to emphasize particularly two of its aspects. The first has to do with the relation, in each case, of the artist to his work. The second involves the connection of this work with the other arts. It is obvious that by reason of its synthetic nature as poem, picture, ceremony, and sermon, the drama has been particularly susceptible to influences external to the theatre. I have, in consequence, tried to keep in mind, for the purposes of this discussion, at least the major tendencies of the aesthetic revolution which formed the background—and occasionally the foreground also—of the development of the theatre in the course of the last century.

It serves, perhaps, no useful purpose in a book directed primarily to English-speaking readers to refer extensively to works written in Danish and Swedish—languages which, for some extraordinary reason, seem to many as remote as Sanskrit. In the present case, there is no alternative. In spite of the attention which Ibsen and Strindberg have attracted in countries other than their own, especially in recent years, the better part of the work of research and criticism has been done by Scandinavian scholars, and only a meagre portion of this work exists in translation. Wherever possible, I have referred to English and German versions; unhappily, this leaves a very significant proportion of necessary text which can as yet be read only in the original.

With respect to the primary texts, I have been able to refer with some consistency to the collected works of Ibsen in Archer's edition, which, with all its shortcomings, has the merit of being, at least, complete and ubiquitous; but I have also referred occasionally to the translations of J. W. McFarlane and Michael Meyer. In dealing with poetry, in those cases where it seemed important that the reader should have the original before him, I have quoted the Danish text of the *Samlede digterverker*, edited by Didrik Arup Seip, and published in 1922. In the case of Strindberg, citation is complicated by the fact that there exists as yet in English no complete edition even of his plays, and the current available translations, while often stimulating, are obviously not intended to serve a scholarly purpose. I have therefore used Landquist's monumental edition of the collected works as a general basis of reference; but for the more familiar plays I have referred to the popular edition of Strindberg's poetic and prose plays published by Bonniers in recent years, and available, I believe, almost everywhere in this country. For the manifest infelicities of the literal translations I have occasionally set before the reader, I hereby solicit his forgiveness, at the same time inviting him by all means to improve upon them if he is so disposed.

It remains only to write a word of thanks to my friends and colleagues, whose interest and encouragement have added immeasurably to the pleasure I have had in putting these chapters together. I am particularly indebted to Dr. Toby Lelyveld, to Dr. Samuel F. Johnson, to Dr. Oscar James Campbell, to Dr. Carl R. Woodring, to Mrs. Kathie Kindquist, and to Mrs. James P. Harrison, who have read the manuscript and made valuable suggestions; to Mr. John N. Waddell of the Columbia University Libraries; to Mr. Emile Capouya, whose gentle guidance and support has been a source of great comfort in my various hours of need; finally, to Janet Cornell, my wife whose expert assistance saved me much tribulation. I am grateful also to the John Simon Guggenheim Foundation which facilitated my work abroad through a timely grant, and to the Administration of Columbia University which made a pleasant contribution toward the expense of preparing the manuscript.

M. J. V.

Contents

Contents

THE FLOWER
AND THE CASTLE

Introduction

A GREAT deal has happened in the theatre since the turn of
the century. The idioms of the stage have changed perceptibly. The texture of drama has loosened. Its forms have developed. Its subject matter has been several times renewed. New
currents are felt; new departures announced. Yet essentially nothing
has altered. The drama of our time is, on the whole, the drama
of Ibsen and Strindberg.

The reason is clear. The cultural transition out of which these
dramatists developed is still in progress. In their plays we see
clearly reflected the tensions between the old world and the new.
These are also the tensions of our time. From a cultural viewpoint,
the First World War appears to have changed nothing, and the
period that succeeded it has not yet acquired a distinct profile.
Three trends shaped the art of Ibsen and Strindberg—naturalism,
impressionism, symbolism. These currents are still dynamically
effective. To them and to their consequences—among which must
be numbered the expressionistic tendency of Strindberg's later

plays—may be related everything, or almost everything, that has happened in the drama of the last half-century.

Long before the time of Ibsen, the ancient edifice was crumbling. By the middle of the nineteenth century the system of values which had stood firm during the long twilight of the Renaissance seemed to be so thoroughly decayed that it would no longer support the weight of a doubt. Yet to this day it has not toppled. Ramshackle as they are, we still inhabit the ancient mansions, marvelling all the time that they still afford a semblance of shelter. It was not too different in the 1860's. The world then must have seemed less critically balanced than it does now, but already it seemed to many to have reached the limit of stability. Romanticism had called everything into question; then romanticism was called into question; then came the turn of positivism, and its consequences, and again a reaction. At the end of the century it was no longer clear what shape Western culture was to take, but already sensitive souls were experiencing premonitions of disaster. *"Nous sommes,"* wrote d'Aurevilly, *"une race à sa dernière heure."* [1] There was no time during the next half-century when these premonitions could be set aside. The significant drama of this period was never far from anxiety. Most often it expressed despair.

After the middle of the century, ideas and systems succeeded one another with bewildering rapidity. In Ibsen's youth, the Hegelian dialectic was supreme. In the 1850's it gave place to Schopenhauer's concept of the blind Will. In the 1870's the pessimism of Schopenhauer was less in vogue than the pessimism of Hartmann. Before long, the social theorists controlled the best thought of the period; then came the turn of the psychologists, then the physicists. Meanwhile, in artistic circles, the enthusiasm for the destruction of the classic modes developed into a frenzy comparable to the madness of those who, in the time of Augustine, collaborated to destroy antiquity in the name of Christ.

In the nineteenth century the new faith was not so clearly defined as in the fifth. If faith in God could not be justified, the only recourse was faith in man. But man, traditionally corrupt and full of guilt, offered no secure basis on which to found a church. A period of remarkable confusion ensued in which the only certainty was that neither the weight of tradition nor the prospect of a chaotic future could be borne with comfort. In these circumstances, every sort of social theory was advanced and explored to justify the demolition of the past and to accelerate the organization of the future. In comparison with the radicalism of those times, the radicalism of the present seems singularly unimaginative.

By the time modern drama may be said to begin, toward the middle of the century, it was generally agreed that the great dramatic forms were lost, perhaps forever. This was attributed to the meanness of the times. "When people," Goethe had said, "compare the pieces of Lessing with those of the ancients, and call them faulty and miserable, what is one to say? Rather let us pity the extraordinary man for being obliged to live in a pitiful time which afforded him no better materials than are treated in his plays . . ." A half-century later, in 1879, Matthew Arnold wrote of the absence of important drama in England:

In England we have no modern drama at all. Our vast society is not homogeneous enough, not sufficiently united, even any large portion of it, in a common view of life, a common ideal capable of serving as a basis for a modern English drama.

For James Huneker, in 1908, the whole spectrum of dramatic activity had a revolutionary look, and he lumped the major dramatists of his day, from Ibsen to Maeterlinck, under the title of "Iconoclasts." At the head of the list he put Ibsen—"the romantic revolutionist and intellectual anarch"—and Strindberg—"the mad genius, the atheist, the socialist." Some two decades later, Bernhard Diebold blamed the irresponsibility of the German expressionists on Strindberg, whom he accused of using sentimental and sensational effects to compensate for his intellectual shortcomings. During the next generation Strindberg's star was steadily in the ascendant; nevertheless, Joseph Wood Krutch, writing in 1953, saw Ibsen and Strindberg in much the same light as Huneker. To him it seemed that while Ibsen was a moral writer, his plays did much to deepen the chasm between the past and the future, while Strindberg saw man as essentially irrational, "neurotic, self-destructive and unhappy." Both writers, in Mr. Krutch's view, marked the end of the ordered, rational, comfortable world of the Renaissance, and to them, as much as to anyone, were traceable the unsettling tendencies of the modern stage. In 1962, Mr. F. L. Lucas treats Ibsen with the reverence due to a classic, but he yields to none in his antipathy to Strindberg.[2]

It is entirely possible that Mr. Krutch is right, though the case is perhaps not so simple as he makes it. Before Ibsen, nobody wrote like Ibsen. But Ibsen did not make a new departure. He merely developed and enhanced the dramatic patterns of his time to a point of great excellence, and succeeded in imposing upon them in a very definite way the cachet of his genius. He was not an original thinker. His drama involved no intellectual innovation; at the most it represents a synthesis of the best thought of his time. For the rest, he inherited the system of Scribe, and shared the interests of the French masters of the Second Empire. Like other northern writers of his day, he came successively under the influence of Schiller, Holberg, Kierkegaard, Hegel, and Brandes. Like Strindberg, he was essentially an impressionist who came at a certain point of his life under the influence of French symbolism. These were also the influences he transmitted. He marks, therefore, neither the beginning nor the end of a tradition, but a particularly eventful phase of its development, and if there is much in his work that seems absolutely novel, it is because greatness is always astonishing.

If Ibsen represents the orderly movement of progressive thought since the time of Rousseau, Strindberg represents the reaction. He took his departure, doubtless, from the same point as Ibsen; but, in time, what Ibsen stood for became hateful to Strindberg. To him also it seemed that the progressive thought of his day ran counter to the moral structure of the universe: in a period of decadence, he thought it was necessary above all to find God. God was everywhere and he was inescapable; but he was elusive. One had to look for him in the middle ages, in the seventeenth century, among the Gnostics, the Cabalists, the transcendental philosophers, and, failing these, in one's heart. Man was pitiable, but God was there; consequently, happiness might be found "on the other side," or at least, blessedness. Thus, far from being the mad atheist that Huneker called him, Strindberg illustrates the development of a highly moral nature, deeply sensitive to the emotional and intellectual currents of its time, which after great spiritual tribulation found its faith and made its peace with God. The process and the type are classical. St. Paul prefigured both, and Strindberg had Paul very much in mind.

Before Strindberg, nobody wrote like Strindberg; but Strindberg, also, said nothing new. It is not his thought, but its effect in the theatre that seems extraordinary. Very likely he is the most influential of the dramatists of the nineteenth century. At the least, in point of influence, he rivals Ibsen. He opened many doors with his diamond; but the doors were there before he came.

The question of what precisely is modern in modern drama obviously admits of no simple answer. In the contemporary theatre there is everything, higgledy-piggledy, and all on an equal footing. Not only is it possible during a single season in New York, Paris, or London to sample almost every style of drama from Sophocles to Genet, but even in a single play such as, for example, Mr. Miller's *Death of a Salesman*, it is possible to review the entire history of the drama from tragedy to expressionism. In this absence of order there is undoubtedly something zestful. Confusion has a vitality that arouses hope. In this respect our time furnishes an interesting contrast to those periods of high dramatic activity— the time of Euripides, the age of Shakespeare, the period of Corneille and Racine—when the conventions of the theatre seemed relatively stable, and people were likely to be shocked by innovations which in our day seem so slight that they need to be pointed out by scholars.

Yet each of these periods in which the drama attained greatness, and a seemingly permanent stability, initiated a period of transition. In the plays of Euripides we see the greatness of Attic culture, and also the germs of its decay. Shakespeare reflects the full glory of the Renaissance, and he foreshadows its passing. In the classic art of Racine is already implicit the romanticism of Rousseau. In Strindberg we see the acme of romantic individualism, and the first signs of the age of Freud. The stages in the evolution of Western art appear to be marked by impressive rituals: one would say that culture too had its rites of passage.

The decisive trend in the drama since the time of Ibsen has been the shift in emphasis from the external to the inner world, from the representation of the movement of a story to the depiction of the movements of the soul. From our viewpoint in the twentieth century, all great drama appears to have mirrored the soul. But the depth of insight which, for us, characterizes the work of the great dramatists was perhaps not their principal concern. It is likely that they had other aims, moral, philosophic, poetic, or simply narrative, and that the depth of psychological perception which astonishes us in their work was a consequence of the writer's genius, but by no means its primary object. In the drama, especially, it becomes evident that a work of art is the result of a collaborative effort which may require centuries for its consummation. Great works seldom spring in all their maturity from the brow of genius. Ordinarily they receive the ministrations of many diverse temperaments over a long period of time before they attain the necessary ripeness. In this manner each age adds its modicum to a work of greatness until, like a painting seen through many glazes, the original vibrates mysteriously in the light of its interpretations. It is now no longer possible, for example, to read *Hamlet* with a fresh eye, and this is doubtless a pity. Whatever it was that Shakespeare meant will remain forever in doubt. Perhaps that is of no great consequence. With time, his play has been transformed into a sacred relic, as potent and as ineffable as the Sangreal.[3]

It is only from the time of Ibsen that we are aware of the dramatist's deliberate effort to represent his own inner life on the stage. Before that time we are aware of the author only if he engages us in argument; we are chiefly aware of the story, not the storyteller. In the plays of Shakespeare we do not find Shakespeare. After reading *Faust* we can presume upon no great intimacy with Goethe. But from the plays of Ibsen it is possible to reconstruct Ibsen, and the plays of Strindberg are Strindberg himself.

In this regard, the drama reflects a tendency common to all contemporary art. Naturalism marked the high point of the artist's concern with the external. So long as the outer world chiefly engaged the artist's attention, a precise and detailed mimesis of nature was essential to his purpose. But after the time of Zola, the artist's eye began to turn more insistently inward. The impressionists cultivated singularity beyond the wildest eccentricities of mannerism, and the symbolists looked beyond reality to something that the eye did not see and the mind could not grasp. These, doubtless, were romantic tendencies. Their origins can hardly be traced with confidence, although their development in the nineteenth century is in some degree measurable. At any rate, in the last decades of the century, poetry became the chief preoccupation of the dramatist—the poetry of words, and, even more especially, the poetry of action—expressed not in terms of a narrative design, but of a more abstruse configuration which reflected the underlying pattern of the psyche.

At the same time, in poetry, serious efforts were being made to convey, through words alone, nuances of experience which had never before been the subject of artistic expression, and which perhaps had never before been considered expressible. Théophile Gautier had said:

Tout homme qu'une idée, si subtile et si imprévue qu'on la suppose, prend en défaut, n'est pas un écrivain. L'inexprimable n'existe pas.[4]

The poetry of the inexpressible, nevertheless, was the goal of the next generation. In a poem like *"Il pleut dans mon cœur,"* Verlaine succeeded in communicating a sense of the sadness that passes understanding; in *"M'introduire dans votre histoire,"* Mallarmé succeeded in transmitting a shade of feeling as subtle as the pleasure of frustration, and in many poems he conveyed an intimation of the nameless agony of creation. It was inevitable that the attempt to describe shades of feeling so impalpable, so far removed from the area through which flow the normal currents of poetry, should result in a complex and difficult mode of expression, a technique of suggestion through image and analogy, and the use of words in other than a denotative fashion. The attempt to do something of the sort on the stage through action does not antedate *The Master Builder*, but after its publication, the drama definitely entered the sphere of modern art.

The effort to develop a new lyricism in the theatre which we associate first with Maeterlinck and the German symbolists, then with Yeats and Synge, and then with such writers as Claudel, Baty, Cocteau, Apollinaire, Giraudoux, and Anouilh, represents a development, but not a break with tradition. Mallarmé felt he was attempting something new; but he did not feel estranged from Baudelaire—quite the contrary; and Baudelaire himself felt close to Banville, Gautier, Hugo, and even Balzac. The group of *avant-garde* dramatists who are now lumped together as "absurdists" is of another stripe.

Traditionally the function of art has been to bring order out of chaos, and to make nature intelligible to man. In the theatre, the modern tendency to demonstrate the absurdity of the world order is most nearly connected with Pirandello, and Pirandello based his demonstration largely on epistemological grounds. In the other arts, the temptation to reduce nature to absurdity emerges most clearly in the Dadaism of Miró and his associates. After the time of that short-lived but exuberant movement there has been an effort to develop the charming irresponsibility of Jarry into a principle of art. It is to this line of endeavor, which dedicates its efforts to the delightful task of bringing chaos out of order, that the new absurdist tendencies of the drama should probably be referred, not to the despair of the existentialists. Far from being a serious expression of an artistic viewpoint such as we occasionally find in Ionesco and in Becket, what these works involve is principally a gesture of derision, the artist thumbing his nose at art, a relaxing but not especially profitable artistic recreation.

The theatre of Ibsen and Strindberg is pivotal in the turn from the drama of the past to the drama of the present; but it is hardly possible to estimate its importance without putting it into its proper perspective. We must therefore step back from them some distance; far enough, at least, to include in our view of their work the main aspects of the dramatic tradition which they inherited. Both of them believed that, up to a certain point, they were working within the traditional forms of drama. It is therefore with these forms that we begin.

Tragedy and Comedy

ANCIENT drama was not realistic. The ancients idealized their characters in tragedy, and caricatured them in comedy. They evidently saw no point in the accurate portrayal of ordinary life on the stage, and nothing of this sort was attempted in the theatre until late in the nineteenth century. For the ancients a play was a ceremony of special character, which had its own reality, hardly to be confused with the reality of life. Renaissance drama, on the other hand, rested on the realistic tradition of the medieval stage. It was therefore more seriously involved with questions of verisimilitude, and the history of drama since the Renaissance shows, in general, a steady development in the direction of realism and the theatrical illusion.

For the Renaissance dramatist, tragedy involved the misfortunes of people of consequence. The adversities of people of no consequence furnished, so far as the theatre was concerned, only matter for comedy. The reasons for this interesting distinction relate to the nature of the tragic and comic modes, and the styles of expression considered appropriate to them.[1]

The classic world view was essentially tragic. The Christian was not. The Christian universe was a moral structure, the history of which had been foreseen by its Creator in most minute detail; therefore all events could be rationalized in terms of God's providence and God's judgments. The solution of a given problem might involve time and suffering, but nothing was more certain than the ultimate reward of the deserving and the punishment of the wicked. If the history of the world were dramatized in these terms, the result, obviously, would be happy. The mystery plays were, accordingly, conceived comedically, and Dante, in synthesizing his universe, called the result his *Comedy*, and composed it, as he tells us, in comic style.

The Christian view of life did not emphasize class distinctions. Originally it had tended, if anything, to abase the high and to exalt the low. In theory, all souls were equally valuable in the sight of God, and all suffering was of equal interest. But the hierarchic view of society which the Romans transmitted to the medieval world was more readily conformable with feudalism than with Christianity, and, in a day when it was considered sweet and decorous, as well as normal, for the poor to suffer, it was inevitable that the sufferings of the great should excite a different sort of interest than the sufferings of the lowly.

Tragedy traditionally had to do with the sufferings of people of the highest class, the misfortunes, as Aristotle put it, of men better than ourselves. The sufferings of heroes, the objects of public veneration, were calculated to elicit a solemn wonder, and the tragedic writer framed his composition in an appropriately exalted style. Comic characters, on the other hand, were treated aggressively. The comedy of Aristophanes was extravagantly ironic. In New Comedy, the characters were commonly depicted as lewd, mean, avaricious or, at the very least, grotesque. Comedy, so the *Poetics* tells us, involved the imitation of men worse than ourselves. It was meant to portray the ridiculous; and, in Aristotle's view, the ridiculous—a mistake or deformity which is not productive of harm to others—was a species of the ugly. It is evident that these definitions reflect Aristotle's tendency to arrange natural data in a scale of excellence. In this scale, tragedy would be a nobler genre than comedy; a tragic action, more beautiful than a comic one; and with reference to the characters, the audience would be presumed to occupy a mean position from which it might observe either with admiration or with amused contempt the behavior of personages who existed, respectively, on the upper or on the lower planes of humanity, but never on the plane of the audience.

Aristotle speaks of the mask of the comic actor as ugly or distorted, and we know that the grotesque appearance of the comic character went beyond the mask. The comedians depicted in the Greek and Roman paintings are short and potbellied. They have a mad look, and the foolishness of their appearance is further enhanced by the indecently short tunic, and the exaggerated sexual appendage which was the mark of the comic actor. The situations of New Comedy, so far as one can judge, were intended to be amusing reflections of urban life. It might be expected that here mimesis would take a more realistic turn than in tragedy; but it is far from clear that such was the case. Just as the supermen of tragedy were represented by great masked figures which moved majestically above the chorus, so the comic roles were played by clowns. In the theatre, Greek art tended to the extreme; and in this respect Roman art appears to have outdone its models. In ancient tragedy the characters were magnified beyond human proportions. In comedy they were caricatured ruthlessly. In the one and the other genre, therefore, mimesis consisted not in the imitation of nature, but principally in the exaggeration of experience in accordance with fixed preconceptions, and with this classic practice, the Renaissance dramatists generally concurred.[2]

The medieval idea of tragedy involved the fall of a great man through some stroke of fortune, or, more commonly, some defect or weakness inherent in his character. It is in such terms, moral and Christian, that such a "tragedy" as Preston's Cambyses is designed, or such a play as Marlowe's Edward II. Seneca's tragedies, however, did not demonstrate this useful concept. On the whole, they were studies in horror, and illustrated the distortion of a personality through the exaggeration of some overmastering idea or compulsion which escaped the tutelage of the rational faculty. The usual pattern of this monomanic type of drama is exemplified in such a play as *Thyestes*, in which the protagonist's insuperable desire for vengeance transforms him into a sadistic monster.

The Middle Ages derived what was known of the classic mode in tragedy principally from the grammar books that survived the destruction of the antique culture. In the more or less fragmentary treatises of Donatus, Evanthius, and Diomedes were found, together with a good deal of rubbish, some useful reminiscences of Theophrastus, Horace, and Cicero, and some descriptions of dramatic practice in the final period of the ancient culture. Early in the fourteenth century, Nicholas Trivet wrote a commentary on the tragedies of Seneca that did much to direct attention to this hitherto neglected body of drama which illustrated perfectly the precepts of Horace in his epistle to Piso, the *Ars poetica*. Not long after, Latin imitations of Seneca began to appear in Italy. Henceforth, the Senecan mode took a foremost place among the patterns for tragedy. In 1498 Giorgio Valla brought out the first full text of Aristotle's *Poetics* in a Latin translation. It had no great effect on sixteenth-century thought, but when Robortelli published his edition and commentary in 1548, Aristotle's treatise rapidly superseded all else as the ultimate authority on classical practice in the theatre. In the course of the century, a vast body of commentary and elaboration grew up around this enigmatic little book, and its "rules" became the foundation of all Renaissance criticism. Horace's authority, nevertheless, was never questioned. In spite of all indications to the contrary, it was taken for granted that Horace and Aristotle were completely in accord, and that together they defined the ideal of the drama. The precepts of the *Ars poetica* were therefore assimilated in one way or another to the rules derived from the Aristotelian analysis, and, thereafter, to be correct meant to be in conformity with the treatises of Horace and Aristotle.[3]

Neither Aristotle nor Horace had discussed comedy. Although the comedies of Terence and, in some degree, the comedies of Plautus, were available for imitation throughout the Middle Ages, medieval comedy in the vernacular was able to develop quite naturally. In the early Renaissance, the theoretical basis of comedy began to take shape along classic lines. Donatus's commentaries on Terence came to light in 1433. In 1427, Cusanus brought a manuscript of twelve plays of Plautus from Germany to Rome. Comedies in the high-spirited style of Plautus now began to be written, first in Latin and then in Italian, French, English, and Spanish. The Plautine plays involved a good deal of bustling in and out of doors, an ingenious but relatively simple plot, and considerable physical movement about the stage. Comedy therefore developed a vigorous style, quite different from the stately declamation of tragedy and much closer to the boisterous tradition of the Middle Ages.

Donatus had given early currency to "Cicero's" description of comedy as *imitatio vitae, speculum consuetudinis, imago veritatis* —phrases which were endlessly quoted by theorists and critics without much reference to the actual practice of the theatre. In a day when fiction was ordinarily justified on the basis of its utility, it became customary to speak of comedy as an art which imitated "pleasing and amusing happenings" for the purpose of exhibiting the follies of men for the instruction of mankind: *castigat ridendo mores.* Comedy thus came to be regarded as a genre devoted to the depiction of amusing deviations from the norms of rational behavior, brought about by such forms of madness as love, jealousy, greed, hypochondria, or simply by a desire to mix things up. Since classic comedy had classified its *dramatis personae* in terms of the mask, and Horace had emphasized the necessity for preserving a properly consistent decorum in characterization, the general tendency in Renaissance comedy was to portray the characteristics of types rather than the singularities of individuals.[4]

Written comedy, *commedia erudita,* as distinct from the comedy improvised by the *comici dell'arte,* was almost completely determined by the practice of the Latin writers. The Renaissance comedic style was fixed along these lines at the beginning of the sixteenth century by Ariosto and Machiavelli; thereafter it varied little. Since the classic models were in verse, there was at first some uncertainty about the use of prose. Ariosto wrote his comedies in prose first, and put them into verse in later revisions. Machiavelli's *La Mandragola* was written in prose, and as this was accounted the best comedy of the age, the use of prose in comedy found a ready sanction. The subject matter of comedy was almost invariably love—not the passion, nor the tenderness of love, but the wiles of love—so that the chief emphasis of the comic plot was on the intrigue—the manner in which the young lover, aided by a clever rogue, found his way into the arms of the lady of his choice in spite of the old men, the fathers and husbands, who generally opposed his wishes. Thus, the basis of the comic plot was almost always some form of trickery.

Generally speaking, the subject of comedy after the time of Ariosto was bawdy. Its matter was either drawn from the *novelle* or imitated from the classics, or else—as in the case of Bibbiena's *La Calandria,* it was a blend of both. About the middle of the sixteenth century, it became fashionable to declare one's independence of the classical models. In their prefaces and prologues, Aretino, D'Ambra, Cecchi, and Grazzini all insist on their complete originality. In fact, nobody broke away from the classical examples at this time.[5] The chief influence on written comedy came from the *comici dell'arte,* whose exaggerations inevitably crept back into the learned comedy which they aped, and these actors were for a time the chief source of originality in the comic genre. Thus Aretino embellished his comedies with elements of farce, humors-characters, and dialect-characters borrowed from the improvised popular comedy; and the stock characters of learned comedy became in time practically indistinguishable from the masks of the *commedia dell'arte.*

The decisive influence in the development of Italian comedy toward the end of the sixteenth century was the Counter-Reformation. As the church became increasingly puritanical during the long session of the Council of Trent, it discouraged more and more firmly the depictions of filial disobedience, and the successful outcome of the intrigues of illicit love which had so far furnished the staple of comedy. The comedic writer was now forced, more or less against his will, to concentrate on innocent love, and the type of courtship which has marriage as its object. Moreover, after the middle of the sixteenth century, the aim of comedy was generally said to be, not entertainment, but edification. The elements of edifying love comedy, however, were hardly to be found in the ancient theatre. They had to be invented or adapted from other genres, mainly from the lyric and the pastoral.

The language of love did not exist in the ancient drama, but it had been amply developed by the troubadours, and Petrarch had crystallized its vocabulary and its syntax for the ages. Accordingly, the troubadour love system was translated bodily into the comedic tradition, but not until it had been rigorously adapted to the moralistic atmosphere of the day. The sentimental bias of the Counter-Reformation now began to be felt in all the dramatic genres. Scenes of pathos and sentiment, at first completely foreign to comedy, soon became its essential feature. In this manner, through judicious pruning and grafting, the modern sentimental love story, with its surmountable obstacles and its happy ending, began to take form in the last decades of the sixteenth century, and by the beginning of the seventeenth it was established as a leading dramatic form even in England.

The inclusion of emotional scenes, often of Hispanic origin and of Hispanic intensity, brought comedy closer to tragedy than it had ever been. Unlike the type of tragedy with a happy ending with which the Renaissance dramatists occasionally experimented, serious comedy could include jokes, low character-types, and *lazzi*, and it was permissible to introduce, also, scenes of terror, narrow escapes, and a high degree of excitement. Contile's *Pescara* (1537) is perhaps the earliest example of this sort of play. The form, once established, proliferated rapidly, and while it was kept theoretically distinct from tragedy with a happy ending, those who wrote it made ample use of the fund of novelistic material which provided also much of the narrative basis of tragedy. It is thus hardly possible to distinguish the serious comedy of Borghini, Parabosco, and Razzi from the type of tragedy that was written in the same period.

The popularity of Spanish comedy, which began to be imitated in Italy sometime before the middle of the seventeenth century, put the finishing touches to the disintegration of the Romanesque style. The antique mode, with its limited subject matter, would probably not have survived the Renaissance in any case; but deprived as it was of its essential character by the policies of the Counter-Reformation, it gave way speedily to the vogue of the three-act romantic comedy in the style of Lope de Vega. In written comedy, the stock cast—the *amorosi, vecchi, servi, capitani, pedanti*, and the rest of the *cinquecento* puppets—now all but vanished from the stage, and their place was taken by Spanish *galanes, barbas, damas, criadas*, and *graciosos*, so that after 1650 the vogue of romantic comedy was almost absolute. In Italian comedy of the late seventeenth century, girls were most often seen disguised as boys; scenes of love were obligatory; there were serious threats and escapes; swords were drawn at every juncture; the *pundonor* was a critical element of the plot; and a high degree of excitement took the place of the suspense attending the intrigues of the clever servant. In this period, only a few stragglers like Oddi persisted in writing comedy in the Roman style.[6]

From the time of Jodelle until the first decades of the seventeenth century, French comedy did little more than to reflect the Italian. It turned then to an imitation of the Spanish style. There followed a period during which French comedy was both broad and coarse, a period dominated by the French *farceurs* and the comedians of the Italian theatre in Paris. It was from this basis that Molière took his departure in order to develop the unique style of comedy which is the chief glory of the French stage.

In his description of comedy, Donatus included a summary analysis of play construction which served to define dramaturgical practice for centuries to come. According to Donatus, a comedy properly consists of a prologue and three parts:

The first part, or protasis, is the beginning of the action of the drama, wherein part of the play is developed and part withheld in order to create suspense. The second part, or epitasis, marks the ascent and further development of difficulties, or, as I have said, the knot of the entire coil. The last part, or catastrophe, is the solution, pleasing to the audience and made clear to all by an explanation of what has passed.[7]

This analysis, closely related to Aristotle's discussion of plot construction in the *Poetics*, bears only a general relation to the modes of storytelling developed during the Middle Ages. The climactic system of Donatus seems inevitable. But in medieval times, stories were rarely told in this way. The interludes and farces were, on the whole, structurally artless. Occasionally, as in the farce of *Pierre Pathelin*, they had the bipartite structure which medieval storytellers appear to have favored in the *chansons de geste*. In the more extensive dramatic forms, such as the mystery cycles, the organization of material is purely episodic in the style of the *roman à tiroirs*, and in many stories the author seems to be at pains to avoid, rather than to achieve, a climax and a resolution. What Donatus describes is the narrative method of Latin comedy, which is related to the design of the Greek romances; and if this manner of telling a story seems most natural to us, it is certainly not because it is psychologically inevitable, but because this classical technique is the basis of the "well-made" story sequence which is still congenial to our time.

Since Terentian comedy was typically a texture of two or more interlaced story lines, the Renaissance dramatists concluded that a complicated *intreccio* was a mark of the kind of ingenuity appropriate to comedy. Ariosto, who developed this technique of storytelling to its fullest extent in the *Orlando furioso*, was also the first to establish the patterns of learned comedy in the vernacular, and his example was very widely followed. Long before the time of English Restoration comedy, Italian writers of the type of

Della Porta carried narrative intricacy to quite extraordinary lengths.[8] Italian practice in this respect found ready imitators. Shakespeare saw no inconvenience in interlacing four separate stories in *The Merchant of Venice* and as many in *A Midsummer Night's Dream.*

The sort of story which Donatus evidently thought suitable for the stage turned upon a conflict of wishes. The protasis defined the situation. In time this part of the play came to incorporate the Terentian prologue also, and thus the protasis developed into the elaborate exposition which eventually became the mark of the *pièce bien faite* of the school of Scribe. The epitasis knotted the action and developed difficulties which were further complicated by the counterturn or catastasis. In the catastrophe, through some stroke of fortune or ingenuity, or, most usually, through an agnition —a revelation of identity—the knot fell apart, and the protagonist attained the object of his desire. The general shape of a comedic plot therefore accorded with the removal of a seemingly irremovable obstacle. Corneille describes the action of *Andromède* in these terms:

L'action principale est le mariage de Persée avec Andromède: son noeud consiste en l'obstacle qui s'y rencontre du côté de Phinée, à qui elle est promise, et son dénouement en la mort de ce malheureux amant, après laquelle il n'y a plus d'obstacle.[9]

In Romanesque comedy, by far the most usual method of overcoming an obstacle was to contrive an intrigue. In these circumstances, the emphasis fell principally on the ingenuity of the effective characters, that is to say, on their cunning, a quality especially suitable to the servile classes. The principal roles in such plays were accordingly those of cheaters and knaves, and the plot took its turns from the strokes and counterstrokes of ingenuity by which such characters strove to overreach each other, either in their own interest or in the interests of those they served.

While comedy was oriented from the first in the direction of cleverness, tragedy remained for a time relatively simple, and the tragedic writer compensated for his lack of intricacy by the use of powerful situations, a solemn mood, and an impressive rhetorical apparatus. Aristotle said little about plot construction; but he clearly indicated the desirability of imposing a causal order on the development of the tragic fable.[10] It was generally assumed, therefore, that in a play each situation was the result of the preceding, and the cause of the succeeding one. Logic accordingly became the essential element in the arrangement of a tragic action.

Classic drama had no act divisions. The number of episodes in the high time of Attic tragedy varied considerably, but it is possible that, by the middle of the third century B.C., tragedy and comedy were regularly divided into five acts. Horace, at any rate, is categorical in this respect, and the Renaissance critics took his rule for gospel, so that in Italy, and, after some decades of experiment, in seventeenth-century France, the five-act structure was regularly imposed on a type of story which, according to the plan of Donatus, was properly divisible in three. Act divisions, accordingly, had no particular significance. The unit of construction was the scene; and by a scene was meant a group of characters on the stage engaged in conversation. The appearance of another character marked the beginning of a new scene; and as each entrance was intended, in theory, to advance the action a step toward the catastrophe, it became usual to think of a play as a mosaic of characters arranged in accordance with principles of design to which the logical exigencies of the plot were sometimes subordinated. In this manner, a distinction arose between the "action" of the play —the substance and necessary sequence of the narrative, and the "plot"—the disposition of characters with relation to the scenes.[11] This practice of arranging plays with an eye to the sequence of characters, the *numérotage*, was still much in use in nineteenth-century French drama. Scribe's collaborator, Legouvé, in a famous essay, describes with admiration the master's method of constructing a play with nothing in mind but the theme, and the order in which, theoretically, the characters should appear and reappear.[12]

It would be reasonable to suppose that after the canonization of the *Poetics*, and the attendant fanfare, Renaissance tragedy would quickly take on an Attic look. Nothing of the sort happened. The first tragedies in the vernacular were either close imitations of Senecan plays or dramatized *novelle* cast in the Senecan mold. For the Renaissance dramatist, on the Continent at least, it was of the first importance to be correct. Therefore the formal aspects of the antique drama received the closest attention, the assumption being that the nearer one came to the classical manner, the more valuable the result would be. The rigid separation of the genres, the five-act structure, the unities, the system of confidants and messengers, the ghost and foreshadowing dreams, the observance of decorum, the alternation of declamatory and stichomythic passages, the use of the chorus—of whose precise function nobody was certain—these Senecan and Horatian elements were supposed to be the sources of what Aristotle had called the pleasure of tragedy, and their presence in a play contributed much to the satisfaction of the experienced reader.

The relation of Renaissance tragedy to the tragedy of the Greeks was thus of somewhat the same order as that of Renaissance epic to the epic of Homer, a largely hypothetical connection which gave people a feeling of tradition but did not seriously affect anyone's practice. Judging by their prefaces, the Renaissance dramatists considered that their tragedies were elegantly classical; but it is obvious that, with the exception of Trissino, they were more strongly influenced by the Senecan horror plays and the medieval story forms than by anything derived from a study of the Greek. There is, in fact, not much in the vernacular before *Samson Agonistes* that makes the impression of Greek tragedy, and nothing after.

The history of regular tragedy begins in Italy at the end of the fifteenth century. It ends, for all practical purposes, in France in the time of the Great Revolution. Its course is therefore a matter of three centuries. The first considerable tragedy in the vernacular was Trissino's *Sofonisba* (1515), dramatized from a story in Livy which Petrarch had elaborated in *Africa*. Trissino followed Greek models. Sofonisba's death was brought about by her lover; the mood of the tragedy was sentimental and pathetic; its inspiration, chiefly lyrical. But Trissino's lead in this respect was not followed. The Italian dramatists felt that tragedy, as Aristotle had intimated, should evoke a sense of horror rather than a feeling of pity. Thus, the favorite motive for Italian tragedy came to be revenge, a completely valid motive for violence in the sixteenth century, for which there was, moreover, the unimpeachable authority of Seneca.

In his *Discourses on Comedy and Tragedy* (1543), Giovanbattista Giraldi extolled the superiority of Latin over Greek tragedy on the ground that Seneca manifested greater prudence, majesty, sententiousness, decorum, and gravity than any of the Greek tragedic writers. It is evident from his discussion that his view of tragedy differed a good deal from ours, but to him also the Senecan plays seemed barely suited to the stage;[13] their form, as well as their subject matter and the manner of their outcome, supports the conjecture that they were poems intended for declamation by a single rhetor, and this seems to have been the idea also of Seneca's first Renaissance imitator, Albertino Mussato. In recitation, naturally, what is properly dramatic would be subordinated to the qualities which Giraldi professed to admire most, qualities which pertain rather to didactic poetry than to acted drama. Horace had laid down the rule that whatever could not conveniently be represented by the actors should be elegantly described by a messenger. It was logical, therefore, to think of tragedy as a series of dramatic declamations, separated by stichomyth and choral songs, leading up to the description or depiction of some gruesome action which could be justified as retributive, and yet provided the sort of thrill considered proper to tragedy. Even when this action, for some reason, proceeded upon grounds other than revenge, it was usually found possible, in accordance with Senecan practice, to motivate the plot through the agency of some vengeful ghost who craved satisfaction. There is, for example, no real connection between the spectres of the first act of Giraldi's *Orbecche* and the action they presumably bring about. Their wrath is ornamental rather than functional, and the same may be said of the ghost of Andrea in *The Spanish Tragedy*. But the idea that tragedy results from the claims of the past upon the present—an essentially classic concept—recommended itself strongly to the writers of serious drama down to the time of Ibsen and Strindberg, and in some measure it furnished a basis for the naturalism of Zola.

The idea of tragedy which Giraldi advocated about the middle of the sixteenth century lasted in Italy until the first decades of the seventeenth, by which time, it is said, Italian tragedy worthy of the name had ceased to exist.[14] Giraldi preferred fictional to historical subjects. He arranged his plays in an involved double-action, with an intricate knot, in a five-act structure, with each act divided into several scenes. The chorus seemed indispensable to him, but he used it sparingly. Since he agreed with Aristotle that the most effective denouement is brought about by a combined recognition and reversal, he brought his plays, as a rule, to a strong climax which was quickly resolved. The aim of tragedy, in his view, was to arouse wonder and admiration, as well as a high degree of excitement. For this purpose, he found love and its consequences most useful motives; and in order to emphasize the pathetic aspects of the tragic action, he followed the medieval tradition which idealized women, particularly in the type of story in which a beautiful woman is victimized by a jealous husband or an irate father. In adapting such themes to the tragic patterns of Seneca, Giraldi depicted his tragic protagonists as monsters of insatiable cruelty, character-types as far removed as possible from the type of tragic hero described in the *Poetics*.

In the Renaissance theatre, the type of the irate father properly belonged to comedy, and in adapting this character to tragic purposes Giraldi was forced into a tone of greater extravagance than was usual even in Senecan tragedy. In his terrible fury, the father who punishes his wayward daughter in *Orbecche* (1541) by serving up her children for dinner comes very close to Punch: he is certainly in no way reminiscent of the stately heroes that Aristotle had in mind. He is grotesque.

The Greek tragic hero was never depicted as evil by nature; it was necessary for tragedy that the hero be, as Aristotle had written, "first and foremost good." Seneca's tragic protagonists were, on the other hand, pathological types. His plays were studies of madness, and it is evident that they were directed to an audience which enjoyed experiencing the strong effects of the arena in connection with a brilliant rhetorical display of edifying nature. This pungent mixture of horror and sententiousness was thought to be pre-eminently tragic and pre-eminently classical. The irate fathers, brothers, and husbands of Renaissance tragedy were therefore made vengeful and cruel beyond the call of duty or reason, and also extremely articulate, and, were it not for the authentication which the history of the period gives them, we should be tempted to think these characterizations completely fantastic. It is only when we read the histories of the Malatesta, the Visconti, and the Sforza that the themes of Renaissance tragedy begin to take on a certain realistic significance.

Aside from revenge, the most popular theme for Italian tragedy, as Giraldi conceived it, involved the persecution of a beautiful woman by a cruel tyrant. The subject, inherently sadistic in its coloring, was most likely borrowed from *novelle* related to the troubadour *razos*, but the form was assimilated to the pseudo-Senecan *Octavia*, in some ways the most influential of the classical plays. As a play, *Octavia* could hardly be more inept; but the spectacle of a beautiful woman tortured by a brutal husband was particularly congenial to a time when the tradition of *fin amor* was still very much alive. In *Octavia*, the husband, Nero, is not jealous, merely cruel; many of the plays, however, which fell into the mold of *Octavia* had to do with the savage revenge of the dishonored spouse. Thus, a good part of Renaissance tragedy, though seemingly classical in subject, and in Senecan form, actually grew out of the lyric tradition of the Middle Ages, and was simply a dramatization of the narrative background of the troubadour *chanson*.

Since Aristotle had treated tragedy and the heroic poem together in the *Poetics*, the Renaissance commentators regularly treated tragedy as a branch of poetry. This had important consequences. The ancients had distinguished three poetic styles—the tragic, comic, and lyric—and Demetrius had added the epic as a fourth style, thus introducing an irremediable element of confusion.[15] The distinction between tragedy and comedy, since it was founded upon a stylistic principle, was thought to be unbridgeable, so that it was considered barbarous to interpolate comic matter in a serious play. Such a distinction seems absurd from a dramaturgic viewpoint, and the Greek dramatists had certainly not observed it rigorously, but the distinction of genres continued to be a cardinal tenet of regular tragedy as long as it was written.

The confusion of poetry with rhetoric which characterizes so much of the literature of the Renaissance was naturally extended to the drama as well. In accordance with the rhetorical extravagance of the Senecan models, magniloquence, hyperbole, and verbal wit became inseparable attributes of the tragic drama, and the ranting actor became a fixture of the stage. The tendency toward an inflated and bombastic style was further magnified by the widespread opinion that the end of poetry was to excite wonder and admiration. Thus everything conspired in this period to make tragedy a high-sounding declamation, and even in the English and Spanish theatres, where the classical tradition played a relatively minor part, the tragic action was devised so as to provide the best opportunities for effective oratory.

Although there was a certain amount of direct Senecan imitation in the early phases of the English drama, it was chiefly through the adaptation of Italian *novelle* and Italian plays that the classical patterns reached the stage in England, and the two main motives of Italian tragedy, persecution and revenge, served to define a good part of the drama of Tudor and Stuart times. The type of English tragedy that most clearly reflected Italian influence centered in a deed of horror or a sequence of such deeds, and their position in the play more or less dictated the order of the action. Since the English playwrights permitted themselves far more scope than the Italians or the French, English tragedy in the time of Shakespeare specialized in spectacles of violence and bloodshed set in a framework of glowing verse, the Elizabethan equivalent of the classical form.

Classical tragedy in Italy hardly survived the Counter-Reformation. For the ancients, tragedy was inherent in the feeling of man's helplessness in the face of implacable fate or capricious fortune. But from the viewpoint of that orthodoxy which the church now actively fostered, a belief in fortune was a denial of God's providence, and a belief in fate was a negation of man's free will. The question of free will and necessity had, of course, been the subject of extensive discussion during the Middle Ages; in the late sixteenth century, whatever smacked of determinism was considered dangerously Protestant. Such ideas were therefore intolerable to the Inquisition. A result was the reinstatement of the medieval idea of tragedy which ascribed the falls of princes to the workings of poetic justice.

Since from this viewpoint the implication was that doom overtakes only those who deserve it, the essential feeling of tragedy was lost, as Aristotle had indicated it must be in such cases, and the tragic play became essentially didactic, an exemplum of the consequences of wrongdoing. The consequence was the speedy attrition of tragedy in Italy and, concomitantly, the development of two new genres, which largely supplanted it. The first was tragicomedy. The second was the *tragedia sacra*. This began to be written about 1575 under Jesuit auspices, and proved to be the only viable form of Italian tragic drama after the Council of Trent.

Thus, in Counter-Reformation times, everything combined to bring about a confusion of the classical genres which the early Renaissance critics had been at such pains to distinguish. Aristotle had declared his preference for tragedy with a sad ending, but he had also acknowledged the taste of the public for plays in tragic style that ended happily. In his *Discorsi* and elsewhere, Giraldi discussed at length the possibilities of this *tragedia di fin felice*, and he offered his *Altile* (1543) as an example of a sort of tragedy which might well be called, as he said, tragicomedy.[16] The distinction between tragedy with a happy end and tragicomedy was in fact easy enough to make, since the latter admitted comic episodes and the former did not, but tragicomedy was not a classical form, and it had no definite style. The term was therefore applied indiscriminately to all sorts of dramatic compositions from Rojas' *La Celestina* to Leoni's *La Converzione del peccatore a Dio* (1591), and until Guarini finally crystallized the genre with *Il Pastor fido* (1590, 1602), it had no specific connotation.

Guarini's innovation consisted in the adaptation of a complex fictional plot of the sort preferred by Giraldi to the type of pastoral love story which Tasso had dramatized in *Aminta*. The result was a bastard form which Guarini called pastoral tragicomedy, thus openly confusing three genres and precipitating a controversy which occupied him for the rest of his life.[17]

Il Pastor fido hardly impresses us in our day as a masterpiece, but its enormous vogue and influence indicates the need for a genre that was neither tragedy nor comedy. It was printed and reprinted in an astonishing number of editions until well into the eighteenth century, and in the development of the consequent genre in France, principally by Alexandre Hardy, it is quite possible to discern the beginnings of modern social comedy.[18]

In France, the beginnings of vernacular tragedy coincided with the first years of the *Pléiade*, a period during which French lyricism enjoyed an especially rich floriation. The French poets of the sixteenth century demonstrated no special aptitude for narrative; it was the lyric aspect of the tragic situation which chiefly interested them. The first experiments in French tragedy had to do with the persecution of beautiful women—Cleopatra (Jodelle), Medea (La Péruse), Sofonisba (Saint-Gelais), Lucrece (Filleul), Mariamne (Tristan L'Hermite)—but for the detailed description, or representation, of the deed of horror which provided the high point of Italian tragedy, the French dramatists substituted a scene of poetic lamentation. The Italian dramatists had thought tragedy should make one shudder. The French thought it should make one cry.

As the interest was shifted in this manner from the horrible to the pitiful, it became unnecessary to depict the chain of events that led to the tragic deed or even to represent the deed itself. The resulting drama, largely devoid of action, took on an elegiacal mood. Jean de la Taille, following Horace, very sensibly justified this practice on the basis of realism.[19] Since it was impossible, he reasoned, to depict violent death believably on the stage, it was better not to attempt this sort of stage business at all. The proper business of the tragic poet was, he believed, in any case, the depiction of mental rather than of physical suffering. It was unnecessary to dwell on the deed of horror. Its consequences alone were essential. Accordingly, one should begin a tragedy toward the middle or the end of the story; indeed, as close to the end as possible. This practice was still recommended in the latter half of the seventeenth century. In his *La Pratique du théâtre* (1657), d'Aubignac advises his readers that a play should begin "as close to the catastrophe as possible, in order to employ less time for the business of the stage and to have more freedom to extend the passions and other discourses which give pleasure. . . . The dramatist must remember to take up the action at its last point and, so to speak, at its last moment." [20]

Since a dramatic action of this sort could most conveniently be comprised within the limits of a single episode, there was hardly room in the play for a reversal of fortune, and all the interest could be focused on a poetic tableau enlivened chiefly by the varying combinations of characters brought upon the stage from scene to scene. The dynamic element in this sort of drama was thus almost completely suppressed, together with suspense, surprise, and other sources of theatrical excitement, and the pleasure of the tragedy was derived largely from the lyrical expression of grief in a situation which tended to become static shortly after the beginning of the play.

The dramas composed on this scheme were directed to a reading public, and very few reached the stage. In the first years of the seventeenth century, Alexandre Hardy, a professional playwright, attempted to adapt these elegant forms to the taste of the paying audience of the theatre in the Hôtel de Bourgogne. To this end,

Hardy made use of the poetic format of the regular drama—the oratorical basis, the five-act structure, and the Senecan system of ghosts and messengers, but not the chorus—and within this frame, he undertook to play an effective story with some semblance of correctness.

Since effectiveness was the prime consideration in the popular theatre, Hardy took no special interest in the unities, but he unified his action, so that his plays told a single story which moved about briskly from scene to scene. The *décor simultané* of the Hôtel de Bourgogne was excellently adapted to the needs of such an action, and the necessary scenic elements were grouped within a single stylized setting which composed them in a manner we should perhaps now call surrealistic, but which had ample precedent in the narrative painting of the early Renaissance. Like a good showman, Hardy used spectacle freely; and since scenes of death and destruction were much to the taste of his audience, he represented such things boldly without regard to decorum. In this manner, by the end of the first quarter of the seventeenth century, Hardy succeeded in making his popular theatre fashionable. His repertory by this time consisted largely of tragicomedies involving a good deal of complication and incident, and in deference to courtly taste, their subject matter was mainly love and honor. If these plays were not especially sensible, they were also by no means dull.

The ancients, we noted, had furnished no precedents for the kind of love literature which was developed in Europe during the Middle Ages. In classic tragedy, love was disastrous. In comedy, it was bawdy. It was sentimental in neither: in the theatre, at least, the ancients were evidently not much interested in lovemaking as such. But the Renaissance dramatists were writing in the wake of the great amatory tradition which had developed in the *midi* of France in the first years of the twelfth century. In the seventeenth century, courtly literature was centered more than ever on the tender passion, and love furnished the prime motivation for all aspects of the drama and the novel.

In tragicomedy, love was depicted, very much as in the chivalric romances, as a noble passion which inspired the gentle heart to high deeds and heroic self-sacrifice. In the new pastoral comedy —which became urbanized with Corneille's *Mélite* (1629)—love was innocent, fresh and poetic, a natural force which culminated in a home and babies. By this time, in England, these romantic tendencies had flowered briefly but effectively, and in Spain, Shakespeare's older contemporary Lope de Vega had already developed fully a style of poetic drama, intricate, witty, and graceful, which centered on questions of love and demonstrated the chivalric virtues.

The interval between 1628, when Hardy stopped writing, and 1636, when Corneille wrote *Le Cid*, was a time of vigorous and uncontrolled experiment in the French theatre. After 1620, tragedy and comedy all but vanished from the stage, the rules were thrown to the winds, and the classical authorities abandoned. But the age had incurably classic tastes, and a reaction soon set in. In the pastoral tragicomedy *Silvanire*, and later in the tragedy *Sofonisba* (1634), both under strong Italian influence, Mairet successfully demonstrated a firmly disciplined style of drama which achieved order and restraint by limiting the action in accordance with the unities, and in which once again effective declamation in high style took the place of spectacle. Mairet's *Sofonisba* was, in fact, one of those works which, without having any special merit in themselves, yet appear to exert a decisive influence on the works of others. In the next few years after its appearance, a dozen attempts were made to rival its success. The last was *Le Cid*, which Corneille produced in 1637. Like *The Spanish Tragedy* in England, it was one of the most spectacularly successful plays in the history of the drama, and it established a concept of tragic form which was to rule the Continental stage until the beginning of the nineteenth century.

Le Cid was at first called a tragicomedy—it was, indeed, what Giraldi called *tragedia di fin felice*, and had a happy outcome, or at least an outcome that promised to be happy. The plot was ex-

tracted from Guillén de Castro's two-part *comedia*, *Las Moce-
dades del Cid*, a rambling play which covered an immense amount
of material and a considerable period of years. Corneille selected
from it a chain of logically related incidents which could, conceivably, have occurred within the space of a day within the walls
of a palace. The setting was simple; in the words of the stage manager: *"une chambre a 4 porte. Il faut un fauteuille pour le Roy."*

In his *Avertissement* to the 1648 edition of *Le Cid*, Corneille
piously attributed the success of the play to the fact that it fulfilled the two principal conditions of tragedy laid down by Aristotle.
The first had to do with the nature of the tragic hero. In Aristotle's view, according to Corneille, "the one who suffers and is
persecuted is neither bad nor entirely virtuous, but one more good
than bad who, by some human weakness that does not amount to
crime, falls into a misfortune he does not deserve . . ." [21] In the
second place, Corneille took account of a passage in the *Poetics*
which Giraldi had also noted, but which not many critics so far had
emphasized: ". . . in tragedy, the persecution and the danger do
not come from an enemy, nor from one who is indifferent, but
from a person who must love the one who suffers and must be
loved by him." [22]

In citing this passage of the *Poetics* with relation to the action
of *Le Cid*, Corneille did a considerable service to the drama of his
time. Tragedy had thus far been thought of, commonly, as a spectacle of unjust and inhuman persecution. Aristotle's idea that the
pleasure of tragedy is derived from the contemplation of the grief
of the doer quite as much as from the suffering of the victim made
the tragic experience infinitely more subtle and refined. It brought
about a complex reaction of pity and terror, and forced the tragic
poet to shift his attention from the sufferings of the unwilling
victim to the dilemma of the reluctant tyrant. Psychology thus
became a central element in serious drama, and for the first time
motivation became a matter of primary interest.

Moreover, in framing the action of *Le Cid* so that the conflicting desires and duties of the characters formed a polygon of

forces, Corneille made manifest for the first time the element of conscious design in dramatic construction, a factor hitherto obscured by other considerations. It was now established that the poetry of drama had to do essentially, as Aristotle had intimated, with the interplay of action and character, and that the rhetoric of drama is primarily the rhetoric of juxtaposed events and not the rhetoric of words.[23]

In medieval literature, the fundamental dramatic conflict had been a moral opposition, the struggle of virtuous and vicious impulses within the soul, made visible through the personification of the conflicting forces. As these forces were the true antagonists, the soul was thought of as a passive entity, standing meekly by while the powers of good and evil struggled for its possession. The soul in Renaissance drama had a more complex and more virile nature. In accordance with the Platonic psychology which Aquinas set forth and the Renaissance developed, the soul was said to consist of three faculties—the intellect, the will, and the desires—and its health was thought to result from the proper subordination of the desires under the will, which was in turn at the command of the intellect. For the Renaissance dramatist the basic psychological conflict therefore involved the opposition of the rational and concupiscent faculties of the soul; the mind, that is, and the heart. The tragic hero was then thought of as a man of noble nature who was at odds not with an external power, but, through some disharmony of his soul, chiefly with himself.

The idea that the struggle of mind and heart was the peculiar attribute of a noble nature had first found literary expression in the medieval love poetry. Through Petrarch this concept gained the widest currency, and it was explored in detail in the *ragionamenti d'amore* of the sixteenth century. In an age that chiefly directed artistic attention toward the ideal, the struggle of the individual to achieve self-mastery was naturally of prime literary interest, and the conflict of mind and heart became a staple of the heroic poetry of the period. These psychological motifs had therefore undergone an ample development in the poetic genres long before they were taken up in the theatre. It was inevitable that in time the representation of the inner conflict of the protagonist should also become the chief business of the dramatist.

The type of conflict developed by Corneille involved the tragic realization that while the triumph of the will conferred greatness upon a noble nature, the cost of victory might be disastrous. In these circumstances Corneille's heroes demonstrated a titanic quality which so far no tragic figure of modern times had achieved. The *Prometheus* of Aeschylus was the supreme classical example of the affirmation of the individual will. Such a figure transcended the familial context of Aristotelian tragedy, and posed the problem of the individual on a scale which dwarfed the well-ordered cosmos of the Renaissance. It was by peopling his hell with just such magnificent unregenerate figures that Dante had given magnitude to his universe; but the Renaissance was too Christian and too deeply authoritarian to make much use of so radical a conception of character. Shakespeare has no such figure as Prometheus; even Milton forebore to advance Satan so far. A great deal of revolutionary ardor was needed for the full artistic realization of this tragic fantasy, and when, in romantic times, it became possible to realize it, it was too late—the art of tragedy was already lost. Modern drama has, consequently, no such titanic protagonists, but with Ibsen the role of the titan devolved upon the poet, and the poet's vendetta against society became the sign of modernism in the theatre.

Corneille went no further in his idea of tragedy than the depiction of the hero's ambivalence, the triumph of his will, and the consequences of his tragic choice. *Le Cid* demonstrated a complex concatenation of motives, all of them logical, clear-cut, completely comprehensible. In this play no one questions for a moment the validity of the social laws which result in the tragic situation. Honor forces Rodrigue to kill the father of the girl he loves, and honor forces the girl to seek the life of her lover. Neither acts according to his desires: the social obligation dictates the course of action. In the circumstances, the situation is insoluble, and but for the intervention of an external agency in the form of the king, it could end only in disaster.

Since *Le Cid* was first presented as tragicomedy—Corneille did not call it a tragedy until 1648—the author did not feel bound by the classic rules, and he felt free to exploit as far as possible the sentimental aspects of an intricate situation. Nevertheless in its elaborate yet perfectly equilibrated design, its disciplined structure, and the artificial but completely winning postures of its characters, the play was so far conformable to the taste of the time that it gave a new aspect to tragedy. After *Le Cid*, tragedy ceased to ape the antique mode, and developed a style of its own, which in turn became classic.

The Greek tragedies had not achieved greatness through the analysis of character. The Greek tragic hero presents, as a rule, the immobility of an archetype, and it is only through some excess or deficiency of temper that he is saved from inhumanity. The conduct of Greek heroes is on the whole exemplary. They are all punctiliously correct people, and the *hamartia* which brings misfortune to them—when something of the sort is at all perceptible—appears to be not so much a flaw of character, as an error of judgment resulting specifically from the characteristic inability of heroes to put themselves in another's place. The heroes of Greek tragedy seem to be remarkably self-centered people. Beyond this, they are characterized chiefly by the nature of their predicament, and in their actors' robes and headdresses, masked, they must have seemed godlike, but interchangeable.

It follows that these characters are, generally speaking, psychologically mobile only within the narrowest limits. As Aristotle had noted, it was not the aim of Greek tragedy to develop the characters, but the action; and the same may certainly be said of the Latin drama. Classic art portrayed characters, not character. The figures of Greek drama fulfill their destinies majestically like chessmen, moving in accordance with their nature, but only through the impulse of an external necessity. We do not understand them;

only their needs are made manifest. The minute and compassionate depiction of individual traits which characterizes the dramatic portraiture of our time has nothing to do with an ideal art which opposes to the inscrutable countenance of fate only the inscrutable mask of the hero.

Le Cid makes a very different impression. In the intimacy of its approach it seems almost modern. At the same time, with its quasi-Roman grandeur, its chivalric background, its Spanish *pundonor*, and its Provençal ideas of love, it belongs essentially to the age of Richelieu. Corneille's point of departure, nevertheless, was the classical tradition, and it is astonishing that he was able to complete at a single stroke the transition, which Hardy had initiated, from the imitative theatre of the Renaissance to something that was vital and valid for its time, an understandable, interesting, and contemporary drama. The characters of Rodrigue and Chimène were perhaps intended to be seventeenth-century counterparts of Roman nobility. They were certainly idealized somewhat beyond humanity. But the actor's mask had at last been dropped; the faces were visible, the eyes filled with light; and one could see, or at least divine, the movements of the soul. These were no longer animated examples of Roman statuary; they were characters who inhabited an age which had known Montaigne.

Although Corneille was not able to equal the vitality of *Le Cid* in his subsequent work, the series of dramas which followed it—*Horace, Cinna, Polyeucte, Pompée,* and *Rodogune*—developed very fully the character-type of the dynamic hero, iron-willed, self-sufficient, master of the situation and of himself. These plays are, consequently, in the nature of examples of virtue, and the virtuous characters deserve, and in general are accorded, happy endings. All these plays were conceived as tragedies and are in tragic style; but their plots, under the influence of Spanish drama, tend toward the complexity of comedy, and have a strong forward impulse. This impulse results from a composition of tensions which bear on each other in a carefully calculated sequence, like the gear-train of a watch.

Corneille did not, of course, originate the syllogistic method of telling a story. It had been worked out long ago by the Italian *favellatori*, and was passed on from Italy to Spain, whose dramatists made a specialty of adapting good stories for the stage. But Corneille showed remarkable ingenuity in adapting his exotic materials to the formal requirements of the French theatre. He was, moreover, a brilliant critic and a convincing theorist, and he was able to establish the basis for the dramaturgical system which in 1876 Sarcey still considered indispensable to the theatre.[24] In England, tragedy developed, of course, along much looser lines; but toward the close of the seventeenth century it had arrived at pretty much the same point as had been reached a generation before in France. Fifty years after the death of Shakespeare, we find Dryden already describing the ideal of play construction in terms of a clock mechanism.[25]

Corneille worked in a stricter, more limited, and less boisterous tradition than Shakespeare. He had quite different conventions to follow, and his plays look nothing like Shakespeare's; yet in theory he was not so far from Shakespeare as one might imagine. Corneille based his idea of drama ostensibly upon the imitation of nature, and his practice on the necessity for verisimilitude. It is clear, however, that in his view dramatic truth was something other than a reflection of observed reality. Situations such as those in *Le Cid*, *Horace*, or *Rodogune* were certainly not chosen for dramatization because they best represented observed experience, but because they were considered especially stimulating examples of the extraordinary, the *mirabile*. Like Shakespeare, Corneille was mainly concerned with the behavior of extraordinary people in extraordinary situations. His tragedies were designed to excite wonder, and his idea of drama involved the arrangement of a sequence of moments of high excitement in a pattern that accorded in all respects with current ideas of formal beauty in the other arts.

What was required for cogency in a play conceived along such lines was not that it should accord at all points, or even at any point, with the norms of external experience, but that it should bear a convincing relation to the norms of fantasy. Its verisimilitude would therefore be a matter of internal consistency; its truth would be a question of logic; its beauty, a matter of symmetrical and harmonious composition; but its power would be measured by the depth of the artist's insight into the unconscious workings of the soul. Tragedy was, after all, a form of poetry; and poetry—as Tommaso Ceva put it two centuries before Freud—was "a dream had in the presence of reason." [26] As such, it would be addressed primarily to the intellect, and was intended to be completely intelligible; but its efficacy depended upon experiences situated beyond the margins of reason, which had to be rationalized, therefore, in more or less specious terms. In this respect, the tragedy of the Renaissance and the following age differed markedly from the type of non-realistic drama, developed at the end of the nineteenth century, which was consciously designed not so much to communicate, as to suggest a truth too deep or too inchoate for expression.

The tragic genre which Corneille developed was intended to be the perfectly calculated expression of a rigorously logical action, an action severely straitened by its rules and concentred in its subject matter, set forth in verse that was tense, elegant, ample, but completely serviceable, with no word that did not relate directly to the matter in hand. Seventeenth-century tragedy was, in short, as far from normal human experience as art could make it. It was a form elaborated by artisans of genius, and what they developed was entirely typical of the period, an art of precise and exacting workmanship, and of high finish, designed to please a discriminating and hypercritical clientele. Racine brought this art to its perfection; but it did not survive him. After his time, tragedy, following the direction which Corneille had given it, became a form which was divested as far as possible of whatever in art is vague and elusive, in short, of dream; and at this point it lost its vitality and most of its interest.

In his analysis of the heroic poem Tasso had written, following Aristotle, that a story must contain everything necessary to its understanding; in its beginning, the cause and origins of the matter treated, and, in its middle, the stages through which the action necessarily passed before arriving at the end which, in turn, must leave nothing unresolved.[27] This was exactly the position taken by Corneille in his critical writings, and it precisely represents his practice. But in order to put before an audience the causes and origins of a story which was all but concluded at the inception of the play, it was necessary to write a careful and lengthy exposition. The exposition came to be considered the measure of the writer's skill. Le Cid unfolded a good part of its action before the eyes of the audience; the preparation, accordingly, was not especially elaborate. In most of Corneille's tragedies, however, the first act was wholly preparatory; all the important characters were introduced in it; and this preparation was framed in such a way as to be interesting in itself as well as to arouse expectation and suspense. The exposition was therefore a very elaborate piece of work in which was inherent, in embryo, the entire development of the play. In this development, the essential element was the logical train through which each event inexorably produced the next. According to La Mesnardière:

The poet should be careful when arranging an action that all his events are so mutually dependent that each follows the other as by necessity. Let there be nothing in the action which does not seem to occur save insofar as it must have occurred by reason of what has already happened, so that all things may be so well enchained that one results from the other by a correct sequence.[28]

In an action so carefully arranged, there would, obviously be no room for chance or accident. Corneille deprecated the action of Horace on the ground that the hero does not fall into his second peril as a direct result of escaping from the first. Moreover, when the plot was complex or double, it was felt that in the interest of unity, the situations must be organically related. "The episode," wrote d'Aubignac, "should be so incorporated with the principal subject that the two cannot be separated without destroying the whole work," and it "must be subordinated . . . in such a way that the events of the principal story are the cause of the emotions of the episode, and the catastrophe of the first must naturally produce that of the second." [29]

The principles of the well-made play, the formulation of which is generally credited to Scribe, were thus clearly laid down in the time of Corneille, in part as a result of his theory and practice, and in part as an elaboration of the *Poetics* of Aristotle and the *Discorsi* of Tasso. Seventeenth-century dramaturgy was essentially syllogistic in character. The sense of doom which the Greeks referred to fate or necessity, and the nineteenth-century naturalists to heredity, the seventeenth-century dramatists invariably ascribed to logic. For the seventeenth century, order was the essence of beauty. Life itself was perhaps chaotic, but in the drama one found that balance and harmony which the visible universe ordinarily concealed from our eyes. Seventeenth-century art improved vastly upon nature. The poet, without relinquishing his function as a master of rhetoric, undertook the construction of a play with the clearheaded calm of one who is prepared to demonstrate a theorem in geometry or a problem in mechanics; and the audience came prepared to take pleasure in the elegance of an exercise which was primarily intellectual, and which, without having much to do with reality, yet helped one to understand life and the ways of men.

In the period following the production of *Le Cid*, tragedy moved progressively deeper into the field of abstract art. The plot of *Rodogune* is frankly posed as a problem in psychomechanics. Cleopatra has twin sons. Both desire to inherit the throne, and both are in love with the Princess Rodogune. But the Empress detests Rodogune. She promises to leave her throne to the son who will kill her enemy, while Rodogune, for her part, offers to marry the son who will kill his mother. The denouement of this remarkable situation brings about the death of Cleopatra by a singular ricochet of forces which results in the most spectacular fifth act of seventeenth-century drama.

Rodogune, obviously, is the result of a purely intellectual approach to art; nevertheless, it makes a very vivid effect, for Corneille succeeded wonderfully well in giving validity to the characters whom he engaged in this frankly contrived situation, and he compensated fully for the abstract quality of the design by emphasizing its theatricality. *Rodogune* is by no means an isolated example of abstract design in seventeenth-century drama. On the contrary, the tendency to emphasize the formal principle, already perceptible as a literary expedient in Counter-Reformation Italy, became progressively more important in the totalitarian state of Louis XIV. Since practically all subjects of current interest were closed to discussion in the theatre, the further a play was removed from reality, the more acceptable it was likely to be. In this period, accordingly, the test of dramatic truth was not the realism, but the elegance, of the abstraction. The moment tragedy was absolved from the necessity for representing nature, it became a mathematical art in which virtually complete freedom of fantasy was permitted in the choice of hypotheses, but a rigorously logical progression was insisted on in the deduction of consequences. Thus, in seventeenth-century tragedy nothing was more ordinary than the extraordinary, and in this respect the drama reflected the general trend of literature in this period.

The first three-quarters of the seventeenth century witnessed the proliferation in every field of art of the pre-eminently theatrical style which for want of a better terminology is called baroque. When Corneille composed *Le Cid*, the praises of Cavalier Marino were still echoing from one end of Europe to the other, the demand for the marvellous in poetry was at its height, and the watchwords of art were *novità* and *ingegno*. In the theatre, the *mirabile* had always played an important role. Since Aristotle clearly indicated a partiality for complex plots which excite wonder, Castelvetro had said that "the end of poetry is the pleasure afforded by the marvellous." A number of later Italian critics also took this position; but there was no general agreement on this point in the sixteenth century. Trissino had objected to the improbable as a fault, peculiar to the romances, which the epic and tragic poet should avoid. Scaliger had written that the poet's aim was to teach, move, and delight, but not to astound or to cause admiration. The very influential Marino wrote, however, "*È del poeta il fin la meraviglia*," a memorable phrase which definitely presaged the new style. In the seventeenth-century theatre in Italy and—save for the brief period during which Racine ruled the stage—in France, the plots of tragedy tended to fall more and more into the class of amazing stories.[30]

From the relatively chaste effects of *Horace* and *Cinna* to the awesome ingenuity of *Héraclius*, Corneille exhibited a taste for complexity and the marvellous that was characteristically baroque. In comedy, an analogous tendency toward complexity might be observed in the plays of Aretino and Della Porta, and in the witty drama of the Restoration in England. In this light, the insistence of Corneille on truth and verisimilitude as the pillars of tragedy takes on special meaning. It becomes increasingly evident that one of the chief functions of the unities was to provide the dramatist with an opportunity for the display of ingenuity in representing within a single room in the space of a day a concatenation of events which would normally occupy a great deal of space and time. Verisimilitude thus became a test for the marvellous, and what was originally devised as a means of enhancing the realism of a dramatic action by limiting its scope became the basis of an art, the object of which was to compress as much matter as possible within the smallest possible compass.

The vogue of the baroque, in poetry at least, did not extend much beyond the third quarter of the seventeenth century. By this time there was a surfeit of Italian *ingegno*, and the reaction set in which was to result in the complete discrediting of the *seicento*. In France the change made itself felt relatively early. In the 1670's, a neo-classical movement led by such influential critics as Rapin, Boileau, and Bouhours developed a full-scale offensive against Italian fancy and Spanish wit. A new wave of classicism now swept over Europe, and for nearly two centuries nobody had a good word to say for the extravagant manner of the *seicentisti*, which nevertheless continued to people the churches and public buildings of the Continent with insistently hortatory figures frozen as if by enchantment in postures strongly reminiscent of the tragic stage.[31]

Among the first to sense the reaction against the current theatricalism of the drama was the youthful Racine. Racine, unlike Corneille, enjoyed the advantages of an impeccable classical education. Nevertheless, he did not restore to the tragic plot that classic simplicity which Boileau advocated. His reform consisted chiefly in shifting the interest as far as possible from the external environment to the inner world of his characters. The ancients had thought of tragedy as the movement of simple beings through a simple action. Corneille had conceived of tragedy as a play of simple beings within a complex frame. For Racine there were no simple beings. All motives were complex, and the dramatic action resided mainly within the individual soul.

Like Corneille, Racine preferred the type of plot in which the tragic hero must choose between the dictates of desire and reason. In such circumstances, Corneille's characters display heroic self-mastery, and move, at whatever cost to their happiness, unerringly toward a rational goal. The climax of their action is therefore a heroic effort which is painful, but restorative, so that, through the catharsis of suffering, they achieve serenity and nobility. Racine, however, was evidently on more intimate terms than Corneille with the irrational aspects of human behavior. He understood more clearly the workings of a master-passion, and he undertook to portray the tragedy of heroes who are somewhat less than heroic. Racine's protagonists are, in general, neurotic characters sick with love. In a hopeless situation, they strive pathetically to do the right thing; but they are not usually equal to the effort:

> Je ne fais pas le bien que j'aime,
> Et je fais le mal que je hais.[32]

In these cases, through all the swings to which reason and circumstance subject it, the heart returns unerringly to the lodestone of its desire, and thus these characters find their doom. Corneille took it for granted that in a noble nature reason must triumph; therefore he saw tragedy in the victory of the will. But for Racine, the source of tragedy was the victory of desire.

It is entirely possible, as has often been suggested, that Racine's early training at Port-Royal disposed him to see tragedy in man's inability to make a free choice. The Jansenists were determinists. Where the will is conditioned by destiny, the efforts of the individual to direct his passions can obviously have no effect. It was not difficult in these terms for Racine to reconstruct the conditions of antique tragedy. In his system, tragedy arises not from the inability of the individual to have his will, but from the bootless struggle of the afflicted soul to regain its health in the face of the implacable destiny which deforms it. The feeling of pity which the contemplation of such a spectacle must evoke is consequently bound up with the deep-rooted sense of the injustice of fate which appears to be the psychic basis of the Greek sense of tragedy. It is perhaps for this reason that of all modern dramatists, Racine seems to come closest to that element in antique tragedy which for us constitutes its universality.

The great innovation of Corneille had been to compensate with psychological excitement for the lack of physical movement which the limitations of tragedy entailed. Racine carried this technique to its logical conclusion. Since the alternation of mental states requires no space and little time, Racine found it possible to represent poetically a wide range of emotional experience with a minimum of physical activity. His dramas consist of a series of carefully disciplined colloquies; but these interviews take place in an atmosphere of feverish excitement; the characters move through their scenes with a degree of courtly composure which barely serves to conceal their inner agitation; and they burst out hysterically the moment they are alone with their confidants. The effect is therefore one of great psychic pressure which is constantly, but only barely, under control. What principally emerges on the stage is the state of mind of the characters. The rest of the spectacle is relegated to the imagination of the audience, directed by more or less elaborate reports and descriptions of action in exquisitely modulated verse. In the hands of Racine, tragedy thus became more than ever an elegant art in which the artist demonstrated his bravura by producing a great effect with a minimum of means.

Of the great dramatists, Racine was, in some ways, the least fortunate on the stage. He had great success with *Andromaque* in 1667. Three years later, with *Bérénice*, he began to encounter criticism. In *Andromaque* the action oscillates energetically from beginning to end. *Bérénice* (1670) has, on the contrary, very little movement. It was founded on a paradox arising from what was called, after Guicciardini, *ragion di stato*: the most powerful man in the world, the emperor Titus, has not the power to marry the woman he loves.[33] With this situation—which Pirandello in some measure recalled in *Quando si è qualcuno*—Racine was able to test the temper of the time. The subject had been proposed by Queen Henrietta of England both to Racine and to Corneille. Corneille's play failed. Racine was extremely successful, but he was reproached for the nondramatic nature of an action which is, in effect, a long elegy of farewell. Characteristically, he defended his plot not on the ground of its profundity, but of its *ingegno*, its skill:

Il y en a qui pensent que cette simplicité est une marque de peu d'invention; ils ne songent pas qu'au contraire toute l'invention consiste à faire quelque chose de rien, et que tout ce grand nombre d'incidents a toujours été le réfuge des poëtes qui ne se sentaient dans leur génie, ni assez d'abondance ni assez de force pour attacher durant cinq actes, leurs spectateurs par une action simple, soutenue de la violence des passions, de la beauté des sentiments et de l'élégance de l'expression.[34]

After *Bajazet* (1672), in which he tried his hand at the complex plotting of Corneille, Racine wrote what is generally considered to be his masterpiece, *Phèdre*. It is, it may be argued, the only profound study of feminine psychology to be put on the stage before *Hedda Gabler*. In spite of the really magnificent characterization, the play was a failure. Racine had written it for his mistress La

Champmeslé, and she is said to have surpassed herself in the role; nevertheless the play had to be withdrawn, while Pradon's *Phèdre*, produced two days later under the patronage of Racine's enemies, had a spectacular success. From a poetic viewpoint there is no comparison between the plays, but it is easy to understand why, quite independently of the extraordinary machinations of the anti-Racinian cabal, Pradon's vastly inferior piece would win the plaudits of a popular audience. Racine depended for his effects on the play of human passions. Pradon depended on an ingenious plot full of turns and surprises. "*Entre M. Pradon et moi,*" said Racine, "*il n'y a que le style de différence,*" but in fact what was involved was a completely different dramatic concept.

Racine felt the setback to his hopes so keenly that he swore never again to write for the stage, and he was dissuaded with difficulty from becoming a Carthusian. In 1689, nevertheless, he was prevailed upon by Madame de Maintenon to write *Esther* for the young girls of her convent of Saint-Cyr. In this, as in his last play, *Athalie* (1691), Racine attempted something in the nature of *tragedia sacra*, and he sought to achieve a more authentic classicism by reintroducing the chorus; but these plays were received by the public with indifference. Thus the process of refinement which had brought regular tragedy to its perfection also brought about its decline.

Racine's popularity, in his time, lasted no more than a decade, from 1667 to 1677. Thereafter, the looser form of tragedy—the spectacular plot, the moving action, the oversized characters, the clear-cut motivation, in short, the style against which Racine had reacted—came once again into fashion. Soon after the success of *Iphigénie*, Madame de Sévigné had predicted, "*Racine passera comme le café.*" She prophesied better than she knew, but her practical nature did not entirely deceive her. It was indeed the line of Corneille and not that of Racine that was followed by the writers of the following age. That line would lead infallibly to the study of Shakespeare, and a new concept of tragedy; but this point was not reached until the possibilities of regular tragedy had been exhausted in a series of fruitless efforts to adapt tragedy to the more exigent tastes of the new century.

Houdar de la Motte was the first of the post-Racinian dramatists to rebel openly against the tyranny of the classical form. In the prefaces to his plays, he repeatedly proclaimed the freedom of the writer to transcend the unities, to represent scenes of violence, and to utilize such visual effects as were already in use in the opera. But in contrast to his revolutionary prefaces, La Motte's actual practice was insufferably tedious, and it was not until the time of Hugo that such enthusiastic ideas as La Motte advocated were actually put into effect. La Motte's only innovation was the suppression of the role of the confidante in *Inez de Castro*. It was a rash departure, but only barely sufficient to assure him a place in the history of tragedy.

The radical views of La Motte did not find favor with Voltaire. He had come to know something of English drama during his three-year stay in England, and he was painfully aware of the necessity for invigorating the French style; but he believed that the special characteristics of French tragedy must be preserved at any cost. The unities were indispensable, he thought, for verisimilitude; the rules of decorum, however, might profitably be relaxed a little to permit the introduction of spectacle. Unfortunately, Voltaire's initial experiments along these lines were not crowned with success. In *La Mort de César* (1743), he imitated Shakespeare by having Antony speak over Caesar's body, but he tried to give the action a classical touch by following Pradon's idea that Brutus was really the son of Caesar, so that the murder of Caesar became a parricide. *Sémiramis* (1748) had four scene-changes, a ghost, and a matricide. In 1759, after overcoming impressive obstacles, he succeeded in clearing the gallants off the stage at the Comédie-Française, so that it became possible for the actors to move about without stumbling over the audience. The result was a loss in intimacy without a corresponding gain in effectiveness. Tragedy was sick with the disease of eloquence. Neither spectacle, nor comedy, nor the grotesque could enliven what was at bottom a motivated series of recitations on topics the possibilities of which had long ago been exhausted.

The Great Revolution did little to change matters in the French theatre, and under the Empire tragedy once again came into fashion. Great actors were now employed to give the imperial theatre the requisite stature and sparkle, and the Kremlin Edict put the Théâtre-Français on a regular and permanent footing. Its productions, in fact, were already taking on a new look. Lekain had instituted a great reform by introducing the use of historical costume. In *Christophe Colombe* (1809), Lemercier went so far as to disregard the unities of time and place entirely—there was a violent reaction in the audience and a spectator was killed. But nobody ventured so far as to question the rules of Boileau concerning the distinction of genres or the distinction of styles. In spite of all efforts to modernize them, the classical forms remained stubbornly classical, an impressive example of generical senility.

The classical idea of drama was attacked first in Germany by Lessing, then by the Schlegels. In Italy, Manzoni had harsh words to say on the subject. The word "romantic," to which Madame de Staël gave prominence in *De l'Allemagne* (1813), began to be used freely, if indiscriminately, with reference to a new concept of art, the precise nature of which was as yet not clear, but which, in contrast to the classic, had disturbingly Germanic connotations. In 1822 Stendhal, in the brilliant essay *Racine et Shakespeare*, came out flatly for the view that classic art was old-fashioned. There was, he argued, need for a modern drama. Racine no longer pleased. Shakespeare did.

In France, by this time, the romantic revolution was in full swing. As early as 1792, Schiller had been made an honorary citizen of France, presumably as a reward for the service he had rendered humanity in writing *Die Räuber* eleven years before. In 1827 Kemble and Miss Smithson brought a repertory of Shakespearean plays to Paris, and set the young men afire with enthusiasm. Two years later, young Alexandre Dumas produced *Henri III et sa cour* at the Comédie-Française. A year after that, Hugo produced *Hernani*.

The characters of the new romantic tragedy were, in fact, much like the characters of regular tragedy, but since they were released from the necessity for observing the rules of decorum, they were able to exhibit unaccustomed vigor. The innovation in romantic characterization was mainly an extension of the revolutionary aspect of Greek tragedy, observable in such plays as *Prometheus* or *Antigone*. The gist of it was to depict robbers and outlaws as great-souled creatures of heroic mold, while those in authority took on the less glamorous aspect of policemen. The consequence was not, however, the abolition of decorum, but the institution of a new convention, in terms of which it became unusual to encounter other than high-minded bandits in the theatre. In addition, the characters of the new romantic tragedy were splendidly self-propelled. They issued from secret doors, masked and caped, sword in hand, made love beautifully and tragically, expressed themselves in high españolistic terms, duelled, swaggered, and died in interesting postures reminiscent of Delacroix.

The unit of construction in these plays was the act, and each act had its own climax, its *coup de théâtre*, and its memorable curtain-line. The situations were improbable, but no more so than those of regular tragedy, and they were designed to elicit admiration, astonishment, and delight. The emphasis, however, was not on the intellectual working-out of a carefully calculated *imbroglio*, but on the emotional experience of living through a series of thrilling scenes.

As it was the emotional experience that was chiefly emphasized in these plays, comic scenes were alternated and even blended with serious matter, and the point of attack was moved back far enough in the story so that its most interesting events could be played. In accordance with romantic practice, the characters were given individuality through the exaggeration of their idiosyncrasies, but characterization continued to be archetypal. The desired effect was tragic. It was certainly not the tragic mood of Racine in which, *"il suffit . . . que tout s'y ressente de cette tristesse majestueuse qui fait tout le plaisir de la tragédie."* Romantic tragedy had too much incident for that; but something of the Racinian melancholy usually colored the last act. The truth is that, in spite of the literary pretensions of their authors, the plays written in this genre in the 1830's and 1840's were, with the possible exception of *Hernani*, remarkably childish. The romantic style in the drama reached its perfection only in the time of Rostand. But by then, romanticism had learned a lesson in common sense from the naturalists, and it was, in any case, too late.

Romantic tragedy dates from 1830. A dozen years later, the failure of *Les Burgraves* initiated a severe reaction in the direction of the classics, marked by the unexpected success of Ponsard's *Lucrèce* (1843), a dreary tragedy in the style of Corneille, which had not even the merit of regularity. The following year, the public was flocking to hear Rachel in the plays of Racine. But a new spirit was already in the air. Novelists and poets were striking out in new directions. Artistic interest was shifting more and more to things of the present: contemporary manners, contemporary problems, and contemporary characters. Balzac's preface to *La Comédie humaine* appeared in 1842. The age of realism was at hand.

It was, however, to be some little time before realism came to the theatre. Aristotle had written of tragedy as an imitation of nature, and Cicero, supposedly, had said that comedy was *imitatio vitae*, but nobody seriously expected the drama to be anything like an accurate transcription of life. There was the world of the theatre, and the world of the actual. They differed in essence. In the theatre all was fantasy and exaggeration. Tragedy was a fantasy of human greatness; comedy, a fantasy of its meanness. There was no genre for the fantasy of the actual, and, for a long time, seemingly, no need for such a thing. When the need was felt, however, a new form came into existence which rapidly overshadowed all that had gone before.

Throughout the neo-classical period it was customary to think of a play in terms of a movement of conventional figures, a kind of animated puppet show. The plots both of tragedy and comedy were largely familial in scope. Tragedy was the domestic drama of kings, just as comedy was the domestic drama of tradesmen. "The difference in these two kinds of poetry," Corneille had written, "consists only in the dignity of the characters and the actions which they imitate, and not in the manner of imitation, or in the things that serve in this imitation." [35] The characters of drama were, in fact, indigenous to their genre—comedy was the play of the gallant, the lady, the old man, the lackey, and the maid; in tragedy, the characters were kings, queens, confidants, and lovers. Each game had its appropriate pieces, the relations of which might be expected to change, but not their essential character and value.

Within this frame of reference, Racine and Molière had already taken important strides toward realism in the portrayal of character. "When you paint men," Dorante says in *La Critique de l'École des femmes*, "you must paint after nature, the portraits must be likenesses, and you have not succeeded if people do not recognize in them the men of the age." Molière began, like Shakespeare, with stock types, but the genius of these writers is apparent in the accuracy of their observation and the acuity of their caricature. The ancestor of Dogberry is possibly the Scythian policeman of Greek comedy, and in Falstaff we may recognize the archetypal *miles*, but these characters are far from animated masks. Similarly in Shylock, as in Monsieur Jourdain, we may see, if we like, the Venetian Pantalone, but these characters have taken on, with the mask, rather more individuality than most people of our acquaintance.

With *L'École des femmes* and *Les Précieuses ridicules*, Molière defined two relatively new genres, comedy of character and comedy of manners. Scarron had already brought comedy indoors, to the bedroom. Molière set *Le Tartuffe*, *Le Misanthrope*, and *Les Femmes savantes* in the living room, and with these plays comedy once for all moved in off the street. It now became possible to play an intimate scene realistically, if one wished, and as comedy lost its public character, it began to take on a new sensibility.

Sensibility was carried into the seventeenth century by the heirs of the romantic tradition of the middle ages, the heroic poets, particularly Tasso, the pastoral writers, and the early novelists, the Scudéry and La Calprenède. In England, the comedy of Etherege and Congreve, like the type of hard comedy which developed in France under classical influence, was based firmly on the idea that in the healthy individual the passions are under the firm discipline of the intellect. Dorimant and Mirabell are well-integrated sensualists who do not fall in love, feel no fear, and have no pity. But the plays in which these characters figure are still relatively abstract compositions, witty anecdotes in which it is unnecessary to assume for a moment that anything is true. The development of realism and the development of sensibility have an understandable relation. The more real a situation appears to be, the less possible it is to view it with detachment; and the closer the degree of identification, the more important becomes the question of psychological validity.

The writers of the new age affirmed the supremacy of the heart over the mind, and thus marked a turning point in the history of European culture. The favorite characters of the new drama were not the strong, the just, or the witty, but the good-hearted, the merciful and compassionate; henceforth, the heart took on a moral aspect independent of the mind. The good heart was obedient to its own categorical impulse, unreasonable and unreasoned, and was motivated principally by love. Its virtue was characterized by a noble excess. The heart, irrational and impulsive, was seen to represent something higher and nobler than reason. It was a more trustworthy guide to action, and reflected a special grace that required no schooling. Like the *cor gentil* of Dante, the good heart was the mark of a natural nobility of character that distinguished the individual regardless of his station in life. From the viewpoint of the intellect, the follies of mankind excited laughter, but the good heart did not know contempt; it knew only compassion.

Under its influence, comedy ceased to be aggressive. It became tearful and joyous, a celebration of the goodness of humanity.

The good heart was awakened in various ways—by a vision of beauty, by the sight of suffering, by a sudden flash of insight into the kinship of humanity, or simply by a touch of grace. The consequence was, a man might suffer in a twinkling a complete transformation of character. Behavior, from this viewpoint, became quite unpredictable. As the idea of the instability of character gained ground with the growth of the romantic interpretation of life, it became impossible in the drama to plot an action with the beautiful precision that characterized the drama of the seventeenth century. Under the influence of beauty, of pity, of conscience, the hardest heart might be expected suddenly to soften, to forgive, and to humble itself in charity. In these circumstances, no character could be considered dependable, and no chain of logic safe. The classical system of playmaking began to show serious signs of erosion. With the advent of sensibility, comedy and tragedy, as distinct concepts, lost whatever validity they may have had.

These changes became perceptible at a relatively early date. Corneille, Racine, and Molière, though by no means free of sentimentality, had affirmed staunchly the autonomy of the classic forms. But as early as 1696, in England, Colley Cibber broke through the hard crust of comedy with a sentimental scene in Love's Last Shift, and his example was soon followed by Farquhar and Vanbrugh, both of whom portrayed the unsettling effects of a sudden attack of goodness on a sparkish character.[36] In 1722, Steele established a landmark with The Conscious Lovers, a deliberate restatement of Terence's Andria from the sentimental viewpoint. A dozen years later, in France, La Chaussée inaugurated the sentimental drama of family life with La Fausse antipathie (1733), a play about two people who fall in love without knowing that they were once husband and wife. La Chaussée, it is true, was less interested in developing serious comedy than in bringing to the stage examples of the marvellous; nevertheless his characters make an impression of humanity which seems relatively new in his time. The next step in the direction of a realistic drama was to place such characters in situations reminiscent of the actual. This involved a complete re-orientation of thought with regard to the theatre, and for a long time no one was willing to venture upon it. In this connection *The London Merchant* took on unexpected importance.

The London Merchant (1731) was based on a popular ballad. It treats earnestly and with some show of actuality the age-old situation of a good but weak young man who is tempted into crime by an evil woman, and it has strong moral implications. It has also a certain sociological interest, for in this play Lillo suggested, for what was perhaps the first time in the theatre, the responsibility of society for the degradation of the individual. Aside from this, *The London Merchant* differs little from the type of cheap melodrama which enlivened the popular stage in the early years of the twentieth century. Nevertheless in Lillo's domestic drama, which he thought "*une chose sublime*," Diderot saw the promise of the serious drama of the future. The cornerstone of this drama was to be the illusion of reality.

In *Les Bijoux indiscrets* (1748), and, later, in the dialogues *Dorval et moi* (1757), Diderot took note of the fact that tragedy was no longer a living art: its plots were contrived, its problems unreal, and its methods unnatural. Tragedy produced no illusion of reality; for Diderot this was an essential defect. He proposed instead a drama of the actual, *le genre sérieux*, a form that would deal convincingly with the facts of contemporary life. "The perfection of a play," he wrote, "consists in the imitation of an action so exact that the spectator, deceived without interruption, imagines he is present at the action itself." [37] For this purpose the stage setting must reproduce exactly the environment of the action. If the scene depicted a room, he thought, then the audience must be considered an invisible presence in that room. The consequence of this idea was to locate the imaginary fourth wall of the room, from one point of view, at the proscenium, but from another, at the extremity of the theatre. Practically, of course, it made no difference where it was, if anywhere: the fantasy accommodates itself equally well to either point of view, or to both at once. It was not until the naturalists of the Théâtre-Libre insisted on subjecting the dramatic illusion to new tests of verisimilitude that the fourth wall began to obtrude itself upon the attention of the audience.

Diderot illustrated his ideas with *Le Fils naturel* (1757), and four years later with *Le Père de famille* (1761). *Le Père de famille* was successful; but Diderot was not talented as a playwright, and his taste, for all his enthusiasm, was not of the best. His ideas with respect to a new concept of mimesis were, doubtless, revolutionary, but his plays illustrated compendiously the dangers of adapting the current stage to middle-class standards. Judging from *Le Père de famille*, the sort of play he had in mind for the new genre would consist of a series of animated tableaux in the style of Greuze's painting *Le Fils punit*. However artificial tragedy had become, it was at least too sophisticated an art to ally itself with the maudlin trend of contemporary painting.

Diderot's ideas caused a good deal of stir in theatrical circles. Three years after the publication of *Dorval et moi*, Voltaire, ever abreast of the current trend, attempted to give definition to the new realism with *L'Écossaise* (1760), a contemporary spy drama, in which people were actually shown in a cafe, eating and drinking. Some years later, Beaumarchais, a disciple of Diderot, produced *Eugénie*, a play in the new genre, which he called a *drame*. He accompanied this "drama" with an essay in which he renewed Diderot's arguments with respect to tragedy, a genre, he intimated, which belonged to a barbarous age, now past:

Everything in these plays seems monstrous to me: unbridled passions, atrocious crimes, these are as far from being natural as they are unusual in the civilization of our time . . . What do I care, I, a peaceful subject in an eighteenth-century monarchy, for the revolutions of Athens and Rome? Of what real interest to me is the death of a Peloponnesian tyrant or the sacrifice of a young princess at Aulis? There is nothing in that for me; no moral which is applicable to my needs.[38]

It was, he added very sensibly, not because a king is a king but because a king is a man that we feel for him:

The true heart-interest, the true relationship, is always between man and man and not between man and king . . . The nearer the suffering man is to my station in life, the greater is his claim on my sympathy.[39]

Although *Eugénie* eventually had some success on the stage, it had no special consequence, and Beaumarchais did not make a second attempt to develop the *drame*. But in 1765, Michel Sedaine, a professional librettist, succeeded in realizing the new genre with a play called *Le Philosophe sans le savoir*. This was not a particularly imaginative work, but it combined the dignity and simplicity of the tragic mode with the realism and actuality of serious comedy, and it provided a viable model for the realistic drama of the succeeding century.

Sedaine wrote his play in five acts, in prose, in a terse quasi-colloquial style which had no literary pretensions. The dialogue is neither spirited nor witty—it serves chiefly to advance the action and to define the characters. The characterization is far from brilliant, but it is convincing; the characters were evidently meant to be real people, and they are believable. The action was devised so that it has a mounting suspense and a strong reversal; but instead of straining for theatrical effect in the tragic manner, Sedaine deliberately understated his scenes and made his points through silence and implication. It was the first serious play in French that was in no sense a poem; for the first time it demonstrated the power of the drama that avoids rhetoric. It was also the first modern play to develop seriously a social problem of some importance.

In 1765 the French middle class had every right to insist on being taken quite as seriously in the theatre as the aristocracy. Sedaine's play not only extolled bourgeois morality and bourgeois courage; it also assimilated the virtues of the middle class to those of the nobility so closely that when the banker Vanderk confesses that, although he is engaged in business, he is in fact of noble birth, it occasions no surprise. The proud fortitude with which

Vanderk carries on at his desk while his heart is breaking is the middle-class equivalent of knightly valor, and the implication is inescapable that the tradesman Vanderk is in every way the equal of the noble Desparville.

Since the virtues of the banker and his son, as Sedaine depicted them, were precisely those chivalric virtues on which the classical drama of the period was based, *Le Philosophe sans le savoir* made a very practical transition from the tragic style to the new drama of the actual. Moreover, the construction of the play, with its symmetrical composition, its unlikely situation, and its surprising reversal, paralleled quite closely the technique of tragedy, while the charming evocations of family life in the first scenes of the play recalled pleasantly the sentimental groupings of the genre painting of the period. But in spite of all this, Sedaine's *drame* won no favor in the literary theatre. The actors of the Comédie-Française preferred the kind of play that gave the necessary scope for declamation: from their viewpoint a play like *Le Philosophe sans le savoir* contained no rewarding roles. The *drame* was therefore relegated to the popular theatre, and it was there that realism had its development, while the Comédie-Française continued as always to specialize in the classical genres. Following Diderot, Sedaine had brought the theatre to the verge of modernity; but the time was not yet ripe. It was to be yet another half-century before any truly significant change took place. The modern theatre begins with Scribe.

The New Drama

BEFORE the time of Scribe, playwriting was a precarious profession in which the dramatist who was neither an actor nor a theatre manager generally had to rely on a patron for his livelihood, or else resign himself to a life of misery alleviated by an occasional windfall. The lot of the dramatist under patronage was not, of course, uniformly wretched. In France in the time of Louis XIV, when the Crown undertook a direct responsibility for the maintenance of the national culture, men of outstanding talent were thoroughly pampered. As royal historiographer, Racine received over a period of ten years a stupendous annual salary, and Molière, during his fifteen-year tenure as actor-manager and royal upholsterer, was able to earn, it is said, 336,000 francs in addition to the 200,000 francs a year he earned as a writer.[1]

Patronage came to an end in France shortly after the middle of the eighteenth century. Thenceforth a dramatist had to look primarily to the public for his livelihood and, as might be expected, popular taste became an increasingly important consideration in the development of dramatic art. During the Great Revolution, the popular audience which the learned drama had displaced once again thronged back to the theatres. The Comédie-Française and the Odéon continued to play tragedy and comedy before empty houses, while the Boulevard theatres—the Gymnase, the Vaudeville, the Gaîté, and the rest—were thronged with soldiers and workmen, the greater part of whom were illiterate.[2] The new audience was partial to strong effects; it was basically moral and conservative in its attitudes; and it vastly preferred song to declamation. The dramatic forms which found special favor in its eyes were the melodrama and the vaudeville. These are by far the most interesting forms of the period, and the most characteristic, and they were pivotal in the transition of the old drama to the new.

Under the Empire and the Restoration the censorship effectively hindered the discussion of anything of current importance in the state theatres. The popular theatre, on the other hand, was considered to have no political significance, and it was virtually neglected by the authorities. Consequently it enjoyed a substantial, if wholly unsolicited, monopoly of whatever was of immediate interest in the drama of the time. In the period between the institution of the First Empire and the July Revolution, aside from the comedy of manners in the style of Scribe, which was occasionally performed at the Comédie-Française, the only living drama was the popular drama of the boulevards.

Plebeian taste in France was not, in this period, essentially different from that of the cultivated classes. The difference was a matter of refinement. The sensationalism and sentimentality of tragedy in the time of La Grange-Chancel and Crébillon found its full scope in the popular theatre. Tragedy died with the *ancien régime;* but its demise was only temporary. It was immediately reborn as melodrama.

Melodrama was not a new idea when Guilbert de Pixerécourt applied the term to the musical play he presented at the Ambigu-Comique in 1797. The word had been used by Rousseau more than twenty years before to describe his *Pygmalion,* a dramatic recitation with intermittent musical accompaniment, and it had since been used in connection with various types of musical spectacle. Pixerécourt's *Victor, ou l'enfant de la forêt* was first written as an opera, with a libretto in the style of *Die Räuber*. By the time this work reached the stage, it had lost its score and its arias, but the musical accompaniment was retained in certain scenes. Melodrama was therefore—largely as the result of accident—a play, embellished with music, and patterned more or less closely on the scheme of *Die Räuber*—the falsely accused hero, the captive maiden, the long-suffering elders, and the cold-blooded villain. Pixerécourt tried to give this form dignity by tracing its origins to the ancient mime.[3]

Melodrama originated as a literary mongrel, and became a popular form by chance; but it was not enough for Pixerécourt to be successful; he aspired wistfully to be thought correct. He therefore confined the action of his plays as far as possible within the unities, and tried to promote his style among the learned. The tastes of the popular audience, however, ran to colorful thrillers, and he had to pilfer the *Sturm und Drang* literature of the Germans, the novels of Mrs. Radcliffe, the English plays of honor and chivalry, and the Spanish *comedias* for suitable material. Like the Spanish plays, the *mélodrames* had a three-act structure. Each act was treated as an entity and had a climactic arrangement. The first act generally established a strong antagonism which precipitated a violent conflict in the second. The third act resolved the situation in accordance with sound moral principles, and the play ended happily with the canonical scene of the distribution of prizes. What this amounted to was tragedy reduced to its least common denominator, enlivened with romantic situations, comic effects, and spectacle, and relieved with a happy ending.[4]

The success of the new form was phenomenal. Between 1798 and 1814, Pixerécourt himself composed and produced well over a hundred plays, and the demand did not begin to slacken until after 1830. It was not long, however, before melodrama attracted first the admiration and then the competition of the French romanticists. They were, after all, dipping into the same sources, if at a somewhat higher level, and the popular character of melo-drama, its crude colors and violent contrasts, its vigor and earnest-ness and, above all, the keen disapproval of the critics, combined to give it glamour in their eyes. Hugo and Dumas presumably based their art upon the practice of Shakespeare and Schiller; in reality they helped themselves generously to the methods and materials of the popular musical theatre. The bandits, rescues, con-spiracies, and ambushes; the daggers, heirlooms, lost documents, and long-lost children of melodrama became the staple also of romantic tragedy. Like Pixerécourt and d'Ennery, the roman-tic dramatists set their scenes in out-of-the-way places and brought about marvellous encounters in tombs, cellars, dungeons, and towers; but their characters, unlike those of the popular theatre, had an air of cultivation, addressed one another elegantly in Alex-andrines, and eventually found their way to the operatic stage.

These attempts to elevate popular drama to the status of a literary genre met with considerable resistance. The return of the public to the theatre, marked by the immense development of melodrama and vaudeville, was felt in learned quarters to be full of menace to the ancient culture of France. The Comédie-Française was the last citadel of the *grand siècle*, and the cultivated classes were determined to defend it to the last from the invasion of the vulgar profane who swarmed in the boulevards. The literary battle which raged over *Hernani* is understandable as a crucial episode in the cultural upheaval which was taking place in the wake of the political revolution. The affair *Hernani* was detonated, it is said, by the passage, "*Est-il minuit?—Minuit bientôt.*" The rhythm of the line is Shakespeare's: "What hour now?—I think it lacks of twelve." [5] Such brevity was an obvious affront to ears accustomed to the *style noble* of tragedy, and the classicists surged forward in defense of the classical tradition and all it connoted. The unities, the distinction of genres, the distinction of styles, suddenly ac-quired both political and moral significance, and the stage of the Comédie-Française took on for a time the aspect of a battlefield.

The battle for the classics was neither lost nor won. By 1830, the cultural level of the popular audience had been raised to the point where it no longer found melodrama inspiring, and the taste which had been nourished on the pretentious rubbish of Pixeré-court turned to something that was, at least, somewhat more reasonable and less pompous. The high astounding drama of Alexandre Dumas and Victor Hugo held the stage only briefly. Then came the turn of Scribe and the *comédie-vaudeville*.

The vaudeville was, to begin with, a short, loosely woven entertainment of provincial origin, based upon a lightly plotted story interspersed with *couplets* of current topical interest. By the beginning of the nineteenth century, it had developed into a form that was substantially the prototype of modern musical comedy. In Paris the demand for this type of entertainment soon reached astonishing proportions. From 1820 to 1850, Eugène Scribe wrote scores, perhaps hundreds, of these ephemeral but eminently profitable pieces. During the whole of this period he was in personal control of the market. The writing of plays had by this time become an important industry. In the past, playwrights had been more or less at the mercy of the theatre managers, and had been glad to sell their compositions outright, or in consideration of the receipts of one, or, exceptionally, two benefit performances. The avidity of the public for new plays was such, however, that Scribe was able to impose upon the managers a system of royalties by which the author received a fixed percentage of the gross receipts of each performance. In this manner, he soon grew rich, and, by organizing a Society of Authors, he made it possible for his more astute contemporaries to follow his example. By 1836, Scribe was so successful a writer that he was elected to the French Academy —which had once refused Molière.

In his inaugural speech, Scribe reminded the Immortals, whom he was about to join, that the purpose of drama was to entertain and not to instruct, and he struck a blow against naturalism a full half-century before it came into being:

You go to the theatre not for instruction or correction, but for re-
laxation and amusement. Now, what amuses you most is not truth
but fiction. To represent what is before your eyes every day is not
the way to please you; but what does not come to you in your usual
life, the extraordinary, the romantic, that is what charms you, that
is what one is eager to offer you . . .

In this oft-quoted statement, which his graver colleagues hastened
to reject, Scribe did no more than to report the condition of the
theatre of his day, which he was in a better position to know than
anyone then living. In fact, Scribe's dramas are full of *meraviglie*,
but his viewpoint was thoroughly realistic. The view of life which
his comedies exemplify is Machiavellian. His world is one in which
God has no further interest, and in which it is a sign of naïveté
to trust in anything but one's own intelligence and strength. In this
jungle, there may be found benevolent creatures of noble nature,
but not many. In general, the spiritual values have become social,
and the desire for peace of mind and a pure conscience which characterized a nobler age has given way to the desire for power, money,
a rich marriage—in short, the desire to succeed at all costs.

The Scribean hero is a person of wisdom and experience who
knows the ways of the world, and is able to play upon the desires
and emotions of his adversaries with the skill of a virtuoso. Most
often his ends are worthy—in the plays of Scribe, the good always
triumph and the mean are punished, so that we are given to understand that even in the jungle, the moral basis of creation affirms
itself. It affirms itself, however, not through the moral superiority
of the benevolent, but through their superior intelligence, which is
another way of saying that evil is a form of stupidity. Scribe's plays
are nearly always formulated in terms of a contest in which the
antagonists are evenly—but not quite evenly—matched, so that
the outcome is often in doubt, and the suspense runs high. Within
this struggle is involved the indispensable love story, the outcome
of which depends on the contest of wills into which it is keyed,
and of which it is a function, for the love story is seldom the central

motive of the play. The lovers are never far from our eyes—the girl, sweet and trusting; the boy courageous and strong—but it is the grown-ups who absorb our interest, and for them love is never a primary consideration.

This technique of storytelling was doubtless an extension of the style which Ariosto had long ago perfected in the *Orlando furioso*, the ultimate pattern of contrivance in the narrative art. Corneille had sanctified such methods to the high purposes of an idealistic age. Scribe had no notion of reconstructing the idealistic world picture. His world was essentially the world of Ariosto, a fantastic creation in which nobody was expected to believe, but which perhaps was true; a creation without moral seriousness, the prevailing mood of which was a sense of irony, which was perhaps a sublimation of despair. The validity of such a world depended principally on the perfection of its internal structure, the co-ordination of its elements. Like the world of Ariosto, the world of Scribe was held together by logic alone. It could therefore not fail to be other than superficial, and was not presented with any pretense of profundity.

In such a world, history would not be the revelation of the divine will, nor the dialectic of economic forces, least of all the evolution of an ethical substance. It would be a mechanical concatenation of cause and consequence, the product of inexorable logic. A prime source of the *mirabile* was therefore the way in which the most trivial causes were seen to bring about the most impressive results. In the first act of *Le Verre d'eau*, the wily Bolingbroke sets forth this viewpoint at some length; he concludes by recalling how he was made Prime Minister because he could dance a sarabande, and how he was dismissed because he caught a cold. The ensuing action then illustrates this ironic view of history—a glass of water spilled on Queen Anne's dress brings about the disgrace of the Duchess of Marlborough, the collapse of the Whigs, the rise of Bolingbroke to power, and a complete reversal of the foreign policy of England. Such revelations were particularly congenial to an age which had survived, over a period of twenty years, the greatness of Robespierre and the greatness of Napoleon, and the ultimate effect was a *reductio ad absurdum* of human greatness. In a universe conceived after the manner of Scribe, nothing could be taken very seriously.

In the system of tragedy which the seventeenth century evolved, the protagonist never addressed the audience directly; he kept it informed of his intentions and his state of mind by speaking to his counsellor or his confidant. The elimination of the confidant would either put the principal directly in touch with the audience or cut him off from it completely. Scribe followed the English practice by choosing the former alternative. The Scribean protagonist thus assumed the role of *raisonneur*. He harangued the audience, informed it of his plans, and by a constant flow of soliloquies and asides kept it continually advised of his progress. The result was to identify the audience so closely with the action that it might well be considered a member of the cast. This system served until the naturalists forced its abolition toward the very end of the century.

The arbitrary design which Scribe imposed upon experience did not exclude the events of experience. It simply gave them an amusing turn by reorganizing them in accordance with the logic of the theatre. Just as in the novels of Balzac we find, for the first time, an awareness of the problems which still confront us, so in the plays of Scribe we find a distorted but unmistakable reflection of the opening phases of our era. Everything which the younger Dumas took up seriously a generation later, Scribe touched on lightly and wittily in his own generation. One has only to read *La Camaraderie* to see how clearly he foreshadowed the social drama of the succeeding age. But Scribe did not consider the stage an appropriate forum for the discussion of ideas. He contented himself with providing a form of quasi-intellectual entertainment which in the name of good sense imposed a semblance of order upon the extravagances of romanticism, and a curb of ridicule on the extravagances of life. He had a first-rate inventive gift. He wrote with brilliance and verve: unhappily, his workmanship was poor. As his vastly varied operations in the theatre involved him in an industrial enterprise of some magnitude, he had not time to give his plays the finish requisite to a work of art. Had he taken pains with them, very likely such plays as *Le Verre d'eau* or *La Bataille de dames* would still be considered masterpieces in their genre, like the English Restoration comedies, which also lack depth and subtlety, and which have plots even less probable than those of Scribe, but which are still accorded the reverence due to works of genius.[6] It is not because Scribe was too much the craftsman that we find his work unsatisfactory in our age, but because he was not craftsman enough.

Scribe could tell a story well. Nothing is more difficult on the stage. He devised a formula which all but guaranteed an effective development; but his subject matter was too often trivial, and his apparatus had already been much handled by hacks. It consisted largely of the menacing secrets, intercepted letters, overheard conversations, *quiproquos* and *méprises*, unexpected encounters, and sudden strokes of fortune which formed the traditional baggage of the professional storyteller. Not even the way in which he arranged his materials was new; he merely elaborated the critical precepts of Corneille and d'Aubignac, adapting the forms of the comedy of intrigue to a romantic subject matter. The result was novel. It was only in the time of Zola that the critics discovered how stale, flat, and unprofitable were the plays devised according to the blueprint of Scribe. In the meantime, this blueprint served as the master pattern of dramatic construction, and it acquired in its day the authority of a science. Until the first decades of the twentieth century, the system of Scribe was *"le système du théâtre."*

In accordance with the practice of Corneille, Scribe employed a five-act structure, with the climax in the fourth act, the denouement in the fifth, and a quick curtain. The first act was mainly expository; its tone was gay. Toward its end, the antagonists engaged, and the conflict was initiated.[7] For the next three acts, the action oscillated in an atmosphere of mounting tension. In the fourth act—"the act of the ball"—the stage was generally filled with people, and there was an outburst—a scandal, a quarrel, a challenge. At this point things usually looked pretty black for the hero. But the last act arranged everything; in the final scene, the cast was assembled, there were reconciliations and an equitable distribution of prizes, and the audience came out of the theatre smiling.

Within the frame of his intrigue, Scribe developed what was virtually a comedy of manners; but there was no point at which the intrigue was suspended—as in the plays of Oscar Wilde—for a display of manners or a discussion of ideas. The innovation of Scribe was mainly that he practiced in fact what the seventeenth-century critics had preached in theory with respect to the pace, excitement, and surprise necessary to a successful theatre piece. Scribe considered it essential that the action proceed smoothly and elegantly from the exposition through the successive stages of complication, climax, peripeteia, and denouement, and to this narrative-progression all other considerations were subordinated.

The unit of construction was now no less than the whole play, but within this unit, the inner structure was very firmly planned. Since, in accordance with classical practice, each entrance made a new scene, the sequence of entrances, the *numérotage* of scenes, was predetermined in accordance with principles similar to those governing the rhythm of units in a design, so that the recurrence of characters from the viewpoint of composition influenced to a considerable extent the arrangement of the plot.[8] The scenes were composed in somewhat the same manner as the play itself, but in miniature. Each scene had its initial situation, its progression, complication, climax, peripeteia, and conclusion, so that it formed an autonomous whole within the total arrangement. It was, consequently, quite possible to come to the theatre in time for the performance of a favorite scene, and to leave immediately after, having enjoyed a complete, and often sufficient, dramatic experience.

Scribe ushered in the era of middle-class theatre. The July monarchy was dominated by an aristocracy of wealth with which the old nobility and the church in the end came to terms. Industrial enterprise now took on unexpected glamour, and the whole system of social values was shifted so as to accommodate a new order of hero. In *Le Philosophe sans le savoir*, Sedaine had foreshadowed the glorification of the captain of industry. The next masterpiece in this genre was *Le Gendre de M. Poirier*, in which Émile Augier showed how a businessman's daughter could give lessons in nobility to a marquis. The way was now open for the development of the tragedy of a banker, such as John Gabriel Borkman, or the tragicomedy of a munitions maker, such as Andrew Undershaft.

After 1852, France became once again a police state. Napoleon III maintained his rule chiefly through an alliance with big business, and his state was in great measure the visible sign of the wave of economic prosperity which lasted into the 1860's. During his reign, Paris became the amusement center of Europe. It was a very gay city, the city of Offenbach, Meyerbeer, and Haussmann; but in this period, it has been remarked, the wrong people were gay: in these years, everything speaks of the growing disillusionment of the intellectual classes. The prevailing mood of the time was critical and analytical rather than creative; and its art, essentially realistic and matter of fact, was didactic, argumentative, and concentrated on the contemporary as the only possible subject of interest.[9]

In the time of Scribe, plays were chiefly directed to the comfortable bourgeois, and drama tended to be relatively sensible; but the age was enthralled by every sort of ingenuity, and in time Scribean contrivance was carried far beyond the limits of Scribe. In this respect, the true heir of the tradition of Scribe was Victorien Sardou, who established himself about 1860 as the grand master of the *pièce bien faite*, and maintained himself securely in this position until the end of the century. Sardou, however, did not really represent his time, nor, indeed, any time. He paid, it is true, lip service to the drama of social problems which was developed during this period, but he was principally faithful to the idea of theatre, a world of fantasy governed by its own laws, its own logic, customs, and traditions, and its own peculiar psychology.[10]

It was Augier and Dumas *fils* who defined the ensuing period in the theatre. They did not, it must be conceded, venture very far beyond the limits of the Scribean system, but they endeavored to bring it into some relation with the social environment in which they lived. Under their influence, once again the utilitarian aspect of the drama was emphasized, this time from a social rather than a moral point of view. The theatre took on a new gravity; for the first time it became possible to take the drama seriously as a social force. But while these earnest playwrights powerfully influenced the course of the theatre in the latter part of the century, their influence was by no means exclusive. The bourgeois drama was at this time undergoing an interesting development under influences which were only partly French and, in the 1840's, a convergent tradition was in process of formation.

While in France bourgeois tragedy had actually developed no further than melodrama, in Germany there had been various attempts at tragedy in a contemporary setting. As early as 1755, Lessing had offered *Miss Sara Sampson* as an example of modern tragedy: in the eighteenth century, seemingly, the tragic situation par excellence was thought to be the plight of a woman in need of a husband. *Miss Sara Sampson* was an attempt to recast *Medea* in modern terms—terms, incidentally, which Lessing borrowed not from life, but from *Clarissa Harlowe*. In our day, *Miss Sara Sampson* is mainly interesting as an illustration of the futility of attempting to revive tragedy by aping the old forms, but the spectacular success of this play inspired Lessing to make a second experiment in this genre. *Emilia Galotti* (1771) was a modernization of the story of that Roman Virginia who was slain by her father out of regard for her honor. Since Lessing set this story at the court of an eighteenth-century Italian prince, it could hardly be called bourgeois tragedy; for that matter, it could hardly be called tragedy.

Schiller's *Kabale und Liebe* (1783) was closely related to *Emilia Galotti*, and it did little to advance the idea of middle-class tragedy. With such plays as *Wilhelm Tell* (1804), *Don Carlos* (1787), and *Wallenstein* (1788, 1799) Schiller taught his successors how to handle ideas in the drama; he taught them also how to handle history; unhappily, it was chiefly with *Die Räuber* (1781) that he influenced the theatre of his time. As far as middle-class tragedy was concerned, the important influence came from Friedrich Hebbel.

In 1843, while Scribe was still at the height of his glory, Hebbel was in Paris putting the finishing touches to a play on a contemporary theme which, he hoped, could properly be called a modern tragedy. Unlike Lessing, Hebbel did not attempt the reconstruction of a classic pattern. The story of *Maria Magdalene* was drawn, he said, from life, and there is cause to believe that the heroine's father, the carpenter Anton, was modelled after Hebbel's own father. The prose was clumsy; the characterizations, crude; and the construction distinctly amateurish—all the events of the play are jumbled together in the last act, as if tossed at random into the bottom of a sack. But with all its obvious drawbacks, Hebbel's play had a quality that brought it close to greatness.

In *Maria Magdalene*, once again, the plight of a dishonored girl provides the substance of the tragedy. The scale is appropriately small. The action concerns an incident in the family of a poor carpenter; but the sequence of events is impressive, leading one to the reflection that the magnitude necessary to tragedy is not an absolute value, but a matter of proportion. The tragic action in *Maria Magdalene* proceeds from the seduction of the girl. The heroine's father threatens to cut his throat rather than face the sneers of the neighbors. In order to keep the scandal from spreading, her true lover, the Secretary, duels with the reprobate who has wronged her, kills him, and is fatally wounded himself. The girl drowns herself in the well, as if by accident, to spare her father the disgrace she has brought upon the family. The girl's seducer is a despicable rogue; but he is of no real importance to the action. The tragic antagonist is society. The tyrant is public opinion. The protagonist is the father, and his tragic flaw is his own sense of middle-class propriety.

The idea of *Maria Magdalene* would seem to be tragic enough for its purpose; but in 1843 it was not sufficient to evoke a tragic mood—it was necessary to make a point. In consequence, *Maria Magdalene*, though framed as a tragedy, may justly be considered the first of the thesis plays. It is indeed into this mold that modern tragedy appears most naturally to fall. In the last act, when the news of Klara's death is brought in by her brother, the Secretary bursts out in passionate self-reproach at the selfish pride through which they have brought the girl to her death. The father stands, stiff and silent, as the girl's body is borne in. Then he speaks the memorable curtain line: "I don't understand the world any more."

Maria Magdalene was the first significant attempt in the modern theatre to revaluate the standards of society with relation to the individual. There was nothing especially original in the idea. Even on the Attic stage it was possible to dramatize the conflict between the laws of the state and the morality of the individual—Antigone is the obvious instance. Something of the sort was occasionally attempted in Renaissance drama also; [11] but it was far more usual, even in the world of Shakespeare, to measure the individual by unquestionable moral standards, and to see that he was properly punished if he was found wanting. The morality of the theatre, for obvious reasons, has at all times been remarkably shallow. Even in such an exceptional play as Heywood's A Woman Killed with Kindness, the impulsive, passionate lady is made to die of remorse. In the theatre of the Second Empire, adulterous ladies, even the repentant ones, did not die of remorse; but the dishonored were seldom the subject of sympathy. In Le Demi-monde, as in the long line of plays on a similar theme from Lady Windermere's Fan to The Circle, the fallen woman is invariably cast out into nether darkness or, at the least, exiled to Italy. Hebbel, however, was thinking of a higher ethics, and he made the point very simply that there is a type of morality which is displeasing to God.

In Maria Magdalene the honest carpenter Anton is not capable of understanding in what way he is wrong, but he understands that in reproaching him for his heartlessness the Secretary is sounding a modern note. It was in fact the note which Ibsen caused, a half-century later, to sound and resound throughout the world, a premonition of that transvaluation of values which was to revolutionize modern thought. In his capacity as a revolutionist, Hebbel was, however, more circumspect than Ibsen. It was with a full awareness of the transitional nature of the period in which the play is set that he conceived his characters and his action; but Hebbel did not go so far as to condemn the moral system by which the carpenter lived, nor the Secretary's preoccupation with matters of honor. Hebbel merely indicated the essential emptiness of these beliefs, and contrasted, in a striking example, the way of Christian compassion with the Pharisaic rigidity that subverts the human impulse. It is, as the title suggests, in terms of the morality of Christ that the play examines the morality of Christians.

In contrasting the heart with the mind, to the disadvantage of the latter, Hebbel clearly manifested the romantic origins of his idea of tragedy. Nevertheless, *Maria Magdalene* is not a romantic play, neither has it much to do with the sentimental drama of the preceding period. In Kotzebue's *Menschenhass und Reue* (1789) the erring woman's sin is forgiven—but only after she has undergone a lifelong penance. Such was the traditional compromise between justice and mercy, both, from the modern viewpoint, equally empty. In Hebbel's play it is not the girl who requires forgiveness, it is society; and therefore the play arouses indignation as well as sympathy. But in Anton, trapped like Creon between two laws, Hebbel achieved, for the first time in a middle-class setting, something like a tragic figure in the antique style.

In a preface to *Maria Magdalene*, Hebbel wrote that the subjects with which domestic drama had so far dealt were not tragic. Tragedy, he wrote, rests on inevitability. A great domestic drama can be created only out of the conflicts peculiar to its world. It is only in this way that the life and fate of an individual become universal symbols. There was nothing new in this thought either— Lessing, Goethe, Schiller, and Kleist had said or intimated as much. So far, however, only Lessing had thought of looking for universal symbols in a middle-class environment, and it cannot be said that he found any. The problem of *Maria Magdalene* was without doubt a universal problem. It was also a problem peculiar to its time. A social code which exacted the blood-sacrifice for a sexual infraction was no longer altogether congenial to a culture which had generated the Romantic movement. In 1843 the right of the individual to live his life independent of official morality had not been extended very far, but already it went somewhat beyond the Mosaic concept. In *Maria Magdalene*, Anton is too firmly rooted in the past to advance even a step with the times. His sin, therefore, is essentially stupidity. The stupidity of a noble nature is, of course, a first-rate subject for serious drama—we have the examples of Othello and Lear. But the stupidity of society is the true environment of tragedy; like the stupidity of fate.

Maria Magdalene was Hebbel's only experiment in middle-class tragedy. In his verse-tragedies *Herodes und Mariamne* (1850) and *Gyges und sein Ring* (1856) he developed further the pattern of she-tragedy which he had initiated with his first play, *Judith* (1840). All these plays deal with the problem of oppressed womanhood, and Hebbel cast them in the mold of tragedy which involves the brutal tyrant and the innocent victim. In each of them the innocent victim exacts a terrible vengeance; nevertheless these plays have, unquestionably, something new and sensible about them. They are essentially modern problem-plays, conceived somewhat anachronistically as tragedies, and placed in a historical setting; but they have all the intellectual characteristics of the *pièce à thèse* of the Second Empire, and in many ways they foreshadow Ibsen.

In the preface to *Maria Magdalene* Hebbel wrote that he hoped to bring out in this domestic tragedy the same point he had made in his historical tragedies—the contrast of older and younger generations. His method, obviously, was related to that of Schiller's historical plays, in which characters are made to represent ideas, and the conflict of individuals symbolizes the clash of ideologies. Hebbel went somewhat further than Schiller in this respect. Under the influence of Hegel, he undertook to dramatize the tension of antithetical forces in the dialectic of history.

In this conception of drama, the moment of time at which the stage is set is of profound significance to the dramatist, for the fate of the individual is necessarily correspondent with the logic of the cosmic process which he exemplifies and symbolizes. In *Maria*

Magdalene the action takes place at a time when the social order based on the idea of the community is in conflict with the individual, who is unconsciously struggling toward the next stage of social evolution. In the despair of those who go down defending the old order by which they live, and which seems to them eternal, and in the martyrdom of those who are destroyed in advancing the new order which is not yet established, but which seems to them inevitable, there is an authentic source of tragic emotion. In such circumstances, the sufferings of individuals transcend the ordinary anguish of life. Such individuals have tragic scale because it is in fact the passion of humanity that is depicted in their passion, and their agony represents the growing pains of the idea of mankind. In this light it makes no difference whether the tragic hero is a king, like Herod, or a carpenter, like Anton; and the drama, whether it be set in a palace or a barnyard, has necessarily the magnitude that is requisite to tragedy.

Hebbel was the first dramatist to arrange a play convincingly in terms of the Hegelian concept. The idea was stupendous, and was certain to have consequences: *Maria Magdalene* did much to pave the way for the renaissance of the drama in the next generation. Hebbel's historical dramas illustrated the same dialectic, and they were much admired in Germany for the beauty of the verse and the elegance of the characterization. The current of European drama, however, was flowing in the direction of realistic middle-class portraiture, and this crude play in prose, which amply demonstrated the author's inability to handle a realistic subject, was eventually judged to be his masterpiece. He had dreamed of breaking new ground with the tragedies of kings. In fact, he succeeded in demonstrating the importance of the tragedy of a carpenter, and *Maria Magdalene* became a landmark in the history of the drama.[12]

In 1831, a dozen years before Hebbel wrote *Maria Magdalene*, Alexandre Dumas the elder had established the farthest limit of extravagance in the depiction of a contemporary situation. His

Antony was presented as a romantic tragedy, and enjoyed a spectacular success at the Théâtre Porte Saint-Martin. It was ostensibly concerned, like *Maria Magdalene*, with a social problem: the questions of illegitimacy and social ostracism bear heavily on the character of the hero and the outcome of the play. Antony is a rich young man of mysterious antecedents and an extraordinarily passionate and fiery nature. Adèle is extremely virtuous. She resists Antony's impressive advances to the utmost of her power, then flees to her husband, the Colonel, for safety. It is in vain. Antony waylays her at an inn and forces her to submit to his passion. She becomes his mistress. The voice of gossip reaches her husband. He hastens home from his post in Strasbourg to retrieve his honor. Antony implores Adèle to elope with him, but she will not abandon her child, and she cannot bear to face public opinion. While the lovers are discussing their dilemma, the Colonel's footfall is heard outside the door. Antony draws his dagger and stabs Adèle to the heart. The door opens. The Colonel cries, "Adèle!" "Dead," replies Antony. "She resisted me, and I killed her."

In a preface to his father's play, Alexandre Dumas *fils* expressed his admiration for this denouement. The ending, he wrote, was certainly unusual, but its logic was superb. A character like Antony could have done nothing else in these circumstances.

Antony is, in fact, pitched well above the gamut of the actual. The hero, portrayed as an *homme fatal*,[13] appears to be quite mad, and in our day it would require much music to make his antics credible. Yet the extravagances of *Antony* hang together quite well once its assumptions are accepted, and Dumas gives evidence of early naturalistic tendencies by assigning his hero's daemonic character to the unhappy circumstances of his childhood as a foundling. For Adèle, as for Klara in *Maria Magdalene*, the fear of scandal outweighs all other considerations. Not so with Antony. Up to the point where the husband's spurs are heard jingling in the hall, the demands of passion are uppermost in his mind. It is only in the face of imminent disaster that he acts to save the lady's honor, and the future of her child, and he does this in the only way possible. His action, like all his actions, is violent, but in the circumstances, not unreasonable. It demonstrates the sort of ingenuity that, in tragedy, was considered *mirabile*. In terms of this extraordinarily romantic character, this extraordinarily romantic action is entirely acceptable, an inspiring example of fast thinking under pressure.

Even in the 1830's it was perfectly evident that *Antony* had nothing to do with the actual. In the world of Louis Philippe such grand passions were encountered mainly in books. Dumas, still young, but by far the best showman of his day, addressed his play to an audience which had recently gone wild over *Henri III et sa cour*, the same audience which had just acclaimed *Hernani*. In *Maria Magdalene*, Hebbel had attempted to give scale to his characters by identifying them with the workings of the cosmic process. Dumas tried to give his characters magnitude by raising their temperature. In 1831 it was not a bad idea; but within a very short time Antony took on a comic look, like the supermen of Orrery and Dryden. Dumas had no doubt carefully calculated the risk. In a speech he put into the mouth of the playwright Eugène in the fourth act of *Antony* he attempted to defend himself in advance against the criticism he anticipated:

The spectator who follows the development of the passion in the actor will wish to stop it where it would have stopped in his own heart. If it surpasses his own power of feeling or expression, he will not understand it any longer; he will say: "That is false. I do not feel like this. When the woman I love deceives me, I suffer, certainly . . . yes . . . for a time . . . but I don't stab her and I don't die, and the proof of it is, here I am." Then come the reproaches of exaggeration and melodrama, and they quite smother the applause of the few who, more happily or less happily constituted than the others, feel that human passions have not changed from the fifteenth to the nineteenth century.

Eugène did not consider that while human passions perhaps do not change, the social environment changes. The energetic postures of Antony, his Satanism, masochism, sadism, and the rest of it, suggested an agreeable fantasy to the spectator in a period in which men longed to live the rich full life of the outlaw and the outcast. This period was of limited duration. The carpenter Anton represented the same moral order which exacted the sacrifice of Adèle d'Hervey, the same idea of honor, and the same absence of common sense. But the audience of 1844 did not wish to see Anton's daughter sacrified, as Adèle had been, to the extravagance of men and their ideas of honor. The same romantic impulse which had given birth to Antony had propagated a wave of egalitarian ideas with regard to women. Audiences were becoming thoughtful. They agreed that Anton did not understand the world any more, and they refused to recognize the inevitability of Antony's behavior. Before long the husband, the wife, and the lover would be expected to sit down more or less amicably, and reason out their difficulties in the manner of Shaw's *Candida*, Coward's *Design for Living*, or Roussin's *La Petite hutte*. Before long, also, in accordance with the individualistic trend of the time, dramatic interest was to shift from the social to the psychological aspects of a situation, from plot to character. According to Dumas, it was Shakespeare who taught him to be a dramatist. The study of Shakespeare made it clear that tragedy is not a matter of splendid dagger thrusts, but a condition of the soul. *Antony* indicates that Dumas had some intimation of this important truth. Obviously, however, there were other considerations uppermost in his mind.

During the period 1845 to 1875 the French stage was dominated by Alexandre Dumas *fils* and Émile Augier. As they wrote far less than Scribe, and took their work more seriously, their workmanship was better than his. Their method was the same. For Dumas, logical construction was the essential element of successful playwriting. The careful dramatist must have his whole action in mind from the beginning—"one cannot begin to write until the final scene, the final gesture, the final words are clear." [14] Sardou was quite as logical as Dumas, and an even better craftsman. He had schooled himself, so he tells us, in the method of Scribe by reading the first act only of the master's plays in order to see how close he could come to working out Scribe's solution in the suc-

ceeding acts. The scrupulous technique which these writers developed resulted in a form of drama very acceptable to an age
that was becoming increasingly scientific. "Love," says Dr. Remonin in Dumas's *L'Étrangère*, "is physics; marriage is chemistry."
Playwriting, he might have added, is mathematics.

Both Augier and Dumas came early under the influence of
Victor Cousin at the University of Paris, and their outlook, like
his, was essentially religious and moralistic. For Dumas, the foundation of the good life was the family. Whatever endangered its integrity was evil. There was in this world nothing more beautiful
than motherhood, no tie more pure and holy than that of brother
and sister. The irrefutable proof of the goodness of woman was her
devotion to her children. "Until she becomes a mother," Barantin
tells Mme. Aubray, "a woman may err . . . the moment she has
a child, she knows her duty." [15] In the theatre of the most dissolute
and extravagant period France has ever known, marriage thus
acquired exceptional sanctity. Adultery was unpardonable.[16] This
stern theatrical puritanism was tempered by a corresponding measure of sentimentality. True love excused everything, every sin, every
fault. "*Il faut aimer*," says Mme. Aubray, evidently paraphrasing
the apostle, "*n'importe qui, n'importe quoi, n'importe comment,
pourvu qu'on aime.*" [17]

The general setting for the plays in which these worthy attitudes
were exemplified was the salon of upper-class society, a large room
with a double door at the rear and an entrance at either side. This
décor, an adaptation of the *antichambre* of tragedy, had the advantage of being unobtrusive and undifferentiated. Plays set in this
environment had a certain abstract quality, like demonstrations on
a blackboard, and their authors contrived them meticulously to
make a point. Scribe had developed his technique in order to tell
a story well. Dumas used it for a peculiar form of the *genre sérieux*,
a quasi-tragic action based upon a social problem, climaxed by a
sermon.

In plays conceived along such lines it was convenient to have
a character who would serve as presenter and preacher, and it was

natural for this character to be the author's mouthpiece. Most of
Dumas's plays center on the *raisonneur*. The character was, of
course, no more new to the stage than was the conception of drama
which gave rise to it. It was the traditional function of tragedy to
teach good morals, and of comedy to teach good manners—on this
idea almost every apology for poetry was based in Christian times.
Renaissance tragedy, both regular and Elizabethan, bristled with
moralizing characters, and such comedic figures as Molière's
Philinte and Ariste were designed to point a moral as well as to
adorn the tale. The *raisonneurs* of Dumas and Augier were, however, more or less directly derived from Scribe, whose heroes were
scrupulous to maintain, as we have seen, a confidential relation with
the audience throughout the course of the play.[18]

Scribe's *raisonneurs* were almost always his protagonists. Dumas
often followed this practice, as in *Le Demi-monde*, but occasionally
his *raisonneur* is a marginal character whose sole function is to
comment on the events of the play. At first the presence of such
characters could hardly be justified in so thrifty a form of drama,
but in time Dumas hit on the ingenious idea of giving this role to
the family doctor, whose presence required no explanation, and
whose opinions automatically inspired respect. Among the first
of these medical *raisonneurs* was Dr. Remonin in *L'Étrangère*.
From him stems that long and illustrious line of stage physicians
which includes Ibsen's Dr. Rank, Dr. Relling, and Dr. Stockmann,
Chekhov's Dr. Astrov and Dr. Chebutikin, and innumerable other
articulate medical men down to Sir Henry Reilly of *The Cocktail
Party*.

In the plays of Scribe, we are hardly aware of Scribe. His
raisonneurs talk to the audience in their own right and for their
own purposes as characters. But both Augier and Dumas had personal business with the audience. In the plays of Dumas, especially, the author keeps himself constantly in view of the public
with an incessant patter of comment and admonition. This technique, of which Wilde and Shaw in their day made extensive use,
is the distinguishing mark of the *pièce à thèse* of the period.

La Dame aux camélias, which Dumas adapted in 1852 from his own novel, was a perfectly straightforward sentimental *drame.* Unlike Shaw's Mrs. Warren, Marguerite Gautier does not attempt to justify her wicked life by an attack on society, nor does she accuse her clients of complicity in her shame. She is a simple soul, troubled chiefly by the fact that nobody loves her, a paradoxical complaint in one of her calling. Marguerite, of course, has a heart of gold, and Dumas treats her with appropriate sentimentality without being in the least aware that in her readiness to sacrifice her happiness not for the good of her lover, but in order to advance the social aspirations of his sister, whom she does not know and can never hope to meet, she is demonstrating, above all, the incredible stuffiness of the author's scheme of morals.

Le Demi-monde (1854) was written two years after *La Dame aux camélias.* Scribe's disapproval prevented it from receiving the highly regarded *Prix Faucher,* but it is generally accounted Dumas's masterpiece. It represents the praiseworthy efforts of an unduly upright man of the world to save an idealistic young officer from the toils of a beautiful woman who is *déclassée.* But although the play was formulated, in the style of Scribe, as a contest, and not at all as tragedy, the relations between Olivier de Jalin, and the beautiful *demi-mondaine* whose attempt to become an honest woman he ruthlessly suppresses, throws the play rather unexpectedly into the tragic mold of the brutal tyrant and the innocent victim. Since in this pattern, sympathy is normally directed to the victim, the play is likely—at least in our day—to make an effect rather contrary to the intention of the author. Nevertheless, *Le Demi-monde* provoked much discussion, and clearly foreshadowed the *pièce à thèse,* a type of drama which was intended to make a point, and therefore made considerable use of the art of argumentation.

In the preface he wrote in 1868 for *Le Fils naturel* (1858), Dumas declared that in this play he had attempted for the first time to develop a social thesis. Diderot had, he continued, in considerable measure initiated the trend toward serious drama; but Diderot, like Aristotle, had thought of the stage chiefly as a source of pleasure. Dumas had a higher aim. Drama, he felt, should have purpose—in Horace's words, utility: "Through comedy, through tragedy, through the *drame*, through buffoonery, in whatever form suits us best, let us inaugurate the useful theatre, even at the risk of hearing the apostles of art-for-art's-sake cry out against us . . ." In the useful theatre everything must be subordinated to the demonstration, "the mathematical, inexorable, and fatal progression which multiplies, scene by scene, event by event, act by act, up to the denouement which ought to be the sum-total and the proof of the whole." [19]

Although *Le Fils naturel* was intended to inaugurate the useful theatre, one may well wonder, on the one hand, in what way this play was meant to be useful, and, on the other, in what respect it was considered logical. The situation on which it is based is an example of the *mirabile*. In his youth, Charles Sternay seduced a poor working girl called Clara and then abandoned her in order to make a suitable marriage. Clara, left to herself, made a fortune, and her illegitimate son Jacques has grown up in affluence, quite ignorant of his parenthood. When Jacques, by an amazing coincidence, falls in love with Sternay's niece, his origin is revealed; but Sternay refuses to acknowledge his bastard, and the engagement is broken off. Jacques, however, is a man of exceptional talent. Without loss of time, he becomes a statesman, saves France, and is universally acclaimed by his grateful countrymen. At this point, his father, who now stands to gain a title through his son's ability, comes forward with open arms and convincing proofs of fatherhood. This sudden access of paternal affection does not have the desired effect. The son obtains a title for his father, then haughtily turns the tables by refusing to acknowledge his paternity.

Though nothing less convincing is conceivable than this sequence of events, it was not so much for its lack of verisimilitude that the play was criticized as for its immorality in depicting so unnaturally the sacred tie that binds father and son. The public, we are told, received the last two acts with pained surprise. According to the critic Louis-Gustave Vapereau:

Un père constamment odieux, un fils, homme supérieur, qui tient en echec la vanité paternelle, ou qui la traite à la fin avec une générosité railleuse, sans jamais ressentir rien qui ressemble à un sentiment filial, celà a paru contre la nature, contre les mœurs et d'un spectacle dangereux.[20]

It seems likely that the daring of Dumas in writing disrespectfully of a bad father had some influence on Ibsen's experiment in the same genre twenty-three years later. The problem of *Ghosts* was, of course, of different nature, but both plays took up the question of a son's duty to respect his father regardless of his merits. Both were thought to be attacks upon the patriarchal basis of European society, and perhaps both were so intended. Dumas, being illegitimate, was obsessed by the question of legitimacy; but he was inordinately proud of his celebrated father. Ibsen was ashamed of his father, and resentful of his extravagance. What is chiefly interesting, however, in a comparison of the two plays is the radical change which took place within a single generation in the type of story which was thought suitable to present a serious theme on the stage.

The pattern upon which Dumas finally settled for the play of social significance of his day exhibited a moral situation in which the protagonist was given a choice of conduct. In this it did not differ essentially from the usual pattern of tragedy. In tragedy, however, the protagonist is usually involved personally and fatally in his decision. In the thesis play, the crucial choice is neither tragic nor inevitable, but only problematical, a juridical matter to be decided in accordance with juridical considerations. Thus, in tragedy everything leads to the disaster, but in the thesis play, to the debate—the obligatory scene is a discussion, and the denouement, a verdict. And since in a play that centers the action in a kind of trial, the advocate is an essential character, the role of the *raisonneur* is, necessarily, greatly magnified. The *pièce à thèse* thus appears to be a development not of tragedy, but of the medieval *exemplum* or the Renaissance *dubbio*, a variety of literary debate of which the most familiar modern example is, perhaps, *The Lady or the Tiger?* [21]

In his later plays, Dumas felt his affinity with the classical theatre more and more strongly, and he tended to arrange his action in accordance with the unities, particularly with the unity of time. This, he considered, was a concession both to logic and to realism. Diderot had made a similar concession for similar reasons, and, in their day, Ibsen and Strindberg came to the same conclusion, matching the time of representation to the time of the action as closely as possible. The growing tendency to observe the unities was not, however, entirely a matter of logic; it reflected the reaction against romanticism which set in strongly sometime before the middle of the nineteenth century, and which was marked, as we have noted, by the unexpected success of the tragedies of Ponsard in circumstances which recalled the success of Mairet some two centuries before. Whatever the cause, the application of the unities to a realistic action in fact resulted in a tightly concentrated form of play which recalled the classical genre.

Émile Augier made his debut in the theatre with some sentimental verse-comedies in the style of Ponsard. *Gabrielle* was his first success. It is a five-act comedy in verse, produced at the Comédie-Française in 1849, which celebrates the advantages of middle-class marriage in a manner which might well be considered comic, were not the author so obviously in earnest. Gabrielle is on the verge of eloping with her husband's secretary, a handsome but impecunious young man. The husband is a prosperous lawyer, a man of no great charm, but of considerable shrewdness; and, without betraying his knowledge of the critical state of his domestic affairs, he reads the secretary a well-conceived homily in Alexandrines on the advantages of comfortable married life as contrasted with the excitements of an illicit relationship outside the social pale. Gabrielle, who is, as her husband knows, eavesdropping, is then left to make up her mind as she pleases. Her choice is soon made, and the last act includes an affecting scene in which she hails her husband in verses worthy of his own, concluding with: "*O père de famille! o poëte! Je t'aime!*"

Gabrielle was crowned by the French Academy. The defense of marriage was an important social concern in a period in which the doctrine was still being vividly preached that love transcends all other considerations. In adorning the brow of the good provider with the poet's laurels, of course, Augier went as far as one possibly could in the glorification of the businessman. His extravagance in this respect, indeed, provoked some smiles, as well as a heavily worded protest on the part of Baudelaire, in the name of poetry.[22]

In 1854 Augier, in collaboration with Jules Sandeau, brought out *Le Gendre de Monsieur Poirier*, which is generally accounted his masterpiece. This was a four-act comedy in prose based upon a novel by Sandeau called *Sacs et parchemins*, and it had to do with an issue that was still of vital interest, the relation of the rich bourgeoisie to the old nobility. The action was contrived very logically, not to say mathematically, so that its antithetical elements are reconciled through a mean which combines the virtues of both, a very neat example of the dialectic of the theatre.

The plot is interesting. M. Poirier, having amassed a fortune, has married his daughter Antoinette to an impoverished Marquis and installed the young gentleman in his house. The newly married Gaston does not bother on this account even to interrupt his liaison with the brilliant Madame de Montjoy, in whose behalf he has involved himself in a duel. But Antoinette gives such impressive evidences of noble character that Gaston ends by falling in love with his wife. It is at this point that his friend comes to accompany him to the duelling ground. Antoinette asserts herself. If he really loves her, she says, Gaston will give up this duel. Gaston gives way; but Antoinette has no idea of actually exacting such a sacrifice. She kisses him, then she says: "*Va te battre,*" a line which, in its day, created a sensation. Luckily, his adversary's apologies are brought in the nick of time, and the play ends happily for everyone, or nearly everyone.

In constructing this play, Augier evidently had an eye to the symmetrical design of classical drama. There are two noblemen, clearly differentiated. Gaston has no *mésure*; his friend Montmeyran is wise and thoughtful. There are two bourgeois: Poirier is narrow and stupid; his friend Verdelet is full of good sense. Antoinette, the central figure, is charming. She combines the nobility and grace one would like to find in a duchess with the practical virtues of her own class. This arrangement makes it possible to alternate the *scènes à faire* with scenes of debate and admonition between Gaston and his confidant and Poirier and his friend. In spite of this highly patterned classical structure, the play makes a very lively effect. All the acting parts are good, and the characterizations, while typical, are worked out in a detailed way that seems exceptional in the drama of the period.

The success of *Le Gendre de M. Poirier* put Augier in the foremost rank of the French dramatists. He continued with a series of social and political comedies in which he turned the spotlight of drama in turn upon each of the chief trouble spots of the day. *Les Effrontés* (1861) depicts the successful efforts of a sharp rascal to establish himself in a position of power by manipulating public opinion through the management of a newspaper. The memorable role in *Les Effrontés* is played by the professional journalist Giboyer, the first of the series of picturesque men of the press who have graced the stage of the last century. Giboyer dresses with conspicuous shabbiness, respects no one, and speaks in the salty manner which stage journalists have affected ever since. He is at heart a devoted liberal; but he has long ago seceded from the corrupt society which betrayed the ideals of the Great Revolution, therefore he feels free to serve with bitter cynicism whatever master pays him best. As might be expected, Giboyer aroused the ire of the contemporary press; and the controversy had scarcely died down when it was fanned into an unexampled blaze of fury by the sequel which Augier produced the following year.

Le Fils de Giboyer (1862) is an excellent example of the type of play which was the staple of the French theatre in the years before the naturalists upset the applecart. The intrigue is of frightening complexity. The unscrupulous journalist Giboyer has all but killed himself in order to give his illegitimate son Maximilien the best education money can buy, and he has caused his son to grow up in an atmosphere of democratic idealism which he himself could never afford. Maximilien believes Giboyer is his uncle, and respects him as a man of great probity of character. The young man is employed as secretary in the house of the deputy Maréchal, a stupid and pompous bourgeois of great ambition. Maréchal is about to make a strongly conservative speech in the house, a privilege secured to him by a baroness who is temporarily in the service of a marquis who desires to do Maréchal a kindness, because he himself is actually the father of Maréchal's daughter Fernande, for whom he has arranged an advantageous match with a titled nincompoop whom the baroness secretly covets for herself. Suddenly Maximilien discovers that the speech Maréchal is to deliver was actually written by the supposedly liberal Giboyer. Exposed as an unprincipled hack, Giboyer breaks down pathetically: "I am not a bad man, only an unfortunate one. My responsibilities have been too heavy: they have ruined me. First I had to labor for my father, and then for my—" Maximilien finishes the sentence for him. He throws himself into his father's arms, and their tears mingle.

This anagnorisis is the heart of the play. Decades of theatregoers were thrilled by it, and the degree of embarrassment it now causes the reader is the measure of the gulf that separates the theatre of a century ago from the theatre of today. The rest of the play is of no particular interest; it develops strictly in accordance with the laws of the drama. The baroness naturally betrays the marquis. Maréchal's Catholic speech is delivered by a Protestant deputy. But Maréchal's disappointment is short, for Maximilien writes him a magnificent liberal oration, as a result of which Maréchal becomes a leading democrat, and Maximilien becomes his son-in-law.

Le Fils de Giboyer was considered a very daring play. The revelation of the martyrdom of Giboyer placated the press, but the implied attack on the integrity of politicians, both clerical and liberal, was not easily swallowed. The antidemocratic bias of this play was characteristic of the genre. It hardly stirred controversy in a period which had fully discussed Tocqueville. Even in the time of Augier the role of the political turncoat was by no means new to the stage: Scribe had made ample use of this character a generation before. But *Les Effrontés* and *Le Fils de Giboyer* fixed the clichés of the modern political satire, which invariably betrays its origins through the traditional complexity of the plot and the indispensable role of the newspaper man, either cynical or idealistic, or both at once. The plots of such plays as *Both Your Houses*, *The State of the Union*, or *Advise and Consent*, however, seem thin and sleazy in comparison with the rich dense texture required of the playwright in the 1850's, when the drama was expected to rival the serialized novel in popular favor.

The development of Giboyer is instructive. In *Les Effrontés* he appears as a cynical character admirably suited to the role of *raisonneur* in a play that deals principally with dirty politics. In *Le Fils de Giboyer* he has become old and pathetic, and his life is analyzed with the understanding sentimentality usually reserved for plays about good-hearted whores. The difference in treatment is caused, naturally, by his relation to his illegitimate son; and from this viewpoint the play furnishes an instructive comparison with Dumas's *Le Fils naturel* of which it is, in a sense, a corollary.

The mainstay of a play of this order is the assumption, axiomatic in a patriarchal society, that no human tie is more sacred or beautiful than that of father and son, so that even criminal behavior is excusable in its interest. The ancestry of this idea is venerable; it goes back as far, at least, as the *Oresteia*, and its viability in our time may be judged from the unfailing success of plays of the type of Robert Morley's and Noel Langley's *Edward My Son*. The insistence with which these values were exploited in the time of Augier, however, provoked a reaction, and in the next generation the naturalistic dramatists did much to dispel the miasma of sentimentality which for centuries had precluded anything like a thoughtful representation of domestic relations in the theatre.

In this, as in so much else, Ibsen marked a turning point in the history of the drama. In the 1920's, playwrights began to be aware of Freud, and before long, the antagonism of father and son, which had seemed so shocking in the time of Samuel Butler, became so much a matter of course in the theatre that it seemed refreshingly novel to hark back to the sentimental relationship of the days of Augier. In the meantime the ambivalence of the father-son relation asserted itself in quite another way. After Strindberg broached the subject in *To Damascus*, the quest for the lost father provided one of the most significant patterns of modern fiction, and, concomitantly, the discomfort of not-belonging became a favorite theme for the serious playwright. Along with this trend, closely associated in the 1930's with O'Neill, and later with Joyce, there was perceptible a marked tendency, particularly on the American stage, to sentimentalize the filial relation. This becomes evident on the contemporary stage even in such disparate plays as Mr. Williams's *Cat on a Hot Tin Roof* and Mr. Miller's *Death of a Salesman*. But while the kind of sentimentality involved in the treatment of Willy Loman and of Giboyer is perhaps essentially the same, there is certainly a difference of degree. Doubtless the tide of sentimentality has to some extent receded in the last hundred years. It is perhaps no longer possible for an audience to indulge itself quite so shamelessly in such displays as made the fortune of Augier; but, of course, this is by no means certain.

Between the type of social drama which Dumas and Augier were developing in the 1860's and the new prose drama of Ibsen and Björnson, there is no perceptible solution of continuity. It was mainly in emulation of the themes and methods of the social dramatists of the Second Empire that the Norwegians developed their style. It may be said, therefore, with some justice that such plays as Björnson's *The Editor, The New System,* and *A Bankruptcy,* as well as Ibsen's *The League of Youth* and *Pillars of*

Society, are essentially French plays with Norwegian characters. Björnson, indeed, produced *Le Fils de Giboyer* at the Christiania Theatre, and in *The New System* he went so far as to plagiarize word for word the famous recognition scene between Giboyer and his son. Similarly, *A Bankruptcy*, which Ibsen followed somewhat closely in *Pillars of Society*, was itself an imitation of Sardou's immensely successful *La Famille Benoiton*. The relation between the French drama of the 1860's and the Norwegian drama of the 1870's and 1880's is therefore at the most a progression. The frontier between the modern drama and the drama of the nineteenth century becomes, however, clearly perceptible in the work of Sardou, and with him also the distinction between the commercial and the art theatre once again becomes important.

Victorien Sardou was the most prolific and also the most successful playwright of the second half of the nineteenth century and, it is commonly said, the most superficial. His career was impressively professional. He made his debut in the 1860's with plays about morals in the style of Dumas; later he imitated Augier's social and political comedies; ultimately he formed the racy style in which he continued to write until 1907, the year before his death. Sardou was in his day a great man of the theatre. He explored every possibility of the stage, kept all the great actors employed in their specialties, wrote about every class of society, enlarged the horizons of the drama in every direction, and succeeded in the course of a half-century in denigrating beyond hope of redemption the tradition of Scribe.

The stuff out of which Sardou made plays was by no means uniformly trivial. He treated with a great show of earnestness and with great popular success the most important themes of his time— politics, religion, money, marriage, and the family. It is possible that if he had contented himself simply with making a fortune in the theatre, he would not have provoked so drastic a retribution as eventually overtook him; but Sardou was hybristic. He gave himself the widest publicity, put on the airs of a great man, and publicly invited comparison with Zola and Ibsen. In 1875 he was elected, like Scribe, to the French Academy. Fifty years later, his laurels were already withered beyond recognition.

Sardou fixed the limit of the art of ingenious narrative, the point at which cleverness defeats its purpose as an element of craftsmanship. By the time of Sardou, the good stories had been told over and over, and the reliable scenes had crystallized into forms which the ingenious writer could arrange in patterns like the tesserae of a mosaic. Even before the naturalistic reaction set in, Dumas and Augier understood that narrative ingenuity would have to serve a purpose other than mere entertainment if it was to maintain itself on the level of art in the theatre. So too in their time did Ibsen, Strindberg, Chekhov, and Shaw. Sardou, however, resolutely held the line of Scribe. During his long life in the theatre he saw the emphasis shift from plot to character study, then to social criticism, finally to symbolism and poetic fantasy. Plots became vastly simplified. Playwrights turned from fiction to fact as a source of wonder. The art of narrative fell into disfavor, and it became a mark of ingenuity to write a play without telling a story. The dramatic tradition we associate with Sardou, however, hardly reflected any of these changes. It continued, and to this day continues, to operate in a world as far removed from art as from reality, cannily supplying the needs of the commercial theatre through a succession of experienced technicians who fulfill their useful and profitable function oblivious of the world beyond the stage, and will doubtless go on doing so until they find, one day, that, without noticing it, they have been superseded by automation.

Realism

I N the 1860's the artistic and commercial aspects of the drama had not yet parted company so far that a writer like Sardou could not insist on being taken seriously. The realistic reaction to the well-made play and the Scribean idea of theatre set in after 1870, and it took some time to define itself. The realists were, to begin with, mainly novelists. They knew nothing of the dramatist's problem, but they had quite definite ideas about the art of story-telling, and initiated their attack, accordingly, by deriding the stale formulas of the theatre, the mechanical concatenation of stock situations, the absence of surprise, and the banality of the play-wright's invention.

This went directly to the heart of the matter. The masters of the drama during this period were professional writers whose livelihood depended on the frequency of their productions. In 1861 Sardou had five new plays running concurrently or successively in Paris; he had three in 1862, two in 1863, and two in 1864. Ten years later, he still had two new plays running concurrently, *Le Magot* at the Palais Royal, and *Haine* at the Gaîté. In these circumstances it would be normal for a writer to draw a little on his memory, and difficult to avoid a certain repetition of effect. It was actually not the vapidity, but the monotony of Sardou's drama that first provoked the animosity of the critics. To say anything new in terms of the well-made play was, in fact, by this time no simple matter. By the time they were cast in the Scribean mold all subjects had a certain family resemblance. It was therefore mainly out of desperation that playwrights turned from art to nature. Quite apart from theoretical considerations, insofar as the theatre was concerned, naturalism was primarily a search for novelty.

Neatness in plotting, we have already had occasion to note, depends largely on the manipulation of stereotypes. Unless it is assumed that, in general, good people act well and bad people, badly, that captains act like captains and tradesmen like tradesmen, it becomes difficult to motivate a story with the sort of precision the well-made play requires. The moment good people begin to act like bad people, they involve the dramatist in questions foreign to the logic of the well-made play. When captains begin to act like tradesmen, they step out of the ordered world of the theatre and enter, as in Shaw's *Arms and the Man*, the uncharted wilderness of reality. Such excursions from the normal are likely to result, however, in nothing more abstruse than a play of mistaken identities. What happens in these cases is simply that one mask is exchanged for another; and the denouement—whatever its intellectual interest—rests from a dramaturgical viewpoint merely on a special type of recognition.

The revelatory technique of Augier, or of Shaw, in which it is shown that a seeming scoundrel is in reality a good man, or that a realist is in fact an idealist in disguise, simply involves a substitution of stereotypes. This introduces an element of surprise; but it in no way alters the basic mechanism of the well-made play. It is only when the idea of characterological types is entirely rejected that plotting becomes difficult, or even impossible. The complex plots of classical comedy depend on simple characters. When characterization becomes a matter of depicting the individual rather than describing the archetype, motivation ceases to be a matter of logic, the events of a narrative are no longer predictable, and the emphasis shifts decisively from plot to character.

The naturalists of the 1870's, looking back upon the realistic novels of Stendhal, Balzac, and Flaubert, could justly accuse the school of Dumas and Augier of being a half-century behind the times. Nevertheless the naturalistic novelists did not evolve anything either new or profound in the way of characterization, and their influence upon the theatre in this respect was not great. In the analysis of character the naturalists depended mainly on the idea of Taine that every personality has a dominant trait, a *faculté maîtresse*, in terms of which all its behavior is understandable. The result of such an idea of human nature was a type of character study which involved a detailed description of traits and mannerisms, but actually came no closer to humanity than the "humours" characters of Jonson or the lively caricatures of Molière.

The naturalists plumed themselves on the scientific objectivity of their portrayals, their rejection of contrivance, their accurate reproduction of speech and manners, their avoidance of arguments and demonstrations. In short, they dissociated themselves completely from the practice of the Second Empire dramatists. The contrast was perhaps not as clear-cut as they pretended. The naturalist plays had no intrigues, but they were certainly contrived. They did not, as a rule, argue a thesis, but they demonstrated and exemplified scientific preconceptions. Their dialogue was far more accurately realistic than the pretentiously archaic language of Augier, but it did not really reproduce colloquial speech. In some respects, nonetheless, the two schools were fundamentally opposed. In general, the Scribeans, for all their irony and seeming cynicism, developed an essentially affable view of human nature. The naturalists, on the contrary, emphasized the sordid and brutal aspects of life.

The two attitudes, "idealism" and "realism," have, of course, developed side by side in European literature since its beginnings. The terms could not be more inept; but the distinction they represent is the most fundamental of all literary distinctions. It differentiates the two main streams of literary thought which, taken together, express the essential ambivalence which characterizes our Western culture. The nineteenth-century naturalists were realists, but they added a nuance. At the root of their objectivity, their plain speaking, their horror of sentimentality, their hostility to convention, and their pessimism it was easy to discern the bitterness of the disappointed idealist. They did not employ *raisonneurs*, and ostensibly they did not preach, but they were moralists. They had simply developed a technique of preaching without seeming to preach.

Francisque Sarcey, writing in 1889, declared that "the pessimists of the Théâtre-Libre invented nothing." But the dissimilarity between the type of drama we associate with the Second Empire and the drama of Zola, Becque, and Brieux fairly leaps to the eye. The plays of Dumas and Augier take place, as a rule, in the drawing rooms of comfortable homes. The characters are principally wealthy *rentiers* whose problems arise chiefly from their social relations. Theirs are questions of love, marriage, legitimacy, adultery, and *déclassement*. Their conflicts are sharp, but invariably polite. The plays of Zola and his followers are set in cheap cafés and the back rooms of shops. The characters are of the lower class, their conflicts are brutal, and their speech is not refined. To some extent, therefore, the down-to-earth tone of the naturalist drama is a matter of decorum; this drama is composed in a style appropriate to a social stratum below that of the polite middle class. Since this class had not been the subject of drama before this time, the appropriate style had to be invented.

Dumas *fils* was the spokesman of the bourgeoisie of his day. In fact, he knew it very little. In his youth he had shared the bohemian life of his father. His later life was spent among the aristocracy. The society he depicted was therefore largely imaginary, like the high society of his disciple Oscar Wilde, and he conceived it in terms of preconceptions derived from literature. Zola's world, though much more carefully documented, was almost as artificial as that of Dumas. Both were literary creations.

It would have seemed ludicrous in the theatre of 1875 to hear laborers and shopkeepers speak in the literary style of the salon drama, and revolting to have them speak the idiom of the street. In France, naturalistic dialogue was, accordingly, a literary compromise, a version of common speech tempered to the tastes of a polite audience. It was the Russian and German dramatists who first made a point of approximating the speech of real people in all its nonsyntactical splendor, yet neither Tolstoi nor Gorki, nor Holz, Schlaf, nor Hauptmann really went so far as to make actors talk or think quite like people. The naturalist position, with its inherent paradox, was never entirely comfortable. In order to make an effect of reality in the theatre, it was necessary to begin with the assumption that the audience was not there; but in fact the dramatist had to reckon at every moment with the feelings of the audience, and on the stage it was never possible to be "true to life."

The word "realism" was not much used in connection with literature before the middle of the nineteenth century. In the late 1850's works of criticism began to appear which identified as "realistic" the style of Balzac, Flaubert, Feydeau, Zola, and the Goncourts.[1] The relation of realism to the art of the ugly was perceived in the early days of the movement. In a satiric comedy of 1852, a character called Realista says:

> Faire vrai ce n'est rien pour être réaliste:
> C'est faire laid qu'il faut! [2]

When the term "naturalism" came into use, it was practically synonymous with realism.[3] In the theatre, as well as in the novel, the realism of this period was actually an aspect of romanticism. Its special interest in the life and speech of peasants and workmen, its revolt against the traditional patterns of play construction, its rejection of the unities, its impatience with the ingenuities of the storyteller make its literary affinities clear. As it has been remarked, a considerable proportion of the novels and plays of the romantic period might well bear, like *Le Rouge et le Noir*, the epigraph which Stendhal borrowed from Danton: "The truth, the bitter truth!" [4]

Zola relates how in his youth he had studied the intricate system called "theatre," the correct methods of preparing entrances, the symmetrical division of scenes, the necessity for, and disposition of, the sympathetic role, and the relative importance of speech and gesture. "We must clear the ground," he adds. "The well-known recipes for knotting and unknotting a plot have served their time; now we must have a simple, broad picture of men and things, a drama such as Molière might have written. Outside of certain scenic necessities, what is called today the science of the theatre is only a heap of clever tricks." [5] It is evident that Zola's celebrated manifesto has something in common with Wordsworth's preface to the *Lyrical Ballads* of 1800, in which the poet proposes to "choose incidents and situations from common life and to relate and describe them, throughout, as far as is possible, in a selection of language really used by men." [6] The romanticism of Wordsworth is doubtless distinguishable from the romanticism of Zola, but it is obvious that in both instances the motive was a desire to find a basis for art on firmer soil than the current traditions of literature permitted, and in each case it was proposed that the artist turn from literature to life as a source of inspiration.

In theory, at least, there was no reason why the life of the middle class could not have provided the subject matter of naturalist drama; but in the time of Zola, as in the time of Wordsworth, the political background had something to do with the choice of subject. The lineage of the naturalist movement, with its partiality for the lower classes, is ultimately traceable to Rousseau, who had actually lived for a time the life of a peasant. The wave of realistic art which culminated in the school of Zola, however, began to be manifested only after the failure of the revolution of 1848, when a group of disaffected artists and writers turned to the lower classes as a source of inspiration and strength. In this movement, the pioneer was the painter Gustave Courbet.

Like Rousseau, Courbet considered himself a man of the people. He had the deepest antipathy for the middle class, its academies, and all it represented. Three of his paintings, exhibited in the salon of 1850–1851, *The Burial at Ornans, The Stone-Breakers,* and *The Peasants of Flagey,* created a sensation, and a strong group of realistically minded writers ranged themselves under his leadership. With his exhibition of 1855 and its accompanying manifesto, it was felt that a critical point had been reached in the history of art, and that realism had at last come of age. "The basis of realism," Courbet wrote, "is the negation of the ideal, and of everything that follows from it. It is only in that way that one can arrive at the emancipation of reason, the emancipation of the individual, and at last, at democracy."

Courbet's ideas were fervently espoused by Proudhon in an essay, published posthumously, in which it was pointed out that Courbet was an expression of his time, and that his work was in complete accord with Comte's *Philosophie positive,* and with Proudhon's *Le Droit humain.*[7] In this way the philosophic and socialistic basis of naturalism took form. The next step was its division into realism as a principle of pure art—the attitude associated with Flaubert, Baudelaire, Leconte de Lisle, and the Goncourts—and the utilitarian realism of Zola, who not only taught "the bitter science of life, the high lesson of the real,"[8] but also thought to improve the human lot through these lessons.

The desire to depict life without flattery, without condescension, and without sentimentality was not new; but romanticism had often been sentimental. The naturalists were determined above all to preserve their objectivity, and they compensated for their romantic background by repudiating sternly the cheap humanitarianism of their predecessors, and by emphasizing both in art and literature the sordidness and brutality of the life of man. There was obviously something perverse about making a cult of the beauty of ugliness, but Zola and his disciples cultivated a scientific air, kept notebooks like researchers, and reaffirmed the proposition of Goncourt that the end of art was *"un document humain, pris sur le vrai, sur le vif, sur le saignant."* In their plays, they avoided discussions and, like the naturalist painters, abstained from preaching sermons. But their scientific postures deceived no one. Naturalism was grounded on the intellectual reaction, which followed the Great Revolution, against the manners and morals of the middle class, to which most of the naturalists belonged. It was the fruit of disappointment and disillusion, and for all their seeming detachment, the naturalists could conceal neither their indignation nor their inherent sentimentality.

The naturalist writers—Taine, Renan, Sainte-Beuve, Flaubert, Zola, Maupassant, and the Goncourts—were not all liberals, but they were all critics of the existing order. The social drama of the Second Empire had dealt principally with individual aberrations from the current standards. After 1875, it was the social standards themselves that came under fire. Accordingly, literature attained a new importance as a social force, and the theatre once again became a storm center, this time for reasons quite different from those which had stimulated the intellectuals of 1830.

In attacking the successors of Scribe, Zola was really renewing an old quarrel. By this time the patterns of classic drama had become almost exclusively of academic interest, and a new classicism had virtually supplanted the old. The rules and unities no longer troubled anyone, but the formalistic patterns of the well-made play had crystallized into rigidity, and its subject matter had become in time as severely limited as that of the earlier drama.[9] The naturalistic position was therefore frankly revolutionist. It reacted not only against the political, but also against the academic standards of the preceding generation, and this reaction was much strengthened by the fact that by 1870 the Second Empire drama had finally evaporated into triviality. It was by this time impossible to deny that the dramatic tradition that was traceable to Scribe in fact led nowhere, and that a fresh start was necessary. In 1873 Zola wrote:

I think we must go back as far as tragedy—not, great God! to borrow
any more of its rhetoric, its system of confidants, its declamations and
interminable recitals—but to return to its simplicity of action and
its single-minded concentration on the psychological and physiological
study of the characters. The tragic form, thus understood, is excellent:
an event unfolding in its reality and arousing in its characters passions
and feelings of which the exact analysis would be the sole interest of
the play! And this in a contemporary setting, with the people among
whom we live.[10]

Zola proposed a form of drama, consequently, the pleasure of
which would be primarily intellectual. The disadvantage of trans-
forming the theatre into a laboratory for the analysis of case histories did not occur to him; on the contrary, he felt that the naturalistic play, like the naturalistic novel, should have the validity
of a scientific observation: "An identical determinism rules the
stone in the road and the brain of man . . . our works have the
exactness, the solidity, and the practical application of works of
science." The idea was inspiring, and Zola was inordinately ambitious for it. His formula for the naturalistic drama—"faire grand,
faire simple, faire vrai"—was intended to result in a new classicism,
a new grandeur, an elegant simplicity, and, of course, a new truth
—the truth of science.[11]

The assimilation of art to science seemed less fatuous in 1873
than it does now. The age of psychology, with its mystical connections, had not yet dawned. It was the writings of the physiolo-
gist Claude Bernard that principally influenced Zola in his scientific attitudes, particularly the Introduction à l'étude de la
médicine expérimentale, and, he was much influenced also by the
genetic studies of Prosper Lucas. It is not clear that Zola altogether
understood Bernard, and one wonders in what way a play could
conceivably approximate the conditions of a scientific experiment.
Zola understood enough, however, to conclude that science was
the key to all human problems, and that the human mind would
in time find an answer, and only one, to every problem of human
nature and every social difficulty.[12]

Since for Zola, the function of art was to tell the truth, the

reality of the theatre could be none other than the reality of experience, and the only valid drama would be that derived from
direct and accurate observation. It was the function of the serious
dramatist to depict on the stage, wholly and unreservedly, without
politeness, ornament, or equivocation, the data which he had collected. The naturalistic play would then be precisely correspondent to the naturalistic novel, a sober, exact, and frank exposition
of the facts of life, brutal, if necessary, but in any case, true.[13]
Science had demonstrated that behavior is determined by heredity
and environment, and not by fate, providence, or chance. Naturalistic drama would therefore exhibit the manner in which the
biologic forces operated, through power and passion, to shape
human lives; and the supreme model in the depiction of life in its
power and its passion, in Zola's opinion, was the Elizabethan
drama—which he knew mainly from the description in Taine's
History of English Literature.

In *La Marâtre* (1848) and *Mercadet* (1851), Balzac had already
indicated the direction which Zola desired to follow in the theatre,
and Zola hailed these plays as monuments in the history of realism.
In fact, *La Marâtre* can be considered realistic only insofar as it is
brutal. It is a *drame* with a tight, well-contrived intrigue, strong
scenes, and a preposterously conventional ending. Like *La Bataille
de dames,* of which it is the "realistic" counterpart, it has to do
with the rivalry of two women for a man; but Balzac took a different view of life than Scribe. In Scribe's play, the two women, both
sympathetic, vie with each other in tenderness and generosity, and
both win a victory. In *La Marâtre* the women fight each other
grimly to the end, and both are defeated. Balzac's dialogue is
clumsy, and his design unnecessarily ingenious, but the play has
the sort of irony that the naturalists enjoyed, together with the
savagely contemptuous view of human nature that had lately
come into fashion. It therefore recommended itself widely, and
even the anti-naturalistic Sarcey wrote that this play was a triumph of realism in the drama.

Thérèse Raquin, which Zola presented in 1873, was a better play than *La Marâtre*, and equally brutal. Though the naturalists professed to report life, Zola did not think of putting an ordinary incident on the stage. He chose instead a situation of the utmost horror, and developed it as if he wished to devise a modern equivalent of Elizabethan revenge tragedy. The play is a study of the morally destructive effects of a bad conscience on a man and woman who were in the first place neither bad nor good. In accordance with Zola's theory of drama, the attention is focused not on the crime which is the center of the action, but on the corrosive effects of this crime upon the criminals. The action is developed in a series of tableaux which depict the desperate monotony of life in a small shopkeeper's family. The details of this environment are drawn in with characteristic thoroughness, but there is very little movement on the stage, and the narrative is almost completely devoid of complication, so that "the exact analysis" of the passions and feelings of the characters is indeed the chief interest of the play.

Thérèse Raquin is evidently in some relation to Dostoievski's *Crime and Punishment*, which was published seven years before; to *The Power of Darkness*, which Tolstoi wrote a dozen years later; and to Ibsen's *Rosmersholm* (1886). The heroes of Dostoievski, Tolstoi, and Ibsen make a very different effect, however, from the criminal lovers of Zola's play. Tolstoi's Nikita is God's creature. The tie that binds him to his Creator is stretched, it seems, to the limit of its elasticity, but it occasions no surprise when he is snapped suddenly back into the arms of the Almighty. The intellectual Rosmer is able, up to a point, to cast off the puritan beliefs of his ancestors, but he cannot divest himself of the intrinsic morality of his nature. God is bred, so to speak, into his bones; and something of the sort may perhaps be said also of the intellectual Raskolnikov.

In *Thérèse Raquin* the absence of God is embarrassing. In the abstract, there is no particular reason why Thérèse and Laurent, people capable of carrying through a murder in cold blood, may not also be capable of enjoying the fruits of their enterprise. Without

God, the intensity of the self-destructive passions generated by their transgression seems extravagant, and, were it not for the ingenious device of embodying the guilt that torments them in the silently accusing figure of the mother, their need for self-destruction would perhaps not be credible. The figure of the paralyzed woman, burning with hatred, belongs, on the other hand, to a rhetorical tradition which comes closer to symbolism than to naturalism. On the whole, the play with which Zola chose to demonstrate the naturalistic position can hardly be considered a cogent example of naturalist drama.

Thérèse Raquin, as it was adapted for the stage, appears to have been an attempt to approximate tragedy on the level of the lowest social class. The design is classic. Thérèse and her lover are trapped between desire and conscience, a situation pre-eminently suited to tragedy, but the psychological movement of the action is too detailed and too precise for tragedy, and too coldly observed; while its design is altogether too ingeniously contrived, and its assumptions too idealistic for a play conceived in the traditions of realism. In accordance with naturalistic theory, the play has no sympathetic roles. The consequence is that the emotional response is chiefly a feeling of horror, as in Senecan tragedy, but with a minimal degree of that emotional identification which tragedy requires. On the other hand, the fundamental tone of the play is didactic, rather than analytic. It is a demonstration of human behavior which admonishes, but does not enlighten. It certainly does nothing to exalt the soul. Yet *Thérèse Raquin* was clearly intended to be something more than a demonstration of the physiology of passion. It was meant to be at the same time awe-inspiring, truthful, and beautiful. Of these objectives, it fulfilled only the first. It was, in many respects, an excellent play; but it attempted to do too many things at once, and in the end it failed to satisfy anybody.

Zola does not appear to have understood that realism is incompatible with the idea of tragedy. Tragedy belongs to the idealistic tradition. The tragic poet flatters mankind by assuming for it a kind of greatness which, in general, we seek in vain among the details of existence. For that reason, the tragic is especially precious as a poetic experience. Viewed realistically, a tragic action deflates. It takes on a clinical character, and, at the most, excites compassion; but it can scarcely reach beyond the bounds of the pathetic. The genre which is appropriate to realism is comedy; from this viewpoint, as the first great realist wrote in introducing the first great comedy of our time,

> Mieulx est de ris que de larmes escripre,
> Pour ce que rire est le propre de l'homme.

The advent of realism in the theatre made it impossible to achieve the magnitude of effect which is essential to the tragic action. It was not the attenuation of the moral system of our culture, nor the erosion of the theoretical basis of the Christian world that made tragedy an improbable art in our age, but the romantic tendency to look at things "as they are," and this fundamental shift in our psychic outlook was evidently a cause, and not a consequence, of the moral transformation of our universe. What the modern critic so often laments in the passing of tragedy is, consequently, not the absence in the theatre of a specially voluptuous type of aesthetic experience so much as the cheerless prospect of the universe which the realistic drama unfolds.

The effort to find a substitute for tragedy when tragedy itself is no longer a viable form seems absurdly compulsive until we reflect that in periods of disillusion it is necessary to find some means of giving worth to human suffering. Tragedy lends dignity to despair, and in some degree it makes it enjoyable. It is the supreme human gesture, the artistic affirmation of man's importance in the face of the powers that dwarf him. It is, accordingly, the most elusive of human sublimations, the most precarious; but also the most precious and noblest, and the most touching in its futility. Zola went back to Racine for his inspiration, but he did not find the secret. Racine in some ways approaches realism; but Racine is deeply compassionate in his view of human nature. The author's attitude in *Thérèse Raquin* is, however, essentially superior; it is the cold detachment of one who patiently contemplates the behavior of laboratory animals under conditions of stress. The play therefore does not dignify the sufferings of its characters, nor can it transform their grief into poetry. It is at the most a splendidly contrived object lesson.

In claiming for this sort of drama "the exactness, the solidity, and the practical application of works of science," the author was doubtless guilty of some pretentiousness. He did, nevertheless, demonstrate the advantage of writing a simple play. *Thérèse Raquin*, bombastic as it is, is perfectly straightforward. The situation is certainly extraordinary: Zola was still thinking in terms of the marvellous; but there are no intrigues, counterintrigues, reversals, recognitions, nor displays of wit. In going back to tragedy for his model, Zola was at least able to free himself from the elaborate superstructure with which the drama of his time had so far been burdened.

The play was hissed. In consequence, Zola wrote nothing more for the stage. But he had sufficiently demonstrated the workings of his idea. He said of his novel *L'Assomoir:* "*Mon livre est le prémier qui ait vraiment l'odeur du peuple.*" In the course of the next generation there grew up a whole school of novelists whose works exuded the odor of common man, and many attempts were made to adapt their material for the stage. But, with the exception of Maupassant, the naturalistic writers did not do well in the theatre.

Augier, Dumas, and Sardou, meanwhile, made haste to catch up with the new realism. They did not, and could not, of course, depart from the patterns of "theatre"; but they saw to it, at least, that their plays were directed realistically. The conventional salon setting lost its abstract quality. There were now real fires in the grates, real champagne in the glasses, real food, authentic costume, and make-up which made the characters look like ladies and gentlemen instead of actors and actresses. Dumas did not attempt to rival the realism of the Théâtre-Libre. He did not place chairs with their backs to a theoretical fourth wall, nor did he ask his actors to warm their hands at non-existent grates with imaginary flues in the proscenium. For Dumas, reality was not the goal of drama, but its point of departure, and, in general, he won his point with the audience. For all their vehemence, the naturalists did not know how to write plays, and they did not learn. In the end it was a writer who did not belong to their group who established naturalism in the theatre.

Henri Becque was a writer of comedies whom a lifetime of frustration sharpened into the greatest ironist of the century. By temper a realist, he was an admirer of Balzac and Flaubert, but he also loved good theatre, and he had the greatest respect for Sardou. His first play was a worthless farce in the style of Labiche. It had just enough success to encourage him to present in 1869 a maudlin drama entitled *Michel Pauper*, which has to do with a poor inventor who drinks himself to death after having discovered a way to make diamonds. This play made Becque a laughingstock in theatrical circles, and after another, and even more dismal, failure, he gave up writing altogether and turned to the stock market for a living. The move proved to be his salvation. As a man of business he conceived a hatred of businessmen so violent that in 1876 he was able to write a masterpiece.

It took Becque six years to get *Les Corbeaux* into a theatre. In 1882 the Théâtre-Français produced it. Three years later, he presented *La Parisienne*. Neither play met with any immediate success. Subsequently he wrote two acts of a satire on the Paris *bourse* entitled *Les Polichinelles*. He did not live to finish it; but he lived long enough to hear himself acclaimed as the greatest dramatist of his time.

Becque was not a good craftsman. His technique was old-fashioned. His principals maintained confidential relations with the audience as in the plays of Scribe, his scenes were formulated in the Scribean tradition, and his dialogue was stilted. But Becque wrote out of a profound sense of life's irony, and he framed his two comedies with a grim humor which skirted the frontiers of tragedy in a way quite new to the nineteenth century. The *comédies larmoyantes* of the end of the previous century had been designed to evoke pity. Becque's comedies made one shudder.

Les Corbeaux was not a well-made play, but it cannot be said that Becque disdained to use *"les petits moyens du théâtre."* The honest manufacturer dies at precisely the necessary moment. His widow and his daughters are helpless because the son is in the army, because the daughter's fiancé is a ninny, because the ladies are as innocent as newborn babes—in short, because this was how Becque needed to arrange his play. One wonders, similarly, at the infallible perspicacity through which a successful industrialist makes sure that he is surrounded exclusively by rogues and scoundrels when he dies. The sublime irony of the curtain line disposes us to forgive everything. It is spoken by Teissier, the most repulsive of all the scoundrels of the play, after he agrees to marry the youngest, and most desirable, daughter of the family he has ruined: "Ah, *ma pauvre enfant, depuis la mort de votre père vous n'avez été entourés que de fripons."*

In this period, every dramatist in France was busily unmasking villains and hypocrites. In the plays they wrote, the conflict was invariably a battle of good and evil, and it was normal for the good to triumph. Evil triumphs in *Les Corbeaux*; but that is not the point. In the world that Becque depicted, the wicked are not conscious of being wicked. They have no moral insight, and feel no guilt. Their lies and rascalities are part of the ordinary routine of business. The result is a world such as not even Tocqueville had imagined, a jungle. It was in this manner that Becque exhibited the middle class of the 1880's.

From a political viewpoint, the play could not have been better timed. The middle class during this period was under attack both from the Right and the Left. The clerical and monarchic interests, on the one hand, and the growing forces of socialism, on the other, were combined for once in a common cause, while the French bourgeoisie, completely secure and entirely in command of the situation, indulged itself periodically in an orgy of self-flagellation.

In the case of Becque, it was not at all clear from which quarter the attack was launched; but it was welcome. *Les Corbeaux* provoked some resentment, like *Le Fils de Giboyer*, but some years after its first production it was accepted as a masterpiece and its author was compared with Molière.

La Parisienne (1885) suggests that, had Becque continued to write, he would probably have developed a magnificent style of sharp comedy. Unlike *Les Corbeaux*, which is dour, *La Parisienne* is gay. The opening scene is celebrated. Lafont is trying to extract a suspicious letter from Clotilde, at the same time administering the traditional moral lecture. "So long as you remain faithful to me," he concludes, "you will be an honest and respected woman. The day you betray me—." Clotilde interrupts: "Be careful. My husband is coming."

In spite of its cynicism, *La Parisienne* is not a shocking play. On the contrary, it is an example of respectable, not to say stodgy, polygamy in the gaslight era. The husband recalls Tesman in *Hedda Gabler*. He is an honest cod who desires above all to dwell in a peaceful atmosphere where he can write books on political economy. Lafont is, naturally, his best friend, and Clotilde acquits herself admirably with respect to each of them, dividing her time equitably between her husband and her lover. She preserves appearances scrupulously. She goes regularly to church: "*Vous ne voudrez pas d'une maîtresse qui n'aurait pas de religion,*" she says to Lafont, "*ce serait affreux!*"

But while Clotilde has succeeded admirably in putting adultery on a moral footing, she has by no means sacrificed her practical bourgeois ideals. In order to further her husband's ambitions in the Ministry of Finance, she finds it necessary to grant Lafont a temporary leave of absence while she bestows herself on a more advantageous suitor. After some months, her mission accomplished, she takes back the good Lafont, so that in the end everyone is happy, and all is once again in order in this best of possible worlds.

It would be too much to expect that a satire of this sort would be received in the 1880's with the same amused complacency that marked the reception of Roussin's *La Petite hutte* in the 1950's. The chief dramatists of the time had founded their fortunes on the ideal representation of the joys of marriage and the home. It was customary to resolve adulterous relations tragically by means of a pistol shot, or sentimentally in a scene of repentance, enlivened by tears and the touching prattle of innocent children. What was amusing in *La Parisienne* was the same thing that had seemed shocking in *Les Corbeaux*, the lack of any consciousness of guilt on the part of the transgressors. *La Parisienne*, indeed, installed adultery securely in the social structure, and laid down standards of respectability in sin, from which reprehensible deviations could be measured. The result, at the opposite pole from the idealistic conclusions of *Thérèse Raquin*, was recognized as truly realistic. *La Parisienne* was dubbed *comédie rosse*, harsh comedy, and it was considered that Becque had invented a new, and very modern, genre. Two years after the production of Becque's play, Jean Jullien imitated its style successfully in *La Sérénade* (1888). The *comédie rosse* thenceforth became a specialty of the dramatists of the newly established Théâtre-Libre.

Meanwhile, in spite of the vigor of their proclamations, the naturalistic playwrights were making no headway in the theatre. The critics, the theatre managers, and the established dramatists were men of experience. They knew—or thought they knew—what was suitable for the theatre and what was not. There were many ways, obviously, of telling a story on the stage, but only one way of telling it properly—on this point there was universal agreement. The system of theatre which Scribe had inherited from Corneille, and which he had transmitted to Augier, Dumas, and Sardou, was supremely French. It was logical, thrifty, neat and elegant, and, above all, it was amply justified by experience. In these circumstances, the hazards of producing the crude compositions of a vociferous group of untried amateurs seemed too great even to warrant discussion, and the works which the naturalist writers submitted for production were therefore returned to them without loss of time. The naturalists were by no means of one opinion, but they were all in the same position with regard to the theatre. They were all unwilling to write in accordance with established practice, and they were all unable to get their plays produced. The rebirth of the theatre in the last decades of the nineteenth century was therefore the result of a typically insurgent movement, small-scale, fervent, and fanatically partisan.

The story of the efforts of André Antoine to launch an *avant-garde* playhouse has a truly classic profile. Antoine was an amateur actor, a man of enormous resolution, brusque, talented, and pigheaded. The fact that for ten years he was an employee of the Paris Gas Company has no special relevance, but it is an indispensable detail. In the early part of 1887, the director of the Cercle Gaulois, Krauss, professed himself relieved when, after making a nuisance of himself for some years, Antoine resigned in order to form an amateur group of his own. That very spring, after a period of incredible exertion, Antoine offered a bill of four one-act plays in a tiny theatre which he had improvised in a room off a dark alley on the Butte Montmartre, the Impasse de l'Élysée des Beaux-Arts.

The offering was a failure. Two months later, Antoine tried again, with better success. He spent a feverish summer reading manuscripts and soliciting subscriptions. In the fall he returned to the fray in a larger house in Montparnasse with the backing of a group of subscribers which at first numbered no more than thirty-five. By the end of the year, Antoine had produced in rapid succession three groups of plays which, in spite of their obvious mediocrity, amply demonstrated the practicability of the new style of writing and the new style of production. By this time his theatre was the center of a storm of controversy, and its success was assured.

While Antoine was quite sure of what he opposed in the theatre, he was happily not altogether clear on what it was he favored. In consequence, he put on whatever captured his fancy. In February 1888, he produced Tolstoi's *The Power of Darkness*, which Augier considered novelistic; Dumas, pessimistic; and Sardou, unplayable. Its reception gave clear evidence that there was an audience for unproducible plays, a public which perversely enjoyed what the experts did not like. At the end of his first subscription year, Antoine found himself in an embarrassing position —he had put on seventeen plays and created a furore, but he was bankrupt. By this time, however, his list of subscribers was so long that he could afford to move into a larger theatre. There, from 1888 to 1894, he produced the series of plays which established naturalism in France.

Antoine's playhouse furnished the blueprint for most of the future art theatres. All his plays were privately performed before a wholly invited audience, so that he was quite free from police supervision. None of his plays was exploited for profit; no new play was played more than twice; and no special effort was made to please the subscribers. As supreme autocrat of his theatre, Antoine consulted primarily his own taste in the selection of plays. He was a good showman, and well aware of the value of shocking his public; but he was also a sincere artist intent on having his way regardless of the result. As his tastes inclined strongly toward realism, he produced the plays written by the followers of Becque—Jean Jullien, Pierre Wolff, Léon Hennique, George Ancey, and others who are now even more completely forgotten—but he was also the first to play Brieux, Curel, Courteline, and Porto-Riche. In addition he brought to Paris for the first time the works of Tolstoi, Ibsen, Turgeniev, Björnson, and Hauptmann. The French theatre suddenly took on a cosmopolitan air.

It was especially in his staging that Antoine's realistic tendencies were manifested. In accordance with the views of Diderot, almost exactly reiterated by Zola,[14] Antoine's settings reproduced reality as nearly as possible. Stage properties were real—real sides of beef hung in his butcher shops, real books were ranged in his bookcases, real plants were set out for his gardens. Since the audience was in theory completely screened off from the play by the "fourth wall" which Antoine fixed at the proscenium arch, the actors faced upstage whenever they wished, and nobody on the stage took any notice of the audience either in theory or in fact. The monologue and the aside were patently unsuited to this new staging, and Antoine's writers ruthlessly severed these bonds which tied the play to the audience. It was, at that time, no easy thing to do. In 1869, Ibsen wrote proudly to Georg Brandes that he had succeeded in completing *The League of Youth* without the use of a single monologue or aside.

More important than the realistic décor was the iconoclastic attitude of the Théâtre-Libre. In the days of Antoine, the phrase "it is not a play" was heard among critics quite as often as it is now. Antoine made a specialty of plays which were not plays. The phrase *"ce n'est pas du théâtre"* became the slogan of the new movement; and Antoine's writers took pains to violate the laws of playmaking whenever they could.[15] In the Scribean drama, logic was king; so it had been in France since the time of Descartes. The naturalists depicted characters who were motivated by passion, impulse, or chance, least of all by logic. Augier and Dumas had consistently idealized marriage and the family. The naturalists took pleasure—as Shaw did after them—in laying bare the economic basis of middle-class life. In Camille Fabre's *L'Argent*, the sacred tie that binds the family together is seen to be money, and nothing but money, so that all family alliances are based on self-interest.[16] In George Ancey's *La Dupe* the elder sister Marie shrewdly advises her younger sister to leave her worthless husband:

ADELE: But you consider only the financial side of the question.
MARIE: What other side is there?
ADELE: A great deal that you don't seem to take into account. First, there is love, the basis of family life.
MARIE: Money is the basis of family life.

The venality of the middle class in these plays is equalled only by its love of comfort, a passion to which all others are willingly sacrificed. In Jullien's *La Sérénade* the honest jeweller Cottin decides that the most sensible way to deal with the energetic youth who is making love simultaneously to his wife and his daughter is to take him into the family, where at least they can all be at their ease. The situation is not altogether unlike that which Pirandello developed in *Pensaci, Giacomino!*, but *La Sérénade*, like *La Dupe*, is purposely left unresolved, because life resolves nothing.

It was this type of play that Jullien had in mind when he coined the phrase "a slice of life." The phrase was not meant to connote a piece of relatively artless reportage such as a dramatized newspaper story. The naturalist plays of the Théâtre-Libre were in fact carefully plotted; but with the sort of plotting which is characteristic of the tales of Maupassant. They were, on the whole, simple, bitter stories involving characters who personified a single trait. These plays had no reversals of fortune, because in life there is no escape from oneself, and their principle of progression was simply a gradual intensification of what was clear from the start. Accordingly, in *La Dupe*, the foolish woman cannot and does not become wise; her innocence is a kind of destiny. Consequently, she is taken advantage of in the end just as she was in the beginning.

In naturalistic drama the worm never turns; the wicked do not repent and are not punished; and Providence never intervenes to save the situation. These plays have no denouement because there is no knot to untie: in the realistic view of the matter, life does not amuse us by tying and untying knots, nor does it exhibit much *ingegno* in contriving destinies or devising parables. The realistic world picture with which the naturalists desired to supplant the conventional fantasies of the theatre was neither pretty nor reassuring. It had the charm of the unpleasant. The naturalists, however, claimed for it an exclusive validity, and in this they were certainly mistaken.

The story of *La Sérénade* would not be out of place among the *novelle* of the *Decameron*, but it cannot be said to belong to life rather than to fiction simply because it nourishes our sense of injustice. It is perfectly normal to devise disagreeable fictions. The naturalistic drama sprang from the side of human nature which looks upon the world with disgust and hostility, collecting examples of meanness, injustice, and iniquity, just as its other side collects examples of virtue, generosity, and nobility. Both sides, obviously,

are capable of initiating fantasies, and it is interesting that since
the collapse of Platonism, reality is particularly associated in our
minds with the less agreeable type of fantasy. For a time, naturalism occupied a dominant position in the theatre, but it was predictable that the ambivalence of which it was a function would
speedily bring about a reaction. In fact, naturalism, in its first
phase, hardly lasted out the decade.

The comedies of the Théâtre-Libre read so much alike that
they might all have been written by the same man. They all share
in some measure the wry smile and penetrating glance of Becque.
What Zola dignified by the name of scientific observation, and
Shaw later called scientific natural history, was at bottom not much
more than the reaction of the *bourgeois revolté* against a system
of values which was taken seriously chiefly in literature. The power
of these comedies lay, therefore, not so much in their truth as in
their indiscretion in saying publicly what, in private, everyone
knew. Obviously, pleasant comedy on this plane was completely
out of the question. The only possible outcome of these attitudes
was some form of unpleasant drama, if not the *comédie rosse* of
Becque, then the type of comedy with tragic characters which was
later developed by Shaw.

In some measure the tragic mood of the 1870's was bound up
with the disaster of Sedan and the failure of France; but it had
other and deeper connotations which caused it to be taken up in
other countries with even greater seriousness than in the land of its
origin. The despair of the period was profound, if ephemeral. It
was the despair of those who were forced by reason to relinquish
their faith in God, and by experience to give up their faith in man.
The naturalists began as reformers, but they had not much zeal.
The middle class was their destined prey, but they were not so
thoroughly partisan as to contrast the sordidness of the wealthy
with the beauty of the poor, like the romanticists of the former
age. In their eyes, all human life was squalid. They faced this fact
with candor and with a certain enthusiasm. The conviction that
the ideals which society cherished were no more than conventions

behind which lurked every sort of iniquity gave them their sense of mission. Their iconoclasm was impartial. They attacked life and art with equal zest, and had a good word for nothing and nobody. In the French drama, after Sedan, optimism became indecent, much as it is in the present day. Pleasant things seldom happened on the naturalistic stage. The duel in the drama of the Second Empire was always providential. In naturalistic drama the hero was invariably killed.

The Théâtre-Libre closed its doors in 1896, after nine years of activity, and Antoine became once again an actor.[17] By the time he entered upon his brief period of tenure as director of the Odéon in 1906, his battle was so far won that Becque seemed old-fashioned, and the disciples of Becque had either vanished or changed beyond recognition. The successful writers of the Théâtre-Libre were by this time entirely absorbed by the commercial theatre, and under their auspices a new style of drama was developing, somewhere between naturalism and the style of Augier. What this amounted to was essentially a play of character with a simple plot of retro-spective nature, with neither *raisonneurs*, arguments, nor displays of wit, and a minimum of contrivance. Its relation to the Scribean tradition was indicated only by the indispensable penultimate crisis and the peripeteia which capped the climax of the action. Such was the style which Brieux, Hervieu, Donnay, and Lemaître be-queathed to the following generation and, in general, this is the basis of the dramatic style of our day.

The new drama of the 1880's thus evolved into a newer drama which represented a compromise, if not a synthesis. The new pat-terns were transmitted by writers whose works are now seldom studied. The powerful social plays of Brieux—*Blanchette, L'Engre-nage, La Couvée, L'Évasion, Les Trois filles de M. Dupont, Les Bienfaiteurs*—did not long outlive Brieux, but his manner lived on in the work of more polite reformers like Galsworthy. *La Course au flambeau*, Hervieu's masterpiece of family life, is read now only by specialists. Maurice Donnay's celebrated *Les Amants* and *La*

Douloureuse are completely forgotten. In our time Curel is remembered chiefly for *Les Fossiles* and *L'Envers d'une sainte*, and Porto-Riche for *L'Amoureuse*, while Lavedan and Jules Lemaître are now merely names. It is dispiriting to remember that barely a generation has passed since these names were chapter headings in the current surveys of contemporary drama. At the turn of the century, a tide of genius rolled over the European stage. When this tide receded, the writers of the Théâtre-Libre were nowhere to be seen.

It was in the German theatre that naturalism had its real floriation, and principally in the work of Gerhart Hauptmann, the leading exponent of this style in the European theatre. Like the rest of his contemporaries, however, Hauptmann was overtaken by the anti-positivist reaction which set in even before the establishment of the Théâtre-Libre and, relinquishing naturalism, he became a symbolist. Thus, strictly speaking, naturalism barely survived its own success.

The return of idealism to the theatre in the 1890's was accompanied by considerable fanfare, amid vastly broadened spiritual horizons. The naturalists had thought of themselves as physiologists. The new movement was much involved with psychology, with hypnotism, and the Hermetic sciences. In the bookshops, the psychological novel and the mystical tale began to outsell the positivistic studies of the school of Médan, and in some quarters the planchette was held to be mightier than the pen. The theatre now blossomed with spiritual plays, mysteries, and moralities rewritten by poets like Hofmannsthal and staged by showmen like Reinhardt. A new moral earnestness made itself felt. There was a wave of conversions. Composers of opera wrote masses and requiems in operatic style. The cathedrals came once again into fashion, and there was a new surge of interest in the Middle Ages and the medieval world picture. People saw ghosts.

In France, after 1892, the symbolic drama of Maeterlinck established its headquarters at Lugné-Poë's newly organized Théâtre de L'Œuvre. The eclecticism of the Théâtre-Libre, however, kept pace with the times. Antoine produced Villiers de l'Isle-Adam along with Jean Jullien. Even in the Théâtre-Français, still operating according to the statutes of the Edict of 1812, important concessions were made to the modern temper. By 1897, it is said, classic tragedy and the romantic drama were played so much alike that they were almost indistinguishable. The same actors played *Phèdre* and *Ruy Blas*, and *L'Avare* was performed as a *comédie rosse*. But these innovations did not suffice to attract an audience which was becoming increasingly aware of foreign literary movements of the first importance. By the end of the century, the French theatre, which for two hundred years had supplied the forms and ideas of European drama, for the first time faced an influx of new ideas and new forms from abroad.

The Norwegian drama which Antoine hastened to introduce to the audience of the Théâtre-Libre did not, however, arouse much enthusiam. Ibsen's *Les Revenants*, in the season of 1889–1890, was received with indifference. It bore too plainly the marks of the well-made play to warrant the full support of the naturalists, and it was not sufficiently ingenious in design to merit the respect of the admirers of Sardou. *Le Canard sauvage* fared no better. It was, so it was said, obviously a *pièce à thèse*, but its thesis was not clear; it proved nothing. For the rest, these things were done better in France.

By the time Ibsen was appreciated in France, his greatness was fully acknowledged in Germany, and even in Russia. In England, in 1890, Shaw began his pro-Ibsenist campaign with a lecture on the socialistic aspects of Ibsen's plays. The following year, he published *The Quintessence of Ibsenism*. It was certainly effective in bringing Ibsen to the attention of the English, but in the long run, it did more harm than good. It was Shaw's special talent to espouse good causes for bad reasons: in this case, he thought he was expounding Ibsen to the English, when in fact he was explaining Brieux and Becque. Nevertheless his enthusiasm was infectious. The English critics began by vilifying Ibsen to the point of indecency. A decade later, it was considered old-fashioned to disparage him, and within twenty years no one doubted that the inscrutable Norwegian was the father of modern drama.

Ibsen

IN 1866, before *Brand* was published, Ibsen looked like a character out of *La Vie de Bohème*, shaggy, black-cloaked, wide-hatted, and vaguely alcoholic. Two years before, he had come to Rome on a tiny government grant. He was ill, uncomfortable, deep in debt, and often hungry. In Christiania, his personal effects had just been sold for debt. In Rome he was at his wits' end to provide for his wife and his little son. He could not even afford to buy stamps: his friend Björnson paid the postage due when Ibsen wrote to him.

The success of *Brand* changed everything. At one stroke Ibsen became an important writer, a national poet with a government stipend. Without delay, he took on an appropriate personality, and costumed himself carefully for the part he was henceforth to play. Carefully brushed and barbered, in velvet jacket, light waistcoat, checked trousers, and shoes of bright patent leather, he stood as tall as he could, spoke seldom, shunned publicity, and made careful investments through his publisher, Frederik Hegel.

The pose of dignified reserve which he struck at this time he maintained scrupulously the rest of his life, emerging from his retirement, when he was asked, only to protest that the world misunderstood him. Nevertheless, from 1866 to 1899, he kept himself constantly in the public eye with a series of plays which appeared in the Scandinavian bookshops every two years in time to catch the Christmas trade.[1] It would seem that further than this he had neither the desire nor the need to exhibit himself to the world, and it would perhaps be indiscreet to look for him elsewhere than in his work were it not that the deliberately enigmatic nature of his performance as an author not only invites, but necessitates a closer view of him as a man. Indeed, he himself at every opportunity called attention to the close relationship between his life and his work, so that one who wishes to understand him, and the nature of his contribution, has no alternative but to consider his work as an extension of his personality.

When Ibsen came to Christiania in 1850 to attend Heltberg's cram course for the entrance examinations at the university, he found Björnson already there. The two were almost exact contemporaries. They were born within four years of each other; both were sons of poor parents; both died at precisely the same age of seventy-eight. There the resemblance ends. Björnson was an immediately acceptable man, warm, eager, earnest, and colorful. His first book was one of his greatest successes and, almost from the beginning, honors and preferment were showered upon him. Björnson wrote the national anthem; he distinguished himself hugely in the struggle for independence; he was the head of the Norwegian liberal party as long as he lived; and was awarded the Nobel prize before he died.

It was quite otherwise with Ibsen. Success came to him slowly and grudgingly. He was not a lovable man, and he led a loveless life, mostly in exile, homeless everywhere, and most of all in his native land. Björnson wrote out of his joy, his exuberance, and his health; Ibsen, out of his desperate loneliness. The result illustrates the advantages of the neurotic personality. Fifty years after his death, Björnson is scarcely read outside the Scandinavian countries, while Ibsen has taken his place among the foremost masters of literature.

Björnson and Ibsen worked along parallel lines in the drama until the 1880's, and up to this point it was Björnson who pointed the direction and set the pace. Both began their career in the theatre with subjects drawn from the history of Norway, conceived in a style somewhere between the manner of Schiller and the manner of Scribe. The year before Ibsen wrote *Brand*, Björnson achieved extraordinary success with a two-act domestic drama in the style of Dumas *fils*, called *The Newlyweds*. Ibsen was impressed. He wrote to Björnson, "Yes, that is how the drama must shape with us now." [2] In 1874, Björnson wrote *The Editor*, and the following year he achieved his greatest success in the theatre with *A Bankruptcy*. Ibsen made haste to follow this lead with *Pillars of Society*, on a similar theme. Björnson's next play, *The New System*, served Ibsen as a point of departure for *An Enemy of the People*. In 1878, Björnson's feminist novel *Magnhild* appeared, and in 1879, his feminist play *Leonarda*. Six months later, Ibsen published *A Doll's House*. By this time Björnson and he were no longer friends, and their political interests diverged sharply.[3] There is nothing in Ibsen's future work that is at all like Björnson's most interesting and most difficult play, *Beyond Our Strength*.

But while it is evident that up to the time of *Ghosts*, at least, Ibsen hopefully followed Björnson's lead, there is a consistency in Ibsen's development as a writer that is altogether lacking in Björnson. In his choice of subject Björnson was often influenced by the latest successes from abroad. Ibsen certainly came under similar influences. There is no doubt, however, that, after a certain point in his life, his choice of theme was dictated by deeper motives than the desire to write a successful play. In a letter of 1870, he wrote Peter Hansen:

Everything which I have created as a poet has had its origin in a frame of mind and a situation in life. I never wrote because I had, as they say, "found a good subject." [4]

Reserved as he ordinarily was with regard to his work, the one thing
he consistently made clear was that the basis of his drama was self-
contemplation and self-analysis. In a speech to the Christiania
Students' Union in 1874, he said:

All that I have written, these last ten years, I have mentally lived
through . . . I have written on that, so to speak, which stood higher
than my daily self. But I have also written on the opposite, on that
which to introspection appears as the dregs and sediment of one's
own nature. The work of writing has been to me, in this case, like
a bath, which I have felt to leave me cleaner, healthier, and freer.
Yes, gentlemen, nobody can present poetically that of which he has
not, to a certain extent, the model in himself.

Such a statement seems hardly novel in an age which has survived
Freud, but in the 1880's it must have seemed puzzling or perhaps
embarrassing; at any rate, nobody seems to have made much of it.
To us it indicates not only the depth of the author's insight into
the nature of literary creation, but also the degree to which Ibsen,
seemingly so reticent in public, felt the need for calling attention
to himself in the theatre. But in spite of the fact that in his elvish
way he explained repeatedly that his plays were at bottom adventures in self-portraiture, he has remained largely inscrutable; and
the principal result of his attempts to explain himself has been to
send his biographers hunting for people with whom to associate
his characters, quite as if he had written so many *romans à clef*.
In this manner, a great deal of interesting material has been brought
to light, but the man himself has not been brought to light, and
perhaps he never will be.

In any event, we do not need to see very deeply into Ibsen's
life in order to read his plays with understanding. For that, what is
chiefly necessary is to learn in what manner he intended us to
understand them. But in this regard, his repeated assurance that
his characters are mainly the result of self-observation takes on a
special significance.

The characters of Second Empire drama were not traditionally
conceived as personal expressions. There is, it is true, a good deal
of autobiography in the plays of Dumas *fils*, but the characters in

the plays of this period are in the main conventional types. After Zola, the naturalists insisted on the precision with which their characters were drawn from life; but observation is not the essential element in the kind of character portrayal that makes great drama. What is essential is a special sort of intuition, the dramatist's inborn ability to see in others the reflection of the complex life which he feels within himself; and the vitality of the resulting characterization depends on his power to transmit to the audience this awareness of the hidden life which humanity shares. When this is done, his characters are felt to have a life of their own; they live, in fact, with our common life, and surprise us with that sense of kinship which is the special attribute of the dramatic experience.

The insistence of the naturalists on the scientific objectivity of their work was in fact a confession of their own artistic sterility. The truth of the theatre has nothing to do with science. It is the result of a direct and immediate intuition. The dramatist's suggestion reaches us long before his explanation, and much more intimately, and it is only when this intimation fails that recourse must be had to the prosaic methods of the logician. In fact, the analytic method of the naturalists resulted in nothing more than the usual gallery of puppets, each doll a personification of its *faculté maîtresse*.

The naturalists of a later day, with the aid of the newly discovered Freudian apparatus, attempted to construct characters of somewhat greater scientific validity. The resulting creations belonged simply to another order of marionette. But the great characters of drama do not behave in the least like puppets. They seem to leap fully and independently into being, moved by a spirit that is more intense than life. There is nothing explicable about the way in which this effect is achieved—it is a magic that defies analysis, but it is through the power of the poet, clearly, and not through the skill of the craftsman that this realization takes place.

The art of characterization, obviously, does not begin with Ibsen; but Ibsen is one of the first dramatists, if not the first, to afford us a glimpse of the workings of the poetic principle. Traditionally, the confessional element in literature was associated with the lyric poets. After Montaigne, the essayists, and after Sterne, the novelists devised for themselves convincing *personae* which permitted them to manifest themselves in public, so to speak, in a congenial disguise. The compulsion to display oneself to society quite candidly is, however, more closely associated with the special sort of masochism we call romantic, and is a comparatively recent phenomenon in literature. If we except such writers as Augustine, Cellini, Pascal, and Casanova as special pleaders, and therefore not quite candid, we are left with few examples of frank self-portraiture before the time of Rousseau. In any case, the drama, perhaps because of its specially exhibitionistic character, was the last of the literary arts to be used in this way.

In using the drama more or less consciously as a medium for the expression of the inner life of the artist, Ibsen made what amounts to a new departure in this art. Ibsen spoke of his plays habitually as poems. They are, in fact, poetic fantasies which have a lyrical nuance uncommon in the history of the drama; perhaps it is new. The extent of his innovation, needless to say, was hardly appreciated by his contemporaries; nor is it fully appreciated now; and Shaw is perhaps excusable for having thought of him primarily as a social dramatist of the naturalist school. Ibsen made few innovations aside from this. He worked almost entirely within the traditional forms; it was by infusing them with his inmost vitality that he gave these forms sublimity. Before Ibsen, the nineteenth-century theatre was a place of amusement or, at the most, a forum for discussion. After *Brand*, the stage became once again a vehicle for the highest expression of the human spirit in art.

Ibsen achieved his maturity as a dramatist slowly and painfully. Before *Brand* his only success in the theatre was *The Pretenders*. It was played eight times in Christiania, in 1864. It was his ninth play; its chief consequence was the modest government grant which made it possible for him to travel to Italy, where, in the summer of 1865, he wrote *Brand*. He was then thirty-eight. The following year

he wrote *Peer Gynt*. It was hardly producible, and it was not produced until Grieg made it into a musical drama years later. In
1869 Ibsen published a prose satire in the French style, *The League
of Youth*. Four years after, he brought out *Emperor and Galilean*
and, two years after that, in 1877, *Pillars of Society*. None of these
three plays can be said to be other than journeyman's work. Finally
in 1879 he hit his stride as a writer of prose drama. *A Doll's House*
was his first solid success in the theatre. It was his sixteenth attempt.
He was already fifty-one.

It would be senseless to suggest that Ibsen was born as a playwright at the age of fifty-one. *Brand* and *Peer Gynt* are unique
masterpieces. All the same, had Ibsen written nothing before 1879,
his stature as a dramatist, outside the Scandinavian countries,
would hardly be diminished. The current critical tendency is to
place more and more emphasis on the early Ibsen, particularly on
Catilina and *The Pretenders*, perhaps because of a feeling that
there remains nothing more to be said about his later works. But
Weigand was doubtless justified in limiting his detailed analysis of
Ibsen's plays to the period beginning with *Pillars of Society*.

Brand was perhaps not intended for the stage. Yet, ultimately,
a playwright intends everything for the stage, and *Brand* has been
played many times in many theatres since its initial production in
Stockholm in 1885. It is a very long play; in Ludwig Josephson's
production it lasted seven hours. One is tempted, in comparing
the operatic lavishness of *Brand* with the thriftiness of *Rosmersholm*, to conclude that in 1865 Ibsen did not yet know how to
write a play. This would be a mistake. The romantic turbulence of
Brand is a source of strength, and it is significant that it was not
until the end of his career, in *When We Dead Awaken*, that Ibsen
once again thought of a character who needed an avalanche in
order to die properly. The record of Ibsen's development from the
romanticism of *Brand* to the romanticism of *When We Dead
Awaken* is not only a reflection of the changing currents of litera-

ture in this age; it is also the measure of the methodical application of an iron discipline to an intensely romantic nature; and this is perhaps the source of the enormous reserve of power which surges behind the quiet conversation of the salon in the plays of Ibsen's middle period.

Brand is far from a consistent statement. It is written in rhymed verse; its scope is epic; it makes use of effects which exhaust the ingenuity of the scene designer; but its mood is, on the whole, the mood of bourgeois tragedy. The story of Brand might have taken place in a country kitchen. The same story, essentially, was in fact set in a living room in *Ghosts, The Wild Duck,* and *Rosmersholm.* The plot of *Brand* served Ibsen thoroughly: it may be said to be, in one way or another, the basis of all his realistic drama.

The setting of *Brand* is Ibsen's favorite setting, a village of a thousand souls huddled in the dark shadow of a northern fjord between the mountains and the sea. To this, his native village, comes a young pastor fierce with zeal, on his way to reform the world in the name of God. He goes no further.

Brand is an extremist. His slogan is "All or Nothing." His love is harsh and his nature uncompromising. Because of his stern sense of duty, he refuses to minister to his dying mother unless she relinquishes all her worldly possessions. He sacrifices his little son, and sees his wife waste away and die in the misty fjord which his vocation forbids him to leave. In obedience to what he conceives to be God's will, he tears down the old village church and builds a new one with his inheritance—it is his idea of settling his mother's debts. Yet when the time comes to consecrate the new church, he perceives suddenly that this gesture is vain, and instead of leading his flock into the church, he leads it up into the high mountains on a pilgrimage to reform the world. The villagers soon grow weary of a journey that leads nowhere. They turn against their leader, stone him, and abandon him to his fate. Brand climbs till he comes to the Black Peak which is haunted by the mad girl Gerd. She has armed herself with a rifle with which to destroy the hawk that obsesses her, the filthy bird which, she believes, is the spirit of evil. The hawk appears. She shoots, and brings down the avalanche that destroys them.

The story is perhaps not entirely sensible, but its point seems clear. Brand is not of this world. He is not quite sure of his goal; he is conscious only of the compulsion that moves him unceasingly toward it. As it turns out, his goal is death. The God toward whom he has striven all his life is as merciless as he. His love is the avalanche. In part, therefore, the play is a parable, a demonstration, of the order of the *Proverbes* of Musset, which demonstrates in terms of poetic justice the working out of an inhuman ideal of rectitude.

It is not easy to decide to what an extent Ibsen came under the influence of Søren Kierkegaard in this period of his life. Kierkegaard is a very difficult writer, and Ibsen by his own admission never read him carefully: "I have read very little of S.K., and understood even less." He evidently understood enough for his purposes.

Kierkegaard's doctrine in *Either-Or* centers on the idea of personality. To live sincerely is to discover what we have in ourselves of greatest value and to orient our lives accordingly. Life thus takes on the aspect of a mission, the essence of which is self-realization. In Kierkegaard's view, man is identical with his mission; his business in life defines him. His goal is to be himself completely, without compromise or reserve, to follow his real desire at every instant with a tranquil passion. It follows that without the complete engagement that such a goal entails, he is nothing.[5]

Since all other considerations are irrelevant to the realization of the true self, there is a certain opposition between mission and happiness. The process of self-realization is one of painful effort, a constant struggle, and it is foreseeable that in this struggle one will not always succeed. But our duty is not measured by our strength. It is always excusable not to be able, but never not to will.[6] It is our duty, on the contrary, to will beyond the possibility of fulfillment, to will the impossible. In the sacrifice of Abraham we see the folly of the human viewpoint. For Kierkegaard the exorbitance of God's demand involves a paradox, and this paradox is the very atmosphere of Christianity.

It seems quite clear that Ibsen's debt to *Either-Or* was considerable: indeed, *Brand* is often cited as the prime literary illustration of Kierkegaard's doctrine, and in Ibsen's day it was even said to be a dramatization of Kierkegaard's life. *Brand* is evidently Kierkegaard's ethical man portrayed in the process of self-realization which, as Kierkegaard warned, leads inevitably to despair. The brief sketch of Einar the poet in *Brand* suggests another Kierkegaardian figure, the aesthetic man, who is also on the way to despair. It is tempting to see also in Brand's final moment the ultimate stage of the Kierkegaardian process in which the ethical man is cast headlong into the paradox of Christianity which is at once the supreme sacrifice and the supreme refuge. But while *Brand* appears to be designed after the plan of *Either-Or*, it would certainly be a mistake to consider Ibsen a Kierkegaardian. On the contrary, it seems that Ibsen either misunderstood completely, or was not at all in accord with Kierkegaard's idea. There is something divine in Brand's mission; it gives him power and courage beyond the capacity of lesser men. It also makes him inhuman; and in the end he makes a bad bargain—he demands all and he gets nothing. It is in realizing himself that he destroys himself.

It was in this situation, particularly, that Ibsen placed the protagonists of his later drama. To be Brand, to be truly oneself, is to invite the avalanche. But to be less than Brand, to compromise endlessly is to be nothing at all—such was the lesson of *Peer Gynt*. To this dilemma, for reasons which were undoubtedly personal, Ibsen returned again and again. It is one of the principal sources of his creativity.

It is astonishing how large a proportion of Ibsen's characters are conceived along Kierkegaardian lines; but it is equally surprising to see what Ibsen does with them. Most of his principal characters regard life as a mission, and most of them seek self-realization through its fulfillment, but Ibsen is testy with these characters. In general, they are either comic or pathetic. They are rarely tragic;

and never successful. Through the pressure of their will, all of them suffer distortion. Brand is inhuman; Julian is silly; Dr. Stockmann is funny; Gregers Werle is repulsive; Brendel, a clown; Allmers, like Rosmer, is pathetic; Borkman and Rubek are brutal. Besides Brand, only Solness, Borkman, and Rubek really inspire respect. All these men have missions in life, real or fancied; and it is not only Ibsen's men who follow this pattern; his women also seek to realize themselves. Hedda Gabler has her mission; so have Thea Elvsted, Hilde Wangel, and Mrs. Alving; Nora expects to find one. Even Aline Solness conceives of life as a duty. It is evident that each of these characters has taken a page out of Kierkegaard's book and, without understanding too well what is involved, each is striving mightily to be himself. To Ibsen this seems, on the whole, comic; occasionally it seems tragic; but never quite sensible.

It is often said that the central problem with Ibsen was the problem of vocation, and that he was particularly involved with the relation of vocation to happiness. Unquestionably there is something of this in Ibsen's plays, but in most of them the problem of vocation is not central, but marginal. While vocation and the paradox of *l'homme engagé* was never far from his thoughts, it seems clear that in most cases Ibsen used the Kierkegaardian formula not in order to illustrate the stages that lead through despair to God, but simply as a device through which to characterize his figures. However incomprehensible Kierkegaard might be as a theologian, he had evidently hit on something that was of value to a dramatist. In order to be at all, it is necessary to be something; and in their efforts to be something, Ibsen's characters in fact become something. It is a very different principle of characterization from that of the *faculté maîtresse* of the naturalists, incomparably more dramatic, and it served the purposes excellently of the existentialist dramatists of the next century.

Unlike the existentialist heroes, Ibsen's protagonists invariably live to regret the sacrifice of love and happiness. In each case the hero, after following the path of complete dedication the better part of his life, turns, when it is too late, toward that dream of happiness which his mission has excluded. Ibsen therefore rejects Kierkegaard's position; and this is entirely understandable, since Ibsen was at no time Christian in the Kierkegaardian sense. Apart from *Brand*, Ibsen's drama takes place in an atmosphere charged with the tensions that subsist between will and desire. The tragedy of man is implicit, in Ibsen's view, in his need to fulfill the one by rejecting the other equally important aspect of his nature, and the pattern of tragedy is seen in the invariable failure of the attempt to synthesize the opposed elements when it is too late.

In Brand's gospel of "All or Nothing" it is easy to recognize Kierkegaard's "Either-Or." But while Ibsen obviously admired the heroic intransigence of Brand, he was entirely clear as to the psychic attributes of such a personality. Brand is cruel to others and cruel to himself, and Ibsen is careful to bring out the voluptuous nature of his suffering, and his pleasure in inflicting pain. Brand says:

> Hvad verden kalder kærlighed,
> jeg ikke vil og ikke ved.
> Guds kærlighed jeg kender til,
> og den er ikke vek og mild;
> den er til dødens rædsel hård,
> den byder klappe, så det slår.[7]

> (What is called love
> I neither want nor know.
> God's love I know,
> and that is neither weak nor mild;
> That is hard, even unto the terror of death.
> That, when it caresses, leaves a wound.)

There is also, Brand knows, another and more tender love; but this love must be deferred. First must come the triumph of will:

> Vandt viljen sejr i slig en strid,
> da kommer kærlighedens tid,
> da daler den som duen hvid
> og bringer livets oljeblad;
> men her, mod slægten, slap og lad,
> ens bedste kærlighed er had! [8]

> (When the will has triumphed in such a struggle
> then comes the time for love;
> Then it descends like a white dove
> and brings life's olive leaf;
> but here, with this lax and lazy race,
> the best love is hate!)

Brand believes that in order to hate the evil in mankind it is necessary also to hate mankind. Christ came not to bring peace but a sword; similarly, Brand's doctrine means eternal war. In his view of life there is no room for love, and this realization is at the root of his agony. He is hard. The good doctor of the village reproaches him for his hardness in practical terms that are made to echo poetically at the end of the play:

> Ja, mandeviljens qvantum satis
> står bogført som din rigdoms rad;—
> men, prest, din conto caritatis
> er bogens hvide jomfrublad! [9]

> (Yes, with regard to what is necessary of human will,
> a great sum is posted to your credit,
> but, priest, your love-account
> is but a virgin-white page!)

His gentle wife, Agnes, also protests at the exorbitance of his demands:

> Og til en slægt, som rådløst faldt,
> du råber: i n t e t eller a l t! [10]

> (And to this race, which falls for lack of counsel,
> you cry: *nothing* or *all!*)

Brand can accept no less than all. In his sight, compromise is the way of Satan. Ibsen symbolizes the spirit of compromise in the hawk, the pursuit of which appears to be the mad girl's main function in life. When she meets Brand, blood-stained and solitary in the mountains, close to the Black Peak that points to heaven, she adores him as the living Christ. But his self-imposed martyrdom is more than he can bear and, like Christ on the Mount

of Olives, he feels a rush of longing for the sun and the warmth of
the world which he has relinquished in the service of God. He
bursts out suddenly, "serene and shining, as if young again:"

> Frostvejr bær igennem loven,
> siden sommersol fra oven!
> Til idag det galdt at blive
> tavlen, hvorpå Gud kan skrive;—
> fra idag mit livsensdigt
> skal sig bøje varmt og rigt.
> Skorpen brister. Jeg kan græde,
> jeg kan knæle,—jeg kan bede! [11]

> (The law endlessly imposes frosty weather;
> Then comes the sun of summer overhead!
> Until today it was worthwhile to remain
> a tablet on which God might write;
> but from today, my life's poem
> Shall bow itself hot and abundant.
> The crust breaks. I can weep,
> I can kneel—I can pray!

It is at this moment precisely that Gerd sees the hawk, symbol of
the sun, hovering overhead, and she shoots it with her silver bul-
let. The shot rings true. There is an answering roar. The hawk
turns white as it falls. It grows vast, a dove, but not the white dove
bearing the olive branch: the all-engulfing dove, the spirit of God,
the avalanche. Brand shrinks back from the almighty force that is
about to take him into its embrace, and in his last moment he
desperately presents his account:

> Svar mig, Gud, i dødens slug!
> gælder ej et frelsens fnug
> mandeviljens qvantum satis—?

> (Answer me, God, in the jaws of death!
> Cannot one buy one mite of salvation
> With the full measure of human will?)

The avalanche swallows him and the whole valley with him. A
voice cries through the thunder:

Han er deus caritatis.[12]

(He is the god of love.)

The meaning could hardly be plainer. Brand's moral credit balance is ample to recommend him to the God who is Will but, as the doctor warned him, he has nothing with which to justify himself to the God of Love.

The strange, but not unprecedented, concept of divine love with which Ibsen ends his play is far from the sentimentality of contemporary Christianity. In Brand's view of the matter, which he renounces only in his penultimate moment, the love of God is not a tender passion. It is hard, so he tells Agnes, and indistinguishable from hate. There is no mercy in it, and no forgiveness. What Brand experiences, therefore, in the end is the love of that God whom all his life he served. This God is also *deus caritatis*, but elemental, icy, irresistible, and uncompromising—love in its aspect as infinite will. Brand discovers the God of Love too late. The thaw comes upon him too suddenly. He has served the wrong God too long. So, in the end, Brand finds God on the heights precisely as he knew him, expounded him, and deserved him—he is loved as he loved.

As it had been pointed out long before the time of Kierkegaard, God is a paradox: he is Will and he is Love. To serve God exclusively as Will is to invite the retribution of the God of Love. It is precisely because Brand's ministry has always been harsh that he has failed in his effort to redeem his flock. God's will is man's strength. But will alone does not save; by itself it can only destroy. That aspect of the erotic which is merely aggressive holds no promise. The spirit of humanity, the eternal willingness to compromise with evil both keeps us from God and shields us from his might. When the spirit of compromise, which is the essence of our humanity, is destroyed, at once we experience the overwhelming rush of divine power, and we are lost in it. In this, God's justice is manifest. If man yearns to be overwhelmed by God, it is just that God should overwhelm him.

In *Brand*, Ibsen exhibited clearly for the first time that ambivalence with respect to the ideal which furnished him with a
basis for his subsequent work in the theatre. All his later plays are
in some way colored by it, and therefore all of them are in some way
Brand. Out of this ambivalence came also the possibility of a
fully realized characterization, one of the strongest in modern
drama. Brand is magnificent; but without compassion, he is hateful. For Ibsen, the Galilean spirit, untempered by the tenderness
which is the human aspect of divinity, is the spirit of death and
darkness, and it can result only in darkness and death. It is the
tragedy of Brand that he is doomed to failure through the very
extremity of his devotion. But the realization that his single-
mindedness has made him morally and emotionally a bankrupt
comes to him only when it is too late. It is at this point that the
wounded God overwhelms him with the love which is the same as
destruction.

From a practical viewpoint, *Brand* is perhaps not a very satisfactory play. Brand is not only difficult to get on with, he is also
difficult to listen to—he talks too much. The stylistic contrast,
also, between the scenes of high fantasy and realism is sharp,
possibly too sharp. The minor and even the major characters, with
the exception of Brand, come close to caricature, and Brand is
exaggerated beyond credibility. Yet few plays in the modern
theatre have the scale and power of this.

Doubtless *Brand* was meant to be taken with complete gravity,
but it is veined with the strange humor which tinges with the grotesque even the most sombre of Ibsen's plays. The relation of
Ibsen's comedy to Becque's *comédie rosse* seems rather explicit;
although A *Doll's House* was written three years before the publication of *Les Corbeaux*, and *Brand* was published seventeen years
before it. The difference between the manner of Ibsen and the
manner of Becque is, however, essential. While Becque's aggressiveness is completely externalized and, therefore, in a sense, discharged by the action, Ibsen's satire is directed in part against his

own fantasy, and this results in the extraordinarily rich and complex characterization which we admire in such plays as *Hedda Gabler* and *Rosmersholm*. Brand, too, is faintly ridiculous. He is the monumental aspect of Pastor Manders; he makes one shudder—but there are moments, clearly, when he makes Ibsen smile.

The relation between Ibsen's idea of himself in 1865 and the portrait he drew in *Brand* has a certain importance for our appreciation of Ibsen's development as a dramatist. The play "came into being," he wrote to Laura Kieler, who was probably the original of Nora in *A Doll's House*, "as a result of something which I had, not observed, but experienced; it was a necessity for me to free myself from something which my inner man had done with, by giving poetic form to it; and when by this means I had got rid of it, my book no longer had any interest for me." "Brand is myself in my finest moments," he wrote some months later. In a letter to Georg Brandes the year before, he had pointed out that the problem in *Brand* had nothing to do with religion: "I could have constructed the same syllogism just as easily on the subject of a sculptor or a politician, as of a priest." [13] Doubtless, Ibsen identified himself closely with the strange romantic figure who was capable of sacrificing his mother, his wife, and his child, and finally himself, to his tragic sense of vocation. Such a projection of the not altogether agreeable facts of Ibsen's early life is an interesting and entirely understandable example of self-dramatization. It is entirely possible, also, that his fantasy was influenced by the hero of Paludan-Müller's *Adam Homo*; but it hardly matters. Kierkegaard had sketched in the necessary outlines: it was necessary only to breathe life into them to evoke Brand.

That this characterization meant a great deal to Ibsen cannot be doubted. As we have noted, a surprisingly large portion of his future work centers upon this image of the resolute idealist he could never quite manage to be. In his later plays, Ibsen tried desperately to rid himself of this obsessive figure. He mocked Brand as Pastor Manders and Dr. Stockmann, vilified him as Gregers Werle, drowned him as Rosmer, pitched him off a tower as Solness, and swallowed him up yet again in the avalanche of *When We Dead Awaken*. One might say he struggled with Brand for thirty years; but he never succeeded in shaking him off. In the end, quite possibly Brand destroyed him.

In a letter of 1858, seven years before *Brand* was written, Ibsen wrote: "Believe me, it is not pleasant to see the world in an October light, and yet there have been times, oddly enough, when I have asked nothing better." The pleasure of seeing the world in autumnal colors, with the memory of a wasted spring, was perhaps more than a conventional romantic pose. This mood appears to have sprung from a source deep in Ibsen's nature and it resulted in the characteristically sombre palette of his later plays. Possibly it indicates also, in a general way, the source of the retrospective method which became his chief technical mannerism. After *A Doll's House* Ibsen often presented his characters in the autumn of their lives, and in his later period, his plays are usually little more than recollections of times long past. The dark valley in which Ibsen spent his childhood, and which, after *Peer Gynt*, he took care not to revisit, save constantly in fantasy, suited his mood admirably. Brand says, toward the end of Act Two:

> Klemt imellem fjeld og fjeld,
> skygget om af tag og tinde,
> stængt i revnens halvnat inde,
> skal mit liv fra nu af rinde
> som en stur Oktoberkveld.[14]

> (Pinched between mountain and mountain,
> shadowed round by roof and peak,
> Locked in the twilight of the crevice,
> from now on my life shall flow
> like a sad October evening.)

This is a sentimental mood and, in truth, Brand is at bottom sentimental. Careful as Ibsen was to sharpen with humor whatever seemed to him even faintly mawkish in his plays, he could not altogether banish from them the crepuscular mood and the romantic self-pity of which we occasionally get a glimpse in his letters. In some measure, no doubt, this mood was literary; it became the prevailing climate of a whole school of Italian poets, the *crepusculari* of the next generation. But it is altogether permissible to find in these passages, if one has a mind to it, a reflection of Ibsen's favorite idea of himself in these years. It is possible that this idea, with its pervasive emotional connotations, was the chief shaping principle of his life for, indeed, his life, like Brand's, passed like a sad October evening in the dark valley he chose to inhabit. The difference was that Brand escaped at last into the high mountains; Ibsen, never.

Ibsen read the story of Peer Gynt in Asbjörnsen's *Norwegian Fairy Tales and Folk Legends*.[15] According to Asbjörnsen, Peer Gynt had lived in the Gudbrandsdal a century or so before, a fantastic storyteller who insisted that he himself had taken a chief part in the old stories he recounted. These were traditional tales, of which the only one peculiar to Peer Gynt was the story of the Great Boyg of Atnedalen. Ibsen, "who had not very much to build upon," [16] adapted this material very freely, using the verse form of Paludan-Müller's *Ahasverus* (1854), and the episodic structure of the dramatic *eventyr*, of the order of Öhlenschläger's *Aladdin*.

Peer Gynt consists of a series of episodes held together mainly by the presence of the central character. The narrative, with its simple epic pattern of departure and return, has a certain logical basis; but no special unity, no climax, and no definite terminal principle, so that it might conceivably have included more or fewer episodes than it has without suffering any essential change. It is evident that here, for once, Ibsen gave rein to his fancy. As a result, *Peer Gynt* has a gaiety and zest which accord richly with the elegiacal note on which the story ends. It is the first, and perhaps the best, example of Ibsen's talent for telling a sad story so that it seems funny: even in his most desperate predicament, Peer Gynt is a clown. It is unmistakable that *Brand* and *Peer Gynt* are companion pieces and supplement each other: "*Peer Gynt*," Ibsen wrote, "is the antithesis of *Brand*." [17] If Brand represents an Ibsen who took himself and his world tragically, Peer Gynt is obviously the Ibsen who gibed at everything and everyone.

Peer is twenty when the play opens, wild, lovable, lusty, a brawler and a braggart. He behaves atrociously, and is soon at odds with all the world, and even with the trolls of the mountain. After his mother's death, he runs off to seek his fortune, an outcast, leaving the young girl Solveig, who loves him, to wait in the cottage he has built for her.

When next we see Peer, he is middle-aged, rich and coarse. He is cheated and cheats, and after a series of remarkable adventures he comes home, shipwrecked, weary, and penniless, just in time to see his house and his legend—a pack of lies and rubbish—auctioned off to the highest bidder. And now at a crossroads he meets the Button Molder, and is given to understand that for him the next step is the melting pot. It is here that Peer's passion begins.

In spite of his supreme effort, Brand proved to be a tablet on which God had not written. Nothing of his survived him; he vanished without trace. Peer is in a similar case, and he too feels, above all, the need for permanence. But in order to endure, it is necessary to be; and in his extreme peril he is forced to cast about desperately for an identity. He has been careful all his life not to commit himself fully to anything. In consequence he has never defined himself, and remains inchoate, a lump of protoplasm temporarily differentiated in the flux of being. There will be nothing to mark his coming or his going—the death of Gynt will mean complete extinction.

But there is Solveig. Old now, and nearly blind, Solveig is still waiting for him in the cottage he built for her in his youth, and never dared to share with her. She is the fixed point in his life. In her mind, Peer exists unchanged and changeless in the image she has made of him, and her love is the one truth that justifies him as a person. It is true that he has no other reality; there is no other permanent trace of Gynt in the world; but no other is needed. It is perhaps not much, but enough to serve as a soul's passport. Thus Solveig, who has played so small a part in his life's adventure, in the end turns out to be the center of his orbit. He thought he had ranged far, but in truth he has not moved; he has been in her arms the whole time. So in the faith, the hope, and the love of Solveig, his wife and mother—"*min moder; min hustru*"—Peer finds at last that self which all his life he sought, and which perhaps at the last crossroads will redeem him from the Button Molder's ladle.

Peer Gynt is evidently a very personal statement. It has the lightness of self-caricature. It has also an unmistakable note of despair. On its face, it is a symbolic description of a journey in search of the self. "Be yourself" is Peer Gynt's slogan. In Eastern philosophies such a search traditionally ends in the discovery that there is no such thing as self, and to the Buddhist this is a supremely welcome thought. In the Christian view, the self is precious. It is God who guarantees our being; we live in him, and he is *deus caritatis*. Peer understands at the last, through a flash of intuition, that Solveig is the anchor of his being, that her love is his only surety, and that through her intercession, the stern father will perhaps forgive him. Thus Solveig is seen in the end to be the eternal mother. In her heart, the boy has never left her; and in the last tableau of the play she sings him to sleep as the sun rises on the end of his life:

> Gutten har ligget til mit hjerte tæt
> hele livsdagen lang. Nu er han så træt.
>
> Sov du, dyreste gutten min!
> Jeg skal vugge dig, jeg skal våge! [18]
>
> (The boy has lain close to my heart
> all the livelong day. Now he is so weary.
>
> Sleep, my dearest boy!
> I shall rock you, I shall watch over you!)

Essentially the story of Peer is the story of the prodigal son, just as *Brand* is, up to a point, the story of the sacrifice of Abraham.

Both stories are, in a way parables; and both characters, caricatures. Brand is stern, austere, solemn. Peer Gynt, even in his most embarrassing moments, is funny. Brand is the caricature of the father image; Peer Gynt, of the son. Brand is the man who stayed at home; Peer, the hero who ranged abroad: both are dreamers, the one dedicated to the dream of death, the other to the dream of life. Brand is the embodiment of principle, of form, unswerving, fearless, noble, and cruel. Peer is his antithesis—an opportunist, a sinner, a haggler, a sentimentalist, a jester—the incarnation of the amorphous, the spirit of compromise, a life without any shaping principle. Brand is the idealist; Peer, the realist: they are extremes, and each illustrates the futility of his effort. Each life, it is seen, can be justified, ultimately, only through love; love not harsh and violent, but tender, compassionate, and feminine, the love of the wife and mother. This alone can save and bless: Brand is overwhelmed by *deus caritatis*; but in *Peer Gynt*, the final tableau is a *Pietà*.

In the service of the ideal, Brand is unwavering—but he has not love, and he is lost. Peer shifts direction with every wind—but in the end love saves him. A good deal of Ibsen's doctrine in these plays may be summed up in the simple words of the Apostle. This seems sensible. Ibsen was certainly no theologian, and the intricacies of the science of God did not amuse him.

That Ibsen showed in each of these characters an aspect of himself is too obvious to require repetition. It is perhaps less obvious that in each of these characters, he meant to portray himself wholly. Nothing tangible, of course, compels us to recognize in either character a likeness, in part or in whole, of the man himself.[19] Yet a writer may, like a painter, use himself as a subject without necessarily painting a recognizable likeness. He may paint himself, if he chooses, ideally or aggressively, knowing that both portraits are exaggerations, but that, after all, likeness itself is an exaggeration.

The man who emerges from Ibsen's letters was a practical man of business, shrewd, but scrupulous in his dealings, frugal, money-conscious, careful in his investments, a man who had struggled the better part of his life with poverty and whose sense of self-preservation was, in consequence, quite highly developed. This Ibsen was a devoted paterfamilias, eager to advance his son's interests as well as his own, assiduous in cultivating the good will of those who could be useful to him, careful of his dignity, easily angered, and an implacable enemy of those who disparaged his work or his character. In the earlier years of his career, he was careful to keep himself well to the fore intellectually, but never to anger the powerful by espousing a liberal cause. As he grew older, and more secure, he veered further to the Right; but never so far as to compromise himself fully. In most respects he was a model bourgeois, with aristocratic ambitions, engaged in a profitable literary venture some steps removed from Grub Street. What differentiated him from his fellows was chiefly two things—he was really an artist, and he was, above all, an individualist.

It is when we read his plays, not his letters, that we see what all this cost him. He was very much Peer Gynt. He was also Brand; and he was Julian the Apostate. His need to be, and to justify, each of these, and also all of them together was evidently not only a source of constant mental torment, but also of a very rich fantasy-life of preponderantly tragic cast. In describing *Emperor and Galilean*, which he had not yet finished, he wrote to Edmund Gosse: "It is a part of my own spiritual life which I am putting into this book; what I depict, I have, under different conditions, gone through myself; and the historical subject chosen has a much more intimate connection with the movements of our time than anyone might at first imagine." [20]

It is quite probable that Ibsen consciously saw himself both as Brand and Peer Gynt, not sometimes as the one and sometimes as the other, but both at the same time; so that it was necessary for him, as artist, constantly to superpose the one image on the other in order to get at something like the truth. The autobiographical intention of the plays is, at any rate, tolerably well documented. *Peer Gynt*, he wrote his friend Peter Hansen, seemed to follow *Brand* "almost of its own accord," and his compulsive state of mind is amply attested by those who, like the novelist Bergsöe, were with him at Ischia while he was working at it in the summer of 1865. The play had much, he told Hansen, that sprang from the experiences of his youth: Aase was modelled on his mother, "with the necessary exaggerations." If in *Brand* he saw himself "in his finest moments," in *Peer Gynt*, evidently, he saw himself in moments perhaps less fine, but equally memorable.[21] Björnson wrote in 1871, when they had ceased to be friends, "Not till *Peer Gynt* did Ibsen become himself, for Peer Gynt was himself." This was doubtless true, so far as it went; but Björnson had forgotten Brand.

When he had finished *Brand* and *Peer Gynt*, Ibsen attempted to synthesize both conceptions in *Emperor and Galilean*. He had begun this work in 1864, so he wrote Björnson, the year before the composition of *Brand*. He finished it with difficulty in 1873, three years after the publication of *Peer Gynt*. It was a work that meant a great deal to him, and it was a failure.[22]

Emperor and Galilean is neither clearly thought out nor forcefully dramatized, but it is quite indispensable in the interpretation of Ibsen's later dramas. The play is in two parts. The first five acts, entitled *Caesar's Apostacy*, carry Julian from his youth in Constantinople to the point, ten years later, when he is proclaimed emperor by the legions he commands in Gaul. The second part is called *The Emperor Julian*. It spans the two-year period of Julian's reign to the time of his death in Persia. Somewhere in the second part, in the course of successive revisions, Ibsen lost the thread of the narrative. He told the story pretty much as Ammianus tells it —though it seems likely that most of what he knew about Julian came from a three-part article published by Listov in *Fædrelandet* in 1866—but evidently he encountered a good many ideas along the way, perhaps too many.[23] At any rate, he was able neither to make a clear and consistent statement in his play, nor to transform his material into a work of art.

Julian develops surprisingly in the course of the action. In the beginning he is fearful, shrewd, opportunistic, resourceful, vacillating, ambitious: we recognize Peer Gynt. Little by little he acquires a sense of mission, and this dedication in the end becomes a madness: we are aware of Brand. Under the powerful influence of the mage Maximus, he hears supernatural voices which bid him establish the Third Empire through the force of his will, by the way of freedom, which is also the way of necessity. In his zeal of reform, he becomes hateful, like Brand; but, unlike Brand, Julian has power, and power betrays him into stupidities of which Brand could only dream.

There are, Maximus teaches, three empires. The first was founded on the tree of knowledge; the second on the tree of the cross. The third "shall be founded on the tree of knowledge and the tree of the cross together, because it hates and loves them both." Each empire claims its martyr. There were the two great "helpers in denial," Cain and Judas. The third martyr, it is implied, will be Julian, whose task it is to destroy the empire of the Galilean on earth, and to establish in its stead the empire which shall reconcile Greek freedom with Christian self-restraint, and thus shall cause the body to accord with the spirit.

In the beginning Julian has a choice. He can remain a Galilean, a slave existing in the shadow of hell, or he can become the emperor, a monarch in a sunlit land. He chooses the latter and directs his affairs so that he is hoisted on a shield in the camp in Gaul. But power corrupts, and Julian is vain. Little by little, his desire to supplant the Galilean as a God on earth leads him into insuperable difficulties. In pursuance of his goal, which is universal freedom, he becomes a despot, imposing his paganism by force on a populace which comes to detest him; and thus he sacrifices everything to his ideal, his friends, himself, and even his own sense of judgment. Julian, indeed, is laboring against the current of history. The world-will at this time is set toward the empire of the spirit. The Third Empire cannot be established by force; it must evolve itself. Unwittingly, Maximus has betrayed him, but not wholly. Julian is not the Messiah who is to establish the Third

Empire but, it is implied, he prefigures him, and this is his glory. In the end, slain by a dart hurled by a young Christian whom he has tortured, Julian dies, "a noble, shattered instrument of God."

According to Ibsen, the play was written "under German intellectual influences." [24] Its basis, presumably, was the dialectical idea of history which was first dramatized by Hebbel, whose plays Ibsen knew through Hettner's *Das moderne Drama*. Thus to the pagan world, the world of delight, is opposed its antithesis, the Christian world, in which the joys of this life must be renounced in anticipation of the joy to come. In his effort to reconcile these antitheses, Julian apes the self-imposed asceticism of the Cynics; he wishes to be another Socrates, another Antisthenes. These efforts at pagan self-discipline please nobody. They offend the Christians, and annoy the luxury-loving pagans. The results, accordingly, are ridiculous, but they do point the way of the ultimate synthesis which one day will result in the autonomy of the individual. Just how this desideratum—the ideal anarchy of the free and self-directed spirit—is to be brought about is at no time clear; and Julian's attempt to realize it is, in any case, obscured by his personal vanity and the childishness of character which appears to be his outstanding trait. Julian fails. But the implication is that one day the Third Empire will be achieved on earth.

Undoubtedly, *Emperor and Galilean* was meant to display a vast historical panorama, but it is chiefly from a psychological standpoint that the play is interesting, and apart from Julian it has no memorable characters. Julian is a complex personality in whom it is possible to detect both the fanatic dedication of Brand, and the self-serving opportunism of Peer Gynt. But, perhaps because of its inherent contradictions, this character is not realized to the point where we can feel its cogency, and matters are not improved by Ibsen's seemingly irrepressible tendency to see the comic side of his protagonists. The effort, however, was ambitious; more so, perhaps, than in any other of Ibsen's plays, and it was partly the magnitude of the task he set himself that was responsible for the failure of the play.

The characterization of Julian was intended to characterize an age; his intellectual discomfort was meant to correspond with the moral and social turbulence of a period in history with which the end of the nineteenth century was in some ways analogous. In the time of Julian, the battleground of the Idea, in fact, extended from Gaul to Persia; but the nature of the battle is not clear on this scale; it is chiefly in the soul of Julian that we are able to discern the struggle between the desire for slavery and the desire for freedom. In this microcosm, the longed-for synthesis, which would be peace, is seen to be impossible; and thus the tragedy of Julian is also the tragedy of his time. It is a fault in the play that, aside from the formal opposition of Christian and pagan, the precise nature of the conflict is never defined. Ibsen symbolized this conflict in terms of Helios and the Galilean, as if its nature was comprehensible in terms of sunshine and shadow, the typical contrast of the Norwegian landscape. Apparently he found these symbols particularly congenial. The series of plays, from *Ghosts* to *The Master Builder*, in which this conflict is developed, do not depart widely from the pattern of *Emperor and Galilean*. In these plays, invariably, the power of darkness triumphs, the empire of the sun for which the hero yearns brings him only misfortune, and the Third Empire which reconciles these opposites remains a dream toward which humanity labors.

Although *Emperor and Galilean* was not published until 1873, it belonged altogether to the period of *Peer Gynt*. By the time it was finished, Ibsen had already laid aside the large canvas of his last three plays and turned to social comedy, a genre which he had as yet not attempted, save for the none too successful *comédie-vaudeville, Love's Comedy*.

Brand made a great stir in Norway. It went through four printings in the course of its first year, and while its critical reception was, on the whole, antagonistic, the younger generation took it to its heart, and it soon became a literary landmark. The reception of *Peer Gynt*, on the other hand, was bitterly disappointing. Björnson was enthusiastic, but his friend, the very influential Danish critic Clemens Petersen, wrote in *Fædrelandet* that the play was a piece of polemical journalism, full of empty riddles, an intellectual fraud, and—since the ideal element was lacking—in no sense poetry. In the course of these remarks on the subject of *Peer Gynt*, Petersen took the occasion also to attack the poetic validity of *Brand*. These adverse views were widely shared. Even Georg Brandes wrote pedantically in *Dagbladet* that, while it had a certain merit, *Peer Gynt* was neither beautiful nor true, and that "the contempt for humanity and the self-hatred on which it was constructed are a poor foundation on which to build artistic works."

Ibsen had poured his heart into *Peer Gynt*, and, while it was too much to hope that it would be completely understood, he had hoped it would find acceptance as a poem. He had expected much from Petersen. His criticism drove him into a fury. On December 9, 1867 he wrote a bitter, inarticulate letter to Björnson, whom he accused of betrayal, and he concluded:

My book is poetry; and if it is not, then it will be. The conception of poetry in our country, in Norway, shall be made to take its shape from this book . . . And tell me now, is Peer Gynt himself not a personality, complete and individual? I know that he is. And the mother—is she not?

However, I am glad of the injustice that has been done me. There has been something of the Godsend, of the providential dispensation in it; for I feel that this anger is invigorating all my powers. If it is to be war, then let it be war! If I am no poet, then I have nothing to lose. I shall try my luck as a photographer. My contemporaries up there, I shall take in hand, one after the other, as I have done with the language agitators. I shall not spare the child in its mother's womb . . .

Peer Gynt marked the end of the first phase of Ibsen's dramatic career. His earlier plays had all been written in verse. He considered himself primarily a poet. Now that he had been assured so emphatically that he had no talent for poetry, he gave up verse, which henceforth he considered unfit for the stage, and in 1870 embarked on a career, as he had threatened, of "photography." [25] In his review of *Peer Gynt*, Björnson had advised him to try his hand at satiric comedy. Ibsen took the suggestion. With the exception of *Emperor and Galilean*, which, we have seen, he had some difficulty in finishing, all the rest of his plays were written in the realistic style of the Second Empire dramatists.

For some time he had thought of himself as the Norwegian "state-satirist." [26] From this time on, his satire developed a keener sting. He had, indeed, no lack of aggressiveness at his command. He detested Norway and the Norwegians with all the fury of a deeply patriotic nature. As an exile, his thoughts were centered constantly on home; but the thought of living there oppressed his spirit, and he could not bear the atmosphere of Christiania. He was not himself, he wrote Björnson, "beneath the gaze of these cold, uncomprehending Norwegian eyes at the windows and in the streets." [27] He felt, he insisted, particularly homeless in Norway, and even in his last play, *When We Dead Awaken*, he expressed his hostility toward the cultural environment out of which, and for which, he wrote.

The first of his contemporaries "up there" to be taken in hand was, naturally, Björnson himself, to whom Ibsen imputed, somewhat gratuitously, the attack on *Peer Gynt* in *Fædrelandet*. In Dresden, during the winter of 1868–1869, he wrote *The League of Youth*. Hegel published it that year. It was in fact a very poor play, a comedy in the French style, and its main point was a somewhat clumsy satirical portrait of the demagogue Stensgård, whose efforts to make a rich marriage are systematically foiled by the playwright. Stensgård's tricks of speech were obviously parodied after Björnson's and, in the October, 1869, production in Christiania, the actor Reimers, who played Stensgård, made himself up to resemble Björnson. Since Björnson had been stumping the countryside for the Liberal party—"his pernicious and lie-steeped clique," Ibsen called it—the allusion, in spite of Ibsen's disclaimer of intent, seemed unmistakable, and *The League of Youth*, interpreted as a blow at the liberals, attracted praise out of proportion to its merits.[28] The play was, as he had promised Hegel, in prose, and "adapted in every way to the stage." It was accepted with alacrity, and played in all the Scandinavian capitals.

The consequence was that when Ibsen came to Christiania in 1874, after an absence of ten years, he was given an ovation because of his supposedly conservative views. In fact, Ibsen was anti-democratic, and at this time decidedly anti-liberal, but the thought of being associated with any party was more than he could bear.[29] The following year, he began work on *Pillars of Society*. Since *The League of Youth* was said to be anti-liberal, he gave the new play—"a counterpart to *The League of Youth*"—a definitely anti-conservative nuance, and he aimed it squarely at the entrenched bourgeoisie whose spokesman he was supposed to be.[30]

Pillars of Society was published in 1877. It developed the interesting thought that a man who is a liar, a blackguard, and an exploiter of human lives can nevertheless be a person of great value to society. Consul Bernick is not really the prototype of Andrew Undershaft in *Major Barbara*. He is in every way a less sophisticated figure, involved in a more conventional action. He is, indeed, a figure out of melodrama; but Ibsen uses him in a very original way. Bernick wants power. He sacrifices every ideal to this desire. His struggle up the social ladder is ruthless. His success is founded on every kind of iniquity. Yet he is an indispensable member of the community, the initiator and promoter of many enterprises, the employer of many people, a philanthropist, a model of respectability, and a pillar of the church.

The picture Ibsen drew of the captain of industry was certainly disquieting, but it was fashionable. The attack on the middle class and its ethics had already assumed great proportions in France, and it had the support not only of the liberals but also of the aristocracy and the church. Ibsen's position was not extreme; it was thoughtful; above all, it was ironic. Bernick was certainly despicable; yet, Ibsen suggested, it is possible that without men of this stamp the national economy would not progress. Like Brand and Julian, and like John Gabriel Borkman, Bernick is a fanatic, completely engaged, and quite prepared to do without the things most people prize—love, friendship, honor—in order to realize himself fully as a man. The implication is that, in some degree, the same is true of all those for whom wealth is the ultimate human value, but Ibsen certainly did not mean to limit his idea in this manner. Essentially, Bernick is simply another version of Brand; a somewhat debased Brand, it is true, but psychologically of the same stripe, another example of the application of what Ibsen had called the Brand syllogism. In identifying the sordid motives of middle-class enterprise with the Kierkegaardian pattern of self-realization, Ibsen did not excuse them, but he made them understandable, and thus rescued them from the sterility of a merely moral interpretation. The process which Bernick illustrates ends, as it must, in despair. It is this crisis which marks the transition from the aesthetic to the ethical stage of his development. But the entire process is shown to take place behind a veil of hypocritical idealism which must be stripped away before anything can be understood.

Pillars of Society was Ibsen's first attempt at social drama in the style of Augier-Balzac. It was hard for him to write it; he revised it over a period of two years, yet it suffers from all the faults of the French style. The plot is quite obviously contrived; the situations are melodramatic; the characters are stock; and the sentimental outcome—with its reminder that the ruthless entrepreneur has a heart and a conscience, after all, like everyone else—is not particularly convincing. But in spite of its manifest weaknesses, *Pillars of Society* marked a forward step in the evolution of this style. It was not as smoothly worked out as its predecessors—Sardou's *La Famille Benoiton* and Björnson's *En fallit*—but it was an honest attempt to analyze a banal situation in terms of its philosophic content, that is to say, its reality. In 1877 this had a novel air. It has still.

Five years before, in 1872, Georg Brandes had published the first part of his *Main Currents of Literature in the Nineteenth Century*. Its viewpoint was realistic, and he emphasized the idea that literature should be useful, and that every poetic composition should serve to advance the frontiers of culture. He felt, accordingly, that the modern French drama was in the lead of contemporary effort, and he urged Scandinavian writers to follow assiduously the example of Dumas and Augier in bringing current social questions to the stage. It was hardly necessary for Brandes to direct the attention of Björnson and Ibsen to the aims and methods of the contemporary French playwrights, but it is not impossible that his words had some weight with them. Ibsen, for his part, professed the greatest admiration for Brandes's book: "It is one of those works which place a yawning gulf between yesterday and to-day." In any event it was precisely three years after the publication of Brandes's survey that these writers turned to social drama in the French style.[31]

Ibsen's realistic plays are, in a sense, the end-product of the French school: he represents its perfection. All his realistic plays are well made; none is free of some degree of contrivance. He worked strictly within the traditional frame of *"le théâtre,"* and even his best and freest plays have that epigrammatic neatness which is the mark of good Scribean craftsmanship. As for subject matter, in accordance with the practice of the school of Paris, almost all of Ibsen's plays after *Pillars of Society* dealt in a provocative way with some problematic aspect of contemporary life.[32]

Pillars of Society touched upon a timely subject. The question of the "Plimsoll coffins," and the agitation through which Samuel Plimsoll eventually succeeded in securing the passage of legislation to assure the seaworthiness of merchant shipping, were being earnestly discussed during Ibsen's stay in Norway in 1874. The subject of his next play, A *Doll's House*, was equally timely. Georg Brandes had translated Mill's *The Subjection of Women* into Danish in 1869, immediately after its original publication in English. The movement for the emancipation of women began to take form in Norway almost at once. Ibsen was no feminist. In the spring of 1877, while he was finishing *Pillars of Society*, the famous feminist Camilla Collett had frequent arguments with him on the subject of what she called his shockingly old-fashioned views regarding woman's place in society. Yet, as early as 1869, Ibsen had written a passage which contained in embryo all the feminist content of A Doll's House. In The League of Youth, toward the end of act three, the young wife Selma is suddenly made aware of her husband's misfortunes, which so far he has concealed from her. She bursts out, quite unexpectedly:

. . . You have dressed me up like a doll; you have played with me as you would play with a child. Oh, what a joy it would have been for me to bear my share of your burdens! . . . . But I will not be treated as a last resource. I will have nothing to do with your troubles now. I won't stay with you!

Georg Brandes had remarked, when The League of Youth first appeared, that this theme might well serve as the basis for a new play. But there is no indication that Ibsen was thinking of writing a feminist play when he first began to work seriously on A Doll's House in the summer of 1879. Very likely, he had a much more abstruse idea of the relation between the sexes than anyone was prepared to cope with in the theatre of the 1880's. The reception of A Doll's House, when it appeared at the end of 1879, must have afforded him a certain amusement. It was successful beyond his wildest dreams, and doubtless for the wrong reasons; but Ibsen bore its success with dignity, and stoically endured the consequences. Eleven years later, in 1891, he accepted without protest an honorary membership in the Viennese Verein für erweiterte Frauenbildung. It was not until nineteen years had passed that he ventured to express himself publicly on the subject of his supposed feminist leanings.

The speech he made in Christiania on May 26, 1898, at a dinner given in honor of his seventieth birthday by the Norwegian Society for the Woman's Cause, occasioned some surprise. It could obviously make little difference to the interpretation of a play which was by this time a landmark in the history of feminism that the author now disclaimed any interest in the feminist cause, but the speech served to shed some light on the author's original intention. Miss Gina Krag proposed a toast to the poet who had done so much for the Woman's Cause. Ibsen answered at some length:

I thank you for drinking my health, but I must decline the honor of having consciously worked for the Woman's Cause. I am not even clear what the Woman's Cause really is. For me it has been an affair of humanity . . . Not all I have written has proceeded from a conscious tendency. I have been more the poet and less the social philosopher than has been generally believed. . . . It is most certainly desirable to solve the woman question, among others, but that was not my whole intention. My task was the description of man. . . . The women will solve the question of mankind, but they must do so as mothers. Herein lies the great task of woman . . .

The first sketch for A Doll's House, labelled "Notes for the Modern Tragedy," is dated October 19, 1878, and it indicates quite clearly the sort of play Ibsen at this time had in mind to write. "There are," he noted, "two kinds of conscience, one in man, and another, altogether different, in woman. They do not understand one another, but in practical life, the woman is judged by man's law as though she were not a woman, but a man." The idea that the sexes have such different psychic patterns that they can never hope to understand each other, and that therefore it is unjust to judge women by male standards, was certainly not new in the 1880's, nor had it, for that matter, been new in the days of Mary Wollstonecraft, almost a century before. But in the theatre such a thought was revolutionary, and it caused a sensation.

For his purposes in A Doll's House, Ibsen depicted a man and a woman of diametrically opposed temperament. His Nora is ostensibly a blithe little sparrow, scatterbrained, flirtatious, and gay. Helmer is stuffy, pompous, and circumspect. Both characters are necessarily exaggerated so that the action of the play can demonstrate to best advantage the contrast between their appearance and their reality. In fact, Nora is a carefully studied example of what we have come to know as the hysterical personality—bright, unstable, impulsive, romantic, quite immune from feelings of guilt,

and, at bottom, not especially feminine. It is a vastly more enlightened conception of woman than the stereotypes of Kotzebue
or Dumas. Helmer, on the other hand, is a typical example of the
compulsive male. The problem is thus not especially a problem of
sex. It would be strange if two people constituted in this way
could possibly succeed in understanding one another.

The idea that a woman is a grown-up child, without mind, but
with much heart, devoid of logic, but sensitive and intuitive, is
traditional in Western culture. It certainly antedates Rousseau,
who is often credited with the formulation of this cliché, by some
hundreds of years. At any rate, such appears to have been Ibsen's
notion of womanhood during the period in which he wrote *A
Doll's House,* so that the characterization of Nora which he finally
hit upon must have surprised him quite as much as it did everyone
else. In a speech about this time in the Scandinavian Society of
Rome, he said:

Youth has the instinct, akin to genius, for hitting intuitively on what
is right. But it is this very instinct that woman has in common with
youth, as well as with the true artist.

Such statements make it clear, at any rate, that from the standpoint of personality, and quite apart from the question of sex,
Ibsen was disposed to identify himself with the Noras and not
with the Helmers of this world.

In its first draft, *A Doll's House* was a conventional domestic
drama of tragic character. The touches of caricature which were
eventually to transform Nora and Helmer were still to come. Torvald was not yet the pompous, self-centered ass of the final version,
nor was Nora as yet the earnest and innocent child who was sure
there could be no harm in forging her father's signature, provided
her motives were good. But in the course of the revision, Ibsen
pushed his characters further and further toward the extreme, so
that they took on comic overtones. At the same time, the gulf
between them was deepened until they quite lost touch with each
other. Thus, though the plot, throughout the revisions, remained

substantially the same, the characters were more definitely molded, and their relation shifted, so as to emphasize as far as possible their psychological disparity. The principal action was made to hinge on a *méprise;* but the misunderstanding, which in a Scribean play would be the result of a purely intellectual error, was in this case founded on a profoundly significant difference of personality, so that no explanation could possibly avail to correct it. Yet, while an action founded on so deep a misunderstanding has, of necessity, a tragic color, the incongruity of feeling and motive is such that in *A Doll's House* most of the significant scenes are comic in tone, and no scene is entirely devoid of humor.

Since Ibsen habitually preserved and dated the drafts of his plays, it is often possible to reconstruct with some accuracy the method by which he arrived at his final version. He generally began with a story, not with a character. The story was usually such that it reflected a psychic conflict into which he had some degree of insight. He then conceived his characters as archetypes moving through the narrative in conventional fashion. The result was something in the nature of a melodrama, straight, obvious, and sentimental.

But once the play was finished, the author's mood changed. He now took up the entire matter from a critical angle, testing with ridicule the situation he had formerly taken seriously, and contemplating the behavior of his puppets with the amused skepticism of a detached and hostile observer. In this mood, the absurdity of the theatrical postures into which human behavior tends to fall became progressively clear to him, and he remolded and retouched his figures so as to bring out more and more clearly the comic aspects of what had originally been conceived as a pathetic situation. The result of this process was the rich ambiguity of characterization which gives Ibsen's plays their unique quality.[33]

In *A Doll's House*, all the touches from which the play derives its charm were added in revision—the amorous scene of act three, the tarantella, the champagne, Nora's little fibs, her coquetry with Dr. Rank, her daydreams of the rich uncle who is to die and leave her a fortune. In the final scene, when the menace of Krogstad is removed, Torvald says, "I am saved, Nora." In the first version he said, "You are saved." In this manner, Ibsen did whatever could be done to heighten the effect of comedy within the tragic situation.

The effect is altogether remarkable; but this sort of writing has, of course, its drawbacks. Nothing is more disarming in the theatre than such evidences of an author's willingness to laugh at his own fantasy, especially when this fantasy has tragic overtones; but nothing is more puzzling. For this reason, doubtless, these equivocal effects are generally glossed over in production, and the characters are pushed unceremoniously back into the stereotypes from which the author was at pains to redeem them. The plot of *A Doll's House* is related comically to a cliché of tragedy—the formula of the tyrant and the innocent victim who in the end exacts her revenge. It is in these terms, accordingly, that *A Doll's House* is usually played. It cannot be denied that the author in some measure invites this interpretation. This seems malicious. All the salt of the play is in the counterpoint of satire which accompanies the tragic line of the action.

The use of the Scribean apparatus to bring about the reversals and discoveries necessary for the development of Nora's character did not require justification at a time when nothing was more common than this sort of contrivance. But Ibsen was evidently concerned in this play not with the management of the narrative so much as with its psychological significance. Apart from his irrepressible tendency to caricature his figures, he had serious reasons for the comic extremes to which he pushed the characterization. Helmer emerges in the final version as a caricature of the archetypal father; Nora as a caricature of the rebellious daughter. Characters conceived after this fashion are obviously capable of transmitting a wide spectrum of symbolic significances, and they elicit a very complex psychic response. It is easy to associate Nora with the impulsive, and Torvald with the compulsive side of human nature; but, if one chooses, one can involve in their relationship the antithesis of mind and body, spirit and matter, heart and mind, light and darkness, and so on to the end of the table of contraries. Since it is precisely in terms of such Pythagorean opposites that we customarily think of the relation of the sexes, marriage may be made to serve as a prime example of the clash of antitheses, and the home becomes the battleground of the cosmic dialectic.

In Ibsen's concept, therefore, the affair Nora-Helmer quite transcends the question of the normal opposition of husband and wife. A *Doll's House* restates the social problem of *Emperor and Galilean* on the elementary level, and indicates the correspondence of the family quarrel with the dialectic of history on every plane of the social structure down to the individual soul. From this point of view the revolt of Nora takes on a certain universality, and it is this which gives tragic magnitude to what might otherwise be considered simply another story of marital incompatibility. It seems clear that in developing his "modern tragedy" in this manner, Ibsen very shrewdly followed the direction indicated by Hebbel in *Maria Magdalene*. He could not have done better.

It is possible to think of A *Doll's House*, therefore, as a kind of dramatic metaphor, a play of symbols, a conceit. The opposition of irreconcilable viewpoints which brings about the dissolution of this union is then seen to be a reflection of the vast conflict which is bringing about a readjustment of social relations on every level. The only possible reconciliation of the spiritual entities which are here displayed in opposition must be, accordingly, in terms of that synthesis which will, in its largest aspect, result in the Third Empire. It is to something of this sort—the miracle—that Nora looks, none too hopefully, as she leaves Torvald's house at the end of the play.

Moreover, since A *Doll's House* was constructed in accordance with a concept which, as Ibsen said in 1891, looked far beyond the question of the advancement of woman's rights, it is hardly possible to assign to Nora the traditionally sympathetic role of the injured wife. As the unwitting, but implacable, representatives of antithetical forces of universal character, Torvald and Nora are equally matched, equally doomed, and equally the objects of sympathy. There is, of course, something undeniably comic about the plight of Torvald who has to listen to a homily on the rights of woman when all he desires is to go to bed with the *raisonneur*; nevertheless, his predicament when Nora leaves him is, if anything, more desperate than hers. Like Anton in *Maria Magdalene*, he does not understand; and it is he, not she, who suffers the major casualty of the battle.

What has happened to Torvald on the domestic level is the equivalent of the fall of a prince in high tragedy. In accordance with the canonical concept of marriage, Torvald has postured consistently as the wise and monumental male, and Nora, suitably conditioned by her upbringing, has thus far accepted this pose as fact. In the desperate emergency in which she suddenly finds herself, her idea of what is about to happen is based on the supposed nature of the ideal Torvald. Just as she had sacrificed herself when he needed help, so, she believes, he will insist on suffering for her in her hour of need. Of course, she will not permit this sacrifice. She will outdo him in nobility by killing herself at the proper time. This is how it seems to her. But the hour of trial reveals the wretched truth of the matter. Torvald is a humbug. He has no idea of suffering for anyone. On the contrary, in the emergency, he thinks only of saving himself; and in the contrast between the romantic splendor of her dream and the squalid reality, Nora suddenly finds herself emotionally bankrupt.

A *Doll's House* thus describes in a very convincing manner the process of falling out of love. Its force, however, lies not in the superficial action, which in any case lacks suspense, but in the psychological undercurrent which it generates. The man Nora loves is a creature of fantasy, constructed partly in accordance with his idea of himself, partly out of her own ideal requirements. When this figment evaporates, she is left with a stranger in whom she has no interest. She realizes at this point that she has been masquerading as a child only because Torvald has been posing as a father. She has been, so she says, "in fancy dress the whole time, not happy, but merry." Even now, she has no clear idea of what, or who, she is; but that is not the point: the moment she becomes aware that she is more of a man than her husband, their relation becomes impossible. She can now no longer endure the passive role that her position entails, either mentally or physically, and she declares the marriage at an end.

It is believable that Nora's sudden educational experience is sufficiently catastrophic to change in the course of an hour the seemingly dependent and submissive wife into a realistic and autarchic individual; but it is believable only provided we assume that this individual was always there. The implication is that Nora, no less than Helmer, was, from the first, other than she seemed. Her childlike pose was a pretense by which she herself was taken in: once she understands this, a general revaluation of her position is inescapable. The moment she doubts the validity of her assumptions, she can no longer accept the authority of father, pastor, or husband. Neither law, nor custom, nor religion will suffice henceforth to keep her in line: she must think for herself. In the end, she is frightened, like a somnambulist who is suddenly awakened in a perilous place—but her future behavior is predictable. She has become a feminist.

This does not mean, perhaps, that she will evolve suddenly, like Mrs. Warren's daughter in Shaw's play, into a kind of man. Nevertheless, the disparity between her way of thought and that of the masculine society which Torvald represents is fundamental, and she must re-orient herself:

NORA: . . . I am all at sea about these things. I only know that I think quite differently from you about them. I hear, too, that the laws are different from what I thought; but I can't believe that they can be right. It appears that a woman has no right to spare her dying father or to save her husband's life. I don't believe that.

HELMER: You talk like a child. You don't understand the society in
which you live.
NORA: No. I do not. But now I shall try to learn. I must make up
my mind which is right—society or I.

For the wife, in these circumstances, the dissolution of the
family may be painful, but it is not tragic. On the contrary, she
throws off her servitude; she is emancipated and strengthened; and
though she leaves the play in some confusion, she is, on the whole,
victorious. The tragedy is, we have noted, mainly the husband's.
He has, of course, the canonical flaw. Had he been the man his
wife thought him, or even the man he thought himself to be,
Nora would perhaps not have left him, and the paternal authority,
in this instance at least, would have remained unquestioned. But
Torvald is an example of the decline of the patriarchal idea. He
is incapable of fulfilling the obligations of a domestic suzerain, and
a woman's gesture suffices to sweep away the vestiges of what was
perhaps once a truth. Torvald is therefore fated, as a husband, to
go down with the patriarchy which he unworthily represents. But
he is a man, as well as a husband, and the idea that in the hour of
trial he was found wanting is a bitter experience for him, even
though he is not altogether clear on what it was he did that was
wrong. There is, of course, nothing novel in his experience: his
behavior, judged by chivalric standards, leaves everything to be
desired. What is new is Nora's assumption that in these circumstances the entire principle of male authority must be called into
question. The slam of the door at the end of the play is therefore,
symbolically speaking, a sound of some significance.

What outraged "all decent people" when A Doll's House was
first published was actually not Nora's desertion of her three children, who are not even differentiated in the cast, but this symbolic
caponization of Torvald. The brutality of Nora's action could
have hardly escaped Ibsen. A Doll's House is a play of bold outlines and sharp contrasts. Torvald is extravagantly fatuous; Nora
is needlessly cruel—Ibsen does not assume the risks of subtlety.
Nor is the play truly realistic. After nine years of marriage, a

woman is normally under no misapprehension as to her husband's possibilities as a man.

As the play is arranged, Nora and Mrs. Linde deliberately lay a trap for Helmer. When he falls into it, Nora presses her advantage to the extreme. In the last scene we see what the little squirrel is really like: she is implacable. At this point, A *Doll's House* takes the form of Hebbel's *Gyges und sein Ring* or *Herodes und Mariamne;* the play of the revenge of the outraged wife, the classical prototype of which is *Medea.* But while Nora contents herself with destroying Torvald only in fantasy, Torvald is denied the honor of being destroyed in a manner suitable to heroes of tragedy—in the end, he is simply ridiculous.[34] The age of the straw men ends, as Mr. Eliot so cogently put it, with a whimper, and in this is seen the nature of "the modern tragedy," as Ibsen conceived it.

In 1881, two years after writing A *Doll's House,* Ibsen published *Ghosts.* He had decided to attempt a play in naturalistic style, on the type of subject the naturalists liked, with a proper scientific background, without contrivance, and without theatricality. "My intention," he wrote to Sophus Schandorf, "was to produce in the mind of the reader the impression that he was witnessing something real." [35]

Because of its Scribean associations, it is now customary to treat A *Doll's House* with some aloofness, but to accord *Ghosts* the reverence due a great landmark in the history of naturalism. *Ghosts* was in fact written eight years after the publication of *Thérèse Raquin* in 1873, five years after *L'Ami Fritz* in 1876, the year before *Les Corbeaux,* and six years before the opening of the Théâtre-Libre, which produced it in its third season. There is every reason, accordingly, to consider it the ensign-bearer of what Zola called, "a methodical and analytical art marching along with science." [36] But while it is true that *Ghosts* depends less than A *Doll's House* on the Scribean apparatus, it is nevertheless a carefully contrived play, and in no sense a slice of life.

In using the retrospective method in developing the story of Mrs. Alving, Ibsen deliberately avoided the naturalistic technique. *Ghosts* conforms in every respect with the classical rules. The result is an effect of compression and austerity unusual in a day when the unities had been largely abandoned. In accordance with Scribe's adaptation of the classical system, every entrance is timed for effect; every effect is prepared and foreshadowed; each scene is a miniature play in itself; and each curtain is brought down with a *coup de théâtre*—the ghosts of act one, the fire of act two, and the precisely timed attack of insanity of act three. What Ibsen had in mind, evidently, was to write a modern tragedy in prose which should reconcile the characteristics of regular tragedy with the advanced technique of the well-made play. The result is a *pièce à thèse* which has the simplicity and repose of tragedy. It is, in fact, a masterpiece in the style of the *drame* of the Second Empire, more perfectly contrived than anything that had been done so far in that genre.

From the standpoint of modern tragedy, *Ghosts* strikes off in a new direction. A woman who has sacrified the best part of her life to a dissolute husband, and who is now forced to devote her remaining years to a son who is doomed to idiocy, or else to kill him, may well be considered the subject of tragedy. But *Ghosts* makes a very ambiguous effect. Up to the point in the third act where Pastor Manders leaves the stage with Engstrand, the play is a comedy. Not only are Engstrand's scenes with Manders written in a broad, comedic style, but the conversion, through Engstrand's machinations, of the Alving Memorial Home into a tavern for sailors is more than an example of dramatic irony— this is the sort of joke that might be told at a party. *Ghosts* may therefore be considered in terms of two interlaced actions, the first of which involves the gulling of Manders, and the second, the ruin of Osvald. Both actions in a sense center on Mrs. Alving, but Mrs. Alving is largely a spectator in each. She is amused by the first, and emotionally devastated by the second, but actually she plays no part in either action: her scenes were played long before this play began. *Ghosts* is the denouement of her tragedy, the result of events long past, which nothing now can change. Like Oedipus, she has no more choices or decisions to make. She has only to wait for the revelation to be made, and the blow to fall.

The polemic character of *Ghosts* is, however, unmistakable. It is the next stroke of the hammer after *A Doll's House*. In leaving her husband, Mrs. Alving followed the dictates of her heart. In sending her back with a sermon, the young pastor, her husband's friend, acted conformably with the fear of public opinion which still characterizes all his actions. Manders's affinity with Torvald Helmer seems clear. He is patterned after the same archetype, just as Mrs. Alving is another aspect of Nora—a Nora who has been persuaded to submit to man's law, but who has inwardly emancipated herself as completely as the vestiges of a dead morality will permit her.

The disclosure of Mrs. Alving's self-sacrifice, and the consequent perversion of nature, is the main business of the play, but Ibsen was doubtless aware that without some developing action, the play would be all exposition. It was this thought that must have prompted the invention of the comic underplot which is ingeniously interlaced with the tragic action in accordance with the best Scribean principles. The consequent mood precisely fulfills the conditions of the grotesque, quite as Hugo defined them in the *Préface à Cromwell*.

As the play was designed, however, it was necessary that the secondary action—the fire, the gulling of Manders, and the defection of Regina—develop on the margin and not at the center of the play. Since the main action took place twenty-nine years before the rise of the curtain, the relation between Pastor Manders and Mrs. Alving has so far faded that all they have for each other now is explanations. These explanations, moreover, no longer matter; nor does the revelation of his father's wickedness make much difference to Osvald. The main source of tragic feeling is, in fact, not the grief of the mother, nor the despair of the son, but the conviction that life has sapped these lives so thoroughly that now nothing matters. In this sense, *Ghosts* is certainly a play of ghosts; and the symbol, like most of Ibsen's symbols, is seen to have a very general application. It is a play of shadows, a drama of dead and dying people, haunted by the memories of worn-out passions and the vestiges of outworn ideals. It is accordingly quite fitting that it should be, in its main aspects, almost entirely static, contemplative, and elegiacal, in the manner of the lyric tragedy of the Renaissance.

The spectacular effect of the final scene inclines one to think of *Ghosts* as a play about the horrors of venereal disease. But *Ghosts* is not, like Brieux's *Damaged Goods*, a modern exemplum. It comes quite close to tragedy, as close perhaps as one can come in a utilitarian age. Regular tragedy dealt mainly with the unhappy consequences of breaking the moral code. *Ghosts*, on the contrary, deals with the tragic consequences of not breaking it. It thus sets up a social principle higher than the official morality of our culture, a higher morality.

The situation is arranged according to a pattern which, after *Emperor and Galilean*, became the intellectual armature on which Ibsen most usually hung his narrative. Pastor Manders is, of course, no more than a caricature of the grim Galilean, but the suggestion is unequivocal:

MANDERS: It is the very mark of the spirit of rebellion to crave for happiness in this life. What right have we human beings to happiness? We have simply to do our duty, Mrs. Alving!

To the duty of self-crucifixion which Manders preaches, is opposed the joy of life which once sparkled in the veins of young Lieutenant Alving, and which his children Osvald and Regina have apparently inherited, along with his other difficulties:

MRS. ALVING: You should have known your father when he was a young lieutenant. He was brimming over with the joy of life!

OSVALD: Yes. I know he was.

MRS. ALVING: It was like a breezy day only to look at him. And what exuberant strength and vitality there was in him!

OSVALD: Well?

The point is that Lieutenant Alving's *joie de vivre* had no chance to develop into anything useful or beautiful in the bleak environment to which he was condemned. As he had no acceptable outlet for his energy either in work or in play, he was forced to turn, like General Saint-Pé in Anouilh's modern version, to the local waitresses and chambermaids, while the puritanical Mrs. Alving nursed her unrewarded passion for the puritanical Mr. Manders. It is not until the twenty-seven-year-old offspring of this unblessed marriage returns from Paris with tidings of sunnier lives that Mrs. Alving understands to what an extent she was instrumental in destroying the life of her husband, as well as her own, by staying with him when she could not bear him. Now she has only the ruins of her life to contemplate, and the sickly son who longs to share the "great, free, glorious life" of those who have successfully achieved a synthesis of desire and self-discipline, the bohemian artists of the Latin quarter. But in this, her second attempt to achieve the good life—this time, for her son—Mrs. Alving is forced once again to concede the triumph of the Galilean. This outcome, she realizes, is perhaps inevitable in the bleak northern country in which the pleasure of suffering is the only permissible pleasure.

The idea that the Norwegian climate was in large measure responsible for the tribulations of its inhabitants appears to have been derived from Buckle's *History*, to which Ibsen, like Strindberg, was indebted in more than one particular. Buckle had emphasized the influence of climate on the temper of nations; accordingly, Ibsen's quarrel with his native land was rationalized, at least partly, in terms of its weather. In *Ghosts*, as in *Brand*, *Rosmersholm*, and *John Gabriel Borkman*, climate plays a major role in the drama. For Ibsen, as we have seen, the conflict between the joy of life and its grimness were aspects of the eternal conflict of light and darkness. *Ghosts* takes place in a gloomy landscape streaming with rain. Osvald longs for the sun; but his mother, like his homeland, has no sunshine for him, no more than she had for his father. She can give him only darkness and death, and this, Ibsen implies, is chiefly the portion of those doomed to live in the cold mists from which he himself had barely escaped, and not un-scathed.

While it is clear from Ibsen's correspondence of 1880 that he had it in mind to present "the black band of theologians who are presently in command of affairs at the Norwegian ministry of culture with a literary souvenir," [37] he must have been taken aback at the violence of the storm which *Ghosts* provoked. Ten thousand copies were printed, but a second edition was not required until 1894, and for a long time no Scandinavian theatre would accept the play. For the first time, Ibsen felt the full weight of public disapproval, and he hastened to dissociate himself from the opinions expressed by Osvald and Mrs. Alving by pointing out that the play was never intended to present a thesis. "There is not in the whole book a single opinion, a single utterance which can be laid to the account of the author. I took good care to avoid this." He adopted, nevertheless, a defiant attitude: "I care no more for this than for the barking of a pack of chained dogs." [38]

All the same, when he published *An Enemy of the People*, the year after the publication of *Ghosts*, he took care to caricature Dr. Stockmann so broadly that this character's radical notions could not possibly be attributed to the author. Dr. Stockmann's opinions were in fact those which Ibsen had repeatedly expressed as his own in poems and letters dating back as far as 1869. In 1882 he wrote his publisher, Hegel: "Dr. Stockmann and I get on so very well together; we agree on so many subjects. But the Doctor is a more muddle-headed person than I." [39] Yet as time wore on, Ibsen leaned further and further away from Dr. Stockmann, and eventually, the public-minded doctor became in his eyes, "*ein grotesker Bursche und ein Strudelkopf.*"

Dr. Stockmann took shape as a comic version of Brand; but his was not a type that could easily be laughed off. In his honesty and his intransigence, as well as in his lack of common sense, Stockmann bears a distinct resemblance to Alceste in *Le Misanthrope*. He is, like Alceste, an idealist of the All-or-Nothing variety; like

Nora, he is naïvely and dangerously romantic. He believes, in his innocence, that the town will honor him for ruining its business, and fails completely to comprehend how unimportant to the local shopkeeper is the risk of a little hushed-up typhoid or cholera in comparison with the bad publicity which would certainly attend the closing of the spa for sanitary reasons. He has, in short, no conception of the realistic viewpoint so necessary to the man of affairs.

Ibsen gives Dr. Stockmann a bad case history. He is, we are informed, a habitual troublemaker, has been dismissed before in similar circumstances, and will no doubt be in trouble again. Evidently his affinity for martyrdom—in which his family reluctantly participates—includes, as always, an element of sadism. His behavior at the town meeting is impressive: but the final tableau in which he is posed monumentally with the wife and children whom once again he has ruined, proclaiming that he is strongest who stands alone, is a masterpiece of comic portraiture. In a letter written to Georg Brandes ten years before, Ibsen had declared with the pompousness of one still young: "To me it appears that the man who stands alone is the strongest." [40]

There is no way of resolving the issue with regard to Stockmann, and Ibsen does not attempt it. The Stockmanns of this world are noble creatures. They are indispensable to society and to progress, and statues must be erected in their honor; but they are also terrible nuisances, and generally make only posterity happy. Stockmann arouses our admiration, but also our ambivalence. Perhaps for this reason he is a perpetually interesting figure, like Don Quixote. Success had relieved Ibsen from the necessity for striking statuesque poses. In 1882 he had no desire whatever to upset a social system in which he was very agreeably situated indeed; but he could not repress a certain admiration for this headstrong character who was willing to sacrifice all he had in order to remain an honest man.

Ibsen had by now accumulated a string of decorations, and was covetous of more. He had discarded the velvet jacket in favor of a long, tightly buttoned Prince Albert and top hat, and he was letting his sideburns grow to majestic proportions. His investments were prospering. He was collecting old paintings. All he desired now was a long period of social and economic stability in which to develop his style.[41] It was natural enough that he should wish to fit Stockmann with a dunce cap. But dunce caps are sometimes more becoming than medals. Stockmann was, after all, the fiery young Ibsen of the 1860's, and there must have been some vestige of him still in the middle-aged individualist who had written in 1871, while refusing to lend a hand in any practical measure of reform: "The state must be abolished! In that revolution I will take part. Undermine the idea of the state, make willingness and spiritual kinship the only essentials in the case of a union, and you have the beginning of a liberty that is of some value!" [42]

The Ibsen of 1882 could look back with amused complacency, perhaps, upon the ideal of his youth—when he had joined briefly in the Norwegian labor movement, and barely escaped imprisonment—but he could not help admiring it. He could not annihilate Stockmann by simply making an ass of him in a play, nor, in fact, could he dispose of him satisfactorily in the play at all. The proof is that, of all Ibsen's characters, Stockmann is the most equivocal and most consistently misinterpreted. Ibsen said that he had Jonas Lie and Björnson in mind when he drew Stockmann. The allusions were natural; but to the end of Ibsen's life, as we can see from *The Master Builder*, Stockmann, like Brand, stood for what seemed to him most manly, and also most dangerous, in his own nature, and he spent a good part of his energy as an artist in apologizing for his failure as a man to live up to this "*Strudelkopf*" whom he had invented.

An Enemy of the People was received with becoming, but not excessive, enthusiasm in the Scandinavian countries, and without any enthusiasm at all in Germany. As might have been predicted, nobody bothered to distinguish Dr. Stockmann from Dr. Ibsen. In the popular mind, Ibsen was now transformed from the staunch conservative of *The League of Youth* into a dangerous radical who would blow up the world if he could. The liberal youth of the Scandinavian countries hastened to rally round this stimulating leader, but they were soon disillusioned. Ibsen was resolutely anti-democratic and anarchistic. Like Strindberg, he sided with Tocqueville, and he took every occasion to point out that the majority was always wrong.[43] Any extension of political liberty, therefore, was in his eyes an extension of the power of the stupid. Besides, as a thorough individualist, he had no interest in political liberties. "I must confirm," he wrote Brandes in 1870, "that the only thing I love about liberty is the struggle for it—I care nothing for the possession of it. . . . Liberty, equality, and fraternity are no longer the things they were in the days of the late lamented guillotine. . . . What is all-important is the revolution of the spirit of man . . ." Two years later, he wrote Brandes, consoling him for the annoyances caused by the reception of the first volume of his *Main Currents in Nineteenth Century Literature*, "Dear friend, the Liberals are freedom's worst enemies. Freedom of thought and spirit thrive best under absolutism; this was shown in France, afterwards in Germany, and now we see it in Russia." [44]

The fact that Ibsen had more than once taken an impossibly extreme position as an excuse for refusing to join in any progressive political movement had not escaped attention. In some quarters it was noted that the All-or-Nothing formula was a useful pretext for avoiding any sort of political involvement. Björnson said, some years later, "Ibsen is not a man, but a pen." In 1882 many of his countrymen shared this idea, and their lack of admiration, manifested from time to time in malicious cartoons and editorials, was not lost upon Ibsen. He was certainly resolved not to be a martyr to any cause; but for a man of so complex a character, martyrdom of some sort was inescapable—even his success was a kind of torment, welcome and rewarding, doubtless, but, as we can see from *When We Dead Awaken*, not without its sacrificial aspect. "There is," he wrote, "of course, a certain satisfaction in becoming so well known in these different countries. But it gives me no sense of happiness. And what is it really worth—

the whole thing?" [45] In the last scene of *An Enemy of the People*, he had found yet another way of saying "Thou hast triumphed, Galilean—" but it was far from enough. His peace of mind evidently required that this be said over and over, and in every possible way. This compulsion was, we have noted, a chief source of his power as an artist. It also measured the scope of his talent.

Long before, in 1869, in a poem addressed to "My friend, the revolutionary orator," Ibsen had defended himself against a charge of political passivity by saying that there had been but one thoroughgoing revolution in the history of the world—that was the deluge; but even that was bungled, since Noah had survived it. "The next time," he concluded, "I shall put a torpedo under the ark." This oft-quoted brag was quite in character for the young Ibsen of thirty-one. *The Wild Duck* shows how completely opposed he was, at fifty-five, to any disturbance of the peace.

Ibsen spent rather more than a year thinking about this play; then he wrote it quickly. In June of 1883 he had written to Georg Brandes that he was contemplating a new play in four acts.[46] A year later he wrote to Theodor Caspari: "I have just finished a play in five acts, that is to say, the rough draft; now comes the elaboration, the more energetic individualization of the persons and their mode of expression." [47] At the beginning of September, 1884, he sent the manuscript to Hegel for publication, with a letter expressing his belief that he had done something new: "This new play in many ways occupies a place of its own among my dramas; the method is in various respects a departure from my earlier one. I do not want to say any more about this for the present. The critics will, I hope, find the points; in any case, they will find plenty to quarrel about, plenty to misinterpret . . ." [48]

He was disappointed in his expectations. Although it was hissed a little at the opening performance in Copenhagen, the play was successful enough in the Scandinavian theatres; but the critics made little of it one way or the other.[49] It was applauded in Berlin, howled down in Rome, received with indifference in Paris, and with frigidity in London. In a review of a series of Ibsen's plays, published in 1889, Edmund Gosse echoed, with characteristic acumen, what many had already said of *The Wild Duck*: "This is a very long play, by far the most extended of the series, and is, on the whole, the least interesting to read . . . There is really not a character in the book that inspires confidence or liking . . . There can be no doubt that it is by far the most difficult of Ibsen's for a reader to comprehend." But Bernard Shaw wrote in 1897, "Where shall I find an epithet magnificent enough for *The Wild Duck!*" [50]

It is not immediately apparent in what way *The Wild Duck* seemed to Ibsen to mark a new departure in his method. Its style seems to be a development of the technique of *Ghosts*, and it resembles that play in more than one respect. Like *Ghosts* it involves a tragic action played, in part, by comic characters, and its effect is similarly strange. Structurally, it falls into the familiar mold of Second Empire drama. It is, in some respects, a *pièce à thèse* which demonstrates the advantages of domestic life, and the folly of destroying the home because of some supposed flaw in its moral foundation. As this thesis involves the idea that the paramount concern of the parents is the happiness of the children, it seems well out of line with the doctrine we associate with *A Doll's House*.

Up to a certain point, *The Wild Duck* was a rearrangement of materials that had already seen service. The chambermaid who was palmed off with a dowry upon the carpenter Engstrand in *Ghosts* becomes here the chambermaid Gina Hansen, who is bestowed in similar fashion upon Hjalmar Ekdal. Captain Alving's illegitimate daughter Regina has her equivalent in Hedvig, who inherits, like Osvald, the paternal infirmity, in this case a tendency to blindness. Haakon Werle appears to be a version of Consul Bernick in *Pillars of Society* and, like him, he has permitted his friend to expiate a crime he himself committed. Gregers Werle is in the nature of a vindictive Osvald come home to confront his father with the sins of his past.

The plot of *The Wild Duck* hangs upon a situation of the utmost banality. A husband discovers that his wife was pregnant by another man when he married her fifteen years before; in righteous anger, he casts her off and disowns his child, who thereupon kills herself. The death of the innocent child reunites the family in sorrow. The moral of the play is then announced by the family doctor: "It is best not to stir up old troubles." The English reviewer in *The Athenaeum* for May 12, 1894, commented: "The play must be a joke . . . it is a harmless, if not very humourous piece of self-banter, or it is nothing."

One might be excused for considering *The Wild Duck* a clumsy travesty. The play has a proper undercurrent of sentimentality, but the plot is all askew. The outraged husband is caricatured to the point of clownishness; the faithless wife is the mainstay of the family; they are all living on the proceeds of the sin on which their establishment is based; and the canonical scenes of accusation and reproach are all comic. Only the child suffers; and the introduction of a tragic note into a distinctly comic situation might well seem an unpardonable incongruity. At any rate, the melodramatic elements of the familiar play of transgression and retribution are obviously deformed in accordance with a new and radical concept. The figures and the design of the narrative are all recognizably traditional, but the manner of their representation goes somewhat beyond the demands of realism. One's first impression is of a familiar scene viewed in a distorting mirror. In fact, the technique is analytical in a manner that suggests the post-impressionists; and it is perhaps to an innovation of this sort that Ibsen referred in his covering letter to the publisher.

It is interesting to see how Ibsen arrived at the novel effect of *The Wild Duck*. He began with a theme on which he had already played several variations. Driven by an exaggerated sense of guilt, the idealistic Gregers comes as a savior to set the Ekdal family free through the truth. In precisely this manner, Julian came to liberate the world, and Brand to save it. The Ekdal family, however, has no use for the truth. It has managed in its misery to find a way of life which approximates happiness, and it would prefer to be left in peace. As old Ekdal demonstrates, the human soul has considerable ingenuity; it can construct a forest in an attic; it can build, if necessary, a world in a shoebox. The illusion serves quite as well as the reality so long as it is not disturbed. Consequently, nobody thanks Gregers for his idealistic efforts. On the contrary, his meddling results only in irreparable misfortune.

The doctrine that Dr. Relling, the *raisonneur* of the play, makes explicit in *The Wild Duck* is thus seen to be the same that was implicit in *Brand* and in *Emperor and Galilean*, and which was advanced cynically in *An Enemy of the People*; it is quite opposed to the idea we associate with the Ibsen of *Ghosts* and *Pillars of Society*. In these two plays it is Ibsen's position that felicity must be based on health, and that health, from the social standpoint, depends upon truth. The superstructure, however elaborate, that is raised on a false foundation must sooner or later topple: a house built on a lie cannot stand. If one is to have stability, the lie must be uprooted, the house must be rebuilt; and the event that brings about this outcome, no matter how disagreeable, is prophylactic and providential. *The Wild Duck*, however, depends on a less heroic concept. Dr. Relling in effect reiterates the words of Agnes when she exclaims at the folly of exacting All or Nothing from the human race in its poverty. In a world miserably patched together of lies and fancies, it is best to let things alone. Men have no use for truth: illusion alone makes life tolerable. "Rob a man of his life-lie," says Dr. Relling, "and you rob him of his happiness." Unlike Gregers, who pins his faith on the surgical efficacy of truth, Relling devises opiates for the incurable. Gregers demands All or Nothing; Relling speaks for the spirit of compromise which is the practical aspect of *deus caritatis*.

To illuminate these ideas in the situation of *The Wild Duck* it was necessary to destroy the theatrical conventions relating to the play of the deceived husband. Dumas would have done this through argument. Ibsen did it through laughter. Gregers reveals his secret to Hjalmar with theatrical impressiveness, and Hjalmar reacts as people do in plays, assumes the appropriate postures and speaks the time-honored lines. But it is clear that he is going through the necessary formalities of the outraged spouse without real conviction, and the resulting scenes are broadly comic. In the midst of a situation that rapidly becomes ridiculous, the action is brought up sharply by the sudden death of Hedvig, and the play acquires abruptly another dimension. The action has proceeded unobtrusively along several levels of reality simultaneously; all at once it is seen that what had no reality for some evidently had terrible reality for others. For Hjalmar, the deception that has shaped his life has not even as much validity as the forest primeval in the attic. His sufferings are largely histrionic. But for Hedvig, his sufferings are supremely real, and she must buy them with her life. The conclusion is plain: in this world it is necessary to look out above all for those who are capable of suffering. These are the sensitive children of life, the nobility of the race, and their lot is tragic. The rest are drugged to the point of insensibility. To expect of them a tragic response to life is to invite absurdity; and this truth is in its implications, perhaps, more poignant than the conventional tragedy of the theatre.

The development of *The Wild Duck*, like that of Turgeniev's *A Month in the Country*, or Chekhov's *Uncle Vanya*, is of the order of a chemical reaction. Into a situation which appears calm and limpid, a reagent is introduced. At once hidden tensions are released, the thing seethes, rages, and gives off fumes. There is a precipitation. Then equilibrium is re-established. Once again calm descends upon the scene, and it is as if nothing had happened; yet everything is changed. It is a simple and effective way of arranging a dramatic action, and quite different from the Scribean contest of intriguers.

The eruption of Gregers into the tranquil world of the Ekdals is very skillfully managed. There is the charming family scene reminiscent of a contemporary genre-painting—the father playing a Bohemian dance on the flute, the mother and daughter grouped happily about him. We are vaguely aware of discordant elements in this scene; nevertheless, it is a tableau suitable for framing. Now comes Gregers, a disagreeable man, advancing "the claims of the ideal," and he reveals their life for what it is—a patchwork of lies and pretenses, a tissue of illusion as pathetic as the imitation forest in the attic.

His motives are decidedly more questionable than Dr. Stockmann's in *An Enemy of the People*; but they are of the same order. Ostensibly he is interested only in truth and justice. In reality, he is a sadistic busybody, and he has personal reasons, besides, for wishing to embarrass his father. Whatever his inner motives may be, however, he has rationalized them in terms of his missionary zeal. He thinks of himself as a rescuer of fallen souls, "a really absurdly clever dog; the sort that goes in after wild ducks when they dive down and bite themselves into the weeds and tangle" at the bottom of the sea. It is in the furtherance of this mission, with its attendant requirements of All-or-Nothing, that he asks little Hedvig to sacrifice the thing she loves most in order to show Hjalmar how much she loves him:

Ah, if only you had had your eyes opened to what really makes life worthwhile! If you had the genuine, joyous, courageous spirit of self-sacrifice . . .

This is the final stage of the progressive vilification of Brand which marks Ibsen's middle period. In *Pillars of Society* the idealistic Hilmar is merely obnoxious with his *ugh* of disgust at the squalor of the world; in *An Enemy of the People*, Dr. Stockmann is funny and lovable in his futility; but Gregers is hateful. It is interesting that he is cast in the first instance as the *raisonneur* of the play.

In *The Wild Duck*, the *raisonneur* of the conventional *pièce à thèse* suffers an interesting transformation. The *raisonneur* of Second Empire drama was traditionally the author's representative, and was therefore intended to inspire respect and admiration. Gregers, however, is unsympathetic. He has, moreover, a rival *raisonneur* in Dr. Relling, who is very likable. Neither, of course, is trustworthy. Of the two manipulators of the plot, the one is fanatic, neurotic, sadistic, and perhaps mad; the other is a drunkard and a disgrace to his profession. These two angels battle for the soul of the hero, which is worthless:

GREGERS: Hedvig has not died in vain. Didn't you see how grief brought out what was noblest in him?

RELLING: Most people feel some nobility when they stand in the presence of death. But how long do you suppose this glory will last in his case?

GREGERS: Surely it will continue and flourish to the end of his life!

RELLING: Give him nine months and little Hedvig will be nothing more than the theme of a pretty little party piece . . . We can discuss it again when the first grass grows on her grave. Then he'll bring it all up, all about the child so untimely torn from the loving father's heart! Then you'll see him wallowing deeper and deeper in sentimentality and self-pity.

Dr. Relling was destined, unhappily, to become a theatrical cliché, and in conceiving him as he did, Ibsen did what he could to dissociate himself from his doctrine. But there can be no doubt that this estimable quack speaks for that side of Ibsen which had by now supplanted Brand as the Ibsen "of his finest moments," an Ibsen who viewed the world from a standpoint somewhere between contempt and compassion, but always with a certain amusement. This is the Ibsen we see in his plays henceforth; until we are confronted suddenly with the agony of *The Master Builder*.

The Wild Duck, like its relatives and descendants, *Il berretto a sonagli*, *The Playboy of the Western World*, and *The Iceman Cometh*, indicates the uses of illusion in a world of unbearable realities, but we cannot conclude from this that Ibsen advocated self-deception as a panacea for the ills of humanity. The play is contemplative, not demonstrative. It has the form, in general, of a *pièce à thèse*, but it is not a thesis play so much as a play of antitheses. It proves nothing: it invites us to think. The mood is meditative, lyrical, a mood of despair. In *The Wild Duck* the priest is drunk, the soldier is broken, the idealist is mad, the doctor is ill. They have all sunk, metaphorically, into the ooze at the bottom of the sea. Here, as in Gorki's *Na dye*, there is the comfort of hopelessness: bad things happen and it makes no difference. There is no indication that out of these experiences will come a better life; on the contrary, the expectation is that after this brief period of turbulence, life will go on precisely as it did before, and in this realization Ibsen finds an authentic source of emotion. Despair, for Kierkegaard, is the terminal phase of each stage of the progress of the soul toward God. In *The Wild Duck* nobody is capable of going beyond the initial stage; but even in the climate of despair it is possible to create a world in which one can live in something like joy.

Of this nature, it is intimated, is the sphere of art, the last refuge of aesthetic man, as pathetic a substitute for nature, perhaps, as a chicken coop in an attic, but very dear nonetheless, and well worth defending. In the absence of God, there is no plausible way of making life seem other than a pointless mummery. Maximus says at the end of *Emperor and Galilean*, borrowing, to express his discontent, a phrase out of Schopenhauer: "What is life worth? All is sport and make-believe. To will is to have to will!" It is evident that in the mood of these plays is prefigured the despair of the existentialist; but Ibsen had no faith in the redeeming power of engagement. In the power of fantasy, however, to find in chaos a home for the soul of man, Dr. Relling sees something godlike. At any rate, this is as close to God as he can come.

In *The Wild Duck* all the characters are formulated in terms of despair; but the source of emotion is the despair of the author, not the despair of the characters. The characters do not complain. It is the author who, by implication, bewails them. The pleasure of the play derives, accordingly, not from the identification of the audience with the protagonist, as in tragedy, but from a feeling of intimate communion with the author in the contemplation of the action, a feeling akin to the pleasure of poetry. As the spectator is never asked to surrender his autonomy, he is afforded an individual experience which is contrapuntal to, but quite distinct from, the emotions experienced on the stage. This technique differs materially from that of Dumas, for example. Dumas, through his *raisonneur*, is often on the stage as presenter and commentator, but the action is always intended to be a realistic demonstration, in academic terms, with a total illusion. Ibsen is never on the stage; but the entire action is portrayed impressionistically, so that we are constantly aware—as in impressionist painting—of the individuality of the author's perceptions. *The Wild Duck* thus marks a subtle, but important step away from the illusionism which especially characterizes realist drama, and it points the way toward a conception of theatre in which the author, rather than the characters, becomes the center of attention, a conception which Strindberg and, after him, Pirandello developed rapidly in the next decades.

The immediate effect of such plays as *Ghosts* and *The Wild Duck* was to stimulate in various quarters artistic currents such as the contemporary naturalistic dramatists had not succeeded in propagating. *The Wild Duck* had influence everywhere, save in France and England, and particularly on Russian drama. These plays, moreover, had interesting consequences of a non-dramatic nature. It was by breaking down the accepted stereotypes of the theatre that Ibsen revitalized the drama of his time, and very likely this is all he meant to do. But the social reflex was inevitable. The revaluation of the clichés of the theatre in time brought about a revaluation of the clichés of real life, which the stage ordinarily reflects and defines. Thus Ibsen, to his embarrassment, found himself once again a leader of public opinion, a position which flattered him, but caused him acute discomfort. As he felt the impulse to be extremely aggressive, yet desired to offend nobody, he was much concerned to resist definition, tacked constantly, changed direction from play to play, and while maintaining a certain general orientation, became exceedingly difficult to follow.

In this respect he differed much from his admirer, Shaw. Shaw began as a revolutionary socialist. He thought of the theatre—at least, in the early part of his career—as an effective means of advancing his program of social reform, and with this design in mind he applied to the stereotypes of melodrama a technique of revaluation very similar to Ibsen's. Yet, as his development indicates, his true relations in the theatre were not with Ibsen, but with the useful drama of Dumas and Brieux. Shaw's purpose in the theatre was from first to last didactic: by temperament, he was a teacher. Ibsen was essentially a poet, and mainly inclined to the school of *l'art pour l'art*. It is, quite likely, to his horror of being pinned down intellectually that we must attribute the curious way in which his plays contradict, belie, and yet complement each other, like the successive images of a kaleidoscope. One would say it gave him claustrophobia to commit himself to an opinion.

In Munich, in the fall of 1885, Ibsen began a new play which, he later wrote Georg Brandes, "simply demanded to be written." [51] The first draft was called *The White Horses*, but in June of 1886 he abandoned the symbolic title along with the draft, and began a new version which, four months later, he sent to Hegel with the title of *Rosmersholm*. In a letter dated 13 February 1877 he wrote: ". . . the play deals with the struggle that every serious-minded man must wage with himself to bring his way of life into harmony with his convictions." [52]

Rosmersholm was, in fact, a variation on the theme of *Emperor and Galilean* in a narrative context which reflected Ibsen's recent visit to Norway, the first in many years. It had also some affinity with *Ghosts*, and it was perhaps to avoid emphasizing the similarity of idea that Ibsen abandoned his first title. As is usual with Ibsen, there is a useful lack of precision in the application of the thematic concept to the details of the story which develops from it. *Rosmersholm* is a complex structure. It is a story of tragic love, a character study, a drama of guilt and retribution, and a meditation on the power of outworn faith. The enclosing symbol of the white horses suggests all these elements, and some others, but, typically, it defines none of them.

The horses symbolize in the vaguest possible way all that is past and dead, and yet dynamically effective at Rosmersholm. They are a principle of vitality for Kroll, who lives by tradition, but a destructive principle for Rosmer, who seeks to free himself from it. Historically, their appearance foreshadows disaster to the men of the house. Thus the symbol, without being in the least clear, suffuses the action with an atmosphere of destiny which recalls the mood of the *Schicksalstragödie* of the early nineteenth century more readily than that of Greek tragedy.

The relation of Rosmer to Julian could not be more evident. Like Julian, Rosmer is apostate, and is seeking that Third Empire which it was not Julian's lot to establish. Over against him is set the Galilean Kroll, as well as the Galilean whom Kroll is able to evoke out of the line of joyless men who have set their mark upon Rosmer's heart and his mind. If the ancient pagan freedom is at all represented in this play, then we must see it in the dissolute Brendel, Rosmer's old teacher, and in him it is depicted as utterly bankrupt, degraded, and inarticulate. The new man, the man of the future, is the plebeian Mortensgaard, who evidently stands for the evolving synthesis of the old and the new, conceived in terms far different from those which inflamed the imagination of the apostate emperor. Mortensgaard is a practical, prudent politician who seeks to combine both sides in support of his policy, deriving strength and respectability from the conservatives he is able to win over in order to advance the liberal cause for which he works. It is part of the tragic paradox of Rosmer that as an avowed liberal he is of no use to Mortensgaard; in helping to bring about the future, he is valuable only insofar as he represents the past.

By this time, the historical dialectic appeared to Ibsen primarily as a tension between the moral and practical aspects of the soul. "The different spiritual functions," he wrote, "do not develop evenly and abreast of each other in any one human being. The instinct of acquisition hurries on from gain to gain. The moral consciousness—what we call conscience—is, on the other hand, very conservative. It has its deep roots in tradition and the past generally. Hence the conflict." [53] The action of *Rosmersholm* proceeds, accordingly, as a psychic conflict in Rosmer, which is reflected on the social plane in his conflict with Kroll. It is not Kroll, however, who destroys him; it is the Galilean within himself: such is the logic of his situation.

It is not, therefore, through the aristocratic Rosmer anymore than through the ambitious Julian that the peace of the Third Empire may be achieved. Rosmer is too deeply rooted to be able to influence the future. His soul has not the elasticity necessary to accept the antithetical elements of his being; with him it is necessary that one side should triumph, and it is the Galilean who triumphs. Rosmer is too elegant, morally speaking, to be useful. The useful man resembles Mortensgaard, the Fortinbras of the play, and not at all the Hamlet-like Rosmer. But Mortensgaard is not dramatically interesting.

Rosmer is interesting. He is the end-product of a long line of high-bred people, one of those sickly souls which Chekhov also, and Thomas Mann, considered the special objects of literary interest. Rosmer is sensitive; his conscience is queasy; he is full of self-doubt and self-criticism. In him we have not so much the protagonist, as the battleground of the evolutionary process. He is not a strong man like Kroll. His faith in God was easily shaken; so too is his new-found faith in man. He is, in short, a man of shaky faith, and his tragedy proceeds from the fact that he can accept no certainty, and yet must have certainty in order to live.

Rebecca West is Ibsen's first version of the fascinating woman who brings death to the man who loves her. Precisely what this figure meant to Ibsen is not entirely clear. Aside from the literary commonplace which couples love and death, there was, in his mind, very likely some terrifying premonition associated with the young girls who, from time to time aroused his interest. That these coquetries, brief glimpses of sunshine in an otherwise gloomy life, were associated with the pagan surge of vitality which the stern Galilean principle within him kept in check can hardly be doubted, and it is reasonable to conjecture that in Julian, Rosmer, Lövborg, Solness, and Rubek, Ibsen intended to represent some versions of himself posed romantically, but uncomfortably, between his own personal devils. On the eve of the publication of *The Wild Duck*, Ibsen quoted a stanza of poetry which sufficiently indicates the degree of his insight into the essential nature of the poetic art:

> At leve er krig med trolde
> i hjertets og hjernens hvælv;
> at digte—det er at holde
> dommedag over sig selv.

> (To live is to fight with trolls
> in the vault of the heart and brain;
> to write—that is to hold
> Judgment Day over oneself.)

In Ibsen's mind, it would seem, the joy of the Third Empire took on the aspect of a deeply exciting young woman whose image he cherished, but whose person it was not permitted him to possess. From this viewpoint, the plays of this period may all be considered as exempla demonstrating the disastrous consequences of a union with this unattainable lady, a consummation which the inner powers would not tolerate for a moment. However it may have stood within his tightly buttoned heart, insofar as is known, Ibsen remained completely faithful all his days to the frugal and unexciting wife of his youth. He never complained of his lot as a husband; it is only his heroes that complain. The beautiful and dangerous ladies who bring a momentary fatal warmth into the breasts of Ibsen's heroes, Rebecca, Hedda, Hilde, and Irene, are all secret agents of the Third Empire and, strangely enough, almost all share the fate of the man they destroy. Of all these *femmes fatales*, only Hilde Wangel survives the doom which attends her coming.

In the cycle of plays which deal with this theme, the form varies only slightly. The protagonists of these plays—Rosmer, Lövborg, Solness, Rubek—are all, for one reason or another, delicately poised men. Each is peculiarly susceptible to the influence of the woman who comes to set him free, and each is destroyed by the effort he is forced to make. They are all examples of highly talented men who are incapable, because of some characterological flaw, of reconciling within themselves their need for freedom and their fear of its consequences, which in each case turns out to be justified.

The narrative patterns conformable with so exigent a formula necessarily varied within relatively narrow limits. The protagonists of these plays are all tied in some way to a woman who gives them no joy. Rosmer cannot extricate himself from the dead Beata. Thea is indispensable to Lövborg. Solness is tied to the desiccated Aline by his imaginary obligation. Borkman—if he may be admitted to this company—is shackled to Gunhild through his crime. Rubek, who rejected Irene, is bound to Maja, who neither loves nor understands him. Into these loveless lives comes, in each case, a beautiful woman whose function it is to save, inspire, and bless—and eventually to kill.

From a metaphysical viewpoint, these ladies are unwittingly in the service of a power which uses them, and, in most cases, uses them up, for purposes beyond their own: their mysterious fascination is attributable to a force outside themselves, with which the soul of the hero is in precise accord. The human wreckage that piles up in the wake of these angels is, accordingly, the debris of the cosmic dialectic which works through the souls of men, presumably toward the betterment of mankind. The lives of these men and women may therefore be considered phenomena of transition, examples that illustrate the cosmic process through which the future grows out of the ruins of the past. It was chiefly to such transitional figures—the "delicate children of life," to use Mann's phrase—caught up in the clash of titanic forces, that Ibsen looked for the characters of modern tragedy.

Ibsen's fatal ladies, therefore, do not share the Gioconda smile of the dangerous beauties of romantic literature.[54] They are not there to ruin men, or to tempt them into the voluptuousness of destruction; on the contrary, they incarnate the dream of normal passion and blessed felicity of the sexually underprivileged male. Even Hedda Gabler, who comes closest to the fascinating malignance of the vampire-woman, is earnestly involved, so she thinks, in the improvement of her lover; she certainly has no idea of destroying him for her pleasure. But while none of Ibsen's ladies is really Satanic, all of them have a piquant trace of sadism which betrays their affinity with the decadent ladies of the romantic school.

Ibsen's male characters have even less in common with the Decadents, but they all suffer from the *mal du siècle* of the nineteenth century. Croce summed up with his customary insight— and his customary prolixity—the Hegelian interpretation of this disease in terms which might be thought to derive directly from a study of *Rosmersholm:*

This malady was due, not so much to breaking away from a traditional faith as to the difficulty of really appropriating to oneself and living the new faith . . . This may have been found possible by robust intellects and characters who were able to retrace the genetic process of the new faith without being overthrown by it, and so through an inner struggle, to reach their haven, and it was also possible in a different way for simple, clear minds and direct natures which at once understood, adopted, and practised the necessary conclusions, illuminated by the light of their goodness; but it was not within the reach of effeminate, impressionable, sentimental, incoherent, fickle minds which stimulated and excited in themselves doubts and difficulties of which they could not get the upper hand, and which enjoyed and sought out dangers and then perished in them.[55]

The sufferings of such minds, Ibsen represented as an individual and relatively secret experience, a psychic crisis. But since this experience is in each case shown to be the reflection of a conflict of universal character, Ibsen found it possible to give tragic magnitude to his figures by associating them consequentially with the cosmic struggle they embodied. The significance of *Rosmersholm* is therefore mainly in its correspondences—the play is a kind of metaphor through which a greater drama is symbolized. The agony of Rosmer is the agony of the world of Rosmer; his end is the end of Rosmersholm; and the end of Rosmersholm prefigures the end of a phase of the world's history.

This idea which, we have seen, Ibsen derived from Hebbel, is the basis of modern tragedy. Through it, it becomes possible to give a heroic cast to the sufferings of soldiers, farmers, stokers, and salesmen—figures which, without these associations, would hardly be capable of sustaining the weight of a tragic action— and in these terms the dramatists of the next generations, from Chekhov to Arthur Miller, attempted to write the tragedy of the common man. It was, however, barely possible to deal realistically with a dramatic action which involved implications of this magnitude. *Rosmersholm* pushed its action to the extreme frontiers of realism. The next stride in this direction was certain to involve Ibsen with the symbolists.

In the Hegelian view of tragedy was implicit the type of the modern tragic protagonist. The Mortensgaards—strong, prudent men with vision; realists, capable of compromise, and unhampered by ideals—were dramatically useful mainly in plays conceived upon the Scribean pattern. They were athletes, apt for a contest. It was obviously they who would inherit the future, and theirs would be stories of success. Nor was there much to be done in tragedy with Vikings of the type of Haakon Werle or Mayor Stockmann, men of robust conscience who took what they needed from life and troubled themselves no more about it. These men, Ibsen seems always to respect; but they were evidently of no particular interest to him. The type of tragic hero developed by Ibsen, and after him by Strindberg, Chekhov, and the rest, is a sensitive and neurotic individual whose spiritual malaise is the motor of the action in which he is spent. The contrast between such a concept of the tragic hero and that of the Greek dramatists is obvious. The hero of Greek tragedy is, in general, a strong man in sound health who is for some reason at odds with fate. He has no spiritual problems. His pressures are external, and would be ended if he had his will. The Greek gods take little notice of meagre types. The man marked out for tragedy is hybristic through his stature, and there is something stimulating in his struggle and his overthrow by a superior power. In a type of drama based on such characters, there is no need for psychological analysis. The interest centers on the contest, and the issues are moral and ethical, involving choices which depend upon reason. Though the answers may not be simple, the questions are.

The heroes of modern tragedy, on the contrary, are ill with a disease of the soul which mirrors the illness of our culture. The adversary is not an external power. The enemy is within themselves. To enter into their struggles, it is necessary to achieve a degree of intimacy which is entirely foreign to classic drama. The tendency in the modern theatre has been, accordingly, for analysis to take the place of poetry; but the great masterpieces are always those which transmit grandeur. It is no accident, then, that of the great figures of seventeenth-century drama the two which seem to us most "modern" are Phèdre and Hamlet, the prototypes of the modern tragic protagonist. Rosmer seems classic to us only insofar as we do not understand him.

In *Rosmersholm*, as in most of his later work, Ibsen made use of an analytic technique in which a pre-existent situation is examined in detail until in the end it is clear. Such a method is essentially expository, not narrative. It consists of a series of explanations, each of which is precipitated by an event; and the events of the action are motivated chiefly by the need to elicit further explanations. In the three days which encompass the action of *Rosmersholm*, no event of any importance takes place. Headmaster Kroll pays several visits to Rosmersholm, and asks some questions. The old teacher Brendel comes twice to borrow money. The rest is explanatory. When the exposition is ended, the play ends, and the principals go out to drown themselves.

These tableaux, which to the eye seem static, derive extraordinary interest from the manner in which the characters little by little reveal themselves. Everything has happened when the play begins. What goes on is, accordingly, a rearrangement of the past, a relocation of events, and re-definition of motives; so that the significant part of a lifetime is relived in the course of these days, and brought to a close. Underlying the short sequence of actual happenings is the very extensive action which took place before the curtain rose, an action which in a more open type of drama would have furnished the substance of the play instead of the exposition. Hardly a detail remains to be added. *Rosmersholm* is, indeed, no more than the epilogue or, at the most, the denouement of Rebecca's over-successful intrigue.

This intrigue involves a time-honored situation—the struggle of two women for a man, and it is described in some detail. In bringing about the death of Beata, Rebecca is doubtless guilty of what Strindberg was to call, in connection with the plays of 1887–1888, a psychic murder—but this is not the subject of *Rosmersholm*, merely its basis. *Rosmersholm* illustrates another application of the technique of *Ghosts*. In keeping the antecedent action off the stage and concentrating exclusively on the denouement—that is to say, on the revenge of Beata, with all that this implies—Ibsen once again resorted to the manner of regular tragedy; but the effect of the action is different from that of Renaissance drama, and it is certainly quite different from that of *Oedipus Rex*, with which it is sometimes compared. Rebecca, unlike Oedipus, knows from the beginning that she is guilty. The dramatic process is therefore not intended to adduce evidence of a crime, but through the application of spiritual pressures, to elicit a confession. In *Rosmersholm* each act represents another turn of the screw; in each act another revelation is wrung out of Rebecca, until in the end the confession is complete, and she is ready to expiate her sins.

There is, however, no compulsion upon Rebecca other than that which arises out of her own psychic situation. Had her conscience been robust, and her aim purely practical, she might, conceivably, have succeeded admirably in her undertaking, and they might all have lived happily ever after. But the machine which brings about the destruction of Rebecca and Rosmer is in operation from the moment when they first meet. For people constituted as they are, there is no possible happy outcome.

Ibsen leaves Rebecca's original purpose in some doubt; if her ends were sordid in the beginning, they are certainly not so in the end. She represents herself as a woman with a mission; and there is no particular reason to doubt her sincerity. She appears to have insinuated herself into Rosmer's house, like the self-appointed agent of a foreign power, in order to convert Rosmer to her way of thought, and thus to work through him in the liberal cause. When she has gained her ends, she finds herself emotionally implicated, and is thus precisely in the position of the heathen enchantresses we meet in Renaissance *romanzi*, who are sent to corrupt the Christian hero but are converted by him instead. But Rebecca is completely dedicated. It would be logical for a penniless adventuress to give up her missionary purpose at a certain point, and to marry her willing victim. Rebecca, however, does not lose sight of her goal for a moment. She cancels all her material gains by persisting in her wish that Rosmer publish his apostasy and his conversion at the first possible moment. In this manner she brings about a catastrophe which everyone desires to avoid, and most of all, herself.

The tragedy of Rebecca, like that of Rosmer, is thus implicit in her nature. She too suffers from recurrent attacks of that integrity which Dr. Relling calls the national disease of Norway. She stops at nothing and refuses to compromise at any point. Even when she understands that Rosmer will demand an All-or-Nothing sacrifice of her, she stands her ground. In consequence, the play includes within the frame of tragedy a *reductio ad absurdum* of the idealistic personality.

There is something especially grotesque in Rosmer, but his pattern of mind is a familiar one with Ibsen's idealistic heroes: in each case the ideal demands a sacrifice. In *The Wild Duck*, the idealistic Gregers needs a blood-sacrifice to assure himself that humanity is noble. Similarly, Hedda Gabler needs to destroy Löv-borg to assure herself that life can be beautiful. Rosmer must have Rebecca die in order to justify his faith in the liberal creed.

Bereft of his faith in God, Rosmer cannot preach his faith in man unless he is convinced of his own goodness. He cannot believe that his influence on Rebecca has been good unless Rebecca proves it to him, and she can prove it convincingly only by dying for him. Before he can save anyone, therefore, he has to kill someone; but, of course, he cannot, in all conscience, survive such an act. He too must die. Obviously, Rosmer is a victim of logic: such are the dangers of idealism. Whether Rosmer serves the old religion or the new, ultimately he is the slave of the Galilean.

"To understand the play," Ibsen said to a Viennese, "you must know the North. The Rosmer view of life ennobles; but it kills happiness." It has been suggested that Rosmer was patterned after Ibsen's aristocratic friend Carl Snoilsky, the Swedish poet, with whom he stayed at Molde in Norway in 1885. Count Snoilsky was certainly of a liberal disposition, but Rosmer's relation to Brand is clearer. Like Brand, Rosmer is cruel.

Most of Ibsen's idealists, in fact, in some degree enjoy inflict-ing pain. In *The Wild Duck*, Gregers's sadism is meant to excite aversion; but Rebecca, Rosmer, Hedda, and the rest of Ibsen's saviors all have their sadistic side, of which they are more or less conscious. When Rosmer has goaded Rebecca into an offer of suicide, he murmurs: "There is a horrible fascination in this . . ." Hilde Wangel finds Solness' suicidal ascent "frightfully exciting," and she feels curiously exalted when he plunges to his death. Ibsen invariably gives his reformers the worthiest rationalizations; but he usually suggests the erotic impulse that underlies their zeal. It is this suggestion that gives pungency to the relations of the pre-sumably sexless Rosmer and the passionate women who die for his sake. *Rosmersholm* has many connotations, psychological and philosophical, but it should not be forgotten that first and fore-most it is a love story.[56]

In June, 1888, Ibsen began work on the play, at first entitled *The Mermaid,* which he published in November of that year as *The Lady from the Sea. Ghosts* had had a first production in Berlin in 1887. It had been shown privately, but Ibsen was much encouraged by its reception, and his mood was hopeful. *The Lady from the Sea* has an optimistic outcome. This was an unusual departure for Ibsen, and the result is singularly unconvincing. The play was, indeed, not especially successful until after its revival in Oslo in 1928. On this occasion, Halvdan Koht remarks, the play seemed surprisingly fresh, and he judged that in the light of recent advances in psychology it had acquired new meaning and new life. Ellida, it was now realized, was ill. Ibsen had discovered the cure. He removed the root of her illness by giving her back her full sense of freedom.[57]

Sometime before he began this play, in a speech made at a banquet in Stockholm, Ibsen declared once again his faith in the new age to come:

I believe that an epoch is about to dawn when our political and social conflicts will cease to exist in their present forms, and that the two will grow together into a single whole which will embody for the present the conditions making for the happiness of mankind . . . I have been charged on various occasions with being a pessimist. And that is what I am, insofar as I do not believe in the absoluteness of human ideals. But I am at the same time an optimist insofar as I believe fully and steadfastly in the ability of ideas to propagate and develop. Particularly and specifically do I believe that the ideals of our age, in passing away, are tending toward that which in my drama *Emperor and Galilean* I have tentatively called the Third Empire.[58]

It was now fully fourteen years since Ibsen had published *Emperor and Galilean,* but, seemingly, he never tired of re-working this theme. *The Lady from the Sea* represents another turn of the kaleidoscope. It portrays the ambivalence of a sensitive soul situated between two poles of desire—the longing for freedom and the need for security. The problem of *Emperor and Galilean* was thus posed in its most miniscule aspect; the cosmic dialectic became here simply a neurotic conflict.

For Ibsen, who had spent his early life hemmed in by mountains both real and imaginary, the sea stood for the illimitable world, for freedom, adventure, passion, and release. It also seemed to him supremely dangerous. The play he wrote in 1888 is a seascape, full of the memories of a summer spent on the Danish coast. The action is conceived in terms of a series of symbols which associate the land with whatever is stuffy, shut in, and oppressive, and the sea with everything that is fresh, vital, mysterious, and free —the contrast serves the same purpose as the play of light and darkness in the earlier works. As he was writing in terms of a neurotic fantasy, Ibsen set *The Lady from the Sea* in an atmosphere that is somewhere between the natural and supernatural, so that the sea, the Lady, and the Stranger have something strange about them that is clearly opposed to the matter-of-fact solidity of land things. The result is a symbolic drama which points unmistakably toward the more abstruse symbolism of *The Master Builder* and *When We Dead Awaken.*

The plot of *The Lady from the Sea* is constructed in the Scribean mode, and the narrative depends upon coincidences and theatrical tricks of the sort Ibsen generally avoided. At bottom, it is the story of a married woman who is obsessed with thoughts of the lover of her youth. When this lover turns up, after many years, to claim her, she decides she is better off with the man she has, and she sends the lover packing. The same theme served Jean-Jacques Bernard in *L'Invitation au voyage* (1924), and it has seen service in many ways and many places. In Ibsen's hands, this story derives significance from the fact that Ellida's former flame is a species of Demon Lover, a shadowy figure of Protean character, who has committed, it appears, an unexplained murder; has suffered shipwreck; is said to have been drowned; and is endowed with a mysterious influence over Ellida. He is, one would say, an extremely interesting person, if he exists; but when he is brought into focus in the *scène à faire* in all the solidity of his flesh, he finds it impossible to sustain the mystery. He is seen now to be merely another man; indeed, a man of unsavory past and uncertain future.

Ellida's decision is thus forestalled by the sudden materialization of her ideal, so that it is hardly necessary to play the final scene, toward which, nevertheless, everything tends. The consequence is that, in spite of the author's desperate effort to sustain the suspense at the end of act four, the last act is quite without vitality.

The scene in which Ellida is called on to decide between the two men in the fifth act has, nevertheless, become classic in its way. It has had a full development at the hands of Giraudoux in *Intermezzo* (*The Enchanted*), in which the sea shrinks into a lake, and the Lady into a schoolmistress; while the Stranger gains immeasurably in interest by turning, in fact, into a spectre. In *Candida*, the Stranger hails not from the sea, but only from the Thames Embankment; but he turns out to be an even more shadowy figure than Giraudoux's spectre: he is Shaw's idea of a poet. In both these plays, the Lady's choice rests mainly upon material considerations. In Ibsen's "auction scene" the deciding factor in Ellida's decision is purely spiritual—it is the freedom to choose her life for herself. She thus recalls Nora in some degree:

ELLIDA: Free—but responsible! Responsible!
STRANGER: (The ship's bell sounds again) Do you hear, Ellida? She
            is sounding for the last time.
ELLIDA: I cannot go with you.

The failure of this scene is assured by the fact that, while from a philosophical viewpoint it is perhaps critical, psychologically it decides nothing. What the author hoped to achieve is clear. Ellida suffers from claustrophobia. Her life has become a prison: in reality, she is imprisoned by her desire to be free. Like Hedda Gabler she longs for adventure and excitement, but this longing is only an aspect of her ambivalence—she is simultaneously fascinated and terrified by the idea of liberty. Like a half-tame bird in a cage, she beats her head against the bars, so to speak, so long as the door is shut; but she has no desire to fly into the uncertain sky when the door is open. In her case, obviously, the solution is a cage with an open door.

The freedom which the Stranger offers Ellida is antithetical to the ordered life which her husband represents. Neither is a solution to her neurotic problem; therefore neither is acceptable. She flies uncertainly from the one to the other, suffering meanwhile not only from her sense of captivity, but also from the feeling that she belongs nowhere:

ELLIDA: Don't you see? In this house I have nothing to keep me. I have no roots here, Wangel. The children are not mine. They don't love me. They have never loved me. When I go—if I go—with him tonight, or out to Skjoldviken tomorrow, I have not even a key to give up, or any instructions to leave behind. I have been outside—outside everything. From the first day I came here.[59]

The poignancy with which Ellida's position is described in these scenes is perhaps attributable to the insight into loneliness which Ibsen had acquired as a voluntary exile from a country in which, he felt, he had never been accepted, and in which, in fact, he found it unbearable to be accepted. Ellida's feeling of not belonging, however, confuses the issue. The fact that, in addition to her other difficulties, she feels that nobody loves her makes her psychic situation somewhat more complex than is strictly necessary, and it is barely convincing that so deep a sense of self-pity can be discharged by young Hilde's sudden display of tenderness at the end. It is chiefly the philosophic aspect of Ellida's dilemma that is clear. From this standpoint her cure depends upon a synthesis of the contraries which life offers her. The true object of her desire is a secure marriage with complete freedom to do as she pleases. This freedom—the Greek spirit—merged with responsibility—the Galilean—will then result in a voluntary assumption of the conjugal discipline. In this manner, presumably, Ellida's spiritual state will approximate the climate of the Third Empire which, as Ibsen defines it, is precisely a state of individual freedom with social responsibility. The solution which Dr. Wangel offers his wife is therefore in the nature of the miracle of which Nora spoke when she left the bewildered Helmer alone in A Doll's House.

While *The Lady from the Sea* dealt quite intelligently with the problem of marriage in a period when the emancipation of women was still an important issue, it cannot be said that it carried its point much further than *A Doll's House* or *Ghosts*. It broke new ground, nevertheless, in one respect—in accentuating the psychic aspect of a problem which in the earlier plays was treated mainly from the social viewpoint. Nora's revolt in *A Doll's House* was precipitated by her disillusionment. Had her husband been worthy, presumably she would have accepted her subordinate position in his house. In *Ghosts*, however, Mrs. Alving was once placed very much in Ellida's position. She had married a man who did not interest her, and was fascinated by someone who did not need her. In *The Lady from the Sea*, the situation of *Ghosts* is reversed. By insisting that she run away with him, the Stranger causes Ellida to discover the attractions of life with an unexciting but understanding spouse. The play thus falls into the mold of Augier's *Gabrielle*, and the maturity of Ibsen's treatment of a problem which in France had so far been treated only in the most superficial way, indicates the remarkable progress which the Northern drama was making in these years.

Hedda Gabler was written two years later, in 1890. It was the immediate consequence of Ibsen's brief romantic attachment to Emilie Bardach, a Viennese girl who in 1889 gave him, as he later wrote: "the happiest, the most beautiful summer of my whole life." [60] The extent of Ibsen's involvement with Miss Bardach is by no means clear. What is clear is that he complained, that fall, that he was unable to work, and, in February, 1890, he firmly terminated what he evidently considered a dangerous or, at least, a distracting correspondence. That spring he began *Hedda Gabler*, a play about academic life. He finished it the following summer. He was then sixty-two.

The idea of a fascinating woman with sadistic tendencies was certainly not new to Ibsen. All his heroines have a trace of sadism, we have noted, although none before the precocious Hilde Wangel appears to be conscious of this source of excitement. Among the women Ibsen drew, in the dramas of this period, Hilde Wangel stands out vividly. She is the first of Ibsen's women—and perhaps the only one—to give the impression that her mind is not completely on the play. The characterization is indeed so lifelike, that one would say she was drawn from life; but that is far from certain. Hedda's provenience is even less clear. The origin of the situation in which she is placed is, however, clear enough. It comes from *The Lady from the Sea*.

Like Ellida, Hedda is a prisoner of her neurosis. She is trapped between the need for security and the longing for adventure; and as each wish inhibits the other, she is able to give scope to neither; consequently, she is restless and ill at ease. Hedda is not called upon, like Ellida, to make a choice. She must work off her malaise in more subtle ways. Like Hilde Wangel she finds excitement in the risks that others take, and creates situations in which she can enjoy these thrills discreetly, from a distance. But even vicarious excitements of this sort involve some element of risk. In the end she finds herself fatally entangled in her own intrigue. One thinks of Rebecca West.

Hedda Gabler is the most complex play that Ibsen attempted. Its première in Munich in January, 1891, infuriated the German critics. "The public," wrote one, "has no desire to solve the conundrums which the dramatist has manufactured, partly out of trickery, partly out of muddled thinking." Seventy years later, *Hedda Gabler* appears to be as puzzling as ever. It has been played as melodrama, as tragedy, even as comedy. Weigand sees it as none of these, but as "a spectacle of life from which we retire with a shock." Wolf Mankowitz wrote in 1947: "In a sense *Hedda Gabler* is a farce." [61]

It is usual to play Hedda as a cold woman of viperish disposition. The result is a stereotype, the vampire-woman of the romantic school, whose long career in the drama and the films at last crystallized into irrefragable outlines. It is indeed not impossible that in characterizing Hedda, Ibsen was in some measure involved with this tradition. Strindberg's *Miss Julie* and *Creditors* had both been written in the summer of 1888, two years before *Hedda Gabler*, and both were played briefly in Copenhagen in March, 1889. There is no doubt that Strindberg's sadistic heroines did much to translate the *dame bête-féroce* from the novel to the stage.

A certain amount of evidence may be adduced to emphasize if one wishes, the similarity between Strindberg's Fröken Julie and Ibsen's Hedda. Both ladies are aristocrats. Both pose the problem of *déclassement*—by this time a most familiar theme in the French drama—and in both cases this problem is emphasized in the title of the play. The deep revulsion against sexuality which troubles Strindberg's heroine is shared by Hedda; like Julie, she is a *demi-femme*. To Strindberg, at least, such insights into the female psyche were of great personal interest, and he advanced his ideas so vigorously that it was impossible not to be aware of them. In Strindberg's opinion, the degenerate female types, in whose portraiture he specialized, constituted a species of humanity which was both dangerous and useless, and in exposing them he felt that he was fulfilling an important obligation to society. "To the mortal hatred of the sexes is added here," he wrote in a letter to Georg Brandes, "the conscious repugnance to reproduce itself which characterizes the defective species (see Schopenhauer on pederasty) . . ." [62] He was especially concerned with women of the type of Tekla in *Creditors*, artists, career women, feminists: "It is through envy that they become vampires—to be avenged in some way. Since they have no ego that is really theirs, they try to appropriate someone else's." [63]

By 1890 Strindberg had repeatedly attacked Ibsen as an instrument of the great conspiracy of women and effeminate men which was steadily undermining the culture of Europe. Strindberg's *The Wife of Sir Bengt* was a first blast against what he considered Ibsen's feminist propaganda. The story entitled *A Doll's House*, in the first part of *Married* (1884), renewed the attack. By 1886 his hysteria had reached its paroxysm; by this time he was speaking of Ibsen as an asexual bluestocking. His enmity, as usual, went well beyond purely literary considerations. Ibsen had long since become his *bête noire*. Since 1882, he had linked him consistently with the conspiracy to which he attributed his literary mishaps, and he was firmly convinced that Ibsen had caricatured him savagely as Hjalmar in *The Wild Duck*. [64]

In these circumstances it would be normal for Ibsen to take some notice of his obstreperous Swedish contemporary, and it was entirely consistent with his practice to redress the balance with respect to his supposed feminism by writing an anti-feminist play. But however we assess his relation to Strindberg, it must be conceded that if he borrowed anything from him, he put it strictly to Ibsenist uses.

In contrast to most of Strindberg's plays, *Hedda Gabler* is deftly and intricately plotted in the French manner. The plot is deceptively simple: it is actually the result of the juxtaposition of several narrative motifs in a firmly integrated design. The play is consequently capable of producing a variety of impressions, each of which has only partial validity, while, taken together, they make an extraordinarily rich effect.

The theme which provides *Hedda Gabler* with its basic structure is derived, we have noted, from *The Lady from the Sea*—it involves the plight of a woman who has made a marriage of convenience, and is obsessed with the memory of a former love. This theme is combined now with another—a woman who commits a crime in order to help her husband is called to account by a blackmailer: essentially this is the story of *A Doll's House*. Interlaced with these two is yet another theme, that of the idealistic busybody who succeeds only in destroying the lives he attempts to reform: the theme of *The Wild Duck*. Out of this narrative complex arises the social question which *Hedda Gabler* poses, the problem of the aggressive woman in a man's world.

The intricacy of the play is further enhanced by the story of Eilert Lövborg and Thea Elvsted, a story which is independent of the main plot, but closely meshed with it. In the configuration

Hedda-Eilert-Thea, Ibsen develops once again the situation of a soul poised precariously between antithetical forces. Eilert is a wild genius. He has been rescued from the gutter by the motherly Thea, and through her influence he has succeeded in submitting to the discipline necessary to a writer. He has in this manner already achieved a measure of success, and is now on the threshold of a really important achievement. From Hedda's viewpoint, however, Eilert's spirit has been inhibited by Thea's ministrations so that his true genius cannot flower. He is well behaved, tame, and productive; but he is productive through the operation of restraints foreign to his nature, and, in her opinion, it is only when his spirit is freed from these artificial pressures that his genius will have scope.

In the projected rehabilitation of Lövborg, Hedda intends to serve neither as his nurse nor as his secretary, but as his inspiration, his angel. It is her wish to bring about in him, through her power of suggestion, that miraculous synthesis of pagan freedom and Christian discipline which is the special grace of the Third Empire. Unhappily, Eilert does not survive the experiment. Freed from the restraining influence of Thea, he falls promptly into his former swinishness, and once again he affirms the triumph of the Galilean.

One might imagine that a play which includes so many familiar elements would make no great effect of novelty. The reverse is the case. *Hedda Gabler* is often said to be unique among Ibsen's plays; and, in fact, its construction is so nearly perfect that it seems quite unlike anything else he wrote. In part the effect of novelty is due to the peculiar design of the action. The plot principally takes its shape from the Hedda-Eilert-Thea triangle, and it centers ostensibly upon Eilert. Normally a character in this situation would be the protagonist of the play, as in *Emperor and Galilean*, and the tragedy would be his tragedy. But *Hedda Gabler* was not conceived in so symmetrical a manner. Eilert is not central in the play. His personal conflict is causally related to the main action, but remains external to it. His fate brings about the catastrophe, not directly, but by a reflex; and this reflex is itself a function of the nature of Hedda.

The death of Eilert, while pathetically wasteful, is not the climax of the action; it is only a step which leads to the death of Hedda. Her fate completely overshadows his in dramatic importance. Consequently, while the principal conflict centers upon Eilert, it is Hedda who is the protagonist of the play. The wisdom of this arrangement is obvious. The story of the decline and fall of Eilert could hardly result in anything more impressive than a melodrama involving the horrors of drink. By giving this theme a deliberately comic nuance, Ibsen purged it of sentimentality; at the same time he caused it to take on a curiously grotesque character, which is magnified through its association with the essentially tragic action which concerns Hedda. In its technique, *Hedda Gabler* is thus reminiscent of *Maria Magdalene*, in which the melodrama of the dishonored daughter gains force and significance through its relation to the tragedy of the father. But while Hebbel's play is discouragingly clumsy in its detail, *Hedda Gabler* is a miracle of fine workmanship. Not the least of its excellences is the superlative characterization of the heroine.

In the Author's Preface to *Miss Julie*, Strindberg had complained of the emptiness of characterization in the theatre of his day. Dramatic characters, he wrote, were traditionally depicted as automata, "men fixed and finished," without the possibility of organic development, who could be characterized readily by means of an idiosyncrasy, a physical defect, or a catch-phrase. "I do not believe," he added, "in simple stage-characters. And an author's summary judgments of people—this man is stupid, this one brutal, this one jealous, this one stingy, and so on—should be challenged by the naturalists, who know how rich the soul-complex is, and who realize that 'vice' has a reverse which is very much like virtue." [65]

Whether or not Ibsen knew this preface, *Hedda Gabler* illustrates quite aptly the sort of characterization Strindberg had in mind. No adjective will serve to characterize Hedda. She embodies neither good nor evil, is both creative and destructive, idealistic and selfish, noble and despicable, and is no more comprehensible on the stage than she would be in real life. She is not a personage abstracted and simplified in conformity with some dramatic concept, but a bundle of unresolved tendencies, a human being in process of development, conditioned by heredity, limited by environment, capable of anything, and striking out blindly in search of fulfillment. If the picture is bewildering, it is because the example is extreme; but we recognize in her the human condition.

Until she seizes on the luckless Eilert, Hedda has no function in the world. She is a woman; and it is her destiny before long to be a mother. This destiny disgusts and frightens her, and she refuses to face even the possibility. Her actions—her vigor, her language, the pistol-shooting with its obvious symbolism—are those of a young boy, violent and explosive. There is no hint that she has ever done more than endure her womanhood. Such a person, though sexually somewhat vague, might go far in the world if she had a proper outlet for her energy; but in her special circumstances Hedda's only possible mode of self-expression is through the men she can influence and direct. Tesman is too blockish to suit her purpose. It is with joy therefore that she fastens on the brilliant, but unstable, Lövborg as the vehicle for her creative efforts. As he has already demonstrated his aptitude for regeneration, she proposes to improve him in spectacular fashion.

Hedda embarks on her task of re-creation with the eager enthusiasm of an artist who has at last found a subject. First she must clear the way by eliminating Thea. She sets about this efficiently, the more so as she has always enjoyed hurting her. Then, without loss of time, she knocks the props out from under Eilert, and launches him on his career as a genius. What she has in mind is a masterwork, the creation of a beautiful, Satanic figure, strong, brave, and self-mastered—Lord Byron, perhaps. This creation will be a spiritual activity very different from the squalid motherhood to which Tesman invites her; and in this process she hopes to realize herself fully, to become herself.

Her connection with Eilert, from a psychic standpoint, is very close. In the conflict which he has seemingly resolved with the help of Thea, she senses dimly the unresolved conflict within herself. As a young girl she too had felt the urge to live fully and dangerously, but she was afraid, and is still afraid:

HEDDA: . . . I am cowardly. But now I'll confess something to
            you . . .
LÖVBORG: Well?
HEDDA: The fact that I dared not shoot you down—
LÖVBORG: Yes?
HEDDA: That was not my most arrant cowardice, that evening—
LÖVBORG: Oh Hedda! Hedda Gabler! Now I see the hidden roots of
            our comradeship. You and I! It was your craving for life,
            after all—
HEDDA: Take care! Believe nothing of the sort! [66]

The suggestion is that Eilert and Hedda are counterparts. Eilert has given way to the passional element in his soul; Hedda, to the need for safety. The Galilean has defeated her; but only temporarily. Her marriage represents no more than an armed truce. When Eilert turns up once again, she resumes hostilities without delay. Her first step is to arouse in Eilert the courage she has not:

HEDDA: Oh yes—courage! If only one had that!
LÖVBORG: What then? What do you mean?
HEDDA: Then life would perhaps be livable after all.[67]

Eilert, however, is not so much in need of courage as of self-control, and Hedda's attempt to live greatly through him is a failure. Nevertheless, Hedda sees the possibility of turning even this defeat into a sort of victory. If Eilert cannot be inspired to live beautifully, he can at least be inspired, so she thinks, to die beautifully; and she sends him off with one of the General's pistols to redeem by a noble act of destruction the mess he has made of her work of regeneration. Eilert, however, has no idea of affirming the dignity of man by killing himself for her sake. He becomes involved instead in a squabble with a whore, while attempting to retrieve his lost manuscript, and is shot ignominiously in the bowels. For Hedda, this is the last straw:

HEDDA: That too! Oh, what curse is it that makes everything I touch turn ludicrous and mean? [68]

There is, indeed, more to come. Her unsuccessful attempt to stage a tragedy now threatens to implicate her in an ugly scandal involving the police, or, worse still, in yet another form of sexual captivity involving Judge Brack. Under these conditions, she sees her way clearly, and with the twin of the pistol she gave Eilert, she achieves that state of self-realization of which he had proved incapable. Thus Hedda finds in death that freedom and that security which she had vainly sought to combine in life.

In this paradox, the play makes its point. Eilert and Hedda are not lovers, but twins. Dangerously poised between the extremes that attract them, each has a kind of bravado which takes the place of courage. They are exceptional people, high-minded and talented, and desire only to live fully and nobly; but the good life eludes them. They are too precariously balanced, and not sufficiently strong; in them, the romantic impulse is a disease. For such people, the Third Empire is not at hand. Yet it is just such people who most desperately seek it, and this is their tragedy.

It would be a mistake, therefore, to interpret this play as anti-feminist. Hedda is not a vampire-woman. If she is dangerous it is because she stands at bay. She is frustrated at every turn. Her plight is desperate. All her aggressions are aroused: she is defending her inmost life. In contrast to this tragic figure, Ibsen sets up the dull, but eminently serviceable, Thea.

Thea is a woman, so to speak, by vocation. She is wholly receptive. Her femininity emphasizes Hedda's sterility as a woman and Hedda's impotence as a man. In destroying Eilert's manuscript, Hedda, evidently, is not striking at Eilert, with whom she is psychically identified. She is destroying Thea's "child" by Eilert, and thereby manifesting her hostility to the Theas of this world, their passivity, and their fecundity—all those things, in short, which are antithetical to her own nature. It is appropriately ironical that this act of destruction is quite ineffectual, since Thea is capable of reproducing Eilert's work in spite of it; and thus it is through Thea once again that Eilert is saved.

The difference between the two aspects of womanhood could not be more emphatically demonstrated. Hedda cannot help a man create, either biologically or intellectually, because, with relation to the man, she desires to arrogate the masculine role to herself. Thea is willing to take the passive role. She is able, accordingly, simply by being a woman, to make men behave like men, and in the end she rescues Tesman from Hedda quite as naturally as once she rescued Eilert from the gutter. By fitting these women into the design of his drama, Ibsen was thus able to say something profoundly sensible about the relation of the sexes and, had he done nothing more, *Hedda Gabler* would have been a superb example of the drama of social problems. But Ibsen went much further than this, and he cast his action in comedic terms so poignant as to be indistinguishable from tragedy.

In weaving a narrative fabric so light and subtle, and yet so dense in texture that it rewards the most careful scrutiny, Ibsen demonstrated his absolute mastery of the realistic style at this point of his life. It is doubtful that anything finer has ever been done in this genre, or anything more intricate. An achievement of such surpassing depth has its drawbacks. On the printed page *Hedda Gabler* reveals the beauty of its design reluctantly and only upon reflection. In the theatre, where the opportunity for reflection is minimal, only the greatest skill will serve to uncover more than a partial aspect of the play. Such are the risks a playwright runs in writing with subtlety for a medium in which it is generally thought safe to seek only the broadest and most obvious effects.

In the fall of 1891, Ibsen and his wife came back to Norway to live. He was now sixty-three, wealthy, respected, and thoroughly decorated; but without happiness. "They live splendidly and have an elegant house," Magdalene Thoresen reported in a letter, "though all is pretty much in Philistine style. They are two lonely people, each for himself, each absolutely for himself." Ibsen's son Sigurd had by now become prominent in the Norwegian foreign service, but the great man himself took no part in the affairs of his country. He was welcomed wherever he went, but the exasperation he had always manifested with respect to his native land did not subside now that he was home. He felt more comfortable in Oslo in these years than he ever had before, but he was not at all at his ease. Six years later, in 1897, he wrote wistfully to Georg Brandes: "Up here by the fjords is my native land. But—but—but—! Where am I to find my homeland?" [69]

In March, 1892, he began work on *Bygmester Solness*, the first of the trilogy which ended, as he later wrote Count Moritz Prozor, his French translator, with *When We Dead Awaken*. According to Ibsen, the nucleus of *The Master Builder* was a poem of two stanzas he had written about this time, picturing an old man and his wife rummaging in the charred ruins of their home for a precious jewel they had lost in the fire. "And even if they find it," the poem concludes, "never will she find her faith again, nor he his happiness." Although the allusion to Solness and Aline in *The Master Builder* seems clear enough, the play cannot be said to center on this situation, nor is there anything of a specific nature in Ibsen's life to warrant a conjecture as to the personal bearing of the poem. On the other hand, it is quite evident that *The Master Builder* is a personal statement.

Innumerable details serve to connect Ibsen with Solness. Like Ibsen, Solness is self-made, ruthless, dedicated, and friendless. "Friends are an expensive luxury," Ibsen once wrote, "and when a man's whole capital is invested in a calling and a mission in life, he cannot afford to keep them." [70] It is said that Ibsen often spoke of himself as an architect and builder of plays, that he too had a fear of heights, and it is certain that he had come to the uncomfortable realization by 1890 that the younger liberals considered him a stuffy and backward old man. The matter was brought sharply to his attention shortly after his homecoming by the young novelist Knut Hamsun who delivered two lectures, both solemnly attended by Ibsen, in which he blamed the backwardness of modern Norwegian letters on the leadership of Ibsen and Björnson, and their lack of psychological insight.

It seems reasonably clear that the writing of *The Master Builder* was a defensive operation, if not a conscious *apologia pro vita sua*. Nowadays no Ibsen scholar seems to doubt that Solness is to be identified with Ibsen. Halvdan Koht believes that Solness is a self-portrait. Professor Bull calls the play "very much the author's personal confession." [71] These conclusions are borne out by a speech, delivered a few years after the publication of the play, in which Ibsen referred to Solness as "a man who is somewhat related to me." Yet it was by no means clear to Ibsen's contemporaries that Ibsen meant to portray himself in Solness. On the contrary, contemporary identifications ranged all the way from Björnson to Bismarck; and in England the *Saturday Review*, with apparent seriousness, conjectured that in Solness, Ibsen perhaps intended to figure Mr. Gladstone.

Whatever we may think of its aptness with respect to Gladstone, the portrait of Solness is hardly flattering to Ibsen, and it is astonishing that he should wish to present himself to the world in this guise. It may be hazarded, however, that Ibsen willingly portrayed himself in this manner in order to forestall an even less flattering characterization, and that therefore somewhere beyond Solness we may discern the true face of Ibsen. Yet, however interesting this type of inquiry may be for the understanding of the man, there is no need to peer behind the portrait of Solness in order to understand the play. Though we may be morally certain that Solness does not, and cannot, truly represent Ibsen if only because no one truly represents himself, it is enough for our purpose that this is how Ibsen meant to explain himself at this time of his life.

Though in substance *The Master Builder* is actually a rearrangement of familiar materials, it is in some ways quite unlike anything Ibsen had so far written. *The Master Builder* is, in fact, the first of the great symbolist plays of the period, the first to make use of the technique of analogy and abstraction, of symbolist imagery, correspondences, the dramatic metaphor, the spiritistic and cabalistic background, mystery, hypnotism—all the baggage of the mystical school. The play itself is clear enough. The chief mystery is how Ibsen came by this apparatus.

In 1892 symbolist drama was at the very beginning of its development, and symbolism had as yet neither a set style nor a firm theoretical basis. The French symbolist poets were not well known outside France. Baudelaire had died in 1867, ten years after the publication of *Les Fleurs du mal*. Verlaine had published *Jadis et naguère* in 1885; Mallarmé's collected works were brought out in 1888. The following year Maeterlinck created a sensation with *La Princesse Maleine*, but it was not until 1890 that Villiers de l'Isle-Adam's *Axël* appeared, and the same year saw the publication of Maeterlinck's *Les Aveugles* and *L'Intruse*. In bringing out *The Master Builder* when he did, Ibsen therefore showed himself to be in the very forefront of the new movement.

Ibsen had no particular affinity with Maeterlinck. He shared with him neither the love of the archaic nor the stately lyricism which characterize the symbolist manner. Yet *The Master Builder* unquestionably shares with such plays as *Pelléas* and *L'Intruse* that equivocal "atmosphere of the soul" in which the symbolists specialized. Apart from this, Ibsen's symbolism was of a different stamp from Maeterlinck's.[72] Save for the strange, spired house which we do not see, but the characters see, *The Master Builder* has a thoroughly conventional setting, and its action is entirely realistic. Yet as the play progresses, it becomes increasingly evident that behind the realism of the play there is a reality of which the action merely intimates the existence. Solness thinks himself more than ordinarily mad; but the strangely exalted mood of the play cannot be attributed solely to his eccentricity: there is the inexplicable presence of the quite solid Hilde to give objectivity to what might otherwise be considered the fantasy of a disordered mind. The play thus unfolds simultaneously on two planes, and it is from the world of the thoroughly matter-of-fact that we are afforded a glimpse of the occult forces which presumably determine the action.

Although this action is firmly anchored in material things, its events are singularly ambiguous, and the dialogue continually suggests a *sovrasenso*: in some passages it is no more than a stream of thought shared by two people. The narrative is modulated and inflected in a manner that foreshadows expressionism. These spires which Solness climbs at his peril in order to converse with God; this strange girl who appears so opportunely to demand the fulfillment of a promise which Solness does not remember making; the supernatural powers which these people seemingly possess; the unreal past which somehow materializes as it is evoked; the Swedenborgian spirits that help and serve; the entire enigmatic sequence in which Solness has his fulfillment and his end—all these are palpably dual in their nature, figmentary, and yet suggestive of a deeper truth than reality usually affords. All this has the efficacy of poetry; and the inscrutability of poetry which declines to be questioned; and all of it quite defies common sense.

On its face, *The Master Builder* has to do with the infatuation of an aging genius with a young girl. The suggestion is therefore irresistible that this story is in some way related to the romantic attachment which Ibsen formed with Emilie Bardach at Gossensass in the Brenner in the summer of 1889. The immediate literary result of that affair was, as we have seen, *Hedda Gabler*. It seems, however, that three years later the memory of those excitements had mellowed sufficiently to inspire a different sort of play.

The relation of Ibsen and the quite youthful Miss Bardach was, so far as one can gather, never such as need have given her mother the slightest concern. The sixty-two-year-old Ibsen had come to Gossensass as a great man, with a festival arranged by the town in his honor, a *Platz* named after him, music, and many speeches. Emilie was eighteen, and she responded to the advances of the elderly poet like a romantic virgin singled out by Zeus for immortality. "He never admired anyone as much as he admires me," she noted in her carefully preserved diary. "But all in him is truly good and noble. What a pity it is that I cannot remember all his words! He begs me so intensely to talk freely to him, to be absolutely frank with him, so that we may become fellow workers together." [73]

It is more than likely that *The Master Builder* was written in the afterglow of this courtship. There is a strong suggestion of the summer at Gossensass in Hilde's description of the passionate behavior of Solness at Lysanger after the church festival, and the whole play seems to reflect the author's regret at his inability to make both ends meet, biologically speaking, in 1889. Nevertheless, Ibsen's discreet romance could have had, at best, only an oblique bearing on his carefully guarded literary life. The basic pattern of *The Master Builder* does not differ significantly from that of *Rosmersholm*, and it has affinities also with *The Lady from the Sea*, and other earlier plays. It is probable, therefore, that the deep-seated longing for a passionate relationship which seems to be at the bottom of all Ibsen's fantasies of this period was the cause, rather than the consequence of the affair with Emilie Bardach— a situation in which we see the poet acting out somewhat timidly in real life a role he had worked out nobly and tragically in his fancy.

In any case, it was not in character for Ibsen to translate his life directly into literature, and he was not pleased when Emilie Bardach sent him her photograph signed "Princess Orangia." It is certain that he had an invincible compulsion to exhibit his inner life to the world; but this compulsion was balanced by the equally powerful necessity to stand well back of the figures through which he showed himself—unlike Strindberg, he was an exhibitionist of punctilious reticence. It seems most probable, for instance, that in portraying Solness' wife Aline, he meant to complain a little of his own wife Suzannah; and that in Hilde Wangel he meant to depict something of the ideal girl with whose earthly avatars he occasionally flirted; but nothing in the play directly connects Aline with Suzannah, nor the daemonic Hilde with that Emilie to whom he wrote in the fall of 1889: ". . . the things we have lived through, I live again and again—and still again. To make of them a poem is, for the time being, impossible." [74]

By the spring of 1892, however, Ibsen had formed yet another friendship. It was now a young pianist called Hildur Andersen, whose family he had known long ago in Bergen, and it was perhaps to commemorate this new association that he brought back into *The Master Builder* the character of the violent young Hilde who had served in *The Lady from the Sea*. Nothing else in Ibsen's career suggests the provenience of this charming figure; and we have to go back as far as *Brand* to find a character who suggests her in any way. It is entirely possible that the hawk-like young woman, for all her vividness, was in great part a creature of his fancy: such girls appear to have fascinated him. The mad girl Gerd in *Brand* shares with Hedda Gabler a disquieting taste for firearms, and, with Irene in *When We Dead Awaken,* an affinity with avalanches. In real life Ibsen courted girls of another stripe, gentle girls who made no great demands either on the man or the poet. But in his plays these girls grow dangerous. They do not excite interest through their femininity. They have, on the contrary, a certain boyish wantonness, a fresh, bold quality that is quite different from the gentle passivity of Ibsen's earlier heroines, Agnes or Solveig.

Technically, *The Master Builder* is another application of the plot-pattern which Ibsen had used repeatedly since the time of *Peer Gynt,* and was to use in all the plays of his last period. Its design is very straightforward. It has no trace of the Scribean imbroglio, and the retrospective elements do not markedly divert the current of the narrative. Like *Rosmersholm* and *Hedda Gabler, The Master Builder* develops the tragedy of a highly sensitive and talented man whose life is bounded by two women, each of whom represents for him a separate but certain doom. Solness, like his dramatic predecessors, is precariously balanced on the edge of life. Aline has drained him of joy and dried up his creative spirit, so that the man wants to die. Hilde, like Rebecca in *Rosmersholm,* comes to set him free from his past, and so precipitates him head-

long into the future. The mechanism is familiar; but the effect of
The Master Builder is not at all that of the other two plays.

The difference is due to the character of Hilde; and it is she
who chiefly brings out the symbolic values of the play. Hilde is
altogether enigmatic. She is certainly a creature of flesh and bone,
with an identifiable father, and a home address. She has a curious
avidity for thrills, as well as a hunter's instinct with regard to men.
She is a bird of prey. She has, however, mystical connotations which
are impressive. The death of Solness, at which she presides, is
for her an exciting and invigorating experience accompanied by
celestial music. This death, through her ministry, acquires sacra-
mental character. Because of her, the Master Builder's feat is in the
nature of a sacrifice and a promise. In his final exploit, Solness
not only vindicates his manhood, but through this demonstration
of courage, he lays the foundation of that airy castle which was his
life's goal, and which others younger and more fortunate than he
will one day bring to completion. If there is a personal allusion
in this, it is entirely understandable; the symbolism, at least, is
clear.

From a philosophic point of view, Solness is represented as having gone through the stages of a process which recalls, though it
does not duplicate, the Kierkegaardian progression. Like Rosmer,
Solness has renounced the service of God and dedicated himself
to the service of man; but he has gone further than Rosmer—he
has also renounced the service of man. After the coming of Hilde,
he has it in mind to serve only posterity—to build castles in the
air, as he says, on a sound footing. As examples of practical architecture, it is true, these airy castles leave something to be desired.
Even in imagination they remain amorphous as clouds, for it is
only in the Third Empire that they will find realization. Such,
evidently, is the kingdom which Hilde was promised and has come
to claim; but she realizes that for the moment, at least, her demands are exorbitant, and she is willing to settle for a secure
retreat where she can find happiness while Solness arranges matters
on earth to her satisfaction.

Solness is not oriented toward happiness. He is strong and can be wicked, but he has neither the Viking's stout conscience nor the pagan's joyous nature. He cannot follow his desire without self-torment. The Galilean is in his heart; and, in the end, his dream of freedom kills him. From a formal viewpoint, the character and the situation fulfill the conditions of tragedy as Ibsen seems to have understood them, yet the effect at the end is curiously cheerful. The reason is that *The Master Builder* takes place in a realm that is just beyond the borders of experience, on the verge of that madness which was for the symbolists the peculiar domain of poetry.

Obviously it is senseless that a master builder should have to include among his necessary accomplishments the ability to climb buildings with a wreath in his hand; whatever the customs of the trade may be in Norway, we may be sure that at no time has the builder's profession depended on such alpinistic feats. Nor, it need scarcely be added, is it customary in the Scandinavian countries to furnish dwellings with church towers. In this respect, the Master Builder's new house is obviously in the nature of an innovation. However bizarre, nevertheless, these ideas may seem from a practical viewpoint, as metaphors they are transparent. It is one thing to aspire, quite another to attain to the heights of one's aspiration. No artist is able to realize in life the ideal he expresses in art. The disparity between what a man says and what he does is the measure of the man, not of the artist. Moreover, the attempt to surmount in reality the peak of one's fancy may prove to be a perilous business for one not properly equipped for the asperities of the ascent, and it seems wicked for people to insist on one's duty to try.

The Master Builder gives these familiar ideas a new formulation. When the play opens, Solness has passed the peak of his trajectory. He is fifty, and he is faced with an unpleasant choice. He must either exert himself beyond his natural capacity, or fall back and let the younger generation tread him down. The time is critical. Like the hero in *Njal's Saga* whom fate has prepared for death, he feels a little giddy—he is *fæg*—and his judgments are no

longer trustworthy. At this precarious moment of his life, Hilde
appears out of nowhere, bright and breezy, to arrange his death
and his transfiguration.

Hilde comes, evoking troubled memories, to enforce the high
promise of youth, which no man keeps. She had made him giddy
once before, exactly ten years before, so she insists, the day he
dared for the first time to climb as high as he built. On that
occasion he had gone so far as to manifest the sudden premature
passion which has engaged him to her. Now once again she makes
his head swim, pointing upward to the height he must reach in
order to find life worth living. It is clear that in his mind the height,
the danger, and the girl are all one, just as before, and the challenge to his manhood is unmistakable. As for the girl, she loves him
with the complete concentration of one who is bent on murder,
and in return for the fullness of her love, she demands All-or-
Nothing. In her light, the man opens like a flower. He feels his
youth surge like fire in his veins. In that moment everything seems
possible: it is the moment of death. Wreath in hand, he climbs the
tower of his house to the very pinnacle, where God is waiting.

In this play, Ibsen manifests a more obvious, and therefore
more deceptive, subjectivity than in any of his former works. Since
in *The Master Builder* everything has a clear relation to the author,
it is hardly surprising that it should be put forward with ambiguous
symbols. The symbols themselves were not quite new. In *Brand*,
it was by shooting at the hawk that Gerd brought down the roof of
the Ice Church. In *The Master Builder*, the mad girl and the hawk
have merged, the Ice Church has become a spired house, and it is
not the avalanche that falls but the man. A good deal has been
written, mostly in English, about the erotic character of this symbolism—the spires and towers have been given an obvious interpretation, and following Weigand's suggestion, more than one
astute critic has found interesting sexual connotations in Hilde's
excitement as she watches Solness climb up his spire. The temptation to psychoanalyze fictional personages is, of course, irresistible;
but the conjecture, for example, that the thirteen-year-old Hilde

experienced a "spiritual orgasm" when she first saw Solness climb up the tower at Lysanger, and that at twenty-three this experience is still the emotional peak of her life seems unduly stimulating.[75]

It is perhaps more reasonable to assume that Hilde exhibits in this fantasy the kind of sexual fixation with regard to Solness that Ibsen probably imagined young girls experienced with regard to himself. Aside from its phallic connotation—which probably would have shocked Ibsen had it been suggested to him—the towered house was evidently meant to symbolize that synthesis of church and home which reconciles in a higher structure the antithetical goals of the Master Builder's previous efforts in behalf of mankind. Not nearly so clear is the question of what it is, precisely, that Hilde requires of her aging lover. The kingdom he had originally promised her, the kingdom of *Appelsinia*, that is to say, of the Orange, is doubtless that Kingdom of the Sun for which so many of Ibsen's characters yearn in vain. Both Hilde and Solness, however, have passed beyond that stage, and Hilde's demands now take a more practical turn. She wants Solness to build her a castle, and she outlines its specifications with the enthusiasm of a demanding, but impecunious client. Her castle must have, she says,

> a frightfully high tower. And right upon the top of the tower there will be a balcony. And that's where I shall stand.
> SOLNESS: How can you wish to stand so high? Doesn't it make you giddy?
> HILDE: I want to stand up there and look down at the others—the ones who build churches! And homes for mothers and fathers and children! And you can come up there and look down too.[76]

The idea appeals to Solness, since it is, after all, his own. He has already expressed his sense of the futility of trying to better the lot of humanity through practical means:

> SOLNESS: Building homes for people is not worth a penny, Hilde.
> HILDE: How can you say that now?
> SOLNESS: Because I realize that people have no use for the homes they live in . . . So when all accounts are closed, I have built

nothing, really. And sacrificed nothing. It all adds up to nothing. Nothing. Nothing.[77]

His despair, however, is only the prelude to a new departure:

SOLNESS: Now I shall build the only thing in which I believe that happiness can exist.
HILDE: Master Builder—you mean our castles in the air.
SOLNESS: Yes, I mean castles in the air.[78]

It would probably serve no useful purpose to attempt any detailed interpretation of this symbolism. What is meant, essentially, is that the poet's dream is a blueprint for the future, and therefore of greater practical utility than any immediately useful effort to improve the conditions of existence. In this manner, it may be, Ibsen meant to justify his own shortcomings as a social force outside the field of literature; but the symbols are vague, and doubtless purposely vague, and it can hardly serve the play to define what the author intentionally left indefinite. Ultimately, it cannot be said with certainty that Solness and Hilde are anything but what they seem—a middle-aged architect coquetting with a young girl on her vacation. These characters cannot be pinned down. The very ambiguity of their relationship is of the essence of the fantasy:

SOLNESS: How have you come to be what you are, Hilde?
HILDE: How did you make me what I am? [79]

Whether Hilde is a doctor's daughter, or a figment of the imagination; another aspect of Solness, or his youth's ideal; the embodiment of young emancipated womanhood, or the emergent soul of Norway; or all of these together, she fulfills her dramatic function admirably. It is her function to tease the mind of the hero, and with it the mind of the spectator, not toward any certainty, but into the doubtful labyrinth of surmise which is, for the symbolist, the *locus* of the poetic experience. *The Master Builder*, obviously, is of a different order of poetry than *Brand* or *Peer Gynt*; no one can say it is less rich nor, for all its vagueness, less meaningful. It does, however, mark the extreme of Ibsen's venture beyond the frontiers of reality. The next play was not so daring.

Little Eyolf was written in Oslo during the summer of 1894, and published in Copenhagen in time, as usual, for the December trade. It is not to be numbered, perhaps, among Ibsen's masterpieces; but if there were any doubt about its authorship, the scenes involving the Rat Wife and the death of Eyolf would amply attest the genius of the writer. It is difficult to say exactly what *Little Eyolf* was intended to be; but there is reason to assume it was an attempt to answer the growing demand for psychological drama, an effort to explore in the theatre those areas which so far had been the exclusive province of the psychological novelists in France.

The dramatic connotations of this play are far from mysterious. The basic situation involves the portrayal of a state of emotional bankruptcy, the predicament of a self-centered man in a situation calculated to excite the deepest feelings. The play is, in this sense, a development of the terminal situation of *The Wild Duck*, transformed and enriched during the process of revision with useful elements derived from *The Master Builder, Rosmersholm,* and *Hedda Gabler.* Conformably with its antecedents, it portrays comically, in a tragic situation, what is essentially a tragic figure—a man with a strong sense of vocation, but no vocation.

The protagonist, Allmers, is a writer without talent who has married a beautiful, highly sexed woman of great wealth. He has now arrived at the point where she no longer attracts him physically. The child of this marriage, Eyolf, has been crippled in circumstances which have aroused deep guilt-feelings in the minds of the parents. The child is a reproach to them; secretly, his mother wishes him dead. But when he is drowned, his death comes between them like a wall. It is another illustration of the sort of psychic crime which Strindberg was to make the subject of *Crime and Crime* some four years later, and there are, indeed, scenes in that play which might almost serve as caricatures of the scenes of mutual recrimination in *Little Eyolf.* Ibsen's play involves, however, a further complication. Allmers, though he feels deeply obligated to his wife, is really in love with his supposed half-sister, whose boyish traits he has exaggerated in order, very likely, to obscure the incestuous nature of his affection. In his mind, also, there is a certain identification between his sister and the crippled boy—they share the name of Eyolf.

The play had an interesting development. The Allmers of the first draft was not the comic figure of the final version. As he was first conceived, he was a respected and prolific writer of philosophical works, who had published much, but failed to complete his masterpiece when he realized it suffered from an essential defect. This character—originally named Skioldhejm—was a frank and earnest man who did not take himself seriously, and was not above scolding himself for indulging childish fancies that he had some great mission to achieve in this world. His wife, also, was not at first the passionate and possessive figure she later became, but a woman of quite normal attributes. Little Eyolf was not a cripple, but merely a delicate child. The ironic quality which gives the play its special flavor was as yet entirely lacking.[80]

The first version of Little Eyolf was a melodrama. In the second draft, Ibsen retouched his characters so that Allmers became pompous and empty, and his life's work, "the great thick book on Human Responsibility," was reduced to a stack of blank paper on which, it is clear, nothing will ever be written. It therefore serves, like Hjalmar Ekdal's great invention, the function of a livsløgnen, a "life-lie." Allmers's sense of dedication, however, goes deeper than Hjalmar's. When his lack of productivity becomes apparent even to himself, he generously renounces his literary mission in order to undertake the education of little Eyolf, who is now to become his father's masterpiece. The premature death of the boy deprives Allmers of this excuse also for his passivity. It then becomes necessary for him to look outside himself for a mission with which to justify his existence. The fact that in the end he finds a solution makes the play unique among Ibsen's mature dramas.

In spite of the optimistic ending, Ibsen treats his hero with scant courtesy. Allmers is depicted as a neurotic, pretentious man of considerable sensitivity, comically self-centered, whose manifold shortcomings are brought sharply into view by the melodramatic postures he affects. Before his marriage to Rita, this man, we are given to understand, was a brilliant student who worked hard to support his half-sister, Asta. Either this aspect of Allmers is vestigial from Ibsen's first version of the character, or the implication is that a rich marriage has ruined him. At any rate, it was a brilliant dramatic feat to exhibit such a character in a situation in which he is expected to feel the deepest sorrow, and it is by turns funny and profoundly pathetic to contemplate the shifts through which poor Allmers tries to rise emotionally to the occasion.[81]

A father's sorrow at the loss of a beloved child is a commonplace of the theatre, a scene so well crystallized by time that it may be considered the tragic counterpart of a *lazzo* of the *commedia dell'arte*. The distress, however, of one who ardently feels the need of a sorrow he is incapable of feeling makes a very curious dramatic situation, belonging to that no-man's land between tragedy and farce in which Ibsen found himself most at ease as a writer. The scenes in which Allmers's embarrassment is portrayed gain unusual richness from the fact that Allmers seems to be observing his own reactions with a certain astonishment. The scene, for example, between Asta and Allmers on the shore of the fjord in Act Two necessarily borders on the tragic:

ALLMERS: . . . Before you came to me, here I sat, torturing myself
            unspeakably with this crushing, gnawing sorrow—
ASTA: Yes?
ALLMERS: And would you believe it, Asta—? Hm.
ASTA: Well?
ALLMERS: In the midst of all the agony, I found myself speculating
            on what we should have for dinner today.

The characterization of Rita, on the other hand, is perfectly direct. She is a forthright woman of more than usual sensuality, and she quite matches Allmers in her egotism. Both she and Allmers are honest people; but in the scenes in which Ibsen causes Allmers and Rita to strip each other of their pretenses, most of what is truly sincere comes from her.

The early scenes in Act One, involving the little crippled boy, are certainly sentimental, but in the last act Ibsen's dialogue achieves that toughness of fibre which characterizes his best work. The play involves the barest minimum of action. After Eyolf's death, except for the rudimentary sub-plot, there is nothing but discussion. It is as if the play were in fact a tableau—the husband and wife eternally exposed to the gaze of the great open eyes of the drowned child, and this, most likely, was the germinal image of the play and the determining factor in its outcome.

Ibsen told Count Prozor that the Rat Wife was patterned after an old woman who came to kill rats at the school he attended as a boy at Skien. "She carried a little dog in a bag and it was said that children had been drowned through following her." It is impossible not to admire the artistry with which Ibsen adapted this fairy-tale character to his needs. The idea of women luring men to their destruction through some obscene magic appears, indeed, to have quite captured Ibsen's imagination during this period. Rita "lured" Allmers to her on the fatal day when little Eyolf was crippled. Mrs. Wilton "lures" Erhart to Hinkel's party in *John Gabriel Borkman*. The Rat Wife, however, is more closely related to the "helpers and servers" of *The Master Builder*. She is a Swedenborgian Rat Wife; and the implication is that she comes in response to Rita's unexpressed summons to rid the house of the little creeping creature that infests it.

The idea that our moral responsibility extends even to the dimly apprehended currents of irrational desire—by no means new to Ibsen—was to become a cardinal element in Strindberg's dramatic system. For Strindberg this idea had moral and metaphysical implications of far-reaching significance. For Ibsen, it was mainly of psychological interest, as a source of the irrational feelings of guilt to which his characters so frequently react. Even with him, however, such ideas bordered on the mystical; and as time went on he used them quite deliberately to evoke the atmosphere of half-reality which suffuses his later plays. It is easy to see that the mysterious coloring of the Rat-Wife scenes, reminiscent of the technique of Poe, is related to the more subtle shading which Ibsen had given his symbolist play of two years before.

The Master Builder ends on a strangely convincing note of affirmation, but the end of Little Eyolf, with all its talk of heights and stars, is far from persuasive. Ibsen was perhaps at a loss to find a suitable resolution for a situation the hopelessness of which was implied from the beginning. According to the logic of the theatre, the obvious solution would be to manage for these characters a purgation of their selfishness through the misfortune which was its consequence. Such would certainly have been the canonical outcome of Second Empire drama, with its characteristic sentimentality and its obligatory moral lesson. It is much to Ibsen's credit that for many years he resisted such facile solutions; but in the case of Little Eyolf, seemingly, the cliché was inescapable, and he brought the play to an end with the traditional fifth-act scene of repentance and reformation. Little Eyolf thus concludes with an embarrassing display of dramatic rhetoric. This outcome would be even more distasteful than it is were it not for the suspicion that, in ending the play as he does, Ibsen was perhaps having his customary little joke at the expense of his characters, and perhaps at ours also.

In his review of the first English performance of John Gabriel Borkman on May 3, 1896, George Bernard Shaw took exception to the shabbiness of the New Century Theatre production, but even more to W. H. Vernon's old-fashioned direction of the play:

The traditional stage-management of tragedy ignores realism . . . it lends itself to people talking at each other rhetorically from opposite sides of the stage, taking long sweeping walks up to their "points," striking attitudes in the focus of the public vision with an artificiality which, instead of being concealed, is not only disclosed, but insisted on—[82]

In taking the director to task for his lack of realism, however, Shaw did both the director and the play some injustice. Of all Ibsen's realistic plays, John Gabriel Borkman is the most artificial, the most contrived, and the most apt for a stylized presentation. Its action is firmly compressed into the space of three hours, with the usual resulting improbabilities. Its effects are operatic; its structure, classically symmetrical. It was, evidently, a forthright attempt at bourgeois tragedy in the grand style.

The four last plays which Ibsen wrote were all more or less frankly experimental in nature. Each explored a new avenue of approach, and while Ibsen did not entirely lose touch with realism in any of them, it is clear that in each he took a step further from the photographic technique in which he had so far specialized. In these years, Ibsen appears to have come in some measure under the influence of Strindberg. He disliked Strindberg, and spoke of him slightingly. For his part, Strindberg had, as we have noted, constituted Ibsen his arch-enemy, and assigned to him a flattering share of responsibility for the decay of European civilization. Nevertheless, in 1895, Ibsen bought a portrait of Strindberg by Christian Krohg, and hung it on the study wall of his apartment on Drammensveien in Oslo.[83] Its "devilish eyes" fascinated him. He wrote: "I am not now able to write a word without having that madman staring down at me."

In 1898 Strindberg sent him a copy of To Damascus II for his seventieth birthday, with the inscription: "To the Master, from whom I have learned much." Contrary to his custom, Ibsen read it through attentively. It would be difficult to show that this extraordinary work had anything like a direct influence on the older poet, or, indeed, any influence. Nevertheless, by this time Strindberg had become a figure of unmistakable importance, and it is possible that Ibsen had felt his pressure perhaps a half-dozen years earlier. It is certainly tempting to conjecture that in Solness' relation to young Ragnar Brovik there is some reflection of Ibsen's relation to this rising young author who also thought of himself as an architect of ideas.

John Gabriel Borkman began to take shape in Ibsen's mind in the spring of 1896. At the end of August, the first draft was finished.

The revision took seven and a half weeks, and by the middle of October the manuscript was ready for the printer.

The theme was one that preoccupied Ibsen with increasing insistence as he grew older—the incompatibility of the desire for success and the need for happiness. The issue as between happiness and power, or, as Carlyle had put it, happiness and blessedness, had interested many before Ibsen first took it up in *Brand*. Milton and Goethe had given it their attention; Blake, Shelley, and Byron had developed it; Carlyle had given it popular currency. In Ibsen's time, Nietzsche brought it once again into focus, and it was soon to provide Shaw with one of his most useful dramatic formulas. In Ibsen's mind, happiness was identified, we have seen, with the pagan world. It was the classic *summum bonum*, static and perfect in itself. The will to power was, on the other hand, romantic, dynamic, Faustian. It symbolized the striving of modern man for self-realization, and readily connected itself with the evolutionary idea of progress; but it was connected also with the senseless drive of which Maximus speaks in *Emperor and Galilean*, the Schopenhauerian Will. In both *Brand* and *Peer Gynt*, Ibsen had contrasted the happy Horatian life with the restless urge to extend oneself as far as possible in the world, the need to realize one's personality at any cost. The issue went deep. As Ibsen appears to have understood it, it represented the conflict between what we should now call the passive and aggressive aspects of the soul, and its resolution was a matter of temperament quite beyond the power of the individual to alter or to remedy, a kind of destiny.

Like *Ghosts*, *John Gabriel Borkman* is a play of the dead. The dramatic conflict is ostensibly the struggle of two sisters, Ella and Gunhild, for the love, or at least the custody, of young Erhart, Borkman's son. In this struggle is recapitulated their former rivalry for the love of the father. Their struggle, however, is pointless. From the beginning, Erhart is lost to them both; and John Gabriel has deeper interests at heart than the love of woman. It has been their lot, therefore, to sacrifice their lives for nothing, and

when at the end of the play these women join hands over the body
of the man they loved, the operatic gesture has the ironic irrel-
evance that is characteristic of Ibsen's sense of tragedy.

The play, in fact, centers on John Gabriel. On the scale of
bourgeois drama, he is a titanic figure at the end of life—the
dominant metaphor is that of the sick wolf padding to and fro
in its cage. Though he is actually a heroic version of old Ekdal in
The Wild Duck, the difference between the two characters is
emphatic. Ekdal, the old hunter, has accepted defeat, and has become sodden and pathetic. Borkman has lost neither his vigor
nor his avidity; it is only that he has taken refuge in madness, or
something near it. Like Ekdal, he has been destroyed by a man
who is now wealthy and respected; but he has not made peace
with his enemy. He has preserved his pride and his hope to the last,
and still considers himself dangerous. Thus, while Ekdal is no
more than a marginal character, Borkman is presented with complete centrality, and easily bears the weight of the action.

In adapting the story of old Ekdal to his present purpose, Ibsen
changed its character radically. Both men were betrayed by scoundrels, but the source of John Gabriel's misfortunes is entirely in
himself. Sixteen years before the beginning of the play, he bar-
tered his love and his chance of happiness to Lawyer Hinkel in
exchange for his support in furthering his career. The power he
gained in this manner he misused in a reckless bid for greater
power; and at the critical moment, Hinkel betrayed him and
ruined him. It is thoroughly consistent with John Gabriel's character that he should have staked his honor as well as his happiness
in order to win the sort of greatness he coveted, and he does not
at all regret the crime which put an end to his career. He is now
quite mad; but his situation in the end would perhaps have been
much the same had he been eminently sane and successful like
Consul Bernick in *Pillars of Society*, a luckier man than he. As
it is, Borkman is drawn in the broadest strokes—a man whose need
for personal fulfillment is boundless and who, even on the brink

of eternity, clings tenaciously to the hope that one day the world will understand how great he is, and how necessary.

Obviously *John Gabriel Borkman* is a study of ambition, an application of the syllogism of *Brand* to the case of an industrialist. This industrialist is given unusual magnitude, like Brand himself. John Gabriel is repeatedly referred to as a king. He speaks of his kingdom, and has the majesty appropriate to his state. The fall of such a figure comes as close to the fall of a prince as one can come in middle-class life, and in every detail his situation recalls the contours of the antique genre. But whereas the line of antique tragedy was usually uncomplicated by a subsidiary action, Ibsen followed seventeenth-century practice by larding the main action with a contrasting sub-plot, and this secondary plot lacks any sort of grandeur.

By comparison with the noble figure of John Gabriel, the counter-image of his son Erhart does not sustain interest. Erhart's need for happiness is as great as John Gabriel's need for power. He is perfectly willing to sacrifice his career in exchange for a few years of pleasure with Mrs. Wilton and her successors. The two men are thus disposed symmetrically with respect to the practical mean. In Ibsen's system, they represent the extremes of personality, and while both are entirely believable characters, the play suffers from the classic, but entirely obvious, symmetry of the design.

As the play is arranged, Borkman and his son balance each other in the composition. The opposition of Gunhild and Ella, twins of antithetical temperament, adds yet another symmetrical pair, and the pathetic figure of Foldal, whom John Gabriel both supports and leans upon, completes what must be considered a very monumental grouping. The final touch seems superfluous. As John Gabriel loses his son, and Foldal his daughter, in the same turn of the action, the two bereaved men are presented in still another balanced figure, so neat that the ultimate effect is rather choreographic than dramatic. Doubtless in the eighteenth century this type of composition would not have seemed unduly ingenious; but in a period which had turned definitely from classical configuration and balance to the asymmetrical groupings of naturalism, *John Gabriel Borkman* was an anachronism.

The elements which made up Ibsen's intellectual baggage were, as we have seen, remarkably few, and one marvels at the ingenuity with which he made use of them. The idea of the *livsløgnen* which served so well in *The Wild Duck* and *Little Eyolf* is also the mainspring of *John Gabriel Borkman*. John Gabriel is kept alive by the idea of the imminent restoration of his reign. Each time there is a knock on the door, he draws himself up to receive suitably the delegation of repentant citizens who have come, so he believes, to reinstate him in his vanished state. He has thoroughly rehearsed the conditions he will impose, even the Napoleonic posture he will assume, and the speech of acceptance. Foldal, similarly, ekes out a miserable existence in the hope of having his tragedy one day performed on the stage. The ladies cling resolutely to their own illusions—Gunhild lives by her faith in Erhart's "mission"; Ella, by her belief in his love.

In *The Wild Duck* the characters are mercifully permitted to preserve what they can of their illusions. In *John Gabriel Borkman* the characters are stripped ruthlessly bare, and the malicious sparkle of humor with which Ibsen habitually relieves his sentimentality is not often in evidence. Even in the grandiose poses which John Gabriel strikes there is only a touch of mockery; the figure is too poignant to be sneered at, and too haughty for compassion.

In the spring of 1898 Ibsen saw *Brand* performed at the Dagmar Theatre in Copenhagen. It was the first time he had seen it, and he was deeply moved by the production. "This," he told the actress Oda Neilson, who sat beside him at the performance, "is all my youth." He lay awake most of that night, we are told, thinking about *Brand* in connection with his next play. It was not until the beginning of 1899, however, that he began work on the play called *The Day of Resurrection*. He worked at it very slowly. By early fall, when the first draft was finished, the title had changed; the play was now called *When the Dead Awaken*. Some months later, the revised draft was complete. The title was now *When We Dead Awaken, A Dramatic Epilogue*.

The relation of *Brand* to *When We Dead Awaken* is quite evident. Both plays have to do with the tragedy of the dedicated man. Like Brand, who could quite as well have been "a sculptor, or a politician, or a priest," [84] the sculptor Rubek is of the All-or-Nothing turn of mind. In his youth he had devoted himself utterly to his career, had sacrificed to it his love and all his chance of happiness. Now, in his age, he has come to realize that his vocation has cheated him of his life. In this he recalls Brand, but Rubek comes closer to Solness than to Brand. Brand finds in the avalanche the goal toward which all his life he has been working. His mission is a failure. His life is wasted. Rubek, on the other hand, has had all the success a man can have; but he has come to loathe the praise that is showered upon him:

RUBEK: The world knows nothing. It understands nothing.
MAJA: At least they can sense something . . .
RUBEK: Something that isn't there—oh yes! Something I've never
    imagined, yes. And that is what they all go mad about. (He
    growls to himself) What is the use of working oneself to
    death to please the masses, the mob, the whole world? [85]

Since his great group, *The Day of Resurrection*, was finished, Rubek has devoted himself single-mindedly to the artist's vendetta against society. His inspiration having failed, he compensates for it by devoting himself to portraiture:

RUBEK: And I find it intensely amusing. Superficially, there are these
    striking likenesses, as they call them, at which people gape
    in admiration. But behind these masks, I have carved the
    righteous and estimable faces of horses, the stubborn muzzles
    of donkeys, the lop ears and shallow brows of dogs, the fat
    chaps of swine, and the dull and brutal foreheads of oxen . . .
    All nice domestic animals, Maja . . . And these disingenuous
    works of art are what our honest citizens commission and
    pay for in good faith and solid cash.[86]

The *Resurrection Day* group was begun under the influence
of Irene, his model, who offered herself to him body and soul in
his youth, and was rejected as an irrelevancy when he had no
further use for her. She vanished, and Rubek went on to finish
his group. Then his creative power faded. In a sense, he died:

RUBEK: (Taps himself on the chest) In here, Maja, in here. There
is a little casket, with an unpickable lock, and there all my
visions lie. When she vanished from my life, the lock snapped
shut. She had the key, and she took it with her. You, my
poor Maja, had no key. Therefore everything that is in it
lies unused. And the years pass, and all that wealth lies there,
and I cannot touch it.[87]

In these words, it is permissible to suppose that Rubek expresses
the despair of Ibsen at the thought of the wealth of poetry within
himself from which he felt forever debarred for lack of proper
inspiration. This nuance we catch for the first time in *The Master
Builder* when Solness announces joyfully that now that his princess
has come to inspire him, he feels his powers renewed, and is ready
to embark on a new career. We hear it again when John Gabriel,
at the end of his life, issues forth with the love of his youth to conquer the mountains which have so far defied him. Rubek voices, in
addition, the more familiar complaint of a wasted life, the sacrifice
of happiness to a vain ideal. The play thus involves two different
but closely related ideas, both of which have a part in *Brand*. In
sacrificing love, the hero not only destroys his life's happiness, but
also his highest creative possibilities. In realizing himself fully,
the artist must draw deeply upon his fund of will, but even more
deeply upon his *conto caritatis*. To be lacking in this respect is to
be lacking in all. "When we dead awaken," says Rubek, "what do
we see then?" Irene answers: "We see that we have never lived." [88]

Rubek, the artist, and Ulfhejm, the bear hunter, are conceived
as contraries; but in one way they are alike. Both have been cheated
of happiness, the one by art, the other by life; consequently, each
in his way has become savage and hostile, an enemy of society. The
play manages a rearrangement of these wasted lives. The man of

action, who has become hateful because his beloved betrayed him, attempts to patch up his life with the help of Maja, who has no aptitude for the life of art. For Rubek, on the other hand, Maja is a source of intolerable boredom, and he attempts to resolve the paradox of the artist in the perilous company of his Irene, who has tracked him down implacably, as Hilde tracked down Solness. As in *John Gabriel Borkman*, the characters are thus disposed symmetrically, two by two, and the action has a choric movement. In the end, the two pairs of characters, conceived as opposites, are brought together in what amounts to a *scène à faire*. The resolution is rapid. Ulfhejm and Maja climb down into the safety of the valley to try their luck at domestic life. Rubek and Irene climb upward through the mist to celebrate their wedding festival on the peak that glitters above them in the sunlight. The symbols are clear. Life, with its happiness, is for those who are suited for it. Art, with its torment, is for those who can endure it. "I was born to be an artist," Rubek says. "And do what I may, I shall never be anything else." [89]

Such, at least, was Ibsen's idea when he completed the first draft of the play in September, 1899, under the pleasant influence of the young dancer Rosa Fitinghoff. But by November 21st, when the final version was finished, a slight, but significant addition had been made to the ending. Rubek and Irene climb, as before, toward the sunrise. Maja is heard singing happily far down in the ravine. "Suddenly a roar like thunder is heard above," and in a moment Rubek and Irene are buried beneath the plunging avalanche of snow. The nun who attends the madwoman makes the sign of the cross, saying, "Pax vobiscum." The last thing we hear is Maja's song floating up softly from the depths.

Evidently the symmetrical solution of his first version did not please the author, and he came to the conclusion that such characters as Rubek and Irene could not resolve their difficulties in the clear light of the sunrise on the mountain peak. Rubek and Irene were brought to an end, therefore, precisely as were Brand and the mad girl Gerd. In the age of naturalism, very likely, no other conclusion was possible. From the naturalistic viewpoint, inherently pessimistic, the doors we close in youth do not open in our age. For this artist who had come to see too clearly the vanity of fame, the pursuit of happiness could be only a source of danger.

The story of Rubek thus turns out to be a variation of the story of Solness, but even more sad. In Ibsen's view such men are morally disturbed beyond the possibility of regeneration. They are heroes for whom the only possibility is an interesting death and peace in a better world. How far Ibsen identified himself and his fate with these fantasies of his later years remains an open question, but, one would say, far.

When Ibsen was sixty-seven, four years before he wrote *When We Dead Awaken*, Georg Brandes sent him an essay on the stimulating effect of Marianne von Willemer on the sixty-six-year-old Goethe. Ibsen was impressed. "When I think of the quality that characterizes Goethe's work during that period," he wrote Brandes, "I mean the sense of renewed youth, I ought to have guessed that he must have been graced with some such revelation, some such reminiscence of beauty, as his meeting with Marianne von Willemer." [90]

He himself had hardly lacked for similar opportunities, but it was apparently not permitted him, anymore than his characters, to succeed in love. After Emilie Bardach, there had been Helene Raff, a young painter; then the young pianist Hildur Andersen. In April of 1898 he met the dancer Rosa Fitinghoff at Skansen in Stockholm, and at once struck up a friendship, which was nourished, through the succeeding months, mainly through the post. The following April, Miss Fitinghoff sent him a blue anemone to mark the anniversary of their first meeting, and he dutifully wrote his thanks, remarking that he always glanced at her letters on his desk before starting his work for the day. As far as we know there was not much more.

The play he composed in these days under the fiery eye of Strindberg, cannot be said to be a great play, or even a very good play, but it has the fascination of a work of genius. Evidently it was written with difficulty, and with a great sense of urgency. Ibsen was not well. He had often feared the consequences of prolonged reflection, and now he feared, we are told, that he would lose his mind before he finished his work. In spite of this, *When We Dead Awaken* shows surprisingly little evidence of any diminution of creative powers; in fact, it has some of his best writing. It is perhaps lacking in the firmness of outline and sharpness of detail which characterizes the work of his middle period, but there is every reason to suppose that this vagueness was intentional, for the play has a Maeterlinckian quality that is quite new in Ibsen. The dialogue is oddly repetitious, and not quite coherent. The account of his life which Rubek gives Maja in Act One is not consistent with the parallel account in Act Two. One never knows what really took place; and it is almost certain this was the desired effect.

Irene is a figure out of Villiers de l'Isle-Adam. Her appearance, her extraordinary history, her mysterious attendant, her obsession with murder, and the proficiency she demonstrates with the sharp, thin stiletto she carries with her even to bed, all raise questions which Ibsen did not bother to answer. The question of her age, which becomes important when the role is cast, has been the subject of much speculation. Ibsen said she was twenty-eight, and she was played at that age in the original production; but when Gunnar Heiberg demonstrated that by Rubek's arithmetic she must be forty at least, Ibsen agreed readily that she must be forty.[91] Others have made her older still: Weigand thought she was forty-eight; Caspar Wrede suggests she might be sixty-five. These calculations indicate the inconvenience of attempting to reduce to realistic terms a play which was obviously intended to be read as poetry. Irene is as old as the ideal of one's youth needs to be when one is no longer young. For Ibsen the ideal was preferably eighteen, but it was enough that the woman was desirable and unattainable:

Hohes, schmerzliches Glück—um das Unerreichbare zu dringen.[92]

Similarly, it is of no importance how old Rubek is. It suffices that he is past his prime, and has not seen Irene for many years.

It hardly matters how many. It is interesting that in this interval Irene has been made to go through all the vicissitudes of a heroine of the Arabian Nights, but it would obviously be a complete waste of time to subject her story to close analysis. One does not study dreams with a computer. Her story is certainly puzzling; but it would have detracted from its mystery to make it entirely sensible, and Ibsen wisely blurred the outlines.

The armature on which *When We Dead Awaken* was hung had no great novelty for Ibsen. A man who is bored with his domestic arrangements meets once again the woman he might have married—if we reverse the sexual pattern, it is the theme also of *The Lady from the Sea, John Gabriel Borkman, Hedda Gabler.* In the present case, this well-studied situation was given a highly original form. The lady out of the past was once the sculptor's model. She is vengeful—she feels that in using her body when he did not desire her love, the sculptor prostituted her. As it seems to her, it was her form—that is to say, her soul—which Rubek infused into the clay. Thus he sent her out into the world a soulless thing, and her transformation was the result of a terrible alchemy —the clay figure which embodied her spirit came alive for all the world; but the woman turned to clay. It is entirely permissible to see in this line of reasoning—in general, so unlike Ibsen's usual train of thought—some trace of Strindberg. But these are, after all, romantic commonplaces.

If we rationalize this story, it becomes a typical tale of the 1890's. The sculptor Rubek apparently took a young girl from her family for what in 1899 would be considered immoral purposes, to serve, that is, as a nude model. The girl concurred in this seduction because she was in love with the sculptor, but when she had finished posing, she realized with a shock that the young man had only a professional interest in her, and that she was expected henceforth to fend for herself. In these circumstances, she felt she had no alternative but to accept a life of degradation as a professional model, or worse. Thus Irene was forced into the kind of existence which brought her eventually both riches and madness.

For this injury to her womanhood, she has avenged herself amply upon mankind in general, but her craving for vengeance is not yet satisfied—it is now necessary for her to destroy the man who, she believes, was responsible for her downfall. In her terrible resentment, she is reminiscent of Ella in *John Gabriel Borkman*, who was treated in somewhat analogous fashion, and who has never forgiven the man she once loved:

ELLA: You are a murderer! You have committed the mortal sin!
BORKMAN: (Retreats from the piano) You are raving, Ella.
ELLA: You have killed love in me! (She moves toward him) Do you understand what that means? The Bible speaks of a mysterious sin for which there is no forgiveness. I have never before understood what that meant. Now I understand. The sin for which there is no forgiveness is to murder love in a human being.[93]

As a result of this crime, Ella says, she has lost the possibility of loving anything, people, animals, flowers; she has lost even the possibility of feeling charity. Ella, however, has no need of exacting any further retribution. Borkman is already ruined. All she wants now is to care for his son, which should have rightly been hers.

Irene represents an extreme extension of this character; and in these terms her strange manoeuvres with the sharp, thin stiletto become intelligible. Although she hated Rubek because he was an artist and not a man, Irene loved the "child" of their spiritual marriage, just as Ella loved Borkman's child:

IRENE: . . . But that statue of wet and living clay, her I loved—as she rose out of that raw and formless mass, a human child with a soul. She was *our* creation, our child. Mine and yours.
RUBEK: In spirit and in truth, yes.
IRENE: It is for our child's sake that I have made this long pilgrimage.
RUBEK: For that marble image?
IRENE: Call it what you will. I call it our child.[94]

It is when Irene understands that Rubek changed his conception of the Resurrection Day figure that she first draws her knife against him and, as he describes the somewhat extraordinary

group he eventually completed—apparently after the manner of
Rodin—in which her figure no longer occupies the foreground,
he comes very close to physical injury. But when Rubek speaks
of the figure of himself with which he has replaced her in the group,
a figure weighed down with guilt, the symbol of regret for a wasted
life, she foregoes her vengeance for the time, realizing that he has
already suffered beyond anything she can inflict upon him at the
moment. There is, however, more to come:

RUBEK: . . . Help me to live again!
IRENE: Empty dreams. Idle, dead dreams. Our life together cannot
be resurrected.
RUBEK: Then let us go on with our game.
IRENE: Our game, yes. Let us go on with our game.

It is clear that their game is to end in death. His mood is hopeful.
Hers is tender, but consistently murderous. She is very much the
femme fatale:

IRENE: Would you like to spend a summer night on the mountain?
RUBEK: (Spreading wide his arms) Yes! Yes! Come!
IRENE: My love! My lord and master!
RUBEK: Oh, Irene!
IRENE: (Smiling as she gropes for her dagger) It will only be an
episode.[95]

The symbolism is transparent. On the realistic plane, it is a
question of revenge, the retribution of a woman with an *idée fixe.*
On the symbolic plane, it is the rejected ideal of his youth which
leads the artist to a height he can no longer scale alone, and from
which there is no escape for him once he has scaled it. It is precisely the same with Solness, save that Solness' sin is not so clear.
In the case of Rubek, everything is simple. When love was offered
in its tender aspect, Rubek rejected it. What he finds now in the
arms of Irene is that devastating rush of cosmic passion which in
Brand called itself *deus caritatis.* Such is the end of their brief
resurrection.

As Ibsen indicated, *When We Dead Awaken* may be taken as an epilogue to his work in the theatre. It represents the terminal phase of his approach to the problem of *l'homme engagé*, and his final word on the subject of the creative personality, two topics which occupied his mind consistently during the period that separates *Brand* from *When We Dead Awaken*. It is astonishing how little Ibsen's viewpoint changed in all this time. In Ibsen's mind, the hero, whether as artist, scientist, industrialist, preacher, or social reformer, is inevitably a tragic figure faced with a mortal dilemma, which Rubek calls his "hell." This figure has its comic aspects. They are emphasized in the case of Dr. Stockmann, minimized in the case of John Gabriel, but the implication is the same: complete dedication makes a man in some degree ridiculous.

Such complete devotion to duty as Ibsen's heroes feel necessarily excludes that displacement of the ego which is the prime condition of love. A man cannot be exclusively dedicated to his calling if he is emotionally identified with another person, nor can he realize himself fully unless he is fully self-contained. The rejection of love, however, does violence to his deepest life. Ultimately, in every field of human activity, it is love that opens the way to one's highest fulfillment. Without love it is impossible to reach out beyond the self; and the self, as Peer Gynt discovers, is, of itself, nothing. Love, above all, releases the soul from self-absorption, and enables the poet, and the hero, to see life in an aspect which justifies the poet's creation, and the hero's activity. Thus, love is an obstacle to complete dedication; but without love one cannot achieve the goal. This, in Ibsen's view, is the paradox of the engaged personality.

At bottom, the nucleus of this complex situation is perhaps nothing more than the traditional conflict of love and duty, the mainstay of the seventeenth-century theatre. In that typically chivalric situation, the hero accepts with tragic grandeur the consequences of the dedication which robs him of felicity. For him that is the end of the matter, and the play leaves him monumentally posed for the admiration of his fellows. In Ibsen's version of tragedy, however, this is the beginning, not the end of the action. The initial choice involves no great effort for his heroes; but the time inevitably comes when outraged nature calls them to account, and for Ibsen, it is at this point that the tragic action begins.

In Ibsen's plays, the emphasis is thus shifted from the moment of decision, which was formerly the crisis of the tragic situation, to the consequence many years later, so that the situation which was formerly considered the kernel of the drama is now uncovered only in retrospect, and what is played on the stage is actually its aftermath. From a formal point of view, the net result is simply a translation of the axis of the story, a shift in the point of attack further along the line of narrative. From the standpoint of substance, however, this shift is of some consequence. In the tradition of regular tragedy, there can be no doubt that in choosing duty rather than happiness, the hero does well. In a world of firm moral outlines, duty and honor necessarily define a man's highest social obligations, and to affirm their claims is to affirm the stability of the hierarchy of values by which our lives are regulated. The hero can have no higher social function than this. To serve this function manfully is to be noble and glorious, and it follows that glory, not happiness, is the lot of great men.

What is essentially at stake, then, in the hero's choice is our faith in the righteousness and permanence of the world order, without which it is possible to define neither greatness nor glory. The right choice of the tragic hero is in each case an act of faith through which, at whatever cost to himself, he affirms the validity of the social ideal, and, ultimately, this is the source of his greatness in our eyes. Consequently, at the heart of tragedy there is always the sacrifice through which the individual assures the wellbeing of the group, and the crisis of tragedy is the moment of this act of faith, the moment of self-immolation on the altar of society.

With the negation of the ideal, this structure collapses. In a world the moral outlines of which have become blurred, such concepts as duty and obligation are reduced to the status of more or less irrational compulsions; honor becomes a matter of personal elegance; and instead of sin, there is only the sense of guilt, which reason can eradicate or assuage. In a relativistic world order, happiness is the only logically defensible goal, and love, with its exclusive power to fix a relationship categorically, is the only constant in the flux of existence. Ibsen's sense of tragedy is thus bound up with the conviction that in a world where all else is vanity, love alone can ensure some measure of happiness; consequently, the loss of love is an irreparable disaster. In the tragedy of the dedicated man, the tragic emphasis is thus shifted from the moment of decision to the moment of comprehension, when the tragic hero attempts to retrieve the irretrievable error which has ruined his life. So it is in *Brand*.

The statement with which Ibsen closed his career as a dramatist thus corresponds precisely with that which initiated it. Love is the soul of humanity, the sun that warms it and gives it life. Without love one is dead. A man may be guilty of every crime and be forgiven, provided he has love; but without love no man has efficacy, and none is saved. This is ancient doctrine, and Ibsen makes use of it without sentimentality. Because of his interest in social questions, and his secret partiality for the writers of the *pièce à thèse* from whom he learned his craft, Ibsen seems to us primarily a social dramatist. The difficulty of this viewpoint is that it makes his drama, taken as a whole, incomprehensible as well as inconsistent. Ibsen was essentially a poet of love. From this point of view, the whole body of his work, from *Love's Comedy* to *When We Dead Awaken* reveals the "absolutely consistent development" which he once assured Lorentz Dietrichson it had.

The idea of the woman who is outraged in her inmost self by the man she loves, and is thereby transformed into a destroying angel, was Ibsen's most useful dramatic concept in the last period of his career. The idea did not come from Strindberg, but from Hebbel, and behind the vengeful ladies of Hebbel's plays, Rhodope and Mariamne, we may discern Clytemnestra and Medea, the outraged heroines of Euripides. The first clear example of this type of character in Ibsen's drama is Nora in A *Doll's House*. It is certainly a far cry from the outraged Nora to the outraged Irene. Twenty years separate them. But there is a sufficient similarity to enable us to understand why it was that in reply to a question regarding *When We Dead Awaken*, directed to him in 1899 by the newspaper *Verdens Gang*, Ibsen wrote: ". . . all I meant by 'epilogue' in this context was that the play forms an epilogue to the series of plays which began with A *Doll's House* and which now ends with *When We Dead Awaken*. . . . It completes the cycle, and makes an entity of it, and now I am finished with it. If I write anything more, it will be in another context; perhaps, too, in another form."

The essential thought of *When We Dead Awaken*, however, reaches back further than A *Doll's House*. It is fully formulated in *Brand* and *Peer Gynt*: life must be lived somewhere between All and Nothing; at the extremes there is only death and despair. For this reason, it is intimated, neither the hero nor the artist can live like other people. It is their doom to live on the brink of existence, in a world beyond life; and they will never in all eternity free themselves, Rubek says, and be granted resurrection. When these dead awaken, their lives are over. Rubek accepts his destiny with pride as well as resignation: he was born to be an artist. So too Brand was born to be a preacher, Borkman a banker, Solness a builder, Dr. Stockmann a reformer—each of these men is tied to a fantasy that leads beyond happiness. For such people, as Ibsen saw it, there is no escape—their calling is their heaven and their hell.

In all likelihood, this line of thought, as we have seen, more or less accurately reflected Ibsen's idea of himself and his career; but it would be naïve to read these plays as a journal of the author's personal experience. It is the playwright's vocation to dramatize himself, but only under the special conditions of the art, and only to the extent that his temper permits. The nature of the fantasy, nevertheless, can hardly fail to mirror in some way the personality of the artist. That is its function.

Until he wrote *The Master Builder*, Ibsen had developed a

superb type of realistic drama with satirical overtones. Toward the end of his life, he felt, apparently, the need to write tragedy. This was not within his province. Tragedy, we have seen, implies faith. In the absence of faith, the tragic is, at the most, pathetic. The permissible limits of the tragic experience are, indeed, surprisingly narrow; they border upon the sentimental, which, on the highest level of art, appears to be completely unacceptable in our cultural environment. There is, however, a form of quasi-tragedy in which we are invited to smile at our emotions before the point of sentimentality is reached. This provides a type of pleasurable experience which is entirely distinct from the pleasure of tragedy, but in some way recalls it. It is on this aesthetic plane that Ibsen excels, and it is mainly this sort of pleasure that his plays give us—the pleasure of a deeply pathetic experience redeemed from mawkishness by our sense of the absurd.

By the time of Ibsen, Dumas *fils* had already developed an eloquent technique of self-expression within the framework of the Scribean play. His manner, however, was characteristically argumentative and oratorical. It was in this style that Ibsen made his debut as a realist, but it was clear even from his early work that he would not stop at this point. His sense of social justice was certainly as well developed as that of Dumas, Augier, or Brieux, but Ibsen was not much interested in social reform. He was what Irene contemptuously accuses Rubek of being—a poet, self-centered; and after *Pillars of Society* his development necessitated a progressively deeper and broader subjective expression. The sequence of plays from *Love's Comedy* to *When We Dead Awaken* may therefore be considered as a process of self-revelation, the result of which is a portrait of the artist, a dynamic likeness, constantly detailed and corrected in accordance with the promptings of his nature.

In the 1860's it was principally along the lines laid down by Baudelaire, through dreams and madness, that the drama could transcend into these hidden areas of the soul which the symbolists desired to explore. In a culture which was thoroughly committed to the rational, all aberrations from the normal and explicable had to be identified as insane. In the first half of the nineteenth century, heroic efforts had been made to escape from the despotism of common sense into the past, the future, and the supernatural. Blake, Coleridge, and Poe, among others, had shown the way to a fantastic wonderland of the spirit, which poets hastened to colonize; but in the theatre the way to the mystical Beyond was not open much before the time of Maeterlinck, and those who were distasted with everyday reality had to content themselves with the medieval fantasies or lyrical robber-dramas of the later romantics. It was, in fact, not until the time of *To Damascus* that it became possible in the theatre to attempt a depiction of the workings of the inner life without recourse to the protective fictions of hallucination and dream. Then, suddenly, a new continent sprang into view which centuries of artistic exploration had so far missed.

Perhaps it was in the direction of *To Damascus* that Ibsen meant to turn when he wrote Count Prozor in the spring of 1900: "If it be granted me to retain the strength of body and mind which I still enjoy, I shall not be able to absent myself for long from the old battlefields. But if I return, I shall come forward with new weapons and new equipment." [96] It was not his destiny to renew the combat. Eleven days after writing this letter, Ibsen suffered a stroke. There was another seizure in January of the following year, and for five years thereafter he was paralyzed and virtually helpless. On May 23, 1906, Ibsen died.

With Ibsen, realism reached its highest perfection as an art form in the theatre, and his manner set the type of the great drama of our time. It is much to the credit of this remarkable man that, in the end, he became dissatisfied with his life's work, and felt that the time had come to begin afresh. From everything he wrote at this time it is clear that he was aware that European drama had reached both a terminus and a point of departure. A new age was dawning for the theatre, an age with which, he knew,

Strindberg was more in touch than he. It was to be an age which would look at nature through the eyes of Cézanne and Van Gogh, and eventually through the eyes of Picasso and Miró, and it is doubtful that Ibsen, so deeply entrenched in the rationalistic tradition of Scribe and Hebbel, could have found the weapons necessary to man the new frontiers. Happily, it was not required of him.

Ibsen belonged to the age of ethical rationalism. Though he repudiated its conclusions, he could not escape its methods. He lived to see the moral and intellectual foundations of art, sapped by the romantics and battered by the philosophers, at last give way. For a time, the supernatural, the abnormal, the artificial, and the occult became the focus of artistic attention. When these ultimately proved to be unfruitful as sources of inspiration, there came the turn of the irrational, the disordered, the undisciplined, and the senseless. In *The Master Builder* and the plays that followed it, Ibsen had indicated the direction the new development would take; but the man who would first strike out into this morass would inevitably be a little mad. Ibsen was too sane a poet to undertake this adventure. It belonged to Strindberg.

Strindberg

IN his grander moments, Strindberg saw himself as the modern equivalent of the universal man of the Renaissance. Like Paracelsus, he had plumbed the mysteries of the universe; like Faust, he had trafficked with the dark powers; like Swedenborg, he had insight into the workings of the elemental forces. He was an alchemist, and made gold. He was a rebel who defied man, and bore the marks of his lifelong tussle with God. He was the great liberator of his time, a martyr and a messiah. His scope was vast; his ambitions, cosmic. The astonishing thing is that, in spite of all this, his capabilities were enormous. He was a megalomaniac who was, in fact, a genius.

Strindberg desired to know everything and to experience everything. After he became acquainted with Nietzsche, he came to the realization that he was a superman, and that his restlessness and his misery, as well as the hostility he invariably aroused in others, were the necessary consequences of his pre-eminence and his power. He had yet another aspect in which he manifested himself willingly to the world, no less grandiose, but somewhat closer to the fact. He was Ishmael, the son of Hagar the bondswoman, the outcast, the disinherited. "I was the son of a servant," says the Unknown in *To Damascus*, "of whom it is written, 'Drive forth the hand-maid with her son, for this son shall not inherit with the son of peace.' " " 'He will be a wild man,' " the Lady adds in the same passage, " 'his hand will be against every man, and every man's hand against him, and against all his brothers.' " [1]

This most romantic of poses was evidently dearer to Strindberg than any other. At any rate, he strove manfully to maintain his status as an outcast as long as he lived, and as matters stood in Sweden during the greater part of his life, this was not difficult. As he grew older and more mellow, and saw his works received with increasing respect, his pose became majestic, imperial; but even to the last he remained Ishmael, the drunkard, the profligate, the scoffer, the son of the servant.

Destiny did not pamper Strindberg. His birth was humble; his childhood, wretched; his character, neurotic and unstable in the extreme. His career was beset with disappointments and frus-trations which would have broken a less resilient nature. In his youth he could not find the money with which to complete his education, and all his life he struggled with poverty. In some respects he was fortunate. He was an extremely intelligent writer, and capable of intense application. Women liked him. He was a handsome man, elegantly dressed, with a high forehead, a magnif-icent mane, a bristling moustache, and glittering eyes. Physically he was not brave; he was, indeed, neurotically fearful, yet his language was bold, and he constantly provoked aggression. In con-sequence, he spent a good deal of his time in terror of reprisals. Aggressive as he was, it is clear that his will to power was not as decisive an influence on his life as his will to suffer; he received the manifold indignities which life showered upon him as his just meed, and the measure of his success. With all this, he had a strain of practical good sense which makes one wonder. He was an outspoken anti-Semite, but this did not in the least prevent him from maintaining cordial relations, through most of the 1880's, with the publisher Karl-Otto Bonnier, whose father, Albert Bonnier, he had caricatured as "Moses" in *The New Kingdom*.

Though his megalomania and his habitual sense of persecution gave his personality a paranoid cast, Strindberg had not that certainty of innocence with which paranoia usually compensates its victims for their sufferings. Between his profound sense of the world's injustice, and the deep conviction of his own guilt, there was an area of uncertainty which he spent much of his literary life in defining, according as his mood was religious, rationalistic, rebellious, or mystical. In these circumstances, he felt all his life an insuperable need to confess, to explain, to justify, to prove, to teach, but, above all, to complain: he was a busy man. An inexhaustible stream of words poured out of him. He wrote as carelessly and as naturally as one breathes, and as copiously, more than anyone can possibly wish to read. His collected works in Landquist's edition run to fifty-five volumes of text, and this by no means includes all that we have from his pen.

These writings range through every possible subject of literary interest. Like Ibsen, Strindberg was a gifted poet. Besides poetry, he wrote novels, short stories, essays, articles, scientific treatises, plays, and innumerable letters. His autobiographical works alone run to ten volumes, the fruit of his conviction, expressed in 1885, that confession is the form of art which comes closest to reality, and that therefore autobiography must eventually supplant the novel. These autobiographical works, couched in novelistic form, were entitled generally in the first volume *The History of the Development of a Soul*.[2]

One might imagine that this extensive biography would be sufficient to furnish a complete commentary on his dramatic writings, but, as Jolivet pointed out, the autobiography is precise only up to 1886, when Strindberg was thirty-seven. Beginning with *Le Plaidoyer d'un fou*, the autobiographical works are only vaguely informative. Some are novels; some are essays. *Le Plaidoyer d'un fou* was written in something akin to madness. *Inferno* is the detailed history of a mystical crisis. *Fagervik och Skamsund* is highly fictional. *Ensam* is a clinical study.[3] From a descriptive viewpoint, the plays are quite as informative as the autobiography, and, so far as the author was concerned, they served a similar end.

In his art, as in life, Strindberg exhibited the most astonishing ingenuity in creating again and again the same neurotic situation, so that, however varied it may seem, at bottom the subject matter of his plays is almost invariably the same. In his historical dramas this situation is necessarily developed surreptitiously and, one might say, accidentally; in the mystical plays it is figured through signs and symbols; in the naturalistic plays, it is set forth and analyzed in a manner intended to recall the technique of the laboratory. But whatever the style or the subject, ultimately the typically Strindbergian pattern takes form, and the characteristically Strindbergian preoccupations come to the fore—the battle of the sexes, the tribulations of the superman, the tussle with God, the power of suggestion, the play of occult forces, the idea of universal history. The amazing variety with which Strindberg was able to put forward the slender stock of ideas which engaged his interest is a proof of the uncanny resourcefulness of the creative personality which is able, in spite of every obstacle, to transform its illness into art.

Although Strindberg's dramatic works, much more obviously than Ibsen's, form a continuous spiritual autobiography, the two men differed completely in the nature of their gifts. Strindberg had neither Ibsen's iron self-control nor his technical command of the medium, his sense of dramatic design, his flair for narrative, or his capacity for invention. On the other hand, he had great power and insight, an invincible compulsion to work, and remarkable originality.

His style is at the opposite pole from that of Ibsen. Strindberg's art is the art of the unbalanced, the disproportionate, the excessive, and immoderate. His characters are generally abstracted and distorted; his situations, overdrawn, hyperbolic, overemphatic. These effects are neither the fruit of an unbalanced mind nor the result of an innocent primitivism. What Strindberg sought in the theatre, if we can take him at his word, was an exaggerated effect, in garish colors, like that of the *images d'Épinal,* a dramatic impression that should be at the same time childishly simple and very strong, and in this respect he approached quite closely the sophisticated naïveté of the post-impressionist painters. The Author's Foreword to *Miss Julie* informs us that his purpose in employing this technique was didactic. It is an interesting rationalization:

Theatre has long seemed to me, in common with much other art, to be a *Biblia pauperum,* a Bible in pictures for those who cannot read writing or print; and I see the playwright as a lay preacher who peddles the ideas of his time in popular form; so popular that the middle classes, which are the mainstay of the theatre audience, may grasp the matter in question without breaking their heads over it.[4]

In accordance with this idea—with its characteristic assumption of superiority—Strindberg generally reduced his action to its simplest terms, juxtaposing his effects so as to bring out most vividly the design he had in mind, with complete disregard for probability or verisimilitude. For this reason, his naturalistic plays, lacking as they are in the ordinary amenities of the craft, have unusual power on the stage; but if they are taken as examples of naturalism, they are bewildering. Their technique is at the same time unnaturally simple and terribly innocent—it is as if we reduced life to the level of a dream. Strindberg's drama has, indeed, a curious fascination, the compelling relevance and urgency of the life we hopefully repress, and it is entirely understandable that in his day he was not always thanked for bringing to mind what people would willingly forget. It has nothing to do with us, we say, it is madness; but this madness of Strindberg poses the question of our own sanity.

In 1869, when, at the age of twenty, Strindberg wrote his first full-length play, Ibsen was already a successful writer, the author of *Brand* and *Peer Gynt.* Strindberg admired these plays very much, and at this time he professed also a great admiration for the works of Björnson. It was in this very year that Ibsen, exasperated by the reception of *Peer Gynt*, turned to "photography" and *The League of Youth*.

Strindberg was scarcely in his adolescence, so he tells us, when he rebelled against "laws, society, morality, religion." [5] This rebellion was rather ostensible than real. Outwardly a freethinker, an atheist, a socialist, and a rationalist, he remained all his life a moralistic, deeply religious man of mystical inclinations, whose every deviation from the moral standards of his childhood was attended by deep feelings of guilt. The chief result of his falling out with God was therefore the psychic discomfort from which he suffered to the end of his days. "My new conscience," he wrote, "told me I was right; my old one that I was wrong; I could not find peace. And I never found it." [6] The conflicts which this early revolt provoked were evidently necessary to Strindberg. All his life, he found God, his adversary, a constant source of stimulation and excitement. It is only at the end of *To Damascus* that the Unknown declares his willingness to make peace, and even then, one suspects, for literary purposes chiefly. But in his last days Strindberg had his Bible constantly beside him; and he directed that his body be buried in the cemetery of the New Church in Stockholm on the side of the poor, "in the field of idleness."

It would be interesting, as well as novel, to attempt a consideration of Strindberg's drama without reference to his life; unfortunately, it is out of the question—the two are so closely intertwined that it is not possible to say where the one leaves off and the other begins. All his work was in some way confessional and apologetic; he managed to be surprisingly personal without being in the least intimate with his public. His three major creative periods were the aftermath, in each case, of his three marriages, and the psychic crises which they precipitated were the immediate source of his masterpieces. It is as if the neurotic attack which shattered him each time had to be turned at any cost into creative channels in order for the man to survive. The work of each of these periods is therefore qualified by the specific nature of the crisis which was its source, and the consequence is that one needs to be tolerably well informed as to Strindberg's biography in order to understand what his plays are about.

Out of the first of these crises came the great naturalistic works of his maturity, during the period 1885–1892. The failure of his second marriage brought about the terrible experience he called his Inferno, and resulted in the series of extraordinary "mystical" plays, almost two dozen in number, which he wrote between 1897 and 1901. The final stage of his career began in 1902, in consequence of his third marriage. Its principal fruit was two powerful novels, A Dream Play, and the group of short "chamber-plays" which he wrote for the Intimate Theatre in Stockholm in 1907. To the psychiatrist this may suggest that in each case he turned his marriage to account in exciting that sense of injustice which appears to have been the root of his creative personality. This is hardly our concern; nevertheless, the entire performance provides a classic demonstration of the relation of art to the neurotic personality, a demonstration too cogent to be overlooked. The study of Strindberg is inevitably a study in biography.

According to his own account, Strindberg began writing plays the morning after an unsuccessful attempt at suicide. At nineteen he had already run a full gamut of failure and frustration. He had been an unsuccessful university student, an unsuccessful schoolmaster, an unsuccessful medical student, and—as far as he went —an unsuccessful actor—a broad background for a very young bohemian. Of his first play we know mainly that it was written in four days. His next play, The Freethinker, was published in 1870, and shows some Ibsenist influence. It involves a young schoolteacher who is made to suffer for his radical ideas, and unquestionably develops in fantasy a personal experience of the author's.[7] This was followed by a one-act play in verse, In Rome, which the Dramatic Theatre in Stockholm presented in 1870, while he was back for another semester's study at the university. The following spring he finished The Troublemaker, a tight play which centered

on the conflict of Christian and pagan in the days of the conversion of the Swedes.

The influence of *Either-Or* and *Brand* on his thinking during
his second period of study at Uppsala is attested by an essay he
wrote in 1871 on the subject of Öhlenschläger's *Håkon Jarl*. Kierkegaard seemed to him, at this time, to be another John the Baptist
pointing the way to the truth. His attitude toward Kierkegaard,
however, varied with the intensity of his own newly found rationalism. In 1872 he said Kierkegaard was the last gasp of Christianity.
In 1886 he called him the last Christian. His estimation of *Brand*
varied in about the same manner, and there is some indication
that he really understood the play. Like Ibsen, he was impressed
with the idea of life as a task and a duty, but, like him also, he
was skeptical of the outcome.

Of the three stages of development that Kierkegaard distinguishes, he decided—so he tells us in *The Son of a Bondswoman*
—that he had lived on the aesthetic level only, "since he had taken
his profession of letters as a pleasure." It was necessary, however,
to take it as a duty. But why—? At this point the chain of reasoning broke off, and when he read the end of *Either-Or*, and discovered that the ethical man also sank eventually into despair, he
found himself bewildered, and decided to remain aesthetic. But
the aesthetic life was not satisfactory. He began to oscillate, he
says, between the aesthetic and the Christian viewpoints, like a
ball thrown from one hand to the other, and the result was, in
fact, despair.[8]

Master Olof grew out of these spiritual questionings. The subject was well chosen. Olof Pederson was a figure of great historical
importance, the reformer who brought about the transition from
medieval Catholicism to the Protestantism of modern Sweden.
In 1537 Olof's behavior so deeply offended Gustav Vasa that he
had him condemned to death. As a result of the judges' intercession, however, the penalty was remitted to a fine, and in the
end, the king took the pastor back into favor. This story fell readily
into the dialectical pattern which Hebbel and Ibsen had already

established for the historical drama of ideas. Master Olof obviously embodied the new spirit which was sweeping across the world in the sixteenth century, and his enemies represented the decaying culture of the Middle Ages. The analogy to the intellectual revolution of the 1870's seemed striking; the subject had modernity, as well as historical interest, to recommend it. It was the first truly dramatic idea that Strindberg hit upon. He made the most of it, and the result was a really fine play. It was not easy to write. Strindberg spent, in all, five years upon *Master Olof*. The first version was in prose, and it underwent some revision. In 1872 he offered it to the Dramatic Theatre.[9]

Unlike Brand, whom in some ways he recalls, Olof is not, in Strindberg's conception, a strong man. He is by turns confident and despairing, a man of mood, whose behavior reflects his inner uncertainty. On either side of him is placed a strong figure—on the one side, Gert the Anabaptist, on the other, Gustav Vasa, the king. When the king assigns him his mission of reform, Olof accepts after much hesitation, and it is only by degrees that he feels himself committed to the propagation of the new faith. The king, however, is not much interested in the religious question. For him the Reformation is a political expedient, and when, after the Diet of Vesterås, the church lands are divided, he rewards Olof with the best church in Stockholm and suggests that he has gone far enough with his religious program. Olof is outraged, and Gert, cast in the role of the Scribean master intriguer, now takes advantage of his indignation to involve him in a plot against the king. The conspirators are betrayed, arrested, and eventually pilloried at the gate of the Great Church of Stockholm, but, in the final version of the play, Olof is persuaded to retract. Thus he becomes faithless to both sides, and the last voice we hear is that of Gert, who calls him renegade. The play therefore centers upon the tragedy of a man who permits himself to be used as an instrument for another's purpose, then revolts when he discovers how he has been duped, but eventually surrenders to the will of his superior.

It is not difficult to trace the sources upon which Strindberg drew for *Master Olof*. The basic idea is doubtless related to that of Shakespeare's *Julius Caesar* and his *Coriolanus;* there are, in addition, distinct echoes of *Brand, Die Räuber,* and *Götz von Berlichingen;* but the general effect is quite original and Strindbergian. In his treatment of history Strindberg was as free as Shakespeare. His characters speak colloquial prose, his scenes are free of the restrictions of French tragedy, there is the Elizabethan juxtaposition of tragic and comic effects. All this makes for a highly unclassical form. The directors of the Dramatic Theatre objected to a tragedy in prose, and disapproved of Strindberg's cavalier treatment of so august a personage as Gustav Vasa. *Master Olof* was rejected.

Strindberg had relied heavily on its acceptance, and this rejection left him in a precarious state both financially and emotionally. For some months he served an apprenticeship as a telegraphist in the weather station on the island of Sandhamn. The following year, 1874, he managed to get a more congenial appointment as assistant in the Chinese section of the Royal Library in Stockholm. The appointment came in the nick of time. Life as a bohemian had brought him to the verge of madness. Now, for a time, things changed. He was accepted, he was a civil servant; he had status, and a salary. The time had evidently come for him to make his peace with society. He hastened to do so.

In these years he had been reading Tocqueville, and in the Second Part of *La Démocratie* he found much to nourish his feelings with regard to the perpetual conspiracy of the middle class against men of talent.[10] These feelings were confirmed also by what he read in Eduard von Hartmann's *Die Philosophie des Unbewussten,* a work then much in vogue, which exercised a decisive influence on Strindberg's thought.

For Hartmann, pain is the essence of conscious being. The primary aspect of the Unconscious—the Absolute—is Will, the creative power, which brings the world into existence. The action of pure Will is absolute pain—therefore, to be is to suffer. In its desire for relief, the Unconscious evokes Reason and, with its aid, Will creates the best of possible worlds. But this results in merely palliative measures. Eventually, when Reason has succeeded in educating the greater part of existent Will with regard to the inevitable misery of existence, through a collective effort, conscious being will destroy itself, the conscious world will cease to exist, and the Unconscious at last will know peace. Meanwhile, the individual must devote himself to the mitigation of pain, improving the lot of humanity through social evolution, instead of striving vainly for an impossible personal happiness.

The relation of this system to the Eastern sources upon which Schopenhauer also drew for his concept of Will and Idea seemed evident to Strindberg. Both systems pointed significantly to the Vedic and Buddhist writings with which he had became acquainted in connection with his work in the Chinese collection.[11] He found Hartmann's pessimism particularly congenial. It was consoling to discover that pain was the inevitable condition of the conscious world, and not his lot alone. Furthermore, he noted, Hartmann considered pain as the motivating force of evolution, "the very vehicle of movement," so that in the interplay of Will and Reason which constituted the rhythm of the universe the truth was constantly advanced.[12] These ideas gave Strindberg a new insight into the historical situation he had developed in *Master Olof*, which he was now bringing himself to revise, more or less in accordance with the views of the Dramatic Theatre, as a verse tragedy.

The new version of 1876 is distinctly Hartmannian. Master Olof is now an idealist in whom the concept of reform arises spontaneously. The king, a more highly evolved being than Olof, is a realist who understands the illusory nature of Olof's mission. Gustav Vasa, however, does not appear on the stage. He overshadows the other characters in wisdom and glory, but others express his views, in particular, Bishop Brask, who speaks in terms reminiscent of the relativism of Buckle, and therefore in some measure recalls Dr. Stockmann:

. . . After you, a generation will come which will upset your work, and all that you consider truth will become a falsehood . . . What then is truth? I have no answer, nor will any man ever have one of all who walk the earth.[13]

In the new version, Olof no longer makes us think of Brand; nevertheless his wife Christine complains that the intellectual element in her husband is beyond the reach of love. This was a consequence of Strindberg's new philosophical orientation. As he noted elsewhere, love belongs to the golden age of childhood, the domain of the unconscious Will, and is, consequently, outside the province of Reason.[14] The note of resignation on which Olof ends the play, however, did not come from Hartmann. It came from Strindberg's heart. It was the sigh of one who felt that his life's adventure was over, and that at last, though he was not glorious, he was safe:

I am calm on the shore where the wave has cast me, for now I feel the ground under my feet. And in my turn I cry, "Good luck" to the hardy voyager who refuses to heed those who have suffered ship-wreck . . .[15]

This elegiacal note was not long suited to Strindberg's temper. The epilogue which he wrote in 1877 to the verse drama includes a little mystery-play performed by mountebanks at the gates of Stockholm in 1542, fifteen years after the Diet of Vesterås. In this play, a minor demiurge who calls himself God creates a world in which mad creatures scurry about comically for his amusement. In pity, Lucifer gives these creatures the apple of knowledge, so that they realize that they are the victims of an evil will, and that the essence of their life is pain. Then Lucifer bestows upon them the further gift of death, the liberator. But in order to keep his creatures alive, the demiurge compensates for each of Lucifer's gifts with a gift of illusion, the most effective of which is love. At the end of the little play, a spectator points mockingly at a fat prelate who is looking on complacently. He is told to hush. It is the *pastor primarius*, Olaus Petri. At this point, the spectators overturn the stage. The play does not please them.

Fame came to Strindberg when he was thirty. In 1879, the publication of his novel *The Red Room* suddenly catapulted him into the public eye. In *The Red Room* the idealist Arvid Falk is a rebel, like Strindberg, and, like Strindberg, he ends by coming to terms with society. A happy marriage crowns his reconciliation with the world, and the epilogue celebrates the joys of the home, and the charms of a lady "whose radiance brightens the street as she passes." [16] The radiant lady was, in fact, Siri von Essen, whom Strindberg had married two years before, at the end of 1877.

The story of this marriage has been so thoroughly publicized that it scarcely bears repetition. Siri's marriage with the young Guards Officer Baron Wrangel was on the verge of dissolution when Strindberg arrived on the scene in 1875, and the divorce took place early in 1876. Siri was an ambitious young actress, and the rising playwright was very willing to help with her career on the stage. It was understood that their marriage was to be a very enlightened modern relationship, a comradeship founded on equality and independence. Siri's stage career, however, did not progress satisfactorily. After four years she left the theatre in order to devote herself completely to her home and her husband. The role of Margaret in *The Secret of the Guild* was written for her during the months in which she was expecting their first child, and it reflects the happy atmosphere of Strindberg's home in these years.[17] So, indeed, do the two plays that quickly followed. In all three plays the problem of life finds its solution in love, work, and the home.

In December, 1881, *Master Olof* was performed at the New Theatre. It was a success, and Strindberg, greatly encouraged, at once set to work on *Lucky Per's Journey*, a moral fairy tale which owes something to Boccaccio, more to Voltaire, something to Wagner, and much to Ibsen.[18] Per is brought up in a belfry, for his father wishes to preserve him from all worldly contact, but his fairy godparents have more ambitious plans for him, and they send him forth, marvellously equipped, on a journey to find happiness. In the course of his journey he discovers the facts of life,

both comic and tragic, and, at last, disgusted with mankind, overwhelmed by nature, and terrified by death, he learns from his own
shadow that man's only refuge is work, and that with this one
can be happy, provided one has love. Armed with this inspiring
thought, Per becomes an unsuccessful reformer, then a successful
Caliph: one might say that this, in contrast to *Candide*, is a success
story.[19]

Lycko-Pers resa was written in 1882. The same year Strindberg brought out *The New Kingdom,* a short work which sur-
veyed contemporary Sweden in a similarly ironic vein. *Herr Bengts
hustru* followed at once, an ambitious play in which Strindberg
attempted to say something masculine on the question of feminism.

Sir Bengt's Wife is set in the same period as *Master Olof.*
The knight Bengt frees a young noblewoman from the convent
and marries her. In due course they have a child, and they are
happy; but Bengt finds himself in financial difficulties, and he
realizes that unless the harvest is good, he is ruined. His wife
knows nothing of this; she knows only that her husband is neglect-
ing her for his work. A sudden storm comes up. Bengt tells Margit
of the danger that threatens them. It is too late: the horses that
are needed to save the crops have been sent to fetch water for
his wife's roses. Bengt raises his hand to strike her. This is more
than the proud girl can bear. She leaves him, and petitions to
have her marriage annulled so that she may return to the cloister.
Her confessor, however, reminds her that there is a cloister where
she can practice mercy as well as humility and obedience; this
cloister is the home. Margit does not submit. Instead she takes
poison. But at the point of death she discovers that she has no
wish to die—her real desire is to live for her husband and child.
Luckily the confessor has the antidote; Margit lives, and is reconciled to her husband. At the end, Bengt says: "I wanted to hate
you because you deserted me; I wanted to kill you because you
abandoned your child, and yet, I love you. Do you believe in the
power of love over an evil will?" She answers: "I believe!" [20]

Needless to say, the knight Bengt and his wife have more to do with the nineteenth century than with the sixteenth. Strindberg says that he put off reading *A Doll's House* until 1881, and there is little doubt that Ibsen's play was fresh in his mind when he wrote *Sir Bengt's Wife.* "It was about this time," we read in *Le Plaidoyer d'un fou,* "that people began to trouble themselves —thanks to a play by the celebrated Norwegian bluestocking— over that good joke called 'the feminist question.' Then all the soft minds suffered the monomania of seeing oppressed females everywhere. As I refused to be the dupe of this absurd story, I was called a misogynist for the rest of my life." [21]

The relation of *A Doll's House* to *Sir Bengt's Wife* is not especially close. Both plays are about women who leave their husbands; but Margit arrives at the point of leaving her home by a different route from Nora, and the two characterizations cannot be said to be in any sense parallel. Margit, indeed, comes closer to Selma in *The League of Youth* than to Nora. While Nora actually takes up her husband's burden when this is necessary, Margit has no idea of doing anything of the sort; and while Torvald is a pompous fool, Bengt is very much the man. The consequence is that, as the two plays are arranged, Nora is justified in leaving her home, but Margit is not. Thus Margit's eleventh-hour discovery that love and the home are paramount to all other considerations has not the force it would have, had she been placed in Nora's position, and the two plays do not really take issue at all on the question of women's rights and obligations.

The play was nonetheless considered a counterblast to *A Doll's House,* and with it the author ranged himself squarely on the side of the anti-feminists. It is difficult to say why Strindberg, who had so far prided himself on his advanced views, should have taken so conservative a position on this point. His daughter Karin believed it was chiefly because Ibsen and Björnson were on the other side of the question; but at this time Strindberg's hostility to Ibsen was not so intense as to color his thinking.[22] It was not until 1886 that Ibsen became identified in Strindberg's mind with

the powers which were secretly persecuting him, and it was in
Le Plaidoyer d'un fou that he first complained that Ibsen had
caricatured him in *The Wild Duck* as a worthless photographer
and sentimental cuckold.[23]

In 1882, Strindberg's attitude toward women was still quite
reasonable. He blamed the libertine French of the eighteenth
century for turning women into dolls, and the stupid gallantry
of his own age for exalting them as angels, and in this he amply
demonstrated his lack of background in the history of the *querelle
des femmes*; but he did not as yet give any sign of the violent bias
which was to distinguish his later writings.[24] The misogyny which
motivated his plays of 1887–1889 was, in any case, not based upon
intellectual considerations. It was founded on the same grounds
that supported the rest of the neurotic superstructure of his singular mentality. Strindberg was not at any time a woman hater. On
the contrary, women fascinated him, and he found it impossible
to resist them. But he evidently found them more interesting as
a source of pain than of pleasure, and he infallibly sought out the
kind of women to marry who would go to some lengths to aid
him in his desire to suffer.

The fantastic nature of the torments he endured at the hands
of the women who loved him is all too clear from his writings,
both public and private. With the skill of the born dramatist, he
was able to arrange situations in real life from which he could conclude that he was being drained intellectually and emotionally;
that he was betrayed, insulted, robbed, and systematically driven
into madness. He was convinced that his cooks starved him by
extracting the nourishing juices from his food before they served
it to him. He suffered from a kind of morbid neatness, and felt
that he was constantly crossed in his efforts at housekeeping. His
temper was unpredictable. A single word was enough to precipitate
a quarrel that might last for days or weeks. The neurotic pattern
that eventually put an end to his marriage with Siri von Essen
was repeated in essence with all the other women he loved. It was
as if he were determined at all costs to arouse the hostility of the

women who attracted him, and he was content only when he had proved conclusively that nobody loved him and that he stood alone.

Since it was also necessary for Strindberg to be universally loved and admired, he was compelled to exhibit his grievances in detail, to justify and to rationalize his actions, and, in order to evoke universal sympathy for his sufferings, to call, not merely on the neighbors, but upon all the world to witness the injustices to which he was subjected. Strindberg's sufferings were, no doubt, intense; but they certainly involved some element of showmanship. In order to suffer properly, it was necessary for him to have an audience of thousands, of millions; and even this did not suffice. His pain must be abstracted, generalized, universalized, until by a Christ-like effort he concentrated in himself all the suffering of mankind. Even so, it was not easy for him to reach the ear of God. For this it was necessary that his complaints be transformed into something so poignant and so beautiful that they could not possibly be disregarded.[25]

The first-fruit of these psychic operations was the series of plays which Strindberg was to write in the years 1886–1888— *Comrades, The Father, Miss Julie,* and *Creditors.* Three of these plays have been called the most perfect examples in any language of the naturalistic aesthetic.[26] It is perhaps not quite from this viewpoint that these works are chiefly admirable; nevertheless they represent a remarkable contribution to the literature of the theatre.

The Red Room caused Strindberg to be called the Swedish Zola, an uncomplimentary epithet; but in fact this novel mainly showed the influence of Dickens. Strindberg began reading Zola in 1879.[27] By 1882, however, his works were beginning to reflect the naturalist position, with its socialist tendencies and its echoes of Rousseau. The class struggle was much on Strindberg's mind in the mid-eighties. From his earliest days as a writer, he had proclaimed—though somewhat wistfully—his position as a member of the lower classes. Now, under French influence, this posture took on a more warlike aspect. He became a socialist.

About this time he formally repudiated his aestheticism and his love of poetry, since these predilections in no way advanced the cause of social evolution. The aristocracy, and more especially the bourgeoisie, now inspired him with loathing. He professed himself disgusted with the vapid culture and empty refinement of the upper classes, and revolted by the literature which was subsidized to pander to their tastes. Only those works, he felt, which seriously considered the problems of the proletariat were worthy the attention of a modern writer. The writer must, above all, be useful to man. Literature must have a social purpose; as Georg Brandes had said, every literary work must "put a problem under discussion." [28]

In this resolute frame of mind, Strindberg came to Paris in the fall of 1883, to study and to write. He had already a very competent grasp of French literature, which he meant to improve during his stay in France, and he dreamed of giving up Swedish as a literary medium, and of becoming a French writer.[29]

Louis Desprez' *L'Évolution naturaliste* appeared in 1884. It was the very last word on the subject of naturalism. Strindberg studied this young writer's work assiduously, and came to the conclusion that he too was a naturalist. His utilitarian views were, however, not quite the same as those of Desprez. He was by nature much inclined to argument, and while he objected to the salon drama of Dumas *fils* as much as anybody, he was much impressed with Dumas's technique. The four plays which he wrote under naturalist influence, some years later, were all conceived, ostensibly, as accurate transcriptions of reality, without any *parti pris*. In fact, however, they were all concerned with problems—indeed, with the same problem—and each demonstrated a thesis, the same thesis. They were, in consequence, far from perfect examples of the naturalist mode. But, unlike Dumas, Strindberg did not insist on using the stage as a forum. The first of these plays involved considerable discussion; after that, Strindberg simply depicted the facts as he saw them, and announced his findings. Nor did he ordinarily indicate, like Dumas, a solution to the ills which he demonstrated. In his view, the case was hopeless. To this extent, at least, he fell in with the naturalist position.

At the time of *Sir Bengt's Wife*, Strindberg's interest in domestic relations appears to have been no more than the normal interest of a professional playwright in a timely subject. The question of the relation of the sexes in marriage was, of course, one of the burning issues of the day, and Strindberg took it up with characteristic energy; but for him the problems of marriage were as yet completely academic. His own marriage had so far turned out admirably. As late as the summer of 1884, after seven years of married life, there was nothing whatever to indicate that a storm was brewing in this quarter.[30]

Early in 1884 Strindberg left Paris, which, he felt, was too refined an environment for a proletarian writer. He needed to be among peasants. He went to Italy. Meanwhile Dumas *fils* published *L'Affaire Clemenceau*, and Strindberg wrote his brother Axel to send him a copy. In Dumas's novel, which did much to fix the type of the *femme fatale* in the popular imagination, the adventuress Iza marries the sculptor Clemenceau for lack of someone better to marry, and then proceeds to betray him energetically with every man who takes her fancy. When she has at last quite unmanned her husband and stolen "his soul and his genius," so that he is incapable of work, she leaves him. He reproaches her bitterly for her wickedness. In revenge, she gives him to understand that their son is not his.[31]

The relation of this novel to the plays which Strindberg wrote in the course of the year 1887-1888 could hardly be closer, but it was not only to Dumas that he was indebted for his material. In Desprez's *L'Évolution naturaliste* he had his attention directed to two novels by the brothers Goncourt, *Manette Salomon* and *Charles Demailly*, in which, Desprez wrote, the theme is "the annihilation of the artist by the woman."[32] Undoubtedly these highly seasoned works impressed Strindberg deeply, for in the foreword to *Miss Julie* he remarks that "the documentary novels of the brothers Goncourt" appealed to him more strongly than any other modern works.

The *femme fatale*, the *femme bête-féroce*, and the *femme-vampire* were all very much in the mode at this time, but there was more than timeliness to recommend this type of heroine to Strindberg. At the bottom of all his misogynistic drama, from *Marauders* to *The Pelican*, there is clearly visible the irresistible fascination which the image of the bad mother aroused in him, a fascination so intense and so inescapable that after he was thirty-five he infallibly projected this image on every woman who engaged his interest. All the rest of his life he was ill with this dream. There is no play of his after 1887 in which he does not protest either overtly or symbolically against the women who, in his fancy, threatened him, dominated him, starved him, drained him, and poisoned him. The women he found were all in some way the bad mother, although ostensibly it was the good mother that he sought, and until the end of his days he was ceaselessly tormented by the menacing figure of the wife, the nurse, and the cook, huge and mighty with the nourishment of which he had been deprived. Even in the organic disease of which, in the end, he died, there is some reminiscence of this malignant phantasm.

In 1884 Strindberg published a collection of short stories entitled *Married*, in which he developed further the idea that the natural role of woman is that of wife and mother. The first of these stories, "The Reward of Virtue," unfortunately included some unorthodox observations on the subject of Christianity, together with an allusion to Jesus as a social agitator. For this bit of bravado, he was amply punished. The book aroused resentment in conservative Stockholm, and the author was duly summoned to appear on a charge of impiety, with the alternative of having his publisher bear the responsibility in the event that he did not answer the summons.

Strindberg was in Switzerland; nevertheless, the summons plunged him into a frenzy of apprehension. He consulted everyone he knew, and came to the conclusion that if he returned to Sweden he was certain to spend the rest of his life in prison. He therefore wrote to Stockholm, assuming full responsibility for his words, but refusing flatly to appear, so that it became necessary for Bonnier to come to Geneva to fetch him.

After a nightmarish journey, they arrived in Stockholm, were welcomed by a socialist deputation, and, in due course, Strindberg stood his trial and was acquitted. But his fears did not subside. On the contrary, they augmented; for he was now convinced that the trial had been engineered by a secret organization of feminists who were determined to exact a terrible retribution for the damage done to their cause by the publication of *Sir Bengt's Wife*. These feminists, he suspected, formed a vast international complex, the ultimate goal of which was the enslavement of man and the re-establishment of the prehistoric matriarchy.[33] It was, as it seemed to him, obviously his destiny to oppose this conspiracy with all his strength, regardless of the consequences, and to this task he now began to bend all his energies.

The Second Part of *Married*, published in 1886, had a distinctly polemic tone. The stories demonstrated that women were incapable of love, or, for that matter, of anything good; it was their purpose, and had been for centuries, to subjugate their husbands; and they were already very close to their goal. The woman question, from this time on, became an intensely personal quarrel in which Strindberg felt himself engaged tooth and nail. Henceforth he was a man with a mission in life, the furtherance of which was indissolubly connected, in Kierkegaardian terms, with the realization of his personality and the affirmation of his existence.

His wife Siri soon found herself in a thoroughly false position. She was not only embarrassed by the necessity for justifying herself as the wife of a professional misogynist, but the suspicion was inescapable that her husband's violent attacks on her sex must be personally motivated by his hatred of her. As might be expected, she reacted violently, and the latter part of 1886 and the first months of 1887 were unbearable for them both. Strindberg had by this time convinced himself that Siri was deceiving him with other men. He was intensely unhappy, and he wrote piteous letters to his brother and his friends begging them to allay his incertitude before he went mad.

In these circumstances, in the summer of 1886, he was once again inspired to write for the theatre. His first play gave him much trouble. It was intended to show that the modern career woman is a parasite and a social brigand, and for his subject matter, Strindberg drew liberally upon *L'Affaire Clemenceau* and *Manette Salomon*, as well as upon his own marital experiences which now, in retrospect, filled him with indignation. He called the play *Marauders*.

The first act of *Marauders* is laid in Stockholm. Axel and Bertha are painters, and Bertha is in financial straits. Axel marries her, declaring that he desires only to be her slave; she obligingly bestows a slave bracelet upon him. Axel is charmed; but the old doctor warns him of his danger. The next four acts take place in Paris. It appears that both husband and wife have sent paintings to the Salon, and, since Bertha fears that hers may be rejected, she prevails upon Axel to intercede for her with a member of the jury. Now comes a report that, in fact, Axel's entry has been refused. Bertha is overjoyed, and when Axel arrives with news that her painting has been accepted, she takes the occasion to point out to him in detail his hopeless shortcomings as an artist. Axel begins to understand that they are not so much comrades as competitors, and when it develops, a moment later, that Bertha has been cheating him also with relation to the household money, he becomes angry, declares his independence, and confesses an infidelity. In the last act, there is a reception, in the course of which Bertha exhibits her husband's rejected canvas in order the better to savor her triumph. It now turns out that there has been an error. It is her canvas that has been rejected, not his. Axel is the better painter of the two. On this note, Axel leaves her, saying that he is willing to abandon the house and its contents to her, but that he has no intention of being plundered any further.

Strindberg's touch in *Marauders* was far from sure. He undoubtedly meant to follow the naturalist formula; but the influence of Dumas was irresistible, and the play was conceived as a thesis play with discussions, *raisonneurs*, and all the apparatus of the *pièce bien faite*. These characteristics it stubbornly retained through all its successive revisions. By the end of 1886, Strindberg believed *Marauders* was ready for production, and he offered it to a publisher. It was not accepted. The following year he revised it; later still, he asked Lundegård to improve it further in a Danish version. Nothing came of this. Eventually Strindberg gave the play a drastic overhauling, cut the first act completely, and suppressed much of the discussion. In this version, Axel becomes quite brutal at the last, and peremptorily orders Bertha to leave his house. When she reminds him of his marital obligations to her, he throws her some coins. In the midst of these conjugal pleasantries, the servant announces a lady. It is Bertha's successor, presumably a less comradely sort of girl than Bertha. "My comrades, I can meet at a café," says Axel. "At home I want a woman." [34] Strindberg entitled this final version *Comrades*, and sent it to Oesterling for publication in December, 1887. It was accepted. By this time *The Father* had already had a successful production in Copenhagen, and Strindberg had entered a new phase of his development as a dramatist.

The Father [35] was written at the beginning of 1887, and proved to be unlike anything Strindberg had so far attempted. It was a play of great power and concision, arranged so that all the force of the drama is concentrated on the final situation, which rises to an almost unbearable degree of intensity toward the close of the curtain. *The Father* has not the polemic character of *Comrades*. It does not argue, has no particular thesis, needs no *raisonneur*, and thus comes much closer to the naturalist scheme than Strindberg's first experiment in this genre. In *Comrades*, the story of Axel's unhappy marriage was presented as an example of social injustice. In *The Father* the same elements are present, but it is the psychological rather than the social conflict that is emphasized, and the narrative consequently focuses on the fundamental question of the eternal enmity of the sexes.

As in *Comrades*, this enmity is identified with the conflict between the great and the small, an opposition which by this time quite overshadowed the class struggle in Strindberg's mind. In spite of his very sincere humanitarian leanings, Strindberg had never been a true socialist; his socialism was in large part a consequence of his need to make a common cause with other victims of social injustice. For a long time he had proclaimed his base origin and his plebeian status. As we have seen, it was fashionable in the 1870's for an artist to belong to the masses, at least in spirit. Now, in the light of Tocqueville's observations on the subject of democracy, Strindberg was able to shift to more congenial ground. The great, the people of intellect and talent, were obviously every bit as much the victims of social injustice as the laboring classes; they were systematically exploited by the vast stupid majority, the small, of which a considerable part naturally consisted of women. As between the sexes, the male was, by reason of his superior endowment, the productive and imaginative element. As such, he was regularly plundered by the parasitic, uncreative sex which he labored to support.

According to Strindberg, it was toward the end of 1888 that Georg Brandes introduced him to Nietzsche, and it was at this time that their brief correspondence began. Strindberg thus became aware of Nietzsche's writings more than a year after *The Father* was written, and shortly after he finished *Miss Julie*. He himself had arrived, he says, quite independently at the idea of the perpetual antagonism of the aristocratic mind and the plebeian mentality with its constituent elements of conventional morality, Christian superstition, and woman-worship. This idea he developed emphatically in two articles which he wrote in 1888, *De sma* and *De stora*, and he illustrated it profusely in a number of other articles and in his novels, particularly in *I havsbandet*, which he published in 1890.[36]

In the 1880's the age of psychology was in its first dawn, and Strindberg, always abreast of current developments, was fascinated by the experiments of Charcot at the Salpetrière and of Bernheim at Nancy. Their excursions into hypnotism confirmed what he had always believed, that every confrontation of individuals implied a psychic struggle, a battle of minds to determine the mastery. The mental struggle for domination paralleled, in his opinion, the physical struggle for survival which Darwin had not long ago described in *The Descent of Man*.[37]

The conditions of human existence were, in Strindberg's opinion, constantly adjusted, and re-adjusted through these psychic encounters, which took place mainly through suggestion, and in this manner, the stronger minds, the more highly evolved intelligences, forced the weaker to do their will. Such conflicts were sometimes carried to the extreme; a man might be murdered by means of a fatal idea cunningly slipped into his mind. In this connection, Strindberg was much taken with a story by Erckmann-Chatrian called *L'Œil invisible, ou l'Auberge des trois pendus*, in which purely through the power of suggestion an old woman causes the guests at her inn to hang themselves from the inn sign, until, one day, she meets with a will stronger than her own, and is forced to follow their example herself. It was, Strindberg reasoned, through the power of suggestion that Iago murdered Othello, and it was thus that Rebecca did away with Beata in *Rosmersholm*.[38] It was equally possible for a person to suck out another's soul by a sort of spiritual vampirism, which little by little reduced the victim to an empty husk, an automaton. This was the way of Tekla in *Creditors*.

In his essay *Modern Drama and Modern Theatre* (1889), which, for the rest, was largely a restatement of the naturalist position, Strindberg argued that in drama the psychic conflict alone is essential. The significant plays are those in which the *mise-en-scène* is nothing, and all the attention is focused on the movement of the souls. Racine, Corneille, Molière required little scenery; a stage and two stools are an ample setting in which to play *Tartuffe*.[39] Since in the theatre the actual encounter of souls alone is important, it is advisable to suppress as useless everything in the play that is not directly relevant to the *scène à faire*. The throng of unnecessary characters employed by Dumas, the host of irrelevant details which the naturalists meticulously reported, were alike dispensable. For Strindberg, as for Desprez, the goal of the playwright was a work of the utmost concentration, in which all is movement, action, and struggle.

The essential characteristic of drama, as distinguished from the novel, Desprez had written, was its concentration, from which it derived its superior energy. Plots should be simple: *"au théâtre la simplicité de la forme s'impose."* A certain amount of analysis, of course, might be necessary for the comprehension of a situation; but the analysis of a powerful feeling, as in *Thérèse Raquin*, was a very different matter from the complex intrigues of the school of Scribe.[40] For Strindberg these thoughts had the force of Scripture; nevertheless, in practice he found it not altogether simple to avoid the Scribean method, which he despised, and the "laws of the theatre," for which he had, professedly, no use.

By 1889 the Théâtre-Libre had been in existence two years, and naturalism had developed well beyond the phase of *Thérèse Raquin*. Antoine's specialty was the dramatic capsule, the *quart d'heure* in the style of Lavedan, Gustave Guiches, Hennique, and Métenier. To Strindberg also it seemed that plays in general were too long and too diffuse. Since, he argued, a play was usually written for the sake of a few climactic scenes, the sensible thing would be to write those scenes and to omit the rest, which at best simply served to dilute the effect. In any case, three acts was enough, as in *Ghosts*. *Rosmersholm* was too long.

Strindberg was thirty-eight when, in the first months of 1887, he finished *The Father*. To a very considerable extent it epitomized the ideas he had absorbed in Paris. After 1870, the prevailing literary mode in France was misogynistic, and the extreme to which this attitude was carried in the course of the century may be gauged from the reception of such a work as Villiers de l'Isle-Adam's *L'Éve future*, in which a mechanical mistress invented by Edison is shown to be in every way superior to its counterpart in nature.

The theatre in these years was particularly sensitive to the anti-feminist trend. Sarah Bernhardt was specializing in the role of *femme fatale*, and the huge success of *L'Étrangère*, which Dumas wrote for her in 1876, doubtless had something to do with Ibsen's characterization of Hedda Gabler. In spite of the fact, however, that in *The Father*, he was simply following the current mode, Strindberg felt that the publication of this play was a proof of reckless courage on his part, and that personal reprisals were sure to follow. On February 6, 1887, he wrote to Bonnier that he had now completed *The Father*, and he added: "I will not permit myself to be silenced on such a capital question, which has been distorted and disguised by writers without virility such as Ibsen and Björnson." [41]

Like *Creditors*, which was written the following year, *The Father* describes a case of psychic homicide, a "soul-murder." The crime is not developed systematically, nor is its malice prepensed. Its horror is augmented by the fact that it is a wholly instinctive reaction. In the beginning, the wife, Laura, means only to defeat her husband, not to kill him. It is really he himself who shows her the way by which she can drive him to madness and death. In a sense, therefore, the Captain commits suicide, and his behavior in the circumstances seems odd, unless we assume that the male in this situation is always destined to die in some such way as this.

The play was evidently designed along strictly naturalistic lines. The etiology of the case is carefully detailed; the viewpoint is objective; the tone, scientific. There is no moral, and the author does not take a hand in the discussion. A single conflict is depicted at the moment of its crisis. The action consists of a sequence of strong scenes bound together by a single developing action, without complication, surprise, reversal, or denouement. In spite of all this, *The Father* does not make the effect of a naturalistic play. Strindberg thought it did; and he wrote most respectfully, offering the play to Zola as an example of naturalistic drama. Zola sent his professed disciple a tactful answer in his best epistolary style; but he did not conceal his reservations. *The Father* was grand, it was simple, it was perhaps true—but it was not Zola's idea of a naturalistic play.

It is probable that after his study of naturalistic technique, Strindberg meant to divest himself completely of theatrical devices; yet *The Father* is by no means free of contrivance. The exposition is developed in the manner of Ibsen, by way of reminiscence. Nobody, however, could mistake this work for Ibsen's. While in *Rosmersholm*, for example, the unfolding exposition serves to illuminate the existing situation more and more brightly until everything is starkly clear, in *The Father* the exposition clarifies only the motive, and the facts themselves are never brought to light. The reason is evident. Ibsen's characters tell each other the truth; they are rational people, capable of honesty, and are meant to be believed. Strindberg's characters are so grossly distorted by their monomania that it is not possible to take them at their word. The spectator is therefore as much on his guard in a play of this sort as a doctor observing the vagaries of madmen.

The plot of *The Father* is extremely simple: a man is driven mad by doubts as to the legitimacy of his child. The idea may have been suggested by Strindberg's own experience with Siri. In any case, the situation was not particularly novel—there were several contemporary analogues. In addition to *L'Affaire Clemenceau*, it is possible that Strindberg had in mind Maupassant's famous story, *Monsieur Parent*, published the previous year, or Echegaray's play, *O locura o santidad*, published in 1877, and promptly translated into Swedish.[42] The central point of Strindberg's play, however, is not, as in these analogues, the character-study of an individual in a difficult situation, but the opposition of man and woman in its eternal and tragic aspect.

For the view he took of this matter, Strindberg had the weight-

iest and most authoritative precedents. The classical position on
the relation of the sexes was unequivocally anti-feminist, and in
Christian times this position was reinforced by all the weight of
clerical authority from the days of Saint Paul. The egalitarian views
attributed to Björnson and Ibsen were, on the contrary, romantic
in origin, and hardly antedated the century. In ranging himself so
decisively on the conservative side of the feminist issue, Strindberg found himself in strange company for a supposedly advanced
thinker, and he was forced to shore up his position with every rationalization he could evolve. In 1886 he had read an article in
La Nouvelle revue by Paul Lafargue which demonstrated the relation of the *Oresteia* to the ancient matriarchy of Greece.[43] This
was all Strindberg needed. *The Father* was conceived as a modern
Agamemnon.

In *The Father*, the immediate question concerns the daughter's
future. Bertha is seventeen. Her father is a freethinker, and he
wishes her to have a liberal education in the city. The mother
wishes her to stay at home and study art. They differ sharply.
The house is full of women. Their interests vary; but regardless of
their disparate viewpoints, the women make a common cause,
while the men are incapable of standing together. It is true that
the contest in *The Father* would be more thrilling if the sides
were more evenly matched, but the conclusion would perhaps be
less emphatic.

Laura, the mother, is not characterized as a person of intelligence; but she has shrewdness. The Captain, on the other hand, is
extremely intelligent, but quite unable to defend himself. The
consequence is that the play falls somewhat inopportunely into
the stereotype of the innocent victim and the cruel tyrant, with
the Captain in the role of the victim.

Although nobody in *The Father* appears to be entirely lucid,
the plot develops with something akin to logic. The Captain's
careless admission that it is impossible to fix the paternity of the
servant's child gives Laura the idea of casting doubt on the legitimacy of their own daughter on the theory that if the Captain is

not the father, he can have no say in the manner of her education. The suggestion throws the Captain into such a dither that his wife is able to provoke him into hurling a lighted lamp at her. This ill-advised action apparently seals his doom. So far, the Captain has shown himself to be considerably more sensible than the rest of his household; from this point on he seems to agree that he is a madman, threatens to kill his daughter, and raves histrionically until his old nurse entices him into a straitjacket. The end is curiously tender. The wife asks his forgiveness for having destroyed him. The nurse takes his head in her lap. Then the Captain has a stroke, providentially, and dies.

The naturalists believed that the conditions of the theatre should come as close as possible to the conditions of life, and they hoped in this way to achieve a more convincing illusion of reality. *The Father,* however, does not in the least depend for its effectiveness on its resemblance to external experience. Its effects follow one another in accordance with the sort of logic to which Kafka has accustomed us—the logic of fantasy—and the result is a type of realism which has nothing to do with reality. As a slice of life, *The Father* is preposterous; but as a juxtaposition of effects, an arrangement of impressions, it has extraordinary cogency.

It would be too much, perhaps, to expect that a work conceived along such lines should also be able to stand the test of reason, and, in fact, *The Father* does not; it has not that sort of verisimilitude. Its exaggerations quite defy common sense, yet they emphasize modes of thought and behavior which we comprehend, and in some measure share. The figures of the Captain and his militant wife are inflated much beyond the scale of ordinary experience, but they are by no means strangers to us. They are ourselves in hysteria, and their power of emotional evocation is immense. We do not believe them; all the same, they make us shudder.

Strindberg's personal difficulties, out of which he made plays, were, after all, no more than the usual difficulties of humanity, exaggerated by a person of abnormal sensitivity to a point somewhere between the horrible and the absurd. In *The Father*, the Captain's feelings are those of a resentful child:

> CAPTAIN: . . . I believe you are all my enemies, you women. My mother was my enemy—she did not want me to come into the world because my birth might give her pain, and even in the womb she starved me, so that I might be born half-grown. My sister was my enemy—she taught me how to be submissive—.[44]

Nothing could be clearer than the psychic motives which control the play. The Captain's tragedy proceeds from a fantasy of the bad mother; and as this fantasy belongs to the infantile mentality which in adult life we normally consign to the psychic under-world, it is understandable that its characters should emerge into consciousness deformed, exaggerated and caricatured like the characters of a dream. *The Father* is an example, accordingly, of a very special sort of mimesis. As in the case of *The Master Builder*, its truth lies not in the accurate portrayal of external experience—the play has very little to do with that—but in the manifestation of the life which underlies experience, that life of which we are not ordinarily aware, but which, the moment it is presented to our attention, we recognize with astonishment as our own.

Strindberg intended in this play to demonstrate a truth with regard to the relation of the sexes. In fact, he demonstrated such a truth, but not at all in the manner which he intended. The photography of *The Father* is not the photography of external surfaces; it is the photography of the x-ray. The play is, in a sense, naturalistic; but the life which it represents is not the life which we see around us. It is the life which ordinarily we do not see which is here suggested in terms of a preposterously realistic action. In this sense, *The Father* becomes comprehensible not as an example of naturalism, but under the aspect of symbolism.

The type of symbolism of which *The Father* is an example has little enough to do, however, with the intimation of the transcendental, and nothing at all to do with the ideal world of Baudelaire and Mallarmé. Its efficacy lies in the suggestion of a horrible reality which normally lies some distance below the threshold of consciousness, and it is therefore, in a sense, realistic far beyond the limits of naturalism. With all its exaggerations, Strindberg's portrait of the father involves something that impresses us as true, even though we do not believe *The Father*. In spite of the childishness of the hyperbole, or perhaps because of it, the play conveys truly and profoundly something of the martyrdom of the male, the torment of the good provider, whose individuality is daily sacrificed to the interests of the family, the children, the mother, and her need to reproduce. Shaw makes this feeling comically explicit in the last scene of *Man and Superman*, the most tragic of his comedies:

TANNER: But why me—me of all men? Marriage is to me apostasy, profanation of the sanctuary of my soul, violation of my manhood, sale of my birthright, shameful surrender, ignominious capitulation, acceptance of defeat. I shall decay like a thing that has served its purpose and is done with; I shall change from a man with a future to a man with a past; I shall see in the greasy eyes of all the other husbands their relief at the arrival of a new prisoner to share their ignominy . . .

In *The Father*, the portrayal does not make us smile. It awakens in us, on the contrary, a feeling of horror which corresponds to our inner sense, as men, of the injustice of the human situation and the cruelty of nature, which ruthlessly—and senselessly—sacrifices the individual in the interest of the species. Very few men, doubtless, permit that sense of injustice to color their entire view of life as Strindberg did; but the feeling which *The Father* exaggerates is nevertheless in some degree universal. It expresses itself in countless ways, not the least of which is the vast anti-marital literature which has accumulated since the early Middle Ages: *Les Quinze joyes du mariage* and *The Dance of Death* are, each in its way, representative examples. In evoking and emphasizing this feeling, with all its wealth of association, Strindberg makes us uncomfortably aware of the undercurrent of repressed indignation which causes every father to feel occasionally that he too is the subject of crucifixion, and it is doubtless in this capacity to evoke a deep-seated emotion that the greatness of the play consists. It is not the exaggeration, obviously, but the validity of the perception that measures the power of the artist.

It could hardly have been shocking in the late 1880's to have it demonstrated in the theatre that the female of the species is more deadly than the male: the whole current of European thought at the time led in that direction. The suggestion, however, was startling that a woman could love a man truly only as a mother, and that therefore the sexual relationship involved for her the shame of incest:

> LAURA: . . . I loved you as if you were my child. But you know, you must have felt it, when your sexual desires were aroused, and you came forward as my lover, I was reluctant, and the joy I felt in your embrace was followed by such revulsion that my very blood knew shame. The son become the lover —oh! [45]

In this situation, Strindberg saw the root of the sexual conflict. In *The Father* the woman is strong; the man is weak. They are in the relation of mother and son. Yet in order to propagate the race, it is necessary for a time that their roles be reversed— the man must dominate; the woman, submit. The conflict is therefore inevitable:

> LAURA: . . . The mother was your friend, look you, but the woman was your enemy,—for sexual love is strife; and don't imagine that I gave myself; I gave nothing, I only took—what I meant to have. Yet you did have the upper hand—which I knew, and wanted you to know. [46]

Upon this paradox, Strindberg intimates, the idea of the family is based, and this paradox is inescapable; it is a sort of grim jest which every marriage perpetuates and transmits. Such, in Strindberg's view, is the human condition, inalterable in its wretchedness. Yet out of this wretchedness, even in the mind of the skeptic, some hope arises. The tragedy of the father has its sacrificial aspect. The Son of Man is endlessly crucified, but in Him, nevertheless, is the hope of mankind. Pain is of the essence of being, but our suffering is not in vain—it is the premonition of our divinity. Therefore here, as in *The Dance of Death*, the father is conscious of his Christ-like role, and with his dying breath this freethinker calls upon God:

CAPTAIN: . . . Oh God, who hold all children dear!
NURSE: Listen! He prays to God!
CAPTAIN: No. To you, to put me to sleep, for I am tired . . . so tired. Good night, Margaret, may you be blessed among women! [47]

This mystical touch in one who elsewhere stoutly affirms his total lack of faith is entirely characteristic of Strindberg's subsequent drama, until his final capitulation in *The Great Highway* makes his position as prodigal son explicit.

In a play by Dumas, the ideas which Strindberg develops with respect to the sexual relation would have been put—assuming Dumas to have been capable of them—into the mouth of a *raisonneur*, the doctor, perhaps, or the pastor. Strindberg permits his principals to lecture the audience in their own right. They take on, in consequence, a dimension beyond their own, and, in addition to their madness, exhibit such wisdom as is ordinarily beyond the capacity of naturalistic characters. In real life, doubtless, there are wives who feel the sort of resentment that Laura expresses; but they rarely analyze its causes. Nor is it common for husbands to manifest the prodigious insights of the Captain, who not only acts like a child, but also knows that he is acting like a child, and explains why.

It is only exceptionally that Strindberg's personages act and speak like real people. In attempting to lay bare a deeper reality than the depiction of the actual permits, Strindberg parted company completely with Zola. From a photographic viewpoint, Strindberg's Captain comes about as close to a real captain as "Le Facteur Roullin," which Van Gogh painted at Arles the following year, comes to a real postman. Both are examples of much the same phase of impressionism, but in the Captain we have already a distinct premonition of the expressionistic technique which was in time to become Strindberg's specialty as a dramatist.[48]

Some months after he finished *The Father*, Strindberg began *Le Plaidoyer d'un fou*, his most considerable autobiographical work. He wrote it in French, in a very commendable, vigorous style. It occupied him until March, 1888, and obviously represented an exceptional outburst of creative energy. *Le Plaidoyer d'un fou—A Fool's Defence* it has been called in English—is a most extraordinary recital, a work either of the most astonishing ingenuousness or the most flagrant charlatanism, and perhaps both. It is a cry of anguish 434 pages in duration, the confessions of a man in the utmost distress, who is determined to spare the reader no detail of his suffering and its causes. In the form of a novel, but with entirely explicit allusions, it relates most circumstantially the story of Siri's seduction, the subsequent marriage, her numerous failures in the theatre, Strindberg's successes, her jealousies, her vampirism, and the agonies she causes him to endure.

Like Laura in *The Father*, Marie has an insane compulsion to dominate her husband. She detests his virility, and reacts violently to his every display of manhood. For his part, nothing gives him more pleasure than to play the adorable child, and he delights in eliciting little gestures of tenderness by appealing to his wife's motherly instincts. She, however, is fundamentally wicked. She deceives him, he has come to suspect, with every man who comes her way, and even with women; but he is never certain, and this uncertainty drives him mad. The idea that his children are not his own is like a dagger in his heart; but his wife will not deliver him from his agony by confessing the truth. In her letters, which he intercepts, he discovers that she wishes him dead; in fact, she has already tried to poison him; and she spreads rumors that he is insane in order to have him put away. With all this, he does not defend himself. He remains alone, defenseless, at the mercy of this vampire who is sucking him dry, hoping one day to be delivered from her evil spell.

The situation in *Le Plaidoyer d'un fou* was entirely typical of the romantic literature of the period. Strindberg's originality appeared, therefore, in putting himself forward personally, amid a wealth of detail, as one who was actually the victim of such a situation. The question of whether the events he related were true or not is, of course, fascinating; but it is completely beside the point as regards Strindberg's development as a dramatist. Doubtless, whatever truth there was in this story was vastly exaggerated. The cliché of the hag-ridden male was currently fashionable; it seemed to fit Strindberg's psychic posture perfectly; and he slipped it on like a coat. As an example of True Confessions literature, *Le Plaidoyer d'un fou* is probably unparalleled, but the circumstances of its composition can hardly detract from the literary interest of a work which was obviously written along the lines of *Manette Salomon*, and which far surpasses it as an example of the psychological novel.

It requires an effort, it is true, to preserve one's admiration for the author of a work of this sort, but our feelings in this regard are based upon social preconceptions which Strindberg perhaps did not share, and which, in any case, for the time he rejected. Strindberg was no ordinary person, and undoubtedly his need to attract attention to himself as an artist in torment far outweighed all other considerations in his mind, including the professional writer's normal willingness to exhibit himself in intimate poses at so much a pose.

It is also very possible that Strindberg, like Rousseau, ended by believing the fantasies he dreamed up for literary purposes: he had to an amazing degree the talent for making life out of literature. There are indications that he shared our uncertainty with regard to his works of this period. While he was still engaged in writing *Le Plaidoyer d'un fou*, he wrote to Axel Lundegård: "It seems to me that I live like a somnambulist; the imaginary and the real are all one for me. I do not know if *The Father* is something I have imagined or if my life was really this . . . By an abuse of the imagination, my life has become as unreal as that of a shadow . . ." [49] It is also clear that in later years he had some sense of guilt with regard to this book. In *To Damascus II,* the Mother brings about the initial rift in the Unknown's marriage by giving her daughter a book by her husband which he had forbidden her to read.

It is certainly strange that Strindberg should have wished to present himself to the world in this piteous guise. Doubtless he had great need to exhibit his suffering—and it is certain that he suffered—the picture he has left us is not altogether funny, after all. It is a far different image from that evoked by Ibsen, passing his life in the twilight of a sad October afternoon. Perhaps it is less carefully posed. At any rate, it belongs to a different genre of self-portraiture.

Between the composition of *The Father* and that of *Le Plaidoyer d'un fou,* Strindberg found time to write a piece of light fiction. *Hemsöborna* is a pleasant story full of colorful situations, and it fell very happily on the literary market. But Strindberg was in pursuit of larger game. In July and August of 1888, directly following the completion of *Le Plaidoyer d'un fou,* he composed two plays, *Miss Julie* and *Creditors. Miss Julie* was a masterpiece.

Miss Julie involves a single event of crucial character. The play has no intrigue and virtually no complication, and, while in the foreword Strindberg acknowledges the influence of the Goncourts, the technique more readily recalls the practice of the Théâtre-Libre dramatists, and particularly the short plays of Hennique and Métenier. The action takes place in a single act interrupted once by an improvised monologue on the part of the cook Kristin, and once by a folk dance. In accordance with naturalist practice, the set is very precisely arranged and described. There are but three speaking parts, but the boots of the absent Count are constantly in sight of the audience, and they have a certain quiet eloquence.

Unlike *The Father*, *Miss Julie* is a beautifully detailed piece of work. The characters are carefully individualized, the motives thoughtfully worked out, and the action moves smoothly and inexorably through the phases of a rapidly changing relationship in which the conflict of sexes is convincingly identified with the conflict of classes. In considerable measure *Miss Julie* recapitulates the first part of *Le Plaidoyer d'un fou*, which has to do also with the seduction of a woman of aristocratic birth by the son of a servant. In both cases, the woman takes the aggressive role, and the man asserts himself with reluctance; but later he takes unseemly pride in having mingled his base blood with the blood of the nobility.

In *Miss Julie*, the scene following the seduction is brilliantly realistic, and very Swedish. Having broken through the social barrier which all his life he has regarded with awe, the lackey begins to dream at once of capitalizing on his conquest, but the high-born girl cannot stomach his rascality, and they are soon at odds with each other. Unhappily, this brilliant scene leads Julie into a long, "scientific" discussion of her mother's infirmities, from which her own proceed. In the course of these explanations it becomes increasingly clear to Jean that life with this girl may not be altogether amusing. Once again the two begin to quarrel. Suddenly it occurs to them that among the consequences of their new relationship there may be children, and this thought sobers them so far that they decide to elope without further ado. But when Julie reappears in travelling clothes, with her father's money in her pocket, and her bird cage in her hand, Jean refuses to take the bird along, and as Julie says she would rather see it dead than abandon it, he chops off its head on the meat block. This symbolic gesture sends Julie into a hysterical tantrum which is interrupted first by Kristin, and then by the bell which summons Jean to attend his newly arrived master. The sound strikes panic into the miscreants. Julie goes into a sort of hypnotic trance and, in an extremity of terror, Jean puts his razor into her hand, and, at her request, orders her into the barn to cut her throat.

In a celebrated passage in the foreword, Strindberg ridicules the summary characterizations of traditional drama, and compares his own: "I have drawn my figures vacillating, disintegrated, a blend of old and new . . ." Indeed, the characterization in *Miss Julie* is complex beyond anything so far attempted in modern drama. Kristin the cook is rather summarily characterized, but Julie and Jean are studied in the most intimate detail. Julie is by turns pathetic, wistful, haughty, and savage, a maelstrom of moods and motives, but even in her utmost degradation she never loses her air of breeding. In the same way, Jean displays all the possibilities of a strong and ambitious nature, with tastes refined and developed through the observation of his masters, the whole limited by the slave mentality which, it is intimated, he will never lose.

In accordance with naturalist practice, the history of Julie's neurosis is scrupulously examined. It is seen that her difficulties are brought about by a complex of hereditary and environmental factors which betrays her into continual contradiction and uncertainty of mood. She has great need to be loved, but this need is thwarted by her innate hostility to men. This hostility is brought to its paroxysm by the sight of the blood on the chopping block when her bird is killed:

I'd like to see the whole of your sex swimming like that in a sea of blood. I think I could drink out of your skull, bathe my feet in the hollow of your chest, and eat your heart roasted whole! [50]

In Julie's uncontrollable impulses, Strindberg sees an example of the way in which the disintegration of the ruling class is taking place. This class is weakened and diluted chiefly through the looseness of its women. It is therefore destined to be overthrown sooner or later by pressures from below, just as Julie is destroyed by forces emanating from the servile types to which she is chiefly attracted. Her shame, her suicide, the prospective ruin of her father, and the extinction of the line she was meant to carry on are all incidents of the process through which the lower classes will ultimately destroy and supplant the nobility.

What we see in *Miss Julie* is thus another aspect of the social dialectic which Chekhov was to describe, five years later, in *The Cherry Orchard*. The wanton self-destruction of Julie makes an altogether different effect, it is true, from the romantic decline of Madame Ranyevsky, but the process and its consequences are, in sum, the same: both women are ruined through an unsuitable liaison. The Frenchified valet Jean has his exact counterpart, also called Jean, in the Russian play; but the analogy between Strindberg's valet and the energetic Lopakhin is less striking. Lopakhin is characterized very generally; what we know of him is that he is shrewd, strong, and realistic; but he is at the same time magnanimous and timid—he dares not marry into the upper class which his class is superseding. Strindberg was more willing to go into details on this subject than Chekhov. His Jean is therefore very precisely drawn and, as one might expect, the pungent blend of moral and mental attributes which he demonstrates is entirely conformable with the self-portrait which Strindberg gives us in *The Son of a Bondswoman*.

Jean is depicted as an evolving personality in a period of transition. He dreams of trying to climb a great tree of which the lowest branch is out of reach. Julie dreams of throwing herself from the top of a column. Nothing could be simpler than the symbolism of these "dreams": the upper class is suicidal, the lower class, aspiring; and this is the consequence of a destiny which, in Strindberg's opinion, is a biological phenomenon.

With all this, it is perfectly clear that the story of *Miss Julie*, like that of *Le Plaidoyer d'un fou*, is another manifestation of the author's ambivalence with respect to the upper classes, a state of mind which vaguely recalls Ibsen's willingness to accept honors from the state while staunchly maintaining his status as an anarchist. In the valet's domination of the Count's daughter, and her subsequent destruction at his hands, Strindberg demonstrates the pride of the superior male; at the same time, *Miss Julie* emphasizes to an astonishing degree the lackey's sense of unworthiness. Jean rises to great heights in the course of the action, but the sound of his master's voice at the end of a speaking tube is sufficient to dwarf him; and when, at the girl's insistence, he commands her to kill herself, his act is apparently disastrous to them both, for in ordering her to cut her throat with his razor, he makes himself, as he realizes, criminally responsible for her death. He arrives, accordingly, at much the same position with relation to Julie as Hedda Gabler to Eilert when she gives him her pistol with which to shoot himself, and with his last word, which is also the last word of the play, Jean presumably puts an end to his own career as well as to hers.

As the play is usually presented, it is our tendency to emphasize the tragedy of Julie, rather than the plight in which Jean finds himself as a result of her seduction. It is, however, with Jean, and not with Julie, that the author is principally identified, and the extraordinary vividness of Julie in these circumstances eloquently attests Strindberg's power as a dramatist. The midsummer night's encounter with Julie disposes of Julie, but it is also a disaster for Jean.

Julie is thus another example of the *femme fatale*, destined to suffer, and to bring misfortune to all those who cross her path. For Strindberg, she is a degenerate, a half-woman—as with Hedda Gabler, the sign of her degeneracy is her unwillingness to bear children, and in this respect she differs completely from Laura in *The Father*. Laura represents the normal woman, instinctively oriented toward motherhood, in which she finds her happiness, her power, and her reason for being. As mother, Laura is entirely capable of love, and even of tenderness. Julie, like Tekla and Hedda, is, however, not capable of any sort of love, but only of that sort of neurotic impulse which has self-damage for its object. *The Father*, for all its horror, was intended as a study in normal psychology. *Miss Julie* and *Creditors*, on the other hand, are both studies in the psychology of abnormal types.

To Strindberg it seemed that *Creditors* was one of the best things he had ever written. "I read it over and over," he wrote his publisher, "and each time I find new *finesses*—it is a really modern play, human, amiable, with three sympathetic characters, interesting from end to end." [51] His enthusiasm seems exaggerated. *Creditors* is a rather dry demonstration of psychic crime, a case of murder—or, at least, mayhem—by suggestion, and the only explanation of the sympathy which Strindberg felt for its characters is that he identified them in his mind with their originals, Siri, Carl Gustav Wrangel, and himself.

In *Creditors*, Gustav has a classical motive for his crime: he desires to be avenged on his former wife and on the man who, seven years before, robbed him of her, and thus subjected him to public humiliation. The wife, Tekla, is an amiable vampire who lives by sucking the energies and picking the brains of the hapless men whom she attracts. When the play opens, she has already exhausted her second husband Adolf. One might suppose that this would be sufficient revenge for Gustav, but Gustav takes a fiendish pleasure in pushing his retribution so far that Adolf is brought to the point of death.

The action is developed with the cold detachment of a scientific demonstration, but it is very doubtful that *Creditors* was seriously intended as a contribution to the naturalist theatre. It is, in fact, science-fiction, a psychological thriller, the first of a long and fruitful line. As such it has unusual interest, but from a naturalistic standpoint, it comes closer to *Swanwhite* than to *Miss Julie*. In contrast to *Miss Julie*, the technique of *Creditors* is careless and unworkmanlike. *Miss Julie* is placed very precisely in its setting. *Creditors* takes place in a vaguely localized hotel room. The characters, with the exception of Tekla, are not vivid. Adolf is wistful; Gustav, diabolic. Both have a deliberately abstract quality which contributes something to the fantastic nature of the play.

Like *Miss Julie*, *Creditors* is based on the story of *Le Plaidoyer d'un fou*. When Gustav first took Tekla in hand, we are told, her

mind was a *tabula rasa*. It was from Gustav that she had all she
knows; she thinks his thoughts and speaks his phrases. Gustav was
stronger than she. With time and training, she grew impatient
of his mastery, and decided she must find someone to master in
her turn. The artist Adolf seemed to suit her purpose splendidly,
but even with him her first steps were uncertain, and it was at his
expense that she gained the strength necessary to overpower him.

Gustav had taught her how to live. Adolf taught her how to
transform her life into art; thus she has become a successful writer.
But the consequent drain on his psychic energy has been such
that Adolf is no longer able to work—he is psychically crippled.
Seven years have passed. The time has come for Tekla to rid herself of this second spiritual creditor just as she rid herself of the
first. This is the moment Gustav has chosen to present his account.

Gustav's first task is to liberate Adolf from the power of Tekla,
and he does so in terms which recall the methods of Thomas Alva
Edison in Villiers' *L'Éve future*, published two years before, in
1886:

GUSTAV: Look you, she doesn't even speak correctly! You see, something is wrong with the mechanism. The watch-case looks
expensive, but the works inside are cheap. It's the skirts
that do it, nothing else at all. Clap a pair of trousers on her,
draw a moustache under her nose with a bit of charcoal,
then sober up and listen to her again, and you will see how
different it all sounds. Nothing but a phonograph, repeating
your own words and other people's, all thinned down a
bit . . .[52]

In this manner, Gustav sets the stage for the scene of recrimination between Tekla and Adolf, which he proposes to witness from
the adjoining room. When this scene is over, he changes place
with Adolf and, to cap his demonstration of Tekla's depravity, he
gets her to agree to a rendezvous with him that night. There is a
crash in the next room. A moment later, Adolf appears on the
veranda frothing at the mouth, and collapses in an epileptic fit.

Tekla is overcome with remorse. "She really loves him," remarks Gustav. "Poor creature!" [53]

The play thus ends on the familiar note: *"Si je t'aime, gare à toi"*; but, unlike the *femme fatale* of Bizet's opera, Tekla is spared by the victim of her passion. It is perhaps for this reason that Strindberg called *Creditors* a tragicomedy. In fact, with its cast of three, its strict observance of the unities, its simplicity of means, and the exhibition of the victim at the end, from a formal standpoint, the play makes us think of antique tragedy. Actually, Strindberg was moving in quite another direction. The classical look of *Creditors* had nothing to do with the classics; it was simply a method of negating the actual, like the early classicism of Picasso and Chirico. Its artistic relations were as paradoxical as theirs: these reminiscences of the past were a form of futurism.

Creditors was first played at the Dagmar Theatre in Copenhagen on March 9, 1889, by the newly organized Scandinavian Experimental Theatre in a bill that included two of the short plays that Strindberg had written earlier that year, *Pariah* and *The Stronger*. The Experimental Theatre was modelled directly on the Théâtre-Libre, and as its first director, Strindberg examined for production a large number of contemporary Swedish plays. The enterprise failed promptly. There was only one performance of *Creditors* that March, and two of *Miss Julie*; and there was a single performance of *Creditors* later in Sweden. That was all. "Look you," Strindberg wrote to the publisher Geijerstam in December, "the small hate everything that is vigorous and denotes talent. That is why we end up as anarchists . . ." [54]

Toward the end of 1888, Strindberg became acquainted for the first time with the tales of Poe. He was profoundly moved, so much so that he felt certain that he had been designated by heaven to carry the spirit of Poe into the next generation. "Is it possible," he wrote "that this author who died in 1849, the very year of my birth, should have been able through a series of media to transmit his still-living flame as far as me?" [55] All the same, there is no trace of Poe in *Pariah*, and none in *The Stronger*. Both are variations on the theme of *Creditors*.

Pariah was an adaptation of a story by Ola Hansson in which an outcast is forced by a superior intelligence to confess a crime of which he is in fact guilty. *The Stronger* is a dramatic *tour de force*, a fifteen-minute play involving two actresses sitting together in a café on Christmas eve. Only one character speaks. The other reacts with silences and gestures. The situation developed in this ingenious monologue is a distant variation of the Gustav-Tekla-Adolf situation. Y is the strong, silent woman; X is feminine and passive. She has married Bob, whom Y rejected. Bob still loves Y; but X has so far adapted herself to Bob's tastes that, little by little, and quite unwittingly, she has made herself over in her rival's image. Her reward for this sacrifice of her individuality is a home, a husband, children, and happiness, while Y remains alone, nursing her bitterness, her pride, and her hatred. The conclusion is plain: the weaker is the stronger of the two.[56]

The third of the one-act plays of this period, *Samum* (1889), was avowedly written in imitation of Poe. It is, in fact, a psychological thriller in which an Arab girl avenges her lover on a French officer by taking the officer into a cave and killing him with hypnotic suggestions. With this not especially noteworthy play, Strindberg's dramatic afflatus seems to have abated for the time, and the four short plays he wrote in 1892, and published the following year under the title of *Drama*, do nothing to enhance his reputation.

In January, 1891, after a sensational trial full of accusations and counter-accusations, Siri at last obtained a divorce, and the custody of the children. For Strindberg, the trial was the climax of a period of terrible bitterness, financial difficulty, and moral distress. These had been years of incessant toil, during which he had produced some of the best work of his life. Everything had gone badly. His plays were produced with difficulty and brought the most meagre rewards. His books hardly sold—Bonnier had decided not to publish *The Father* or *Miss Julie*; henceforth, Geijerstam became Strindberg's principal publisher. As the author of *Married*, Strindberg was constantly subjected to public humiliation. In these unhappy circumstances, between 1889 and 1890, he composed his great novel *I havsbandet*—later translated into English with the title *In the Outer Skerries*. Its hero is a superman, in whom we have no great difficulty in recognizing Strindberg. After a successful love affair, this hero suffers a complete nervous breakdown, and spends his time wandering disconsolately among the astonished fisherfolk, until he finds the strength to sail away alone with only the stars to guide him.

By this time, in France, the wave of realism was spent. Ten years had sufficed to exhaust its initial impetus; in another ten, virtually nothing remained of the writers of Médan. In the theatre, the naturalists had gone out of fashion even before Antoine closed his doors, and the disciples of Becque were casting about for new styles and new subject matter.

The influence of the idealistic revival was felt almost at once in the Scandinavian countries. As early as 1890, the young writers Werner von Heidenstam and Oscar Levertin had collaborated in an energetic attack on the literary spirit of the 1880's, in the course of which they called for a rebirth of beauty and of imaginative literature. Strindberg, however, declined to lend his authority to any such movement. He was, he insisted, and always would be a naturalist. By 1893, however, his naturalist phase as a dramatist was pretty well at an end. When next he wrote for the theatre, it was in a far different idiom.

Between 1893 and 1897 Strindberg wrote nothing for the theatre. This interval marked the crisis of his career, the mental cataclysm, the Inferno, which divided his life in two. Its first consequences were the three autobiographical novels he wrote between 1897 and 1898—*Inferno, Legends,* and *The Combat of Jacob* —through which he gave the world tidings of his terrible spiritual adventure. At the end of this period, he turned once again to the theatre. He was now a symbolist, a mystic.

The subject matter of Strindberg's mystical dramas was new only to the stage. The literature of dreams and visions in this period was fed mainly through two sources—the new symbolist poetry which stemmed from Baudelaire and the Decadents, and the writings of the very active school of Gnostics and spiritists which included Sâr Péladan and the members of the *Salon de la Rose-Croix*. The relations between poets and spiritists in this period were particularly close, and the two joined readily in the reaction against positivism and naturalism which took place toward the end of the 1880's. In 1889, when Paul Bourget somewhat spectacularly summed up the grounds of this reaction in his novel, *Le Disciple*, the new wave of poetic spiritualism was flowing full and high.

Baudelaire had already laid down the lines which poetry was to follow in the course of the next half-century. In poetry, the realist spirit was still represented by the school of Leconte de Lisle; but in the hands of Rimbaud, Verlaine, and Mallarmé, the new poetry veered sharply away from the concrete, the objective, and the rational into the dark realm of the psychic otherworld which only the imagination illumines. Baudelaire had repudiated nature as infamous; before long, it was subjected to a general attack. Mother Nature, so long inviolate, was now dematerialized by the symbolists, vivisected by the impressionists, and disintegrated by the scientists. On every hand, reason and art collaborated to strip the solid world of its flesh and even of its bones.

In the face of this wholesale devastation, the meticulous descriptions on which the Parnassian poets and the naturalistic novelists had prided themselves were seen to be useless. For the painter as well as the poet the forms of nature dwindled first into riddles, then into symbols; finally they became stereotypes. In time, new stereotypes replaced them, shapes which might provoke a yawn, but which at least owed nothing to nature, and therefore defied analysis. Beyond these intimations there shimmered the ever-beckoning mirage of the eternal.

In the light of the ideal, material existence was seen to be a bore or else a trap: it was advisable to reject it the moment it seemed interesting. The lovers of Villiers's *Axël* kill themselves the instant after they find each other, since life can give them nothing more beautiful than the promise of this moment. Axël says, in the celebrated passage:

As for living, our servants will do that for us! Just as in the theatre, in a seat far from the aisle, one sits out, in order not to disturb one's neighbors—out of courtesy, in a word—some play written in a wearisome style, of which one does not like the subject, so I have lived, out of politeness . . .

The symbolists thus went somewhat further than Baudelaire, to whom they owed their being. Life nauseated Baudelaire, but that perverted puritan was by no means indifferent to it. Insofar as nature was evil, it fascinated him, and he taught that this evil must not be resisted, but transcended.

After Villiers de l'Isle-Adam, the sensualism of the ensuing age was regularly said to be a way of arriving at God. The symbolist poetry thus had a purpose beyond itself. It was intended to be an exploration of eternity, a realm which was, according to the teachings of the influential mystic Eliphas Lévi, chiefly accessible to the poet and dreamer. After Hugo, poetry turned away from the common things of this world. The poet ceased to be a lover, a teacher, or an orator. He became a mage and a seer, and his gaze sought out worlds beyond life.[57]

It is this admirable, this immortal instinct of the Beautiful [Baudelaire wrote], which makes us consider the earth and all its sights as a glimpse, a correspondence of heaven. The insatiable thirst for all that is beyond life and which is veiled by life, is the most vivid proof of our immortality. It is at the same time by means of poetry and through poetry that the soul glimpses the splendors situated beyond the grave. And when an exquisite poem brings tears to the eyes, these tears are not the evidence of an excess of delight, they are rather the proof of an irritated melancholy, of a postulation of nerves in a nature that is exiled in the imperfect and which desires to possess immediately on this very earth the paradise which is revealed to it. Thus the principle of poetry is, strictly and simply, the human aspiration toward a higher beauty . . .[58]

These ideas were rapidly expanded into something that approximated a philosophical system. It is a system that seems strangely inappropriate to its late nineteenth-century context, the more so as it was sometimes advanced with a certain asperity. "All visibilities," wrote Aline Gorren, "are symbols. Our business is to find out what these symbols are. Any book that does not directly concern itself with the hints concealed beneath the diversified masks and aspects of matter is a house built of boy's toy blocks . . ."

As the poet's interests became progressively more esoteric, poetry became more and more difficult to write, and even more difficult to read, and the distance that divided the artist from ordinary people widened immeasurably. So long as the imitation of nature remained the controlling principle of art, the artist served a necessary ministerial function: he represented nature to mankind in intelligible terms, and mankind to nature. Now this link parted. If the visible world was no more than an obstruction to the eye, then art must look beyond nature for its subject, and the poet became indistinguishable from the priest or the medium.

Plato, an enemy of poets, had taught that reason was our only clear window upon reality; but to the disciples of Baudelaire, reason revealed nothing of interest. In their view, the only human faculty in touch with reality was the imagination. Blake had said, long before, that it is only through the imagination that eternity reveals itself—for Rimbaud, also, the image was all that mattered. Following his example, the new poets now devoted themselves exclusively to the quest for the image, the symbol of the unseen, and with this, poetry cut itself off completely from the world of bread and cheese.

As the viewpoint shifted, the nature of art shifted also. For the artist, the soul and its consciousness ceased to be a reflection of the world: the world became a reflection of the soul, the mirror of its images. Nature, consequently, became an individual enterprise, the result of introspection, and the singularity of the poet's impressions were considered to be the mark of his talent and the measure of his insight. Thus art became a revery the elements of which were linked not syllogistically, but through the occult play of association, controlled sometimes by a conscious purpose, more often, not. "To work blindly, aimlessly, like a madman—," Baudelaire had written. "We shall see the result." [59] The result was, in fact, Mallarmé.

Mallarmé was Baudelaire's prophet; but Mallarmé was eminently sane. It was the young prodigious Rimbaud who captured the popular imagination, and his personal drama, set forth convincingly in *Une Saison d'enfer*, became a blueprint for poets. "I have cultivated my hysteria with joy and terror," Baudelaire had written in 1862.[60] Among his disciples, it was understood that a poet was at his best when he was poised most becomingly on the verge of madness. Along with that air of misfortune, which for Baudelaire was the chief mark of beauty, some touch of madness now became indispensable to the artist; and poets and painters everywhere made efforts to live in accordance with the divine frenzy which inspired and consumed them.

Compared with the romantic fury of this period, the madness of the Renaissance seems the merest affectation. Renaissance poets had affected a Platonic frenzy, almost invariably the result of love, and this madness seldom lacked aim or method. But the visions of Rimbaud were altogether unlike the visions of Dante or Petrarch, and, for that matter, not much like the visions of Coleridge or De Quincey. The poetry of the Renaissance, like its drama, was primarily addressed to the intellect, and the pleasure of art was considered to be essentially an intellectual delight. Therefore Renaissance man, however mad as man, had to be sane and workmanlike as artist—the striking example is Tasso.

After Rimbaud, the contrary was the case. In order to have the necessary insights, the artist must be mad even if the man were sane; and in order to circumvent the rational principle, abnormal states were systematically induced, as Baudelaire had taught, by means of hashish, opium, and alcohol. In any case, so far as was possible, the rational in art was given up. The irrational became the true sphere of creative activity, and suggestion took the place of communication.

In this climate of opinion, love, with its insistence on the desirability of the beloved object, became an anomaly. The central tenet of Renaissance art, the perfectibility of man through love, had lost much of its charm in the course of the eighteenth century. The whole idea was now felt to have been a childish illusion, and the long Petrarchan tradition came to an end. For Baudelaire, a sad and deeply religious sensualist, and for his followers, love was pleasurable, an opiate and an irritant, but it was fundamentally evil and its pleasures were perverse. Like other promptings of nature, however, it was not to be rejected, but turned to the account of the spirit.[61]

After Baudelaire there was no great love poetry; but in the theatre, love continued to hold the stage. It was an indispensable dramatic motive, the only sure way to hold an audience. The symbolist drama, however, emphasized to the full the traditional link of love and death. For Ibsen, as we have seen, as early as *Brand*, love was synonymous with health and salvation; it was the sun of heaven, the warmth of life. Yet, although in his symbolist plays love is invariably represented as the hero's ultimate hope and only sure refuge, it is also, infallibly, the mainspring of his destruction. Strindberg came even closer to the current fashion. In *To Damascus*, the first of the plays that followed the Inferno years, love leads the benighted traveller a dance that ends nowhere, and at the end of the trilogy, the Unknown takes regretful leave of this vain hope of happiness, and turns, somewhat grimly, to God.

Inferno, written in French, and published in France in 1897, is a remarkably detailed account of Strindberg's psychic experiences of the years 1893 to 1897. The record of these years of his life, in which he steered a narrow course between the vapors of alcohol and the hallucinations of insanity, is in itself one of the most extraordinary accounts in the history of literature, and it is a mine of information for the student of Strindberg's drama. Nearly all his mystical plays are in some way related to it, just as all his naturalistic plays are connected with *Le Plaidoyer d'un fou*. The two autobiographical novels, with their satellite plays, thus form two distinct complexes in Strindberg's career, closely related, but independent.

The plays of the post-Inferno period involved a whole new series of dramatic conventions. Since these plays were set in a realm that is neither real nor unreal, there was obviously no need to make them conform to the norms of experience. On the other hand, Strindberg made no attempt to relieve the narrative of its actuality: the difference between the naturalistic and the mystical plays is therefore largely a question of the kind and degree of control exercised by the reality principle. The naturalistic plays were fantasies projected upon conventional reality, and therefore had to accord with it in most respects. The mystical plays did not need to be assimilated to reality in any way. They had the validity of dreams, and required, in order to be convincing, only the verisimilitude appropriate to fantasy. Strindberg thus initiated a theatre of the soul in which the laws of revery, or something near them, were substituted for the laws of nature; but in which the action was nevertheless conceived as real, manipulated by the intellect, and directed to the intellect. These plays are, therefore, almost completely intelligible, like the poems of Mallarmé; and where we fail to follow the sense, it is usually because the poet has deliberately chosen to suggest an area for meditation rather than to communicate a meaning.

Strindberg thus transcended naturalism in his mystical drama without essentially changing the naturalistic method. His dream-characters are as well documented as any other characters—they eat, drink, make love, and quarrel like people, but they inhabit a different world. They are phantasms; and, as such, a step removed from such imaginary characters as are confined to the normal categories of time and space. In *Là-bas,* Huysmans had quite appropriately called his method "a sublimation of naturalism." In Strindberg's dream-plays, similarly, the intention is seldom other than realistic. The outlines are precise, the characters are in sharp focus, and the dialogue is, for the most part, easy and colloquial. The result is that realism of the unreal which is Strindberg's specialty, and which, in time, came to be called surrealism.

By the time Strindberg published *To Damascus,* in 1897, the scene had long been set for an innovation in dramatic art. Ibsen had developed symbolism in one way, Villiers de l'Isle-Adam in another, Gerhart Hauptmann in still another. The types of symbolic drama which Maeterlinck had brought to the stage in 1889 with *La Princesse Maleine,* and in 1890 with *L'Intruse* and *Intérieur,* had all but run their course. So far no one had entirely broken with tradition. There was nothing, or almost nothing, in the theatre to prepare one for *To Damascus.* It entered the history of dramatic literature like a rocket from another planet.

The particular form of Strindberg's innovation was partly the result of the artistic influences to which he exposed himself after his return to Paris in 1894, partly the consequence of his own exalted mental state. Under the succession of blows which fate had dealt him after his initial successes of 1887 and 1888, his mind, if we can believe him, had all but given way. But as he drew closer to the edge of despair, he felt within himself a compensatory surge of hope which sustained him marvellously in his wretchedness. With each failure, he became more firmly convinced that he was God's favorite son, marked out for adversity in accordance with some providential plan. Each fall from grace deepened the abyss which separated him from the world and confirmed him in his individuality. He had gathered from Schopenhauer, Nietzsche, and Feuerbach that in life nothing is of consequence save the individual ego. It was, he felt, his mission as an artist to shake off one by one the conventional masks thrust upon him by slaves, and to show the world his true face, the face of a free man, in all the uniqueness of its beauty. His misfortunes were therefore the necessary concomitant of the refinement of his spirit. The secret of life was the Will to Power. The goal of the great man was to dominate the minds of lesser men through the power of suggestion, and also, if necessary, through the power of gold, which a man could contrive to make, with a little patience. Self-fulfillment was a man's only happiness—to grow and to dominate. These ends could be attained through the development of the intellectual faculties, through knowledge and wisdom.

In 1896 Strindberg read Balzac's *Séraphita,* and *Séraphita* led him to the study of Swedenborg and the mystical writings of Josephin Péladan. Through these studies, he began to understand that the evolutionary process through which the superman comes into being is the natural expression of the divine will. The purpose of God in disclosing to Swedenborg the secrets of heaven could have been none other, it appeared, than the acceleration through him of the evolution of the human species.[62] In Péladan's *Comment on devient mage* Strindberg read that *magie* meant "the art of the sublimation of man." All the bits and pieces of wisdom which his mind had sorted out over the years now came together in a clear and consistent revelation of truth. The idea of a malicious God which he had cherished in the days of *Master Olof* was obviously an immature fantasy; God was the end of the human quest. But the mystics too were wrong. One did not sink into God like a stone; one sought him by all the ways of the intellect. The mage forged ahead through knowledge toward an ideal that was completely realizable in this world. For Strindberg, as for Péladan, there was no doubt of the successful outcome of this process; one had only to persist.

The idea of conflict was indispensable in Strindberg's system. On the cosmic plane, the development of the personality, it seemed to him, was a consequence of the psychic struggle of man and God, just as on the social plane it was the result of the psychic struggle of man and man. This battle must be fought to the uttermost. In wrestling with God, the individual must put forth all his strength, and this was a dangerous business to be undertaken only in the utmost peril of life and limb: thus in *To Damascus* the Unknown emerges from the combat in the dark ravine half dead, smitten in his mind and in his thigh by his terrible antagonist.

It was in these terms that Strindberg's many misfortunes now became comprehensible to him. All his difficulties were the result of the conflict with God which, as Ishmael, he had invited and provoked in his youth. He had refused to conform. As a result of his provocation, all the inferior creation, all nature, the servile spirits, and even the Almighty, were in league against him. He had deliberately chosen to assert his superiority, a Godlike act, hybristic in character. He had no choice now but to conquer or to perish. There was no turning back.

The circumstances of Strindberg's existence in the years during which these thoughts took shape in his mind shed a curious light on the development of his genius. It must be remembered that, for all his eccentricity, he was a very bright man and a great poet. It is never easy to understand the mind of an artist: with Strindberg, the difficulty is compounded by the peculiarity of his gifts, for, in addition to everything else, he had a keen sense of humor and a very sound, not to say shrewd, practical sense. No man could say in his case where the madman left off and the mountebank began.

"There are times," remarks the Unknown in *To Damascus*, "when I doubt that life has any more reality than my works of imagination." Pirandello's chief stock-in-trade as a dramatist was this very doubt; but with Pirandello the doubt was carefully nurtured and husbanded and, in any case, it was a philosophical matter, a question of logic. For Pirandello, reality had to be demolished anew day by day, and only his compulsion to do this seems irrational. With Strindberg, this uncertainty was the very condition of his being. For him, the frontiers of reality, which ordinarily are so carefully guarded, stood open, and, if we can believe him, it was well-nigh impossible for him to distinguish shadow from substance. This situation, unquestionably, he wilfully complicated—there is a certain prankishness in even his most solemn flights which is by no means reassuring. But there is no reason for skepticism with regard to the essential nature of his inferno. The man suffered, if not the tortures of the damned, at least something suggested by them.

In 1892 Ola Hansson collected 1,500 crowns by subscription to enable Strindberg to move from Stockholm to Berlin where, it was considered, his talents would be better appreciated. This "charity" brought Strindberg, so he wrote, "a second spring," and he set out for Berlin with high hopes for the future. His literary invasion of Germany, however, did not work out in accordance with the plan. In spite of Hansson's impressive journalistic efforts to smooth the master's way in Berlin, the visit resulted in no substantial gain. On the other hand, Strindberg never forgave Hansson for the "begging letter" which had published his need to the world. There is an echo of this affair in the Second Part of *The Dance of Death*, and in *To Damascus*, Strindberg casts himself, among other roles, as the Beggar.

In Berlin, at the café Zum schwarzen Ferkel, corner of Unter den Linden and Neue Wilhelmstrasse, Strindberg met regularly with a coterie of German and Scandinavian writers and artists, most of whom, it appears, he ultimately succeeded in annoying.[63] In these days also he met and, in the spring of 1893, married the young Austrian writer Frida Uhl.

This second marriage, shorter than the first, but almost equally stormy, provided the impulse and subject matter for Strindberg's second great creative period and the immediate stimulus for the torments of the Inferno years. The marriage itself formed the subject of his novel *The Quarantine Master*, which he completed in 1902. Meanwhile a visit to England, with his bride, to arrange for a production of his plays ended in complete failure. He left London in a bad mood for Hamburg, thence he went to Rügen, then to Mondsee near Salzburg; finally to Dornach on the upper

Danube to stay with Frida's grandparents. By this time Frida was expecting a child, and Strindberg was beginning to identify himself with Buddha, the Superman.

In May, 1894, his daughter Kerstin was born. Although he was normally very fond of children, Strindberg was bitterly jealous of this intruder who had come to supplant him, as he thought, in his wife's affections. The short interval of peace at Dornach came to an end, and in the fall of 1894 he left once again for Paris. Since he was, as usual, in desperate need of money, he persuaded himself that the easiest way to come by it was to make gold, a project he had long cherished; and before long he was involved with crucibles and alembics.

These chemical operations turned out badly. He came to L'Hôpital Saint-Louis in January of the following year with his hands badly burnt, and with symptoms of mental derangement so severe that it was thought advisable for him to undergo a course of treatment. It was only partially successful. In 1896 he spent some months with his friend the celebrated Dr. Eliasson at Ystad in Sweden, and before long he was sufficiently restored so that he was able to visit his wife and daughter at Lund. By the end of 1897 he was well enough to return to Paris.[64]

He was now completely incapable of creative work. In his dark period, he had practiced the Black Art. The elemental powers, as he was well aware, exact a terrible price of those who disturb them unsuccessfully. He had brought evil on himself; and in *Legends* he gives us to understand that in consequence of his transgressions he was possessed by a fiend. Nevertheless, like Faust, he had gained through this traffic unusual insight into the nature of things. With the aid of Swedenborg's *Arcana cœlestia*, he had succeeded in tracing out the parallelism of heaven, earth, and hell, and he was now able to see how the great chain of being is traversed from end to end by a single spiritual force, so that all the forms, from the stones to the angels, are in some degree sentient and animate, and all life is one. The knowledge he gained in these years, he published in a series of extraordinary works on astronomy, botany, and chemistry—it would be a mistake to number them among the major scientific contributions of the age, but they are invaluable to the student of nineteenth-century symbolism.[65]

With his new knowledge, he considered that he was at last ready to demonstrate the scientific basis of religion, and, accordingly, Strindberg set out to demonstrate the workings of the supernatural in terms of logic and scientific method, particularly with respect to the fundamental problem of good and evil. It had become clear to him that men live several lives simultaneously, by means of their *Doppelgänger*. The events of one life appear in the other only in the form of dreams, vaguely recollected; nevertheless, men are responsible in one life for the evil committed in another, and these unremembered sins are the source of the unlocalized guilt-feelings and anxieties from which all men suffer, as well as of the frequent sense of *déjà-vu*. Moreover, as the Vedic writings make clear, the cosmic law involves a retributive principle, so that as one life spends itself in action, a new life automatically takes shape. The world is, in consequence, a hell in which we expiate the evil of past existences, and the evil we suffer is caused by the workings of the corrective spirits whose charge it is to purify our souls through pain. Thus all the events of our lives have symbolic significance. All is moral and meaningful; and to the enlightened mind, life is a journey of discovery, the progressive revelation of the universal will.

It was in this frame of mind that Strindberg composed the *First Part* of *To Damascus*. In March, 1898, he sent the play to his publisher Geijerstam, with a letter which differs significantly from the enthusiastic letters with which he usually recommended his manuscripts: "I am enclosing a play; good or bad—I absolutely don't know . . . If you think it good, submit it to the theatre." [66]

The play was, in fact, a most extraordinary piece of work, mysterious and elusive beyond anything that had so far been done in the theatre. In form it was a species of *eventyr*, a series of dramatic episodes set in the format of an imaginary journey. This was, of course, a familiar genre to the author of *Lucky Per's Journey*

(1882) and *The Keys to Paradise* (1892). The literary ancestry of *To Damascus* is thus traceable to Ibsen and Öhlenschläger; but, unlike *Peer Gynt* or *Aladdin*, which are fairy tales, *To Damascus* has the immediacy of a barely sublimated experience, a true story in an atmosphere of unreality.

It is not altogether impossible that in devising the pattern of *To Damascus* Strindberg gave some thought to *The Master Builder*, which Ibsen had published six years before. Both plays are extremely personal in nature, both have Swedenborgian associations, both involve a struggle with God. In both, moreover, there is a man under a curse, and a mysterious woman who comes in the nick of time, as the agent of supernatural powers, to bring about the purification, and eventually the death, of the protagonist. The similarity goes no further than this, and in any case is of little importance; but it is interesting that Strindberg should have followed Ibsen's design even in its general outline.

The *First Part* of *To Damascus* is, from a formal viewpoint, meticulously planned. The action progresses through a series of nine scenes from a city street to the refectory of a convent; from this point, the hero retraces his steps scene by scene until he arrives once again at the point of departure. Here the play ends, precisely where it began. The narrative, however, is not resolved; the action ends on a suspended note which clearly implies a sequel. Indeed, within a few months, the *Second Part* brought the story some steps further toward a resolution, and in October of 1898, Strindberg wrote his publisher that perhaps both parts might be played, with a few cuts, in a single evening. But the last scene of *Part Two* leaves the end still in doubt; it is not until *Part Three*, finished in 1901, that the action of *To Damascus* comes to a close.

The protagonist of the play is called simply *Den okände*, the Unknown. This character is evidently Strindberg; he is, at least, a fantastic version of Strindberg, and the play develops, in a sharp, unearthly light, the stages of his marital misadventures, his renunciation of love and marriage, and his final withdrawal from the world.

The connections of this story with the realities of Strindberg's life have been traced as far as is possible, and perhaps somewhat further.[67] The Lady of the first two parts, Ingeborg, seems to have been chiefly modelled on Frida Uhl; but she bears also certain obvious resemblances to Siri von Essen. In the *Third Part*, the Lady is clearly identified with Harriet Bosse, Strindberg's third wife. These ladies are not differentiated in the play; they are all simply The Lady: evidently all the women in Strindberg's life were, in his mind, aspects of Eve, the woman who, as wife and mother, tantalized, tempted, and tortured him all his days. The birth of Strindberg's daughter Kerstin, and its singular consequences, are, mainly, the subject of *Part Two*. The *Third Part* is a less literal transcription of reality, and, with the exception of the meeting with his eldest daughter, and the episode concerning Harriet Bosse, it has few very definite connections with the facts of the author's life.

To Damascus I reflects, more or less exactly, the course of Strindberg's wanderings of 1893, together with the sense of persecution and terror which colored them. The street of the first and last scenes has been identified with the street in which Frida Uhl lived in Berlin in the month preceding their marriage; the scene "By the Sea" is very likely related to the brief, happy time they spent together in Heligoland where their marriage took place; and the scenes following it recall the various stages of their journey to Dornach and the neighboring village of Klam. In a dozen ways, the Unknown conveys the sense of being hunted across the land by an invisible Huntsman, and it is with difficulty that he makes his way through the inimical forces that cluster about him, merging and dissolving like evil mists. In the course of these journeyings everything is real, more real even than reality; but the topography is the topography of dreams.

The technique of the later *Dream Play* is already implicit in

To Damascus, but Strindberg did not as yet intend to represent dramatically the consciousness of a dreamer. Here it was his idea, rather, to indicate in symbolic fashion the correspondences and interweavings of the various lines of destiny which formed, as he thought, the texture and pattern of his life, and to suggest the moral significance of events which had originally taken place within the actual borders of his experience, or just beyond. *To Damascus* is not a dream. It is an abstract reconstruction of life in accordance with an underlying pattern of meaning which comes to light as the play progresses. While *A Dream Play* develops a sequence of events localized wholly within the mind of the invisible actor, *To Damascus* conveys a sense of external reality which, though acted upon and colored by the insights and intuitions of the visible protagonist, is actually independent of him.

In the *First Part,* the Unknown meets the mysterious Lady on a street corner within sight of a church, which he refuses to enter, a post office, which he dares not visit, and a café, where they refuse to serve him. A party of brown-clad mourners enters the café, after attending the funeral of someone who was either a carpenter or a carpenter-ant; it is apparently a matter admitting of some doubt.[68] The Lady now comes back from the church to join him. The Unknown falls speedily in love, and before the scene ends, he agrees to free her from her husband, the Doctor, whom she calls a were-wolf—it seems clear that this husband combines, in a single dangerous figure, Baron Wrangel, from whom Strindberg liberated Siri, and Dr. Eliasson, of whom he had conceived a terrible fear during his stay in the hospital at Ystad.

Together, the Unknown and the Lady journey first to the home of the Doctor, then to the seacoast, and finally to the home of the Lady's grandfather, the Forester. It is no accident that their path repeatedly intersects that of certain personages who mysteriously resemble the Unknown—a Beggar, a madman called Caesar in token of his megalomania, and a Dominican, who is actually the *raisonneur* of the play and utters all the wise sayings. These figures, it would appear, are the Unknown's *Doppelgänger,* aspects of himself leading independent existences which are not yet fully integrated in a single personality. At the same time, they are spirits leagued together to encompass his ruin, which is also his salvation.

The Lady's husband, the Doctor, stands in a close relation to the Unknown. Once, long ago, when they were children together at school, the Unknown had done this man an injury greater even than the injury he does him now by stealing his wife. At that time, the Unknown had damaged a library book and concealed his guilt, so that his friend was punished for it. The sin was trivial, but it has colored both their lives, for the Unknown has never lost his feeling of guilt and the Doctor still nourishes a sense of the world's injustice. As for the Lady, the Unknown surmises from the first that she has been sent into his life providentially, in order to purify his soul.

This function, she serves admirably. Turned against the Unknown by her mother, the Lady proceeds to torment him until he can no longer endure her presence. By this time, though he does not know it, he has come some distance toward purification, and this is the result of his unremitting struggle with the Power which tortures him through its manifold agencies, of which the Lady and her mother are but two. The critical phase of the struggle takes place in a ravine near the home of the Forester. The Unknown is found there, unconscious, after what appears to have been a terrible struggle, and, crippled in body and in mind, he is borne to the Convent of Good Help, where little by little he regains his strength. So, at last, in the refectory of the convent, he comes face to face with himself; and, under the influence of the Dominican, all the evil of his past life rises up spectrally to curse him.

The Unknown now returns to the Forester's cottage, humbled, thoroughly anathematized, but still unconquered, to resume the unequal contest with God. But he is beginning to understand. In the eleventh scene of the play, which is crucial, the Mother tells him that he is already on the road to Damascus, and that he must now seek out the instruments of his salvation—first of all, his

wife and her husband, whom he has wronged. He duly seeks them
out, but no one forgives him. What is more, he cannot forgive
himself, and in this pitiable condition he finds himself, in the
end, with the Lady on the street corner where he started. The
Lady persuades him to collect the letter which, he knows, is waiting for him at the post office. When he opens it, he finds that the
money, of which they were in such dire need throughout their
journey, was there all the time. The Lady goes gratefully to burn
a candle in the church. He steps into the church with her but, he
reminds her, not to stay.

In this doubtful fashion, the *First Part* ends. But while the
outcome is deliberately left in doubt, it is clear that the play reflects certain changes in Strindberg's thinking. Most significant,
after so many years of skepticism, is his acceptance of an essentially
Christian teleology. We have seen that the plays of his first period
reflect Hartmann's position that pain is the natural condition of
existence, and that there is peace only in non-being. Strindberg's
second creative phase, however, was dominated by the idea of the
ethical purpose and the moral structure of the universe. But in
taking this more hopeful viewpoint, he did not entirely relinquish his former pessimism. In this newly moralized universe,
nature appears no more benign than it did before. The world, as
always, is full of misery; but this misery is now seen to have a purpose. It is through pain that guilt is expiated and the soul purified,
as, step by step, it learns through suffering to know and to accept
God, who epitomizes all human suffering. The net result of Strindberg's conversion was therefore to sanctify pain and to dignify
humiliation in terms of the divine plan, and thus to give significance to what was formerly a senseless torment.

Similarly, the sexual relation, which Strindberg had thus far
considered, in Baudelairean terms, as a fascinating, but tragic
paradox, now seemed to him to be an essential part of the process
of purification. Woman, he realized, is God's angel, sent to man
for his sins, in order to refine and to humble his soul through
suffering. The process, as Strindberg saw it, is not quite as Dante

described it; but it is evidently in some relation to the medieval idea of the refinement of man through the pain of love. In Strindberg's view it is through the purgatorial pains of marriage that the soul is refined of its pride and egotism. The road to Damascus is consequently enlivened by the incessant bickering of the pilgrims.

The transformation of the captivating angel into the self-centered fury who makes a hell of our domestic life is explicable, moreover, in terms of the transfer of evil from the soul which is undergoing purgation to the soul which is administering it. In changing her husband little by little into a saint, the Lady becomes bit by bit a devil, and in this process her character as vampire becomes comprehensible and benign: it is her function to suck out of her husband's soul the poison which is in it, and to store it up for a time within herself; this is a Christ-like act of self-sacrifice. The she-monster is thus in reality a kind of saint; though not the kind of saint one loves to touch.

Finally, since it is natural to resist suffering with all one's might, it is only through a relentless chase that God drives us to him. The proof of God's love is the agony he inflicts upon the object of his affections. The elect is hunted, dodging and doubling piteously, to the steps of the temple. He is driven into it only after passing through the full extremity of despair. With this conclusion, Strindberg was able to bring the Kierkegaardian ethos into a neighborly relationship with the Swedenborgian view of nature. The result was a strange, but consistent system which afforded him the greatest satisfaction the rest of his life.

In the *Second Part* of *To Damascus*, most of these motives are developed in detail. The Lady of *Part Two* closely resembles Laura in *The Father*. She intercepts her husband's letters, frustrates his scientific ambitions, and humiliates him in every way in order, so she says, to suppress everything that might minister to his pride. Her former husband, the Werewolf, now reduced to despair by his wife's desertion, providentially appears from time to time to add to the torments of his successor in her affections. The Unknown, like the protagonist of *The Father*, thinks to distract himself by engaging in scientific research. He has already succeeded, as he thinks, in making gold. His experiments, however, are interrupted by his wife's pregnancy; and when the Mother gives him to understand that the child cannot possibly be his own, he flings off in a fury.

The third act opens with an extraordinary scene which fully anticipates the technique of A Dream Play. A banquet is being given in honor of the Unknown, but even while the frock-coated professor is elaborating his encomium of the man who has at last succeeded in making gold, the guests are transformed as if by enchantment into a motley array of tramps and beggars, the banquet hall is seen to be a room in a low dive, and the Unknown is arrested because he cannot pay the bill. After this débacle, his humiliation might be thought to be complete, but even in his prison cell he hears the horn of the pursuing Huntsman.

Meanwhile, his child is born, and the Unknown abandons it. When next he is seen, he is in a state of terrible degradation. It is, presumably, at this point that his pride at last is broken, and his sanity is restored, for now the madman Caesar kills himself, and the Dominican, who is somehow merged with the Beggar, comes to take the Unknown to the convent toward which all this time his path has tended. The Unknown is thus, it is suggested, no longer at odds with himself, and the Christian monk in him at last has the upper hand in this newly integrated personality.

To Damascus III, from a dramatic viewpoint much inferior to the rest, was written some years later in a somewhat different style, and was first published in 1904. It brings the tale of the Unknown to a definite conclusion. In the first act, the Unknown arrives, still under the tutelage of the Dominican, at the banks of a mysterious river, which suggests Lethe in Dante's Comedy. Across the river, on a mountain above the clouds, is seen the monastery which is their goal. While they are waiting for the ferryman, the Unknown meets his eldest daughter, Sylvia, now grown to womanhood, finds her completely indifferent to him, and takes final leave of her. Then the Lady appears. Her little daughter is dead. She herself has suffered deeply, and, through her suffering has purged herself of evil, so that she is once again young, pure, and beautiful.

At the instigation of the Tempter, an argumentative personage who dodges somewhat ineffectually in and out of the action, the Unknown decides to make one last try at life with the beautiful Lady. But the happiness of their first days together soon turns into boredom and discord. The Unknown finds himself involved a third time in the agonies of marriage, and at last he agrees that the time has come to give up the struggle for happiness once and for all. In the last scene, after justifying the inconsistencies of his behavior by passing in review a gallery of great men of history who were more inconsistent than he, the Unknown puts aside the Tempter and accepts at the hands of the venerable Prior the mystical death which is the prelude to his new life in Christ. There is not much enthusiasm in this acceptance. The Unknown accepts peace in Christ only because he is sick to death of the world. He achieves salvation not through conversion, but through exhaustion. He has been literally hunted to death, and the last words of *To Damascus* are: "May he rest in peace. Amen."

If *To Damascus* is the ancestor of the *avant-garde* drama of our time, it is evidently not so by reason of its form. In this respect, it belongs to the allegorical tradition of the Middle Ages: it is a play of quasi-abstractions which represents in quasi-allegorical fashion the progress of a soul weighed down by pride, beset with ambition, and subject to temptation. It also illustrates the progressive integration of the various aspects of a schizoid personality into a unified and harmonious whole—it is a description of the illness and the cure of a tortured soul, and thus it employs a very ancient technique for a very modern purpose. The characters are partly individuals, partly personifications, somewhat like the characters of Bale's *King John* or the Digby *Saint Mary Magdalen*, and the situations with which the hero meets are occasionally reminiscent of the situations one encounters in such works as *The Faerie Queene*.

It would be stretching a point, perhaps, to suggest that *To Damascus* is a multiple allegory, like *The Faerie Queene* or *The Divine Comedy*, but its result is precisely that polyphony of significance which multiple allegory was designed to produce. The resemblance may not be entirely accidental. *To Damascus* was written in a period that witnessed a general revival of interest in allegory, and the habit of thought we associate with allegory. It was conceived in accordance with the theory of correspondences and the doctrine of signatures. In consequence, its action lends itself readily to analysis in accordance with the system of interpretation which Dante set forth in the *Convivio*. It is astonishing that in harking back through Baudelaire, Balzac, Swedenborg, and the Paris Gnostics to the metaphysics of a bygone age, Strindberg should have brought out of his Inferno a quasi-medieval work that was to furnish the blueprint for the most advanced drama of the twentieth century, and perhaps for the Joycean novel as well, but, astonishing as it may be, such seems to be the case.

Whatever its formal relations may be, however, *To Damascus* is, in substance, essentially modern and unorthodox. It is probable that Strindberg knowingly followed the medieval style—the influence of the *Divine Comedy* could not be clearer—but he followed it as freely as did the painter Rouault. *To Damascus* breaks repeatedly through its veil of abstraction, and though it traces the journey of its protagonist from the "dark wood" of the street corner, through the infernal regions, to the pure heights of the celestial city, its mood is as different from that of Dante's *Comedy* as is the mood of Joyce's *Ulysses* from that of the *Odyssey* which in similar fashion it mimics. The Unknown sees a good deal in the course of his journey, but he does not see God. *To Damascus* ends not in paradise, but in death, and by death is meant, obviously, that withdrawal from the world and its concerns which Strindberg from time to time believed he had achieved in his later life. In the end, he finds peace and inner harmony, but not joy, and his desire at no time merges in the love that moves the sun and the other stars.

From the dramatic standpoint, curiously enough, the central action of *To Damascus* bears an unmistakable relation to the familiar theme of regular tragedy, the persecution of the beautiful innocent victim by the cruel tyrant. Since in this case the tyrant is none other than God, and the victim, Strindberg, the outcome cannot be other than good; but it is obviously not a happy outcome. The play is Christian enough; but there is something undeniably embarrassing in the sense of injustice which the Unknown carries with him into the very bosom of the Creator. In the end, the action is resolved; but it is not quite clear that the hero is resolved; on the contrary, the implication is that, although he has surrendered, he is not reconciled.

This effect results, in part, from the fact that, in spite of the cosmic breadth of the canvas, *To Damascus*, insofar as it is tragic, is essentially domestic tragedy. It is through his wives, chiefly, that the Unknown is brought to his knees. He has some public humiliation, but his spirit is not broken; he never becomes abject. He goes down, still bickering, into the grave. The last view he has of life on earth is of a bridal couple,

. . . what is loveliest and most bitter, Adam and Eve in paradise, which in a week will become a hell, in a fortnight, paradise again.

For the Unknown, the grave is the only sure refuge from the joys of marriage, but he accepts it reluctantly. At the very last the old gambler is tempted to try his fortune yet once more; but, with the good sense of the experienced playwright, he hastily admonishes the inner Tempter: "Stop! Or we shall never come to an end!"— and he permits himself to be wrapped in the funeral vestments. The idea of the purgation of souls through the pains of marriage has, after all, its comic side. There is no reason to believe that Strindberg was blind to it.[69] We should be disposed to take the final scene of *To Damascus*, with its sombre procession and its funereal air, somewhat more seriously were there not about it some suspicion of that impudent wink which was Strindberg's special *cachet* as an artist.

To Damascus marks a turning point in European drama. Although the occult style in poetry dates back at least as far as the *trobar clus* of the twelfth century, dramatic style has always been relatively clear. The development of the art of motivation and the analysis of character was based, we have seen, on the assumption that motive and character are intelligible and that, in consequence, through observation and reason human behavior is in some measure understandable and even predictable. From this standpoint, drama, like science, is a clarification of experience. With *To Damascus*, however, Strindberg inaugurated a more arcanic tradition in the drama.

In *To Damascus*, Strindberg for the first time abandoned the principle of logical sequence in favor of a relatively free structural arrangement in which the selection and disposition of elements is dictated not by a syllogistic principle, but mainly by a necessity arising from the writer's inner sense of design. By releasing the narrative, in this manner, from the conventional categories of realism, with its rigid chronology of cause and consequence, Strindberg was able to anticipate on the stage some of the rhetorical effects of post-impressionist art. But unlike the mannered painters of a later day, he had no idea of making a purely decorative use of such devices. His rhetoric was always employed in the service of an idea; and in this he came closer to Cézanne than, for example, to Matisse, or to Gauguin, whom he knew well, but did not admire.[70]

To Damascus is, at bottom, the dramatization of a conceit—analogous therefore to such poems as Herbert's *The Collar* or Thompson's *The Hound of Heaven*, quite as much as to the *Comedy* of Dante—and in the juxtaposition of seemingly unrelated elements within the conceptual pattern we may often discern examples of what may be termed dramatic metaphor. Much in *To Damascus* seems spontaneous or arbitrary, but the fact is that the narrative sequence is at all times under intellectual control; and what appear to be accidental or merely decorative associations are in reality excursions artfully contrived to extend or to enrich the central thought which the narrative develops.[71]

It is evident that no mere love of novelty led Strindberg into the intricacies of this sort of writing. It was in order to reveal what the realistic method cannot reveal, and to capture nuances which elude direct expression, that Strindberg went beyond the realism of his first period. Since it was his object to represent on the stage a psychic experience far more complex than anything the theatre had as yet seen, he was forced to experiment with a much more complex apparatus than any dramatist had so far employed. For his purposes he levied largely on the rhetorical techniques of poetry, but even more on the rhetoric of dreams, a form of experience of which Western drama had made use from its very first days, but which no modern dramatist had so far treated other than superficially.

Even before the Inferno years, Strindberg had given evidence of an astonishingly keen intuitive faculty. In *The Father*, the Captain's observations on the behavior of woman as mother and mistress may hardly seem remarkable in the light of modern psychoanalytical literature. Similarly, in *To Damascus*, Strindberg's reference of a life-long feeling of guilt to a trivial misdeed of childhood, his awareness of the search for the elusive mother in the various embodiments of the Lady, his depiction of the integration of the disparate elements of a split personality, his intuition of the part played by an unfaithful mistress in stimulating the unconscious homosexuality of the men who share her [72]—these may strike us as ideas common enough to the thought of our time. But it is noteworthy that these observations were arrived at poetically, not scientifically, some years before Freud published any of the writings which now serve to illumine the world of the unconscious.[73] In the case of Freud, these discoveries were the result of clinical observation and a brilliant application of scientific method. But the intuitions of Strindberg were purely the result of his genius.

For Strindberg, *To Damascus* inaugurated a period of intense literary activity. Immediately after finishing the *Second Part* in the fall of 1898, he began work on a novel, *The Cloister*; after that he wrote two plays, *Advent* and *Crime and Crime*, published together under the title *Before the Highest Court* in 1899. Both plays belong to the Inferno complex, though they represent it in quite different ways.

Advent is a sort of miracle play with autobiographical allusions —Strindberg called it a Swedenborgian drama. It has to do with an unrighteous judge and his wife, unpleasant people who mistreat their son-in-law and cause him to be separated from his wife and children. God sends the Other, a fallen but repentant spirit, to drive these evil-doers, through tribulation, into the fold. Through the stern ministrations of the Other the judge is paralyzed and blinded, and eventually tried by the former victims of his injustice, while a grand spectral ball is organized in hell in honor of his wife. The infernal regions, however, are not what they once were. Since the harrowing of hell, Christ has forced evil to serve his purpose. Consequently there is no longer evil in the world; what seems to be evil is simply the evidence of God's discipline, and thus at the proper time, Christmas is celebrated in hell, complete with a crèche, and a choir that sings the *Gloria*. The relation of this play to the rest of Strindberg's œuvre, and the nature of the author's revenge upon the Danish court of law which deprived him of the custody of his children seems too clear and too quaint to require elaboration.

Crime and Crime is seemingly in naturalistic style, but it differs significantly from the plays Strindberg wrote under the influence of the Théâtre-Libre a decade earlier. Unlike those plays, it is firmly localized: the action takes place in Paris, in and around Montparnasse, and the entire narrative has a flavor of the Latin

Quarter and the *vie de bohème*. As in *Creditors*, the plot centers on a psychic crime, in this case a murder; but the play is substantially a study of guilt and retribution, and the religious aspect of the case absorbs much of the author's attention.

Crime and Crime follows closely the lines of a play by Octave Feuillet, called *Dalila*, which was unexpectedly revived, much to Strindberg's chagrin, at the Théâtre de la Renaissance in March, 1899.[74] Strindberg called *Crime and Crime* his "boulevard play." Indeed, this moral tale of a man led astray by a *femme fatale*, with its conventional adjuncts, the faithful friend, and the compassionate abbé, was admirably suited to the boulevard audience of the day. Evidently, Strindberg saw more in this banal tale than meets the eye, and he retold Feuillet's story with an intentional air of naïveté which is completely foreign to the original. *Dalila* is a typically commercial drama of the period, while *Crime and Crime* makes the primitivistic effect of the later paintings of Van Gogh.

The narrative makes no concessions to verisimilitude. In two days' time the hero, Maurice, is shot up from obscurity to the pinnacle of success, dashed down to the depths of the most terrible degradation, then borne up once again to his former height, while his friend Adolphe experiences analogous changes of fortune in counterpoint. The minor characters have the simple and earnest bearing of puppets. Their entrances are timed precisely for effect; their sentiments are conventionalized according to type; everything is done to give the play an effect of the *guignol*, and though it differs markedly from the marionette plays of Maeterlinck, *Crime and Crime* makes an excellent puppet show. Of all Strindberg's plays, it comes closest to his idea of drama as a medium of instruction for those who do not read.

The plot is typically Strindbergian. Like the Unknown in *To Damascus*, Maurice makes off with another man's woman, and finds punishment for this sin in the very relationship which he has thus created. The play is a demonstration of the workings of sin, and in the violent peripeties of the action are discernible the operations of the divine plan which merges these destinies briefly in order to turn them, each in its way, into the path of righteousness. In these terms, the reason for the studied unreality of the action and the strange rigidity of the characters becomes comprehensible.

Although the action is realistically conceived, the total effect is far from realistic—the technique, indeed, is the technique of symbolism, and the play is deliberately removed a certain distance beyond the plane of actuality. The action is therefore drastically simplified, and the characters abstracted to the point of caricature, for the author is concerned here with the pattern they trace rather than with those details which for the naturalist constitutes their reality. The technique has much in common with that of *To Damascus*, and serves the same purpose. In both plays, the protagonist is oriented, through misfortune, toward God; and, in both, he stops short of complete submission. Just as the Unknown of *To Damascus I*, chastened by his sojourn in hell, returns to find the money he needs waiting for him at the post office, so Maurice is delivered from his inferno to find himself once again rich and respected, and he too consents, gratefully, to pass through the church, but not, as he says, to stay.

Crime and Crime is, in sum, a kind of exemplum conceived in the spirit of the early Renaissance painters: it makes us think of Giotto, Uccello, Fra Angelico; in terms of theatre, it has the charming naïveté of *Nice Wanton*. In twentieth-century art this style had its counterpart in the reconstituted innocence of the later Gauguin, Van Gogh, Matisse. Not long after the composition of *Crime and Crime*, Matisse wrote:

Quand les moyens se sont tellement affinés, tellement amenuisés que leur pouvoir d'expression s'épuise, il faut revenir aux principes essentiels qui ont formé le langage humain. Ce sont, alors, les principes qui "remontent," qui reprennent vie, qui nous donnent la vie.

It was in accordance with such ideas that the post-Inferno plays were written. Whatever the professed intention may have been, these plays were new departures from first principles. It is obvious that anyone who could write *Miss Julie* would not consider *Crime and Crime* a work of art in the same style. This play is, in fact, at the opposite pole, technically, from *Miss Julie*, and expresses more clearly the reaction against the school of Scribe. *Crime and Crime* is not, perhaps, as successful, artistically, as *Miss Julie*; but that is quite another matter. This style of art was new, and its forms were not yet clear; only the intention is clear. In spite of the idea expressed in the Author's Foreword, *Miss Julie* is too sophisticated a work, too complex, and too closely bound up with the actual and the specific, to point a simple moral or to convey a simple thought. *Crime and Crime* is exactly suited to this purpose. It is from this point of view that its charm becomes apparent.

This play is thus rather more interesting than at first appears. Some years after its publication, Shaw made a new approach to comedy by rationalizing melodrama. Strindberg was on another tack. By exaggerating the conventional effects of melodrama well past the point of credibility, he succeeded not only in giving to a banal action the fabulistic quality of a fairy tale, but also the glaring realism of a nightmare. This impression is accentuated by the fact that in *Crime and Crime*, under the conventionally moralistic surface of the action, we are conscious of an entirely unconventional current of sensuality, the presence of which indicates its relation to the symbolistic literature of the period.

Since the time of Baudelaire the literature of wickedness had vastly multiplied, but Strindberg was the first since Webster to bring the poetry of evil to the stage. In the opening scenes of *Crime and Crime*, Maurice is made to savor the pleasures of sin as if he were tasting caviare for the first time. In the later scenes we find him enjoying no less voluptuously the pangs of suffering and remorse. Somehow, this puppet-like character succeeds in conveying as clearly as the carefully individualized Miss Julie the irresistible fascination of wickedness for those who are not wicked. Although these aberrations are rationalized, as in *To Damascus*, in terms of the Swedenborgian idea of the chastening function of evil, *Crime and Crime* has a perverse quality which we do not find in *To Damascus*, and which makes it more or less unique among the plays of this period. Just how this nuance was intended to emerge in the theatre, we do not know, but we know that the author did not mean Maurice's brief excursion among the flowers of evil to be treated with Norwegian solemnity, that is to say, in what he believed to be the manner of Ibsen. He wrote expressly that he would prefer the play to be played in "Swedish style," ironically, and with a touch of comic skepticism.[75]

The end of 1897 brought Strindberg's period of suffering for the time being to an end. Indifference, more than anything, had driven him to the verge of insanity. It seemed that the louder he shouted, the less attention was paid to him. Now suddenly he was rescued by success. *Master Olof* had been briefly welcomed on its initial appearance. All at once, its merits became apparent and, at the end of 1897, it had a magnificent run of fifty-three performances at the Vasa Theatre in Stockholm. Strindberg lost no time in turning this success to account. In 1899 he wrote, in quick succession, four masterpieces in the historical genre, each of which served, in one way or another, to round out the autobiography which was his chief concern as a writer.

In 1900 Strindberg left the university town of Lund, and came to Stockholm to live. That fall he wrote *Easter*, a play in three acts set in a university town. It clearly reflected his convalescence and the optimistic direction his thoughts were now taking, and it found ready acceptance. It was first presented in Frankfort in March, 1901, and was played that same year during Easter week in Stockholm. The role of the hypersensitive Eleanora was acted by the brilliant young Norwegian actress Harriet Bosse.

Like *Crime and Crime*, *Easter* is a modern exemplum, designed to illustrate the manner in which pride is humbled through suffering. The two plays follow the same general pattern—in each case the protagonist is brought to a desperate pass, and is then rescued by a sudden peripeteia. Like the Borkmans in Ibsen's play, the

Heyst family is expiating a misdeed on the part of the paterfamilias: the elder Heyst has been convicted of embezzlement and is serving a term in prison. The family keeps up appearances as best it can. The son Elis is a schoolmaster. The daughter Eleanora has been sent to a mental hospital. The cloud that hangs over the family is embodied in the person of Mr. Lindkvist, a brutal creditor who has obtained an execution against the family property, and is sadistically biding his time to serve it.

The three acts of *Easter* correspond to three movements of Haydn's *Seven Words of the Redeemer*, of which a movement is played as a prelude to each act, so that the play is an entertainment of predominantly musical character. After the introduction, *Maestoso adagio*, the action begins. It is Maundy Thursday, the sun is warm, the windows are open, spring has come. But things are going badly—Elis's pupil, Benjamin, fails his Latin examination; Eleanora comes home unexpectedly from the asylum; Mr. Lindkvist has been seen prowling ominously in the neighborhood. On Good Friday (*Largo No. 1. Pater dimitte illis*), things get worse. It now appears that Eleanora is being sought by the police for breaking into a florist shop and stealing a jonquil. Elis has cause to suspect that his fiancée, Kristin, is partial to his friend Peter. Mr. Lindkvist looms so near that his malignant shadow is literally cast over the scene as he stands outside the window in the light of the streetlamp. The family is evidently on the brink of disaster; but on Easter Eve (*No. 5. Adagio*), all is arranged happily. The affair of the florist is pleasantly settled. Kristin is seen to be devoted to Elis. The menacing Mr. Lindkvist, after terrifying the family with various legal documents he draws from his pocket, turns out to be a loyal friend of the father. He meant them no harm at all. It was his intention merely to give Elis a lesson.

Mr. Lindkvist, who haunts the play like a bogey, only to reveal his heart of gold at the end, is a character out of Dickens; but here, as always, Strindberg lapses into sentimentality for a specific purpose. In Swedish, Lindkvist means linden twig: Mr. Lindkvist's function is symbolized by the Lenten birch which Elis has received in the mail from an anonymous donor, and through him, in the last days of Lent, Elis's pride, self-pity, and anger are beaten out of him, until he recovers the sense of humility that is suitable to the season.

Like the Dominican confessor in *To Damascus*, Mr. Lindkvist sees all, knows all, and in the end arranges everything. As a character, he is entirely human; nevertheless, he appears to be possessed of clairvoyance, has mysterious insights into the souls of those whom he persecutes, and even knows what they are thinking. It is quite clear, therefore, that this strange person is meant to embody one of those corrective spirits through whose agency God's purposes are achieved on earth. From a naturalistic viewpoint, Mr. Lindkvist, it is true, does not make good sense; but the play cannot be judged in this way. Like *Crimes and Crimes*, it has the innocent quaintness of religious drama and, since Mr. Lindkvist serves a supernatural purpose, it is reasonable to allow him the sort of latitude that supernatural characters require.

The mad girl Eleanora is one of Strindberg's most enchanting characters. Strindberg himself repeatedly alluded to Eleanora's connection with Balzac's Séraphita, "Swedenborg's niece," the androgynous angel; but the character seems closer to Maeterlinck than to Balzac.[76] Like Mr. Lindkvist, Eleanora is supernaturally sensitive, but she is sensitive in quite another way—she understands the language of the flowers, and is so close to the heart of the world that all its suffering is concentrated in her soul.

It is possible that in creating this poignant character, Strindberg was thinking, as he wrote Harriet Bosse, of his own sister Elisabeth, who was sent to Uppsala Asylum while he was at Lund recovering from his illness.[77] But it is even more likely that he was thinking of himself, for he, too, understood the allegorical language of flowers, and lived close to the heart of the world; and he had strange intuitions concerning his destiny and that of others. On February 25, 1901, in a letter written to Harriet Bosse after she had undertaken to play Eleanora, he included, in his usual style of mystification, a paragraph which perhaps refers to his own spiritual status in this world:

Why did I send you the bizarre *Prince de Byzance*? That is a very long story that would begin with Eleanora's close kin, Balzac's Séraphita-Séraphitus—the angel for whom no earthly love exists because he-she is *l'époux et l'épouse de l'humanité*. A symbol of the highest, most perfect type of humanity, which has figured lately in the contemporary literature; and which by some is thought to be coming to earth to live. Ask no explanation now, but keep the word in your memory . . .[78]

By spring of 1901 Strindberg was thinking amorously of Harriet Bosse, whose luminous portrait is sketched in *To Damascus III*, and who had already played the part of the Lady in the Stockholm production of *To Damascus I*. It was, strange to say, in the first months of his acquaintance with her, at the end of 1900, that Strindberg wrote the *First Part* of *The Dance of Death*, the most gruesome of his plays on the subject of marriage. In the first weeks of January, 1901, he finished the *Second Part* and subsequently offered Miss Bosse the role of Judith, which frightened her. In March he asked the young actress to marry him. She was then twenty-three:

He told me how hard and severe life had been for him—how he longed for a ray of light: a woman who could reconcile him to humanity and her sex. Then he placed his hands on my shoulders, looked at me long and ardently, and asked: "Would you like to have a little child with me, Miss Bosse?" I made a curtsey and answered, as though hypnotized: "Yes, thank you!"—and we were engaged.[79]

Immediately after the "naturalistic" *Dance of Death*, Strindberg turned again to the style of *Advent*, and by the end of April, 1901, he finished *The Crown-Bride*, a grim peasant-tragedy with a decidedly Christian coloring and a strong element of the marvellous. It made no great noise in the world. On May 1st, 1901, he was married.

The Dance of Death does not have, seemingly, the religious turn of *To Damascus*, nor does it entirely reflect the anti-feminist attitude of *The Father*. Its point appears to be the plight, tragic and comic, of two people shackled together by time and passion, utterly weary of their marriage and each other, and yet helpless to escape. For these characters marriage seems to be neither a refining nor a chastening process, but a state of unendurable boredom which fosters every form of malignancy, and is therefore even more dangerous to the bystander than to the participant. The situation which *The Dance of Death* depicts is tragic, but the play is not a tragedy; it is a sort of farce, the first example, perhaps, in modern drama of the tragic farce.

The action takes place in a symbolic setting, the living room of an old tower, guarded by an armed sentinel, on an island fortress nicknamed "Little Hell." It is, in effect, a corner of hell, shared by the elderly Captain and his wife Alice, two people whose destiny it is to torture one another as long as they live. The Captain has not been advanced, and despairs of promotion. The wife is a former actress, still attractive, and full of regrets. Both are failures, nourishing delusions of grandeur, tense with hatred and bitterness, seedy with ennui, miserably poor, and too weary even to quarrel.

Into this environment comes Kurt, an old friend of the family who has been posted to the island as Quarantine Officer. His presence acts upon this seemingly stable situation as a reagent, and at once it begins to seethe. The Captain has a bad heart, and is on the verge of death, but he cannot resist the exciting opportunity of goading first Kurt and then Alice into a series of evil actions. The tension mounts. Alice denounces her husband to his colonel as an embezzler of military funds; she takes Kurt for her lover, and openly taunts her husband with his disgrace. The Captain draws his sword to kill her, then collapses in a death-like swoon. Kurt, overcome with disgust, leaves the two to their fate. The moment he is gone, they become calm; they joke and laugh together: the incident has united them, and once again the grim game begins. They plan to celebrate their silver wedding as if nothing had happened.

Through this pattern are shot the threads indispensable to Strindberg's art. According to Alice, the Captain is a man-eater who destroys the lives of others because his own life lacks interest. For her part, she does what she can to accelerate his destruction, not because, like Laura in *The Father*, she needs to prove her mastery, nor because, like Ingeborg in *To Damascus*, she means to chasten his pride, but simply because she cannot bear him. The Captain, however, refuses to die; he seems to leap back and forth with ease across the frontiers of being. These leaps are involuntary. He is jerked from death to life like a puppet on invisible strings, and there are times when, in the same strange fashion, he is made to dance.

He dies midway through his dance, actually, toward the beginning of the play; but he revives soon after, and when he comes to himself, his mood is changed. Now he no longer seems sane, and it is, in fact, as if he were possessed by a demon. His wife suggests he is now a vampire, but she talks at random; it is clear she does not understand. In fact, his behavior is not that of a vampire, but of one whose erotic impulses are entirely involved with cruelty and the desire to suffer. In the *First Part*, the Captain appears to have no further purpose than the satisfaction of his sadistic tendencies. It is only in *Part Two* that we are given the clue to his moral function.

Part Two takes its departure from the situation of the *First Part*, but its style and its intention are new. The *First Part* ends in a stalemate which presumably will last indefinitely. In the *Second Part*, the Captain is much altered—we find him mysteriously invigorated, decorated, and prosperous, and with the greatest gusto he proceeds to ruin his friend Kurt systematically and in detail. He then moves into Kurt's house, possesses himself of his furniture, and arranges to have Kurt's son Allan ignominiously posted, with the aid of charity, to an infantry regiment in Norrland.

Kurt bears all this, and more, with the patience of a saint. The Captain, meanwhile, has arranged a shameful but profitable match between his aged colonel and his young daughter Judith. But, at the last moment, Judith discovers that she really loves Allan, and she acts decisively to thwart her father's intentions. The Captain's fury at this unexpected setback is so great that he suffers a stroke in consequence, but even in his mortal agony, he continues to struggle. His wife taunts him with his helplessness; paralyzed, he spits in her face. She boxes the dying man's ears and pulls his beard. It is only when he is borne off at last to die that her hatred leaves her. In a little while, the young Lieutenant in attendance comes to announce that the Captain is dead. Strangely enough, his last words were, the Lieutenant reports, "Forgive them, for they know not what they do." Kurt tries in vain to fathom the meaning of this exhortation. Meanwhile a change has come over the house: with the Captain's death, all its evil has evaporated, and its tensions have relaxed. The peace of death descends upon it, and with it come the sweetness and the sadness of death, and its dignity. The dance is over.

It is the Captain's last words that furnish the clue to what has happened. The Captain really died in the midst of his dance, in the first part of the play:

CAPTAIN: Well, my dear, when I had that first attack, I passed over for a while to the other side of the grave. What I saw I have forgotten, but the effect has lasted . . .

The implication is that the Captain was sent back from the other side of the grave for a purpose, and that he is no longer as he was. Indeed, from this time on, he acts the part of a chastening spirit, like the Other in *Advent*. Through the Captain's malignant influence, Kurt, who has sinned with Alice, is purified to the point of sainthood, while his persecutor, by sopping up and concentrating in himself all the evil of his surroundings, becomes progressively uglier and more hateful.

In the end, his malignance benevolently touches all those with whom he comes in contact. By arranging an outrageous match for his daughter, he causes her to triumph over her own evil tendencies; by humiliating young Allan, he brings out unexpectedly all the sweetness of Judith's nature. Even his wife, having thoroughly vented her malignance upon him, emerges from the ordeal of marriage purged of evil, resigned and calm. As for himself, his final agony is as terrible as a crucifixion; indeed, it is a crucifixion, for, having laden himself with all the evil his soul can carry, he dies as a scapegoat, a *pharmakos*, supremely self-sacrificial. His last words are therefore entirely appropriate to the occasion. Through his wickedness, he has redeemed them all, and it is only after his death that some realization of his worth dawns upon the others:

ALICE: Riddles! Riddles! . . . Do you know, it is very strange, but the Lieutenant's simple words—and he is a simple man—still echo in my ears, but now they mean something. My husband, the love of my youth, —yes, you may laugh, but he was a good and noble man—in spite of it all.

KURT: In spite of it all. And a brave man too. How he fought for his own existence and for what was his!

ALICE: What anxieties! What humiliations! Which he cancelled— so he could pass on.

KURT: He was one who *passed over*, that's the crux of it. Alice, go in to him!

ALICE: No. I can't. For while we have been talking here, I've had a vision of him when he was young. I saw him—I can see him now—as he was when he was twenty . . . I must have loved that man.

KURT: And hated him.

ALICE: *And* hated him. May he rest in peace!

It is in this fashion that Ingeborg, grown hideous through the evil she has absorbed, appears to the Unknown in the second act of *To Damascus III*, pure and beautiful as she was in youth, with all her evil and her ugliness purged through suffering. But while, very likely, *To Damascus III* furnished the philosophical basis of *The Dance of Death*, the *Second Part* of this play is obviously related to the situation in *Creditors*, in which a man wantonly ruins another out of revenge. In order to utilize that situation for his present purposes, it was necessary for Strindberg to make Kurt as meek and passive as Adolf in the earlier play, while the Captain is unexpectedly characterized as a man full of energy and extraordinarily full of evil, somewhat like old man Hummel in *The Ghost*

Sonata. The action of *Part Two*, with its underlying moral intention, thus proceeds on the plane of conscious exaggeration which is characteristic of Strindberg's technique at this time, and the result is a series of scenes in bold and garish colors, with great contrast and emphasis, and not the slightest verisimilitude.

The weeks preceding Strindberg's marriage were a period of great happiness. He felt young, gay, and at peace with the world, and in this pleasant mood, he composed the fairy play *Swanwhite* for his bride, with the intention of having her play the title role. As it turned out, she did not play it, and it was not produced until 1908, at Strindberg's Intimate Theatre, sometime after their divorce.

Strindberg had first read Maeterlinck in 1894, with considerable distaste. Six years later, he read *Le Trésor des humbles* and was so completely won over that he translated it into Swedish. It was under the influence of Maeterlinck, he told Schering, his German translator, that *Swanwhite* was written. But while *Swanwhite* is entirely characteristic of Strindberg, there is very little in it to remind one of Maeterlinck.

Swanwhite is a naturalistic fairy tale with quite transparent autobiographical allusions. The prince who comes to court the young princess Swanwhite in the name of his king, only to fall in love with her himself, has curious affinities with the Unknown of *To Damascus*, as well as with its author. He is a very imaginative, but not very brave prince, and everyone is unjust to him. What is more, he has qualities not altogether usual in fairy-tale princes— he bickers unpleasantly, for instance, with his princess over a trivial difference of opinion arising out of a misunderstanding. Through the evil influence of Swanwhite's wicked stepmother, he is confined to a prison tower so that his hair turns gray and his skin withers before its time, and eventually he is drowned in the coracle that bears him away from the palace. Through the power of love, however, Swanwhite brings about his resurrection, restores his youth and his good looks, and they are married and live, presumably, happily ever after. The personal allegory is perfectly transparent. It was more or less in this fashion that the lovely Harriet Bosse restored the aging poet, after his self-imposed period of incarceration, to youth and the joy of life.

In the unhappy upbringing of Swanwhite is reflected a good deal of the detail of *The Son of a Bondswoman*. Swanwhite's mother, like Strindberg's, died young, and the wicked stepmother, through her magic, which is evidently of the order of hypnotism, has complete control over Swanwhite's father, the duke. The stepmother naturally detests Swanwhite, and hopes to advance her own ill-formed daughter at the expense of the true princess. With this end in view, she provides Swanwhite with a minimum of soap and water so that her feet are always dirty, and her underclothes will not bear inspection. In a passage of a sort uncommon in fairy tales, the stepmother reveals the reasons for her wickedness: it is because she was crossed in love early in life that her goodness turned to evil. Thus, when Swanwhite saves her at the last from the accumulated fury of the duke, her hard heart melts, and she is suddenly transformed once again into her true self, which is beautiful.

What all this amounts to is a bourgeois *drame* in a Hans Christian Andersen setting, and the result is neither good domestic drama, nor a convincing fairy play; nor is it an especially good example of symbolism. *Swanwhite* is, in fact, chiefly interesting for the insight it affords us into the manner in which the technique of *A Dream Play* developed in Strindberg's mind. *The Crown Bride* and *Swanwhite* cannot be said to be successful plays, either of them, but from a technical viewpoint they repay study as the bridge that leads from the technique of *To Damascus* to that of Strindberg's most authentic masterpiece.

A Dream Play was written during the period of disenchantment that followed the first days of Strindberg's marriage.[80] Miss Bosse had been swept off her feet by the glamorous recluse, but she found life with him intolerable. As a successful young actress, she was accustomed to a stimulating social atmosphere, and a host of admirers. Strindberg was ringed about with a thousand fears and furies. He had a horror of meeting new people, and a morbid fear of travel, and he was insanely jealous.

They were married in May and lived happily till June. In June they quarrelled. In August they went together to Berlin. At the end of August, Harriet left him. His efforts to effect a reconciliation are preserved in a heart-rending correspondence.[81] Having left the apartment Strindberg had furnished for her at Karlavägen 40, in Stockholm, Harriet took lodgings and manfully sustained a bombardment of letters from her husband. At first these letters were urgent, passionate, insistent; little by little, as the fall wore on, they took on an elegiac tone. By September all hope of reconciliation was gone. Miss Bosse was expecting a child. Strindberg was writing *A Dream Play*.

He finished it in January, 1902. It was not written easily: his mind was troubled, the technique was new, and he began without knowing too well where he was going. The play went through successive transformations.[82] From the various drafts which Strindberg preserved, it is evident that he did not plan it originally as an uninterrupted dream, nor was the heroine at first conceived of as a visitor from outer space. Strindberg's diary indicates that it was not until after the play was finished that he reread the myth of Brahma and Maya, and became involved with Eastern writings, until suddenly he perceived "the explanation of my Dream Play, and the significance of Indra's daughter, and the door's secret: nothing." [83]

In its original conception *A Dream Play* was written in somewhat the same style as *To Damascus*, to which Strindberg refers in an Author's Note as his "earlier dream play." One of the first drafts was entitled *The Drama of the Corridor* (*Korridordramat*) in allusion to the stage-door alley of the opera house where the Officer waits interminably for his beloved Victoria. A later draft was called *The Growing Castle*, and this in turn became *A Dream Play*. In the final version, Strindberg's talent for organizing a bundle of disparate elements into a unified system functioned bril-

liantly, and for once he was able to fuse into a single poetic concept all he had gathered from Hartmann, Schopenhauer, Nietzsche,
and Swedenborg, together with some half-digested notions out of
the Upanishads and the Mahayana scriptures, and some odds and
ends of socialist thought, the whole colored by his recent disenchantment and his habitual sense of the futility of the human condition. The result of this truly supreme effort is, from a philosophic
viewpoint, a glaring example of uncritical syncretism; but there
can be no doubt of its value as poetry. A Dream Play is the most
exasperating and also the most impressive piece of dramatic writing of our time.

The panorama of human misery which Strindberg unfolds for
the edification of the god Indra is by no means systematic; but it
certainly covers the ground. The traumata of childhood, the con-
tagion of evil, the antagonism of the great and the small, the
tragedy of marriage, the discomforts of domestic life, social injustice, the benign function of pain, the moral structure of the
universe, the meaning of life, le goût du néant—it is a compendium
of Strindbergiana. Casting the play in the form of a dream made it
possible to achieve the greatest flexibility of structure, without
sacrificing either the unity of the style or the unity of the action.

Strindberg had experimented successfully with this form in
To Damascus, and it provided the model, but in A Dream Play he
went further. To Damascus is a sequence of scenes strung together
on a thread of narrative, slender enough, but traceable, so that the
episodes are presented chronologically in a more or less clearly
articulated train of events. In A Dream Play the narrative element
is minimal. The drama is a mosaic of images arranged rhythmically,
but without strict chronological succession, in a spatial frame that
has no special dimension. The result is intended to approximate
revery, but it is far from the jumble of freely associated images that
throng to the mind when we are not thinking. It is, on the contrary, a carefully ordered syllogy of experiences, lyric rather than
dramatic in quality, without logical implication, but with an extremely high degree of resolution.

Strindberg appears to have realized before anyone else that dramatic realism, with its implied certainty of means, was a mirage which sooner or later must be dispelled, just as the *certezze* of the Florentine masters of perspective were dispelled in time. The Scribean theatre had attained a certain perfection with Ibsen, but, as Ibsen must have realized when he wrote *The Master Builder*, this formal perfection, like the "scientific" perfection of Renaissance painting, rested upon artificial conventions which greatly limited the possibilities of the art. The *trompe l'œil* of the theatre obviously has its uses; but the tricks of realism can no more guide the writer in conveying the subtle nuances of his thought than the tricks of perspective can assist the painter in conveying a feeling of sky or of receding atmosphere.

In the theatre, undoubtedly, realism can achieve certain pleasing effects through the mechanics of motivation which the nineteenth century perfected, but these effects have little to do with the type of reality which is the subject of poetry. The search for dramatic realism initiated by Diderot and his followers led infallibly to the search for dramatic truth, but this quest led far beyond the point which Diderot set for himself as the goal of the dramatist. By the time of Ibsen, the theatre of Diderot had been fully realized. The result was a technique which, at best, perverted the drama by imposing on the theatre the function of a peep-box, just as the search for spatial illusion perverted the true nature of pictorial representation on a flat surface.[84]

The revolution in dramatic art which Ibsen and Strindberg inaugurated thus paralleled quite closely the revolt against the limitations of academic painting which was developing in their day, and its purpose was much the same—the attainment, not of greater realism, but of a deeper truth, a wider basis for artistic expression, and a more complete utilization of the possibilities of the medium. Cézanne did not seek to imitate nature, but to create, as he said, "a harmony parallel with nature," a second reality, achieved, as in the case of El Greco, through distortion, exaggeration, and the emphasis of the meaningful.[85] The *Dream Play* makes very much an impression of this nature. Moreover, with relation to the subject, in this type of drama, neither the eye nor the mind of the beholder is thought of as fixed. Since, in *A Dream Play*, the images of the fantasy have not the rigorous order of the events of a story, they can be presented as a picture in which the eye of the beholder is directed from shape to shape, but in which it is at liberty to roam at will, assembling and resolving the units into patterns, the meanings of which are suggested, but not forced upon the mind.

Among the consequences of this technique was a regression from the three-dimensional solidity of the naturalistic theatre, with its emphasis on the backs of the characters and the stage furniture, to the earlier idea of the two-dimensional stage-picture, in which the characters emerged at the most into bas-relief. This made it possible to emphasize the symbolic aspects of the play to a degree hardly conceivable in realistic drama, in which the author is ordinarily so completely preoccupied in specifying his action that it is all but impossible for him to pass from the thing seen to the universal values of the fable. The reaction against the "specified particulars" of the naturalistic mode made itself felt in the drama as early as *The Master Builder*. Thus, what Eric Newton had to say of the modern trend in European taste with regard to painting twenty years ago might be applied without altering a syllable to the type of drama which Ibsen and Strindberg developed about the turn of the century:

Its direction has been steadily towards puritanism of outlook and classicism of form. It concerns itself with essentials, not with accidents; with generalizations, not with particular instances; with fundamentals, not with surface truths; with things digested by the mind, not merely seen by the visual eye. It has in fact retracted its steps from the purely visual world of nineteenth century art . . .[86]

It is reasonable to call the technique of *A Dream Play* expressionistic, if only to distinguish it from the impressionistic tendencies of the period. But while the term existed in Strindberg's day —it is said to have been coined in 1901 by the painter Julien-

August Hervé, and to have been taken up soon after by Matisse [87] —it probably would have meant little to Strindberg, and less to Ibsen, although both were in close touch with current trends in painting. In Strindberg's time the ideas that were to be associated with this term by the German expressionists a decade after his death had certainly not crystallized into anything like a complex. Nevertheless, everything indicates that *To Damascus*, *A Dream Play*, and *The Ghost Sonata* were the chief literary precursors of the short-lived, but influential drama of Hasenclever, Wedekind, Werfel, Toller, and Kaiser.[88]

Like *Peer Gynt*, *Lucky Per's Journey*, and *To Damascus*, *A Dream Play* traces the steps of a mythical journey. The plot—if it can be called a plot—is rudimentary, another and more abstract version of the narrative which underlies the action of *To Damascus*. *A Dream Play* develops the situation of a lady who becomes, presumably, the mistress of an officer, through whom she meets a lawyer, who marries her. She bears him a child. But in time she finds life with the lawyer unendurable, and she sets off with her first love on a long journey which she does not enjoy, but in the course of which she meets a poet, whom she finds congenial. The lawyer now attempts to assert his conjugal rights, whereupon the lady puts an end to her troubles by withdrawing from the world. Such, at least, are the bones of the action; and seldom has a plot had less relation to a play.

Though *A Dream Play* in many ways recalls *To Damascus*, the narrative patterns necessarily differ a good deal. *To Damascus*— the story of a man hunted by God—belongs to the tradition of the medieval chase-allegory, and, very properly, has a medieval coloring. *A Dream Play* belongs to the *topos* of the visitor from another sphere. Since, in this play, the Daughter of Indra is on a sight-seeing tour of the Christian world, she grows and develops, but she maintains her identity from beginning to end; she is, essentially, a constant in variable circumstances, and in this she somewhat resembles the Unknown in the earlier play. She is, however, unlike

the Unknown, fundamentally an observer, and her perceptions
are therefore much more objective than would be the case were
she the primary subject of the action as he is. Nevertheless, in a
general way, it is as if in A Dream Play the story of To Damascus,
or something near it, were told from the viewpoint of the Lady.

The play, we are told in the foreword, is intended to produce
on the stage the effect of a dream.[89] Its shapes arise out of chaos
half formed, with wisps of chaos, so to speak, still clinging to them.
In its effects of abstraction and its bizarre groupings, it clearly announces the art of the twentieth century; yet its subject matter and
its mood are unmistakably romantic. It is, moreover, as I have suggested, only seemingly amorphous. Its episodes are grouped quite
systematically within the rigid frame that encloses them. It has a
beginning, middle, and end; and its conclusion follows from the
données of its beginning in a way that is by no means characteristic of dreams. Beyond doubt it was a brilliantly revolutionary departure in its day, far ahead of the theatre of its time. It is only
when we compare it with more completely developed examples of
the genre it inaugurated—the brothel scene in Ulysses, for example
—that its connections with the romantic tradition of the nineteenth century become apparent.

It is customary to say that in this play Strindberg explored the
workings of the subconscious during sleep,[90] but it must be obvious that the unconscious elements of A Dream Play do not come
into consciousness here any more readily than they would in any
other play. A Dream Play is a play, not a dream. It is a montage of
scenes in prose and verse composed in accordance with a conscious
artistic aim, and for a wholly rational purpose. The play has therefore the enigmatic character of a work of art, and not at all the
enigmatic character of a dream, and while much of its beauty, and
its power, are derived from what is suggested by and to the unconscious, on the whole it is directed to the intellectual faculty
and is meant to be understood.

Within the mythological frame which Strindberg imposed
upon it, A Dream Play consists of a series of vignettes abstracted

from the autobiographical sources which customarily provided him with his subject matter. It is, like *To Damascus*, essentially a personal statement, the complete comprehension of which would entail an impossibly intimate knowledge of the author's life and works. Consequently, although it has been the subject of the most careful study, much of the detail remains, and very likely will always remain, puzzling.[91] Underlying the entire conception is the Brahmanic myth of self-sacrifice, to which Strindberg gave a vaguely Christian tone. As he understood the myth, the diversification of Brahma was the result of a sexual act, a seduction, and in the union of Brahma with Maya, the world mother, was figured the primal union of spirit and matter, corresponding to the creation of the world.

The Daughter's name, Agnes, was doubtless suggested by Agni the fire-god and heavenly messenger, often associated mythologically with Indra, the principal god of the Vedas, lord of the sky and the lightning, and dispenser of the fructifying rain. The Daughter's incarnation in *A Dream Play*, and her life on earth, is a species of sacrifice in the course of which she experiences all the evil she can bear in order to carry to her heavenly father a full report of the miseries of mankind. Through Agnes, Strindberg once more rationalizes the desire for suffering as a spiritual yearning for deliverance. The Daughter says, in words which come somewhat closer to Hartmann's *Philosophy of the Unconscious* than to the Upanishads:

But in order to be freed from the earthly element, the descendants of Brahma sought renunciation and suffering . . . And so you have pain as the deliverer . . . But this yearning for pain comes in conflict with the longing for joy and love . . . now you understand what love is: the highest joy in the greatest suffering, the most beautiful in the most bitter! [92]

Strindberg's position in *A Dream Play* is thus entirely consistent with his earlier views on the subject of pain and pleasure. Deliverance is a matter of freeing the spirit from its material involvements. This necessitates suffering. Pleasure binds us to the flesh; pain liberates us from it. It was through woman that the spirit was first entangled in matter, and it is through her that it is trapped in the flesh forever in the irresistible process of reproduction. But woman, who seduces the spirit through joy, also chastens it through suffering, and thus she teaches us the way of renunciation by which the spirit may be freed from the misery of being. Meanwhile the lot of mankind is pitiable, for man is continually torn between the craving for joy, which enslaves him, and the desire for suffering, which liberates him from the flesh. Such, according to the Daughter, is the answer to the riddle of life—as much of it, at least, as the Poet is privileged to hear.

There is nothing to indicate that Strindberg's acquaintance with the complexities of Eastern philosophy was other than superficial; but it was amply sufficient to support the poetic groundwork of A Dream Play. The Daughter's explanation of the riddle of the universe is based on the fundamental myth of atma-yajna, the act of self-sacrifice through which God brought the world into existence, and through which man eventually resumes his godhead. In the beginning, according to the myth, the Consciousness behind the universe, in the guise of Brahma, created the world by an act of self-forgetting, or self-dismemberment, through which the One became many. The diverse universe was the result. But this diversity of nature is only a seeming, maya. Accordingly, all attempts at definition and classification are merely an expression of the viewpoint of the beholder. In reality, there is only the flux of being; the forms exist only with relation to one another; and the play of contraries is simply the result of a poetic fiction, since order would be meaningless without disorder, and good would have no special character without evil.

The play of God does not go on eternally; only for countless kalpas of time: ultimately, the God comes to himself again, but only to forget himself once more in the endless game of improvisation. In the meantime, the individual consciousness, "that which knows" in each mind, is none other than God himself, the primal consciousness, and each individual life is a role in which the mind of God is absorbed in the course of the play which is our reality. Thus, the one divine actor plays all the parts, and when the play of existence comes to an end, the individual consciousness awakens to its own divinity.[93]

The sacrificial act by which God gives birth to the world, and by which men in turn reintegrate themselves into God, involves the giving up of the individual life. This act is the same whether it be considered from the standpoint of creation or of cessation. For Strindberg this act had an erotic connotation. He symbolized it through the Growing Castle, where life begins and, in its flowering, ends. The Swedenborgian influence is seen in the manner in which the correspondence is indicated between the dream of man and the dream of God, the micro-macrocosmic relation. In Strindberg's play, the dreamer—with relation to his dream—is Brahma; and his single consciousness becomes multiple as he bodies forth through his fancy the dream-characters who live their independent lives while his mind is absorbed in them, and yet have no being aside from his.

The dreamer's personal experience, moreover, has universal character. In his dream, all begins and ends, and begins again through the Growing Castle, which endlessly initiates the cycle of birth-and-death, samsara.[94] In the Mahayana scriptures, the castle is sometimes used as a symbol for the personality, the ego, in which the individual fortifies himself against the external world, isolating himself in the belief that there is a sacred difference between one individual and another, while the truth is that there are no individuals; and the external world is merely the externalization of mind, which casts its shadow, as the French symbolists would say, in order to see itself.

The characters of A Dream Play thus stand in a complex relationship to one another. They are at the same time different and the same, many and one. In To Damascus, which makes use of a similar relationship for symbolic purposes, these identities are rationalized in metaphysical terms, though even there we are aware of the psychological undercurrent as one by one the personalities of the Unknown are integrated into his single person until at the end only the Tempter remains unresolved. In *A Dream Play*, the identification is wholly psychological—all the characters, and all their experiences, are manifestations of the personality of the dreamer, from whose sole consciousness they derive their being, and whose fantasy is their life.

Aside from the Daughter of Indra, *A Dream Play* has four principal characters: the Officer, the Lawyer, the Quarantine Master, and the Poet. Whatever else they may be or represent, these characters, evidently, are four aspects of the author, the dreamer, and in their composite life is indicated his manifold nature.[95] Moreover, since Strindberg cherished the idea that men lead several lives simultaneously, the four characters are thought of sometimes as four independent personages, sometimes as a single individual, depending on the circumstances. It is much the same in *To Damascus*. Here, the Officer represents the romantic hero, the Lawyer is the bickering husband, the Quarantine Master, the merciless critic, while the Poet is the lover of beauty in his creative aspect, and is consequently more closely identified with the author, as dreamer, than the others, since *A Dream Play*, in a strict sense, is the Poet's dream.[96]

To the Daughter of Indra, however, the dream gives a degree of autonomy that the other characters have not. She is the subject of all the dreamer's experience, the mirror which reflects his consciousness, and she is also, like the Lady in *To Damascus*, the woman he has endlessly wooed and lost. In that play, the Unknown has relations with the Lady in her various guises, chiefly, but not exclusively, as himself; but in *A Dream Play* the dreamer wins and loses her as Officer, Lawyer, and Poet in turn: he experiences her from every angle. Ultimately, of course, she too is an aspect of the dreamer; but, it is implied, an aspect of his truest and inmost self, which is conversant with God.

It is consistent with this idea that the Daughter is the only personage who develops organically in the course of the action; and this action is, on the whole, her biography. In the beginning she is relatively innocent, eager to experience life, energetic, and full of curiosity. At the end, she is weary and heavy with suffering, but yet as knowing and as fierce as Beatrice in the *Purgatorio*, whom she recalls:

DAUGHTER: . . . Look into my eyes.
POET: I cannot endure your gaze.
DAUGHTER: How then will you endure my words, if I speak in my own language? [97]

In keeping with its dream-like character, the action of *A Dream Play* involves a wealth of detail, not all of which comes into focus, and not all of which admits of a ready interpretation. The Daughter of Indra is first seen outside the Growing Castle in which the Officer is found imprisoned. She appears in the company of the Glazier (*Glasmäster*), whom she calls father. There is no certain way to identify the Glazier, whose diamond is capable of opening all doors, including the doors of the castle. Possibly this character was suggested by Baudelaire's prose-poem *Le Mauvais Vitrier*; possibly, Strindberg had in mind the great Leverrier, director of the Paris Observatoire; there are certainly other, and perhaps better, possibilities.[98]

With the Growing Castle, we are on safer ground. The figure appears to have been suggested by the vaulted roof of the cavalry barracks, with its crown-shaped cupola, which Strindberg could see above the treetops from the window of his study at Karlavägen 40 in Stockholm.[99] In *A Dream Play* the castle grows quite appropriately out of the heaps of manure and straw that accumulate around stables, and, since it is a growing thing, it is topped by a blossom. The symbol of the flower, rooted in the soil and aspiring to the heavens, was a favorite figure with Strindberg: in *The Ghost Sonata*, there is the shallot which grows out of the lap of Buddha. The phallic character of this symbol need hardly be pointed out; doubtless Strindberg intended to suggest through it the reproductive process by which through pain the material world little by little becomes spirit.

In the interior of the castle, the restive Officer somewhat hesitantly permits the Daughter to draw him into the outer world, in order that he may see how, in spite of the pitiable condition of mankind, love conquers all. The allusion is clear in this scene to the role of Harriet Bosse in drawing Strindberg from his self-imposed seclusion, and the feelings of guilt and impotent fury which his seclusion involved.[100] Having liberated the Officer, the Daughter passes, without any transition, from the castle to the stage-door corridor of the opera. There is a giant monkshood growing behind the gate; for Strindberg, the monkshood, with its charming blue flower and its deadly root, was a symbol of worldly desire. The Officer appears, top-hatted and frock-coated, bearing a bouquet of roses: he has come to wait for his beloved Victoria. He has been waiting for her to come out, we learn, for seven years, and while he waits, he is overcome with a longing to see what lies beyond the mysterious clover-leaf door which opens off the theatre alley. The tempo of the action is suddenly accelerated. Day follows night, flash upon flash. The Officer comes and goes. His hair grows white. His clothes become shabby. His roses wilt. Victoria never comes out. The Officer preserves his good humor; he does not despair, but at last he insists on having the mysterious door opened, behind which, he is told, is the answer to the riddle of life. He sends for a locksmith. Instead, the Glazier comes with his diamond. He is about to open the door with this instrument when a policeman commands him to stop in the name of the law. The Officer resolves that the law which forbids us to know the riddle of life must be changed, and he dashes off, in the company of the Daughter of Indra, to find a lawyer.

The opera corridor now literally dissolves into the law office. The clover-leaf door, which remains on the stage as a visible reminder of the unsolved enigma of existence, thus becomes the door to the Lawyer's document file. For a time, the Officer gives place to the Lawyer as the focus of attention, and the Daughter becomes the principal witness of the Lawyer's pain. Like the Lady of *To Damascus II*, the Lawyer has grown hideous because of the evil absorbed from his clients. The law office suddenly turns into a church; the clover-leaf door becomes the entrance to the vestry; and the Lawyer, who is passed over in the conferring of degrees which takes place in the church, is crowned not with laurel but with thorns. The Daughter sits at the organ, from which she elicits screams of human pain; then the organ turns into the resonant wall of Fingal's grotto, which is called the ear of the world. In this symbolic setting, the Daughter joins her destiny to that of the Lawyer, so that she may experience with him the supreme joy of life, which is love and marriage. The scene at once dissolves into the squalid apartment which they share, and in which the Daughter has so far savored the joys of marriage that when the Officer comes to her rescue, she gladly goes away with him.

The Officer means to take the Daughter to the beautiful seaside resort of Fairhaven. Instead, they land at Shamestrand. There they meet the Quarantine Master. In this worthy, whom the Officer greets as "old chatterbox" (*Ordström*: literally, word-stream), we are invited to recognize Strindberg in person. He is in blackface, because, as he says, he finds it best to show himself to the world a shade blacker than he is; and he tells us that it is in order to forget himself that he has taken up masquerade and play-acting. Now the Poet appears, his eyes on the heavens, and a bucket of mud in his hand, and gradually the suggestion takes form that it is essentially he who is the dreamer whose dream we are witnessing. There ensues an interlude in which a pair of lovers, one of whom is the Officer's beloved Victoria, are mercilessly fumigated by the Quarantine Master, in spite of the Poet's protests.

The symbolism once again grows transparent. The fumigation scene is evidently intended to represent comically the inner conflict of the dreamer in his trinary capacity as hero, critic, and poet. As the hero of the play, he recognizes his lost love, and he feels jealousy; as poet, he feels compassion; but in his capacity as national watchman, it is his duty to apply the severest measures to prevent the spread of the disease of love. While the lovers go sadly into the quarantine shed to be purified of passion, the Officer prepares to take up the hated profession of schoolmaster in order to support his mistress. Accompanied by the Daughter, he enters Fairhaven, the earthly paradise, a rich resort where a ball is constantly in progress. As it turns out, nobody is happy in Fairhaven; and the Officer suffers deep and undeserved humiliation as a student in the very school where he meant to teach.

The dream now becomes fragmentary. The cry of human anguish swells higher, and the Daughter, utterly weary, and faced with the obligation of returning to the Lawyer's home, yearns mightily for the peace of the upper world. To be rid of the Lawyer, and his domestic entanglements, however, she must retrace her steps until she is once again her own true self. She begins the backward journey in the company of the Poet. They find themselves first in a Mediterranean resort where two coal heavers demonstrate how society makes a hell of paradise. Then they are once again in the marine grotto, and the play begins to unwind. The Poet presents the Daughter with a petition for the lord of the universe. From the grotto they witness a shipwreck at sea: Christ himself appears on the waters, but his appearance merely serves to inspire the mariners with terror. While these visions appear and dissolve, the ship's mast turns into a tree, the cave turns into the opera-house corridor, and now the Daughter summons the chancellor and the faculties of the university to witness the opening of the door which conceals the secret of the universe.

Time rolls back. The Officer appears, young and fresh, with his bouquet of roses for Victoria. Before the assembled faculties, constantly at odds with each other, the Glazier solemnly springs the lock with his diamond. The door swings open: there is nothing behind it. The university faculties grow angry. They threaten to stone the Daughter. But by now the Daughter has recovered herself sufficiently so that she offers to reveal the secret to the Poet if he will come with her into the wilderness. The Lawyer opposes this, asserting his claims and the needs of his child. It is in vain. The corridor scene turns back into the Growing Castle. The Daughter reveals to the Poet the secret of the origin of pain, the nature of love, and the source of power; but she stops short of the ultimate answer, and the riddle remains unsolved as she shakes the dust of the world from her feet and prepares to enter the fire which will make her one with the air. The flame springs up spontaneously. While the characters of the play appear one by one and cast into the flames the poor things they have prized on earth, the Daughter speaks her farewell to mankind:

DOTTERN: . . . O, nu jag känner hela varat's smärta,
så är det då att vara människa . . .
Man saknar även det man ej värderat
man ångrar även det man icke brutit . . .
Man vill gå bort, och man vill stanna . . .
Så rivs hjärtats hälfter var åt sitt håll . . .
. . . Farväl!

(DAUGHTER: . . . Oh, now I know the whole of the pain of existence.
This, then, it is to be a human being . . .
To regret even what one never valued,
and feel remorse for what one never did . . .
To wish to go, and to wish to stay,
Thus the heart is cleft this way and that . . .
. . . Farewell!)

She enters the castle. Silhouetted against the wall of human faces, the castle burns, and as the flames rise high, the chrysanthemum bud that tops it bursts into flower.

The symbolism of A Dream Play thus ranges from the simplest and most amenable sort of signification to the most baffling. The train of thought that underlies it is at once straightforward and labyrinthine; yet the general impression is one of spontaneous improvisation. This is unquestionably the effect Strindberg aimed at, and the degree of success he attained is the more remarkable when we consider that the play was not developed from a unified conception, but is the result of the assimilation of several quite independent ideas, the full significance of which was avowedly not realized by the poet until after the play was substantially finished. The Growing Castle and the Corridor Drama were not, in the beginning, related at all; the unifying figure of the Daughter of Indra came quite late into the frame, and the Mediterranean episode was interpolated, unfortunately, without much reference to the organic nature of the whole. In consequence, the progression is not uniformly smooth, nor is the play consistently meaningful. The first two scenes are original beyond anything that has ever been done in modern drama; the kaleidoscopic sequence that separates the first grotto scene from the second makes the effect of a series of exempla; the Mediterranean scene is in an obviously discordant style of allegory; the end is magnificently Wagnerian. The whole work, with its recurrent figures, transpositions and inversions, its thematic development, and the management of its modes and rhythms, makes less the effect of a dream than of a musical composition, a symphony, perhaps, or a tone-poem. A work of this sort might not be expected to convey very much to the mind by way of meaning. Its power of suggestion, however, is enormous, and this is to a considerable degree the result of the intricate scheme of correspondences by means of which the action and its symbols are laced together.

The Growing Castle, for example, evidently symbolizes the aspiration of the earthbound spirit, rooted in matter, and striving eternally to rise above it. The Officer who is liberated from the castle exemplifies a similar aspiration in the living individual, drawn out of himself by a vision of divine beauty into the hurly-burly of life. These two ideas are certainly not precisely correspondent, but they are related, and the result is a composite metaphor which has great cogency. Like the Castle of Alma in *The Faerie Queene*, the Growing Castle is the soul's prison; but the Growing Castle symbolizes also, and in quite another way, the aspiration of the flesh through which the germinal substance seeks its fulfillment. This is a visual figure, and the superposition of this image, with its wealth of erotic implication, involves the suggestion that the physical desire for procreation through beauty is identical with the longing of the spirit to expand and to exalt itself beyond its bodily confines.

It is precisely the point of A Dream Play that this identity of aims involves a tragic paradox. In man the inclination of the flesh is toward woman, but the aspiration of the spirit is toward God. The two desires, and their consequences, are quite distinct. The one tends to bind us ever more firmly to the earth, the other to deliver us, and the confusion of the two desires is, inevitably, a source of pain. Yet, in the nature of things, this confusion is inescapable, for it is to woman that we turn, first of all, for a glimpse of paradise. Man seeks his happiness in woman; it is exactly for this reason that happiness eludes him, for woman, the representative of the material principle, cannot deliver the spirit through love. She can only imprison it. Her beauty, therefore, though it is God's beauty, is a snare; and though the spirit is irresistibly drawn to it, it must transcend this beauty or suffer disappointment. The elucidation of this time-honored mystery, the root of The Divine Comedy, seems to have been Strindberg's chief concern as a dramatist in the post-Inferno period.

The opera-corridor episode, half comic, half tragic in mood, is closely related to the episode of the Growing Castle. It illustrates, sardonically—as, indeed does all the rest of the play—in what way love conquers all. Doubtless, also, this episode reflected Strindberg's mood during the rehearsals of Easter, when he played stage-door Johnny for Harriet Bosse, as, in his youth, he had for Siri von Essen. Harriet Bosse notes that, in fact, Strindberg's curiosity had once been aroused by a disused door with a clover-leaf airhole cut into it, which led off the theatre alley where he was accustomed to wait for her. Since it was out of such details that Strindberg created the symbolism of these scenes, their interpretation is no simple matter, and the ever-widening ripples of significance tease the mind beyond certainty into precisely the mood which the symbolists considered proper to the poetic experience.

In the Officer's unwearied attendance upon the elusive Victoria we may certainly see the unhappy plight of one who had spent a lifetime, as it seemed, waiting in theatre corridors for a lady who never came; beyond that, the figure unquestionably symbolizes Strindberg's inhumanly protracted wait for a victory in the theatre, a period during which he had ample time to ponder the riddle of the closed door; beyond that still, is suggested the predicament of man waiting eternally for the One who never comes. But while this web of meaning gives the play something of the rich texture we admire in the intricately loomed allegories of a former age, A Dream Play differs from these allegories even more markedly than does To Damascus. The Romance of the Rose, for example, is also, ostensibly, an erotic dream; but as a dream it has no verisimilitude; it is actually a play of abstractions arranged in a perfectly logical sequence, and would lose none of its quality if the dream framework were dropped. The logic of A Dream Play, which is also not a dream, comes somewhat closer to the logic of revery. The action involves effects of the sort actually experienced in dreams; it has something of the local color of dreams; and the result is something which is much less precise and more mysterious than allegory.

The flowering of the Growing Castle illustrates this point clearly. The symbol is obviously crucial to the total conception. It may be variously interpreted. From the moral standpoint, it suggests the liberation of the spirit, its release from matter, and its resumption into Godhead, its reawakening. But this moral superstructure evidently rests upon a deeper basis. In his celebrated production of A Dream Play, Olaf Molander piously changed the flower into a cross. The association of a Christian symbol with the assumption of the Daughter of Indra may be regarded as a somewhat arbitrary display of creative showmanship, but we must remember that Strindberg himself saw no inconvenience in presenting Indra's Daughter with a view of Christ walking on the waves. Moreover, the Growing Castle is not, like the Castle of Alma, a rigid figure which can admit of but a single interpretation. If one wishes to crown it with Christian significance, it will serve.

Nevertheless, in poetry, the preferable interpretation is that which gives greatest efficacy to the figure, and the efficacy of the figure ordinarily depends more on what is suggested than on what is rationally conveyed. On the intellectual level, there is no particular objection to the substitution of the cross for the flower, save that Strindberg did not write it so. Moreover, the cross is immediately comprehensible, while the chrysanthemum bud by itself tells us nothing. But for that faculty of the mind which is able to understand without understanding, and is therefore chiefly amenable to suggestion, the bud-capped edifice which grows until the moment of conflagration, and then bursts into flower, is not only comprehensible, but unmistakable.

Into this symbol is gathered, at the end, all the force of the play. The dream of life is essentially erotic. The Officer, the Lawyer, the Quarantine Master, the Poet himself, are all aspects of the lover. The Daughter of Indra, like all Strindberg's women, offers herself freely. She offers herself, in fact, to each in turn—to all save the Quarantine Master, who is an enemy of love—and in the end she offers herself to the burning tower. It is precisely at the moment when she unites with it that the castle bursts into flower. The suggestion is tolerably clear—it is in the moment of orgasm that mortality merges with immortality, and pain with peace. The moment of flowering is extraordinarily ambiguous. It is release and captivity, pain and ecstasy, death and resurrection. The quest for the secret of life which lies concealed behind the clover-leaf door which connects the theatre with the law office, and also with the church, the grotto, and the home, ultimately leads us to the *linga*, Siva's symbol, in the supreme moment which brings about the union of form and matter, Atman and Maya, the creative spirit and its creation, together with all the tragic implications of this union—for the individual, birth, suffering, old age, and death; for society, greed, cruelty, injustice, hatred, and violence. The process is clear. But the riddle remains unanswered. The clover-leaf door conceals nothing.

Nevertheless, the significance of the conceit is unmistakable.

In the final moment of conflagration, all the elements of this creation, the physical, the spiritual, the concrete and the abstract, are fused in the bud which all this time has been maturing, and which is now offered up to the lord of heaven. In this respect, at least, the figure is superbly precise. The golden bud which crowns the castle in the beginning grows little by little as the fantasy of life develops. When the pain of life is more than the soul can bear, it flowers. For Strindberg, at least, this was the way of creation. Therefore the petition which the Poet addresses to God in the scene in Fingal's grotto seems pathetically insufficient to the Daughter:

DOTTERN: Är det så du ämnar nalkas
              stoftets son, den allerhögste . . . ?

DIKTAREN: Hur skall stoftets son väl finna
              ord nog ljusa, rena, lätta,
              att från jorden kunna stiga . . .
              Gudabarn, vill du vår klagan
              sätta över i det språk
              de Odödlige bäst fatta?

DOTTERN: Jag vill!

(DAUGHTER: Is it so that you intend to approach,
              son of dust, the All-highest?

POET: How shall the son of dust ever find
              a word so bright, so pure, so light,
              that it may rise up from the ground . . . ?
              Child of God, our complaint will you
              set over into the speech
              that the immortals best comprehend?

DAUGHTER: I will!)

Indeed, at the proper time, the Daughter translates the Poet's complaint into the language of the gods by taking it with her through the fire—thus, through her example, the Poet learns how the thing is done. It is in fact through the artist's experience of evil, the artist's pain, his passion, that poetry is made; but the complaint which ultimately reaches the All-Highest is nothing like the poor jingle lost in the confused roar of Fingal's cave. To reach God one must pass through the fire. What the Daughter of God takes with her into the burning castle is the dream of life in all its wretchedness. But what comes out of the purifying flame is something precious and beautiful; not pain, but the flower of pain; not evil, but the flower of evil; the golden flower, the poem.

A *Dream Play*, "child of my greatest pain," was Strindberg's most ambitious attempt to formulate the passion of the artist in modern conceptual terms. Others had written of this, but it is safe to say that nothing of this magnitude had ever been conceived for the stage. A *Dream Play* is perhaps not wholly successful; but there is nothing in the modern theatre to surpass it.

The years following the publication of A *Dream Play* were heavy years for Strindberg. The success of *Master Olof* in 1897 had encouraged him to consider himself a master of historical drama, and he had proceeded at once, full of enthusiasm, to dramatize in his own terms the history of Sweden. The result was the brilliant series of historical plays which forms so significant a part of the Swedish national heritage. Four were written in the same year, 1899: *The Saga of the Folkungs, Gustav Vasa, Eric XIV,* and *Gustav Adolf.* This series was followed by *Engelbrekt* in 1901, and *Charles XII,* the same year.[101] *Gustav Vasa,* his masterpiece in this genre, was performed with a magnificent cast at the Svenska Theatre in Stockholm in October, 1899, and was an outstanding success, but the *First Part* of *To Damascus* aroused no great interest when it was first performed the following November, and the failure of *Engelbrekt* in November, 1901, was a bitter disappointment. After this disaster, Strindberg found no one willing to produce *The Crown Bride, Swanwhite,* or A *Dream Play,* and the three historical dramas with which he rounded off his cycle— *Kristina* (1903), *Gustav III* (1903), and *The Nightingale of Wittenberg* (1904)—fared no better. Once again, he fell into a severe depression, and now he felt more certain than ever that he was the victim of a far-reaching conspiracy to ruin him. The fruit of this crisis was the novel *Black Banners*, after *Le Plaidoyer d'un fou* the most intemperate of his works.

In 1907, after arranging with some difficulty for the publication of this novel, Strindberg was at last able to organize, with the help of the young actor August Falck, a little theatre in Stockholm in which to show his plays. It was his second venture as a theatre director. The first, the Scandinavian Experimental Theatre he had organized in Copenhagen in 1889, had barely lasted a month. The Intimate Theatre opened its doors on November 26, 1907. It was a remodelled store with a shallow stage and 161 seats, and its lobby was decorated with a bust of Strindberg. Its ideals were not very clearly defined in anyone's mind, but Strindberg was much impressed by Reinhardt's work at the Kleines Theater and the Kammerspiel-Haus, and he warmly recommended Reinhardt's methods to Falck and the group of actors assembled under his direction. The memorandum he addressed to this group was much less precisely worded than the foreword to *Miss Julie* which he had written almost two decades before, but it was full of good sense:

If one asks what is the object of the Kammarspel, I will answer about like this. In the subject, we seek a powerful motive, significant, yet precise. In the writing, we avoid the obvious, all calculated effects, passages written for applause, brilliant roles, tirades for stars. The author must resist the shackles of set forms: it is the subject that dictates the form. In sum: freedom of execution, limited only by the unity of the conception and the sense of style.[102]

The four short plays he wrote in quick succession in the early part of 1907 for the projected Kammarspel theatre—*The Storm, The Burnt House, The Ghost Sonata,* and *The Pelican*—bear a certain family resemblance to one another, but they differ a good deal in their style. They are all one-act plays, of about the length of *Miss Julie*; but unlike *Miss Julie*, all but the last require scene-changes and intermissions, and all are divided into three scenes, save *The Burnt House*, which is in two. Ibsen had thought of his plays as poems. Strindberg evidently thought of his as in the nature of musical compositions, and he referred repeatedly to the chamber plays of 1907 as his sonatas.

The analogy of the chamber plays to chamber music is by no means clear. These are essentially full-length plays in miniature, and the acts are called scenes chiefly because of their brevity—in other respects, the construction does not differ materially from the normal construction of Strindberg's longer plays. Save for *The Pelican*, which has a cast of five, the chamber plays have full-sized casts requiring a dozen or more actors, and all of them require elaborate settings. Mallarmé had spoken of poetry which would approximate music in its freedom from subject matter, and its direct effect upon the emotions, but the chamber plays all have a very definite subject matter, though none can really be said to develop a plot. What chiefly distinguishes the manner of these pieces is that all involve a play of fancy centered upon a theme arising, in general, from a personal grievance which the action symbolically settles. They are all, accordingly, in the nature of meditations on a topic related to injustice or wickedness and conceived fancifully in terms of a dramatic situation of domestic character.

It is possible that in Strindberg's mind, the Beethoven sonatas, to which he was passionately addicted, with their antiphonal effects and thematic parallelism, the interlacing of their melody lines, and generally climactic development, had a certain dramatic significance which is not immediately apparent. He may well have thought of the themes and figures of this music as actors entering a scene, speaking, involving themselves, and then disengaging and retiring, only to make subsequent entrances, until all is gathered together and resolved at the close. Something of this sort may well have been in his mind in the composition of these tripartite plays in which the intention appears to be, not to tell a story, but to evoke an emotion in terms of a certain composition of events.

From a substantive viewpoint, there is nothing especially novel in these plays, and Strindberg appears to have felt that he was recapitulating rather than inventing during the period of their composition. "I have been working," he wrote Schering in March, 1907, "with the feeling that these are my last sonatas." [103] ". . . And the feeling has come over me that I have done my tour of duty and have no more to say." [104] The idea that he was actually evolving a new dramatic style does not seem to have occurred to him at this time. In *The Ghost Sonata* he thought he was developing further a style of dramatic writing that approximated music. In fact, with this play he invented dramatic surrealism, and anticipated the expressionist movement of the 1920's.

All four of the plays of 1907 are extensions of Strindberg's intimate life. Their general theme is the contrast, tragic and comic, between the decent appearance which people normally present to the world and the sordid reality which this appearance conceals; and, very likely because of the author's consciousness of his own keenness of vision, two of these plays include characters who have clairvoyant powers. Strindberg's favorite setting in these plays is a house. His houses, viewed from the street, present serene façades of unquestioned respectability. In the course of the play, the façade is penetrated, and what lies behind it is brought to light. It is then seen that each apartment has its secret and each closet its skeleton.

The metaphor seems obvious. The house, like the castle of *A Dream Play*, symbolizes for Strindberg the outer shell which the individual inhabits and within which he shelters his soul from the public gaze. Within this shell, behind this mask, are hidden his uneasy conscience, his misdeeds, his guilt, his shame, in short, his self. Each individual is, in this sense, a house, a castle, and every house is a fastness in which are stored the accumulated miseries of those who dwell there. When these things are brought to light, in each case the result is prophylactic, a purification, and a renewal of hope and beauty.

In these plays, most often, this purification is brought about by fire, or something like it. In *The Storm*, the end is peace and the serene light of evening. The orchard in which *The Burnt House* stands flowers prematurely after the burning. *The Pelican* ends with a purifying fire which is associated with a dream of summer and joyous childhood. A *Dream Play* was in rehearsal during the period when these plays were being written, and it is quite evident that all four plays are in some way related to the burning castle and its flower.

In *The Storm*, Strindberg publicly settles his accounts with Harriet Bosse for having left him, presumably because of the disparity in their age. The first scene is laid in the street outside the house, and the lighted interior of the ground-floor apartment is plainly visible through the open windows. The Gentleman—in whom we may easily recognize Strindberg—is an aging recluse who lives a lonely, but contented life in this apartment, tended by a young and pretty servant. It is the end of summer, oppressively hot, with a hint of lightning in the air.

The Gentleman's apartment has been kept exactly as it was when his young wife left him ten years before, and he himself has preserved tender memories of his lost love. The basement of the house is occupied by a pastrycook. New tenants are keeping what looks like a disorderly house on the floor above the Gentleman's apartment, behind red blinds which are always drawn. The scene now shifts into the Gentleman's dining room, and the narrative develops quickly. The lady who lives upstairs turns out to be none other than the Gentleman's former wife, Gerda, reduced to living in humiliating circumstances with a gambler who beats her. This man is planning to run off with the pastrycook's young daughter, and he intends to take with him also his wife's eighteen-year-old daughter, whom he proposes to exploit for immoral purposes.

In these distressing circumstances, Gerda appeals for assistance to the man she has wronged. Somewhat haughtily he comes to her rescue, and through the intervention of his brother, the Consul, the gambler's wicked scheme is defeated. The last scene takes place once again in the street. The thunder shower has come and gone. Once again peace settles upon "The Quiet House." The Gentleman is now purged of his painful memories, and as the streetlight is turned on for the first time that fall in this land of the midnight sun, he settles back gratefully to enjoy the autumn of his life, all passion spent.

In the course of this somewhat fanciful action, Gerda is roughly handled by the author. She is depicted as a strumpet, or something near it. She begs her former husband's pardon very humbly; asks to be taken back, and is coldly rejected; and she grows bitterly jealous of the pretty servant who looks after the Gentleman. The infantile nature of this revenge-fantasy is entirely characteristic of Strindberg. The play, moreover, is repetitious, and shows every sign of hasty workmanship. Nevertheless, in its very naïveté it has a penetrating Kafkaesque quality which is memorable. It is, in a very real sense, theatre reduced to its first principles.

Something of the sort may be said also of *The Burnt House*. It belongs to the genre of scenes of childhood revisited, a theme especially congenial to Strindberg. In this play, after many years of absence, the Stranger returns from America to visit his father's house and to renew the memories of his childhood, only to find that the house has just burned down. Now the walls alone are standing, and the neighbors are picking over the charred remains of the furniture, so that all the secrets of the house are revealed. The house, it develops, was occupied by the Stranger's brother, a dyer, whose wife was involved amorously with a young student who lodged with them. The fire was apparently accidental, but the Dyer has made it seem that the Student set it, and, in consequence, the Student is arrested for arson. It now turns out that the Stranger's seemingly irreproachable home was in fact a nest of thieves and smugglers. The walls were double and were stuffed with contraband yarns. Everything in the house was false, the antiques, the occupants, their reputation—it was all a web of lies and deceit.

The Stranger now reveals that he hanged himself as a child, and was dead for a time. When he revived, he had extraordinary faculties, the ability to read people's thoughts, and to see through their pretenses. Like the Gentleman in *The Storm*, and the Captain in *The Dance of Death*, he is a kind of ghost. He cares about nothing, and takes life with amused cynicism—one suspects he is meant to be a self-portrait of the author. The Student, indeed, is perhaps his illegitimate son, but he can do nothing to save him, and he troubles himself very little on his account.

In the end it is discovered that the insurance premiums had not been paid on time, so that the Dyer is ruined, as he richly deserves. The scene so far appears to be one of unrelieved gloom, yet, strangely enough, the fire which has destroyed all this tissue of lies and crime, has also caused the orchard to burst prematurely into flower. Out of all this evil, good has come, or, at least, beauty.

THE STRANGER: Suffer. But hope!
THE WIFE (Giving him her hand): Thank you.
THE STRANGER: And for consolation, remember—
THE WIFE: What?
THE STRANGER: That you do not suffer innocently.

The Ghost Sonata is constructed along somewhat different lines, but its technique is a further development of the abstract method of *A Dream Play*, and the effect is really quite extraordinary. Strindberg thought very highly of this work. He wrote to Schering: "In writing it, I suffered as if I were in kama-loka (*Sheol*), and my hands (literally) bled . . . I hardly knew myself what I had written, but I felt something sublime in it that makes me shudder." *The Ghost Sonata* has, in fact, something sublime in it that makes one shudder, but it is as difficult for us to say what it is as it was for Strindberg.

Unquestionably the play has many faults. Its underlying narrative is fantastically complex. The relation of its three movements is neither close nor entirely apparent. Its effects are hyperbolic in the extreme, and convey a sense of horrible absurdity. Nevertheless, the play transmits an unforgettable experience, a momentary glimpse of the world through the eyes of madness.

With this play Strindberg initiated a style of drama that had not before been attempted, but which had everything in common with the current trends in painting, sculpture, and music, and it presaged a most interesting development of the art of the theatre. Yet the play remained unique. Neither Strindberg nor the followers of Strindberg were able to fulfill its promise, nor has it yet been fulfilled by those who, like Ionesco, Becket, and Genet, have in late years attempted to mine this vein.

Like its predecessor, *The Ghost Sonata* has to do with the exploration of a house. The principal character is the Student, a Sunday's child, endowed with unusual perceptive powers. In *A Blue Book,* Strindberg tells how sometimes at a gathering he would experience a momentary acuity of perception in which he could see the guests quite naked and hear the thoughts they did not speak.[105] The Stranger in *The Burnt House* boasts of such powers also, but he makes no use of them. The Student, however, can see ghosts and other apparitions that others do not see; he feels the mysterious influences that are at work upon him; but his psychic powers are evidently limited, for he is easily taken in by old Hummel, the villain of the piece.

The Student's explorations begin on the street corner outside the Colonel's door, and proceed step by step toward the heart of the house, which is, as always with Strindberg, quite close to the kitchen. There is a certain logic in this progression, but in *The Ghost Sonata* the narrative thread is slender out of all proportion to the weight of reminiscence that is charged upon it. Moreover, since the third scene depends upon the first, but is more or less independent of the second, the play has not a powerful forward thrust, but makes rather the effect of a montage than of a sequence. This is perhaps the result of the musical form ABA which Strindberg had in mind in the composition of the piece, for while the Student is the principal character of the first part, he does not appear in the second, and the characters of the second part do not appear in the third. Aside from this arrangement, there is little here to make one think of a musical composition—on the contrary, the effects are predominantly visual; the technique is, if anything, painterly; and the impression is rather that of a triptych than of a sonata.

Underlying the action is an intricate web of antecedent material, unfolded mainly in retrospect, and involving therefore a prodigiously weighty exposition. The three scenes of the play actually form the epilogue of the story, somewhat in the manner of Ibsen, and the attention is directed to this narrative only to the extent necessary to rationalize the effects produced on the stage. The action involves mainly two stories. One concerns the machinations of old Hummel; the other has to do with the Student's ill-fated romance. These stories are interlaced through Adele, who is Hummel's daughter and the object of the Student's courtship, and her death represents the final collapse of Hummel's carefully-laid plans.

It develops that Hummel was once the lover of Bengtson's cook. In time, he went to Hamburg and became a loan-broker, committed a crime which was discovered by a milkmaid and, to keep this lady from denouncing him, enticed her out on the ice one day and drowned her. Meanwhile Hummel's fiancée was seduced by the Colonel. In retaliation, Hummel had a daughter by the Colonel's wife, and palmed the child off on the Colonel as his own. It was about this time, apparently, that Hummel involved his friend Mr. Arkenholz in the speculation which ruined him. Hummel is now a very old man, and is forced to carry on his intrigues from a wheelchair, which his servant calls his war-chariot. The Student is the son of Mr. Arkenholz. Hummel has been observing him for some time, and he has plans for him, which now begin to mature.

In the first scene, we find Hummel in his wheelchair contemplating from the outside the Colonel's beautiful house, which he plans to appropriate. It has, as is usual in these plays, several tenants. A caretaker lives in the basement. The caretaker's wife has had a daughter by the Consul who formerly lived in the upper story. This dignitary has just died—it turns out later he was strangled by Hummel—and his illegitimate daughter, called The Lady in Black, plans to elope with the Consul's son-in-law, the Baron. The Colonel occupies the ground floor with his wife and his supposed daughter, Adele. Old Man Hummel, having secretly bought up all the Colonel's outstanding obligations, now plans to bring about a marriage between Adele and the Student, whom he intends to make his heir. In this manner, Hummel proposes to acquire the Colonel's family as well as his home, and thus to take into his hands all these destinies which time has intertwined with his own.

Although he is a little troubled by the ghosts that haunt him, Hummel develops his plans with admirable efficiency. In due course, he invades the Colonel's house, takes possession, proves the Colonel to be a scoundrel and an impostor, and insists on attending the Colonel's tea-party. The servant Bengtson, once Hummel's master, and now the possessor of his guilty secret, calls this party a *spöksupé*, a ghost supper, because the guests always look and act as if they were dead. These festivities are normally presided over by the Colonel's wife Amelia, who is shrunken into a mummy, prattles like a parrot, and spends the greater part of her time in a dark closet, exhibiting to the world only a statue of herself as a young girl.

In the presence of this surprising character, the living symbol of the depressing effect of a bad conscience, Hummel proceeds to threaten the Colonel's guests with exposure, *seriatim*, but at this point, the mummified Amelia unexpectedly intervenes. Putting aside her parrot guise, she denounces Hummel as an adulterer, a thief, and a murderer, and calls upon Bengtson to corroborate her charges. Hummel collapses. Amelia then hynotizes him into disgorging his bundle of incriminating documents, and orders him into the closet to hang himself behind the death-screen.[106]

The last scene takes place some days later in Adele's room, which is filled with hyacinths and ornamented with a large Buddha image which holds a flowering shallot in its lap. The scene begins lyrically with a musical prelude and a recitation. The Student courts the girl tenderly; but after a certain point she does not seem properly responsive. The Cook, the family incubus, now makes her appearance, huge and menacing. For years, it turns out, she has sucked the family dry by extracting the nourishment from the food she serves them—it is for this reason that they all look starved, while she herself is of exceptional solidity. The appearance of the insubordinate Cook has an extraordinary effect on the budding romance. Adele complains bitterly of the burdens of housekeeping and the drudgery of life: she cannot bear, she says, the thought of marriage and the nursery. The Student, sadly disillusioned, bursts forth in a passionate tirade against the horror of the world in which all beauty is deceptive, and all creation is cursed and damned. Since he is clairvoyant he sees the ugliness and the disease which the girl's beauty conceals. It is more than she can bear. The girl wilts before his eyes like a blighted flower, and before he has finished, she calls for the death-screen. Bengtson places it around her. The Student invokes Buddha:

. . . wise and gentle Buddha, sitting there waiting for a heaven to grow out of the earth, grant us the purity of will and the patience to endure our trials, so that your hopes may not be lost.

A harp begins to play by itself, and the Student recites the paraphrase of "The Song of the Sun" from the *Elder Edda*, with which he began the scene. Then he takes leave of the dying girl:

Poor little child! Child of this world of illusion and guilt and pain and death, this world of eternal change and disappointment, and never ending misery! May the Lord of Heaven have mercy on you in your journey . . .

The scene dissolves into a view of Böcklin's sombre painting, *The Isle of the Dead*, with its cypresses, and the black gondola gliding across the dark sea.[107]

It is safe to assume that a dramatist of Strindberg's experience would hardly expect an audience to absorb the immense tissue of plot which underlies the simple action of *The Ghost Sonata*. Very likely what he had in mind was to present in a very special way a sequence of what seemed to him particularly significant situations. These scenes could have been presented, of course, without preparation, in the manner of the *Quarts d'heure* of the Théâtre-Libre. Strindberg evidently preferred to tie them together in a causal sequence. The intricate plot serves much the same purpose, therefore, as the canvas of a painting, the carefully prepared but largely invisible support of the visual composition.

Most of the elements which form the texture of *The Ghost Sonata* are familiar. As in *Miss Julie*, the young woman is presumably the daughter of an aristocrat, expensively nurtured, but psychically fragile to the point of morbidity, and for this reason unmarriageable and degenerate. She is called the hyacinth girl, and the hyacinth apparently symbolized for Strindberg the type of beautiful, but soulless womanhood which he had described in *Miss Julie* and elsewhere.[108] Adele, like Julie, pays with her life for the sins of her mother, and she illustrates the decadence of the noble classes, just as Hummel demonstrates the vigor of the servant who rises through force and fraud to displace his masters. The fact that all the nobility in this play apparently consists of former domestics serves to emphasize the universal nature of this process. From this point of view, it becomes apparent that *The Ghost Sonata* is in some respects a rehandling of the material that went into *Miss Julie*.

What is chiefly interesting about *The Ghost Sonata*, however, is not so much the insistence with which Strindberg clung to these familiar notions as the very novel way in which in this case he presented them. The idea of a vampire hovering over a houseful of ghosts, with its reminiscences of Poe, and the macabre fiction of the period, unquestionably fascinated Strindberg; but it was obviously not in itself enough to hang a play on. Moreover, Strindberg had before him the example of Ibsen's *Ghosts*, which his title recalled, and to the plot of which his own plot bore a certain relation, since both plays have to do with the sickly offspring of a bad marriage. Strindberg developed his fantasy, therefore, in terms of a solidly realistic situation, abstracted his characters from life, and endowed them with impeccably naturalistic motives which accord strangely with the visionary character of the fantasy.

The vampire Hummel takes on the shape of the valet Jean at the end of a long and fruitful career as a scoundrel. Aged, but still militant, he now aspires to graft his stock upon a noble genealogical tree, and thus to achieve vicariously the status which fate has wisely denied him. This is a situation entirely typical of Second Empire drama, and the complex narrative that underlies it is reminiscent of the plotting of such plays as *Le Fils de Giboyer*. It is, of course, characteristic of Strindberg that instead of achieving his purpose in a business-like way, Hummel needs to offer himself the luxury of annihilating his rival, his rival's family, and his friends in detail, thus provoking nemesis in the person of the parrot-like Amelia whom once he wronged, and whom he continues to wrong. In any realistic presentation this blatantly melodramatic situation would hardly support one's interest. The exceptionally fantastic nature of the scene, however, transposes this action to a plane so remote from experience that our ordinary responses no longer serve to evaluate it, and it is entirely acceptable as a nightmare. Thus it is that, conceived in terms of the sort of macabre childishness which we associate with the fantasies of Kafka, or the more violent paintings of Van Gogh, *The Ghost Sonata* has extraordinary efficacy as drama, in spite of its obvious puerility from an intellectual viewpoint.

The Ghost Sonata is theatrically successful in about the same measure as *A Dream Play*; that is to say, it is full of promise, but nobody has as yet succeeded in producing it well. In this play, Strindberg indicated, more clearly than ever before, the way in which the gulf between the inner and the outer world might be spanned by a dramatic action. The method had been explored, of course, in his previous dramas—notably in the interior of the castle at the beginning of *A Dream Play*, and in the banquet scene of *To Damascus II*. But *To Damascus* was presented mainly as a parable, and *A Dream Play* was intended to make the effect of a dream. In *The Ghost Sonata*, however, Strindberg put fantasy and reality on an equal footing, without attempting to distinguish the one from the other, and in thus merging the two forms of experience, he created something which quite transcends the normal categories of the stage. There is, I have suggested, good reason to call this genre surrealistic, if only to distinguish it from the style of the earlier plays, both of which were, on the whole, extensions of existing poetic traditions, while *The Ghost Sonata* was in many ways really new.

With these plays, a new chapter opened in the history of the drama. The rejection of the principle of logical sequence, and of the spatial and temporal categories which, in the interests of realism, had so far been cherished as indispensable to the theatre, was now seen to entail no greater inconvenience than the abandonment of the classical unities. Furthermore, the possibility of bringing together in the theatre things which in real life are not normally related opened the way for the elaboration of a new rhetoric of purely dramatic character. In the circumstances, it is hardly surprising that while *The Ghost Sonata* and *A Dream Play* occasioned some astonishment, the full extent of Strindberg's innovation was not realized for a decade or more, and it is perhaps not yet fully realized.

The last of the chamber plays of 1907, *The Pelican*, did not fulfill the promise of *The Ghost Sonata*, nor was it written in quite the same style. It is a quasi-realistic play with ghost-effects, a further extension of the theme of the vampire-woman. In this case, the lady is another version of the bad mother who, in contrast to the self-sacrificing pelican of the Christian bestiary, nourishes herself at the expense of her husband and her children. *The Pelican* is, indeed, an exceptionally virulent attack, in which Strindberg vents his ire upon the mother, in somewhat the same fashion as he squared accounts with the wife in *The Storm*. These are retributive fantasies, and the process of sublimation cannot be said to have gone so far in either of them as to result in a work of art. They are chiefly valuable, accordingly, as fully-realized examples of that intermediate phase of creation, somewhere between revery and art, which ordinarily does not crystallize into permanent form.

The Pelican was the play with which Strindberg chose to inaugurate the Intimate Theatre. There are indications in the text that the play was first intended to be called *The Awakening*; in the course of the action, at any rate, the bad mother, recently widowed, is little by little awakened to a sense of her guilt by the extensive and repeated reproaches of her children, by the brutality of her son-in-law, with whom, it is suggested, she has had sexual relations, and by the ghost of her husband which intrudes from time to time, *poltergeist*-fashion, to emphasize a favorite point. The nature of these reproaches is primitive in the extreme, and thoroughly familiar—the mother systematically starved and chilled her family, while she herself ate well and kept warm; the food she served was without substance or taste, and its poverty was disguised with Worcestershire sauce and cayenne pepper. The result of these maternal iniquities is the daughter's sterility and the son's drunkenness. Driven at last to the wall, the mother disclaims responsibility for her misdeeds on the ground that the evil in her nature is an inheritance from her parents, who in turn derived it from theirs, so that the guilt ultimately reverts to the first man and woman. There is evidently no remedy for so venerable an evil save purification by fire, and in the end the drunken son sets fire to the house, the mother leaps from the window, the boy and girl huddle together blissfully in the warmth of the burning house, and this warmth brings them a vision of summer and the happiness of childhood in the days when their father was alive.

The Black Glove, a five-act Christmas play in prose and verse written in 1909 along Dickensian lines, closed the series of plays that Strindberg wrote especially for the Intimate Theatre, a venture which, in the course of its brief existence, brought Strindberg several times to the verge of bankruptcy, but did much to advance his reputation in the Scandinavian countries. Before he was finished with it, he assumed the title of *régisseur*, but there is no evidence that he actually undertook the direction of any of the plays save *Swanwhite*, and the chief fruit of his technical collaboration was the series of memoranda and other messages of admonition directed to the actors which, taken together, form a very sensible and useful manual of acting, in many ways reminiscent of the method of Stanislavsky.[109]

In the fall of 1909, when he was sixty, Strindberg published his last play, *The Great Highway, A Travel Play with Seven Stations*. By this time, he had attained to a certain degree of resignation, if not of peace. His divorce from Harriet Bosse had been made final in 1908, and she had immediately married the actor Gunnar Wingard. Strindberg could not bear to have any of his wives re-marry—he took it in each case as a breach of faith—and the pain that Harriet's marriage caused him, already anticipated in *The Storm*, is clearly reflected in *The Great Highway*.

His financial responsibilities in connection with the Intimate Theatre had caused Strindberg to abandon his apartment at Karlavägen 40 quite suddenly in the summer of 1908. He moved into a small suite of rooms on the fourth floor of the house in which the actress Fanny Falkner lived, and arranged to take his meals with her family. This new abode he called his "Blue Tower." Miss Falkner, whom he also came very close to marrying, has left a vivid description of his life during this period, his strange habits, and his morbid fear of coming into contact with people who might sap his psychic energy or steal his thoughts.[110] *The Great Highway* mirrors his state of mind at this time in much the same way that *To Damascus* mirrors the Inferno crisis, but it makes an altogether different effect.

In *The Great Highway*, the Hunter has found it necessary to retreat to the heights in order to breathe, but he is now impelled to come down once again into the valley and cast an appraising eye on the Land of Desire. Like its predecessors in this genre, *The Great Highway* represents a mythical journey; but this time the voyager mainly revisits the scenes of his past life, and his adventures have a nostalgic quality which is lacking in the earlier plays. Since the Hunter's wanderings take him over familiar ground, the reader, as well as the Hunter, frequently experiences a sense of *déjà-vu* which is entirely appropriate to a work that was evidently intended as a final recapitulation, an epilogue.

The great highway is life itself, the road midway between birth and death, and the principal character, the Hunter who is also the Traveller, traverses a good piece of it before he decides to retrace his steps to the lonely but hygienic heights whence he came. His purpose in revisiting the dark valley, from which twelve years before he had escaped, is to live out his life among men, as the good Hermit of the mountain advises:

> . . . lev livet ut, gå ner igen, det är ej farligt;
> landsvägen dammar, borsta av dig;
> det löper diken utmed kanterna, fall i!
> Men res dig. Där finns grindar,
> spring över, kryp inunder, lyft på haken;
> du råkar mänskor, tag dem du i famnen,
> de bitas ej, men bits de, bettet är ej farligt,
> får du en dusch, låt rinna av! [111]

> (Live life out, go down again, it is not dangerous;
> if the road is dusty, brush yourself off;
> if there are ditches along the edge, fall in!
> But get up. Where you find gates,
> spring over, creep under, lift the hook;
> if you meet people, embrace them;
> they do not bite, and if they bite, bites are not dangerous;
> if you run into a shower, let it run off!)

The Hunter's goal, as it turns out, is a mirage, the longed-for Land of Fulfillment which may be glimpsed from the heights, but is nowhere to be seen from the road below. In search of this elusive paradise, the Hunter traverses six stations on the road: the Place of the Windmills, Eselsdorf, a Passage in Tophet, the Columbarium outside a crematory, the Last Gate—from which the Land of Fulfillment is visible in the clouds—finally, the Dark Wood, where, at last, he turns to God. There is no doubt of the retro-spective nature of this journey; it might have been called Inferno Revisited.

The first scene, "On the Heights," recalls the grandeur of *Brand*. At the end, the Hunter sets off hopefully in the Traveller's company, and the play takes on a jaunty air. The first stations along the road involve scenes reminiscent of *Lucky Per's Journey*, episodes that sparkle with wit and are boisterous with clowning. In the fifth scene, "The Park Outside the Crematorium," the tone deepens; thereafter the action becomes progressively sombre. It ends with a cry of anguish.

Aside from the detail, *The Great Highway* ends much like *To Damascus II*, though in a mood that is infinitely more intimate and sincere. It winds through a landscape for which *To Damascus* prepares us, but the journey is blessedly free from the literary disquisitions which mar the end of the *To Damascus* trilogy. Its di-gressions are perhaps not all equally successful; but on the whole this play makes an effect of life, and, most of all, it makes an impression of the most candid self-portraiture. In the Hunter of *The Great Highway*, it is not difficult to make out the poseur, the braggart, the mountebank, the shyster. The author makes us fully aware of his self-pity, his sentimentality, and his compulsion to argue interminably in his own defense; but we are aware even more vividly of the idealist and the poet, his misfortune, his pain, and, most poignantly, of his profound humanity. No writer makes so much the impression of belonging to the human race.

Like its original, this portrait is a very complex and most un-even piece of work. Moreover, the play is almost too personal a confession to be generally useful on the stage, and it makes un-conscionable demands on the reader. It is, nevertheless, a great masterpiece of autobiographical writing, and, as a theatre-piece, it is doubtless unique.

The special quality of *The Great Highway* becomes apparent when we compare it with *When We Dead Awaken*, which Ibsen had published fully ten years before. Both plays are in the nature of epilogues, of generally tragic character, and quite obviously personal and apologetic. In both, the hero journeys into the past in search of life and the happiness which has eluded him; and, although they were written by practical men of the theatre, both plays make extravagant demands on the physical resources of the stage.

Here the resemblance ends. The characters in which Ibsen and Strindberg present themselves to the world at the last are diametrically opposed conceptions. The Hunter complains of having lived too much; the Sculptor of not having lived at all: perhaps they mean the same thing. The Hunter's tragedy is that he is not the man he meant to be. It is the tragedy of the Sculptor that he has become exactly what he intended. "And now," the Woman asks the Hunter in the last scene of *The Great Highway*, "are you dead?" "Yes," the Hunter answers, "but not spiritually." With Rubek, it is quite the other way: it is spiritually that he is dead. The climax of the Hunter's drama is the scene of the red cottage by the sea, with its bright birthday table and the child—a scene out of Kotzebue, almost too idyllic for comfort, and directly inspired, we know, by a sentimental scene painted on a cheap dinner plate which had come by chance into Strindberg's possession. In comparison with *When We Dead Awaken*, with its unforgettable figures and its Wagnerian climax, *The Great Highway* seems overstrained, sentimental, crude. Yet, with all its faults, it is to this day vibrant with the life of the man who wrote it, bitter and fierce with the zest of failure: *When We Dead Awaken* is cold and calm; and sick with a surfeit of success.

In *The Great Highway*, the Hunter appears in many guises. We know them all. He is the Traveller, the Oriental, the Wandering Jew; but chiefly the Outcast, the Scapegoat, laden with the sins of humanity and signalled out for sacrifice. In the Tophet scene, he tells Möller the Murderer that, twelve years before, he had pilloried himself in public and done away with his old self.[112] Now he is a new man whom Möller cannot know. Even so, his

travail has not come to an end. In his former life, as the Woman
of the Seventh Station remembers, he had been lawyer for the
defense, evangelist, architect, and theatre-builder. All that is over;
but still he is there, and active, the soldier, *l'homme engagé:* "I am
a fighter and so I live. But *I* do not exist—only what I have
done." The Hunter is without means; but when the Tempter
comes to offer him the position of court Architect, on condition
only that he conduct himself like other people, he refuses scorn-
fully: he is not like other people and never will be. His individuality is more necessary to him than his life—therefore for him the
end of the great highway can be only "the crystal air of the snow-
white height," where one day the Hermit will write his epitaph
on the snow:

> Här vilar Ismael, Hagars son,
> som en gång nämndes Israel,
> emedan han fått kämpa kamp med gud,
> och släppte icke striden förrän nedlagd,
> besegrad av hans allmakts godhet.
> O evige! Jag släpper ej din hand,
> din hårda hand, förrn du välsignat!
>
> Välsigna mig, din mänsklighet,
> som lider, lider av din livsens gåva!
> mig först, som lidit mest—
> som lidit mest av smärtan
> att icke kunna vara den jag ville!

> (Here rests Ishmael, Hagar's son,
> who once bore the name of Israel,
> because it was granted him to wrestle with God,
> and he ceased not to struggle until he was spent,
> vanquished by his almighty goodness.
> O Eternal One! I shall not let go your hand,
> your hard hand, until you bless me!
>
> Bless me, your creature,
> who suffers, suffers with your gift of life!
> Me first, who suffered most,

who suffered most because
I could not be the man I wished to be!) [113]

Strindberg wrote these words in 1909. They were spoken publicly for the first time in February, 1910, on the stage of the Intimate Theatre. Two years later, on May 14, 1912, Strindberg died.

His was a strange, uncomfortable life, and he died an uncomfortable death—he passed with difficulty into that Beyond toward which so long his thoughts had tended. In Sweden not too many took account of the event. But almost at once his legend began to take shape, and in the course of the next decade it was generally agreed that a great man had died. Even so, a good many years had to pass before it was fully realized how great an artist Strindberg had been, and how powerful his influence was to be on the coming age. It is perhaps not fully realized even now.

The Flower and the Castle

A S we look back over the history of the drama in the last half-century, Ibsen and Strindberg seem at the same time surprisingly far away and disconcertingly near, like figures within reach of the hand, seen through the wrong end of a glass. It is astonishing to consider that out of two great wars, a long series of social and political cataclysms, and the unexampled widening of the horizons of knowledge, so much new subject matter has come into being, and, insofar as the drama is concerned, so few ideas.

Four trends, it was suggested in the beginning, have principally affected the course of modern drama: naturalism, impressionism, symbolism, expressionism. These words are not only embarrassingly imprecise, but, beyond a certain point, their associations are meaningless. In terms of those who principally expressed these tendencies: Zola, Ibsen, Maeterlinck, and Strindberg—to say nothing of Dumas and Sardou—our view of modern drama may be brought into a sharper focus, but one cannot be certain that had these authors not written, the drama of our day would have presented a different face. The principal currents of art in the latter half of the nineteenth century were certainly transmitted to the theatre by these very authors; but not only through them. The impulses they conveyed, and which others in time developed, were organic tendencies common to all the arts of the time, and it is safe to assume that in one way or another they would have found their way to the stage regardless of who served them.

These influences were all in some measure hostile to tradition, and they encountered resistance. The ideological conflicts which Ibsen and Strindberg brought to the theatre were episodes in the cultural upheaval attending the disintegration of the medieval world picture. Naturalism began as an attack upon the bridge of idealistic preconception which for centuries had connected the artist with nature. The impressionists pressed the assault so far that the whole thing crashed down, and the traditional concept of nature with it.

The various forms of post-impressionism—expressionism, surrealism, cubism, abstractionism, and the rest—were attempts, more or less desperate, to reconstitute these ruins in terms of some principle that would sustain belief. Inevitably there were those who found joy in sheer destructiveness, a delight in absurdity for its own sake, and a noble satisfaction in thumbing the nose at absolutely everything. These attitudes developed in time into a style of art which, like virtue, is its own reward. Its basis was not necessarily profound. It must have been pretty good fun, at fifteen, to write *Ubu Roi*. It is not at all necessary to assume that despair is the exclusive source of what is now called, somewhat compendiously, the Theatre of the Absurd, any more than it is necessary to treat the vagaries of the Dadaists of the 1920's as if one were involved in the exegesis of Scripture.[1]

After the time of Baudelaire, art became a frantic search for novelty. The art dealer, the publisher, the public, the artist himself joined in the cry: *"Du nouveau! Du nouveau!"* This avidity for the new was symptomatic of the uneasiness of a period that was resolved to make a virtue of its discontent. The medieval craftsman and the Renaissance artist had not looked so assiduously for novelty. In a world in which it was firmly believed that the best had already been and the wisest had already been said, there was no obvious advantage in looking to the future. The Golden Age was in the past. It was needful only to recover it.

A consequence of the social cataclysms of the early nineteenth century was the breaking of the chain of imitation which had served so firmly to bind the present with the past. Romanticism involved a rejection of the classic mode, but also a frantic effort to find a foothold somewhere else. This effort proved to be fruitless. In the absence of an established tradition, art could offer no firm basis for the elaboration of form. Style succeeded style, and the end of the romantic effort was inevitably the cult of the self, with its accompanying moods of confusion and despair. The era of certainty thus ran its course, and with it ended the age of the sublime style and the finished masterpiece. Toward the end of the nineteenth century, art, in all its branches, became a provisional response to a world that was in itself a provisional response.

The aversion from tradition, which became progressively more emphatic as the century drew to a close, reflected psychological changes which, doubtless, had deeper roots than anyone at the time imagined. In the 1870's, Mallarmé was teaching that what had been said in poetry had been said too often and too thoroughly to bear repetition. Poetry had become in time, it was felt, a parroting of meaningless saws and empty sonorities. It inspired nausea among the *cognoscenti,* and their mood foreshadowed the surfeit that was to afflict the visual arts also, about the turn of the century, and music, not long after.

Both Strindberg and Ibsen felt the need to break with tradition. Twice in their lives they thought it necessary to embark in new directions. It was not easy, however, to turn one's back on the past, and the road into the future became more doubtful as time went on. The naturalists became impressionists; the impressionists became symbolists; before long, symbolism was in its turn rejected. Maeterlinck was unable to follow the path he himself had marked out in *Le Trésor des humbles,* and, in his age, he retracted the theories he had so fervently advanced in his youth. Mallarmé best illustrates, perhaps, the artist's embarrassment in this period of confused aims and uncertain pressures. In such poems as *Le Pitre châtié,* and *Le vierge, le vivace, et le bel aujourd'hui,* we have a clear intimation of the agony of the poet, silent and frozen in the desperate effort to express a half-felt reality in a language which was not yet invented.

The realism of Balzac and Flaubert, the naturalism of Zola and Maupassant, were consequences, more or less direct, of the empirical aspect of romanticism, the effort to direct attention peremptorily to the facts of life, and to find in the thing seen the truth which formerly had been felt to reside only in the unseen archetype. But the meaningless confusion of the phenomenal world proved to be of little use to the artist. Before long, writers and painters grew tired of enumerating facts; and the classical tendency to organize experience into intelligible patterns made itself felt once again in an attempt to penetrate into the heart of things through ways other than the intellectual. Symbolism was thus, from a practical angle, the reverse of naturalism; but it had in common with naturalism an insistence on the necessity for a fresh and intense experience as the basis of art. The naturalists had attempted to analyze experience physiologically. The symbolists specialized in psychology, and extended their researches to the psychology of plants and other forms of creation, and finally to the psychology of the universe. At this point they became involved with the occult sciences.

The impressionists also had scientific pretensions. The word "impressionism" was coined by the journalist Leroy in *Le Charivari* apropos of a little canvas which Monet had ingenuously entitled *Impression* in the 1874 exhibition. The term never acquired an exclusive connotation, but, before long, it was applied to a complex of attitudes which exerted an influence on every branch of art.

The impressionists were, at first, primarily empiricists who emphasized close and honest observation of nature. Their aims were not other than mimetic; they differed from the academic painters largely in the degree of their insistence on painting what they saw. Monet, for instance, appears to have had at first no idea save the representation of the object as it really appeared to the eye, and Manet began by extending the tradition of Velásquez and Goya. But it was soon observed that things appeared differently at different times and in different circumstances, and while the impressionists had very little in common, they agreed on a style that treated its subject in each case as a special instance, emphasizing above all its particularity. In this manner they fell in readily with the tenets of Flaubert and Zola. For a time, therefore, the impressionists in painting made a common cause with the naturalistic novelists.

The emphasis which the impressionists put on the look of things, however, inevitably involved an accentuation of the subjective factor. In this manner the individualistic basis of impressionism came rapidly to the fore, and what had at first purported to be a style of austere and impersonal objectivity now revealed itself as an approach to experience which derived its energy principally from the idiosyncrasy of the individual. Here the impressionists and the naturalists parted company.[2]

From a psychological viewpoint, impressionism was essentially a revolt against convention; that is to say, against the despotism of the ideal; and, practically, against the Academicians who had constituted themselves its custodians. It was, in short, a calculated affront to the official art of the state, and for a time it reflected the zestful mood that results from the flaunting of authority. Thus it fell in with the other revolutionary tendencies of the period.

Its effects were doubtless salutary. The impressionist painter tried to paint what he really saw; the impressionist writer looked on the world with a sharpened sensual awareness. These attitudes had their inconveniences. There was little stability in a world viewed through impressionist eyes: what they saw varied from moment to moment in accordance with the conditions of the environment. In the drama, from this viewpoint, it became impossible to fix character, or even—as Strindberg pointed out in the foreword to *Miss Julie*—to describe it. For the eye, only the surface could be said to exist, and even that became ambiguous after the divisionists and vibrists demonstrated the nature of the visual illusion. The analytic tendency of impressionism thus brought about, ultimately, a dissolution of the subject, and what had begun as an attempt to represent nature more truly, ended in the destruction of the conceptual basis of nature itself.

For centuries, the ideal had been the anchor of Western culture. The system of values, moral and aesthetic, which had been handed down from the time of Plato, furnished a basis for human behavior on every plane of activity. Now all was called into question. In the absence of fixed standards, art became increasingly insolent and increasingly aggressive. The artist acquired a noble belligerent air; but the cost from a psychic viewpoint was heavy. It was impossible to feel at home in a world that was no longer intelligible, or even sensible. The individual became increasingly aware of his individuality, of his autonomy, but also of his impermanence, his loneliness, his helplessness, and even his unreality; for to be impermanent is, in a sense, not to be at all. Such is the plight of the hero in *Peer Gynt*.

For Ibsen, love was the one element of permanence in a world in which everything passes ultimately through the Button Molder's crucible: in *Dover Beach*, Matthew Arnold said the same thing precisely in the very year *Peer Gynt* was written, in 1867. But in the world he made for them, Ibsen's heroes are not able to realize themselves through love. They are, above all, individuals; and individualism and love are demonstrably at variance. In the incompatibility of the need for love and the need for self-fulfillment, Ibsen saw a prime source of tragic experience. His heroes, whether they are men of action or men of art, are made to discover in their final hour that to be oneself is to lose oneself, and that in striving to live greatly, they have forgotten to live at all.

It is as a sculptor that Ibsen presents the artist, at the end of his life; but Rubek's ideas of sculpture seem as strange as Solness' notions of architecture: one would say they were both rescued from symbolism in the nick of time by death. Ibsen had dreamed in his youth of becoming a painter, and had studied briefly, but seriously, with several masters.[3] Judging from what can be seen of his early efforts, one would say it was as well that he turned to writing as a profession; but in his plays his potentialities as a painter are clearly realized. His compositions are brilliantly conceived, meticulously planned, and boldly executed. His landscape, it is true, after *Peer Gynt*, has a certain sameness and absence of color, the result perhaps of the sombre light in which he imagined it. But his portraits are superb; they carry exceptionally well, the more so as they involve, in general, some element of exaggeration or caricature. In his later work, it is true, we do not read the faces so easily; the features become less obvious, and take on progressively an enigmatic quality which perhaps reflects the enhanced subjectivity of the artist.

Until the close of the nineteenth century, dramatic characters were largely generic in nature. They were, that is to say, in the nature of personifications embodying standard patterns of human behavior. These types were defined authoritatively in such works as the *Characters* of Theophrastus or La Bruyère, which were in turn based not so much on observation, as on the *Ethics* of Aristotle, and similar books. There is a good deal to be said for this mode of characterization. It was simple and effective, and it rested on the accumulated authority of centuries.

From the time of Theophrastus, moralists, character-writers, physiognomists, physiologists, and, most of all, artists and poets had collaborated in the differentiation of human types; and in the theatre, the body of information that had been adduced in this manner vastly facilitated the work of the actor in the interpretation of a role. Since actors were generally cast according to type —as, indeed, they usually are to this day—the actor and the role were usually identical. An actor had a specialty, and played nothing else, and the dramatist most often conceived his characters with the idiosyncrasies of definite actors in mind.

For the impressionists, however, there were no types. Not only was each character *sui generis*, but in their view no character could be said to be the same from day to day or even from moment to moment. A person was defined by his behavior at a given time, and nothing more; and behavior might be expected to vary without reference to any consistent rule or pattern. There was, accordingly, no way of classifying characters. Thus, with the advent of impressionism, the classical theories of characterization were called seriously into question and, while it was predictable that from a practical standpoint the old masks would not be abandoned, the classical theories were dealt a blow from which they never entirely recovered.[4]

In this respect, as in most, Ibsen avoided an extreme position. He was, without doubt, generally an impressionist; but his characters frequently represent recognizable patterns of behavior, the more readily as they are so often caricatures, and therefore involve a rather definite preconception on the part of the author. Yet, on the whole, with Ibsen, nothing is quite finished, neither the portrait nor the story; both suggest the flux of being rather than its stability. It is rare that Ibsen ends a play with a posed tableau as in *John Gabriel Borkman* or *An Enemy of the People*; more often the final curtain comes down on an effect of less than complete finality, as in *A Doll's House*, *Ghosts*, or *Little Eyolf*, so that the play makes an effect of life rather than of a carefully contrived and completely finished work of art.

It is rare also that Ibsen's characters are independent of their physical surroundings. Not only has Rosmer the quality of the bleak northern landscape against which he moves, but, by a kind of reflex, he himself characterizes his environment, much as Cézanne's portrait of Madame Cézanne (1877) characterizes hers. Something of the sort might be said with equal justice of Brand, Mrs. Alving, or Ellida Wangel. It is, as a rule, not easy to visualize

Ibsen's characters apart from their immediate situation. None of them has the fixed expression of academic portraiture. They are creatures in motion caught in a situation which serves to define them momentarily, but there is no guarantee of the consistency of their behavior. Nothing authorizes us to assume that Hedda Gabler would ever, in a similar situation, repeat her performance—the character is not conceived or presented in such a way as to warrant a prediction of any sort; but we know exactly what to expect of a Cyrano de Bergerac or a Comtesse d'Autreval.

The practice of bringing a play to a close without resolving the narrative was, of course, in complete accord with the principles of realism. The slice-of-life technique, however, had little in common with the powerful dynamism of Ibsen's plays. At the end of *Thérèse Raquin*, or, for that matter, *Les Corbeaux*, there is no more to be said: the last words sum up the action with the force of an epigram. But *A Doll's House*, *An Enemy of the People*, or *The Wild Duck* end on suspended chords; and even the pistol shot which ends the story of Hedda Gabler begins the story of Tesman and Thea. In the hands of Chekhov, Ibsen's heir, this technique resulted in the most perfect examples of the impressionist mode in the modern theatre.

Strindberg's practice was of a different order. Ibsen preserved, from first to last, the superior pose of a sophisticated reporter, observing the behavior of humanity with an untroubled eye. Strindberg viewed life with the feverish interest of a precocious child. The result was a very special sort of sophisticated primitivism. It is clear that during his periods of crisis, at least, Strindberg occasionally experienced the kind of hallucinatory experience, usually associated with childhood, which is sometimes called eidetic. It is this sort of visionary re-creation, apparently, which furnished the experiential basis of the post-Inferno plays, several of which include a character who sees what others cannot see.

It is perhaps for this reason that Strindberg insisted, even toward the end of his life, that all his plays were essentially naturalistic—accurate transcriptions of observed reality. Even in his earlier drama, however, he was accustomed to develop his fantasy without much regard for the accepted norms of art, and the world he depicted naturalistically in those plays is not the world that is usually depicted on the stage—it is a world of strange shapes, a sharper and more extravagant world than the world we know, a world brought to us by a bad lens of high power. This distorted world, with its thoroughly contagious hysteria, also involves an unmistakable element of absurdity, like the fantastic landscapes of Henri Rousseau, or the pink hyperbolic nudes of Renoir's last period. It is entirely possible that, had Strindberg not been rescued by the mystical crisis which motivated his symbolic plays, his style would have culminated in a *reductio ad absurdum* of humanity in general. As it is, his naturalism ends in something not far from that.

In the 1890's the practical applications were still unclear of those works of art for which Zola had claimed the exactness and solidity of works of science; and even less clear than before. Observation, logic, and experiment had brought the generation of 1870 no further than a sense of the squalor and confusion of existence. "Materialism and positivism," Edouard Rod wrote in 1891, "no longer answer any actual need." Time did little to improve matters in this respect. Fifty years later, we find the critic Eric Newton writing, somewhat more subjectively, but to much the same effect: "This intense pursuit of the thing seen that characterizes the whole of the impressionist movement is not particularly sympathetic to me." [5] In 1891, when Jules Huret queried the leading French writers of his day as to the future of literature, almost all of his sixty-four authorities hastened to assure him that naturalism was dead.[6]

By this time, the shortcomings of the outer world had been amply demonstrated by the realists in every field of art; the political climate had altered perceptibly since the disaster of Sedan; and a wave of optimism swept over Western Europe. For two decades art had sought truth in ugliness and horror. It was the need to recover the beauty of the world that gave the impetus to symbolism, and the quest for that truth which the observation of material things had failed to disclose led inevitably to the inner world, the domain of that creative imagination which so far had created so little.[7] The symbolists found it necessary to give this world some degree of objectivity. They attempted to localize it in time and space, and thus found themselves thrown unexpectedly into a former age. The Hermetic books were sought out, republished, reinterpreted. Surrounded by throngs of spirits, bailiffs, and admiring ladies, the new mages stepped in and out of their pentacles and circles, lecturing in phrases that nobody understood, and interpreting visions that nobody saw.

The symbolist movement was first identified by Moréas in 1886, two years before the publication of *The Wild Duck*, in an article in *Le Figaro*.[8] He defined it as the attempt to replace outer reality as the subject of poetry by the "idea." The movement as such was attributed to Verlaine, but Verlaine was not a reliable symbolist: in the nineteenth century, the real father of symbolism was Baudelaire. "All the visible universe," Baudelaire had written in his *Salon de 1859*, "is only a store of images and signs to which imagination gives a place and a relative value." [9]

For the poets of the Parnasse, as for the naturalists and the impressionists, sense-experience was the ultimate reality. The symbolists considered, on the contrary, that the outer world was simply an appearance, a blurred intimation of the transcendental. It was useless, in their view, to imitate the external; the artist's task was to reveal its essential form, its idea. Such a task was evidently beyond the reach of natural science, which had promised everything but had so far failed to answer even the simplest questions about the nature of reality. But the poet had resources which the scientist had not—he had the power of imagination. This was not necessarily creative. "Things exist," Mallarmé wrote. "We do not need to create them; we need only to grasp their relations." [10] But while for Plato the relations of things could be grasped only by the intellect, the symbolists abandoned the intellect to the scientists, and depended for their insights upon the non-intellectual faculties, upon imagination, intuition, vision, and hallucination—or direct communication with the other world.

The significant difference between the symbolists of the Middle Ages and those of the nineteenth century was that whereas the medieval poets knew the truth, and had only the problem of finding suitable symbols in which to body it forth, the symbolists of the time of Mallarmé had no idea of what the truth might be, and therefore used the symbol mainly as an instrument of exploration, following it from thought to thought wherever it led, setting down what came to them first, and worrying later about what it might mean. Accident thus became an important element in creative technique.

In describing the imaginative artist, Baudelaire had come close to defining the basis of expressionism: "*L'imagination est la reine du vrai, et le* possible *est une des provinces du vrai. Elle est positivement apparentée avec l'infini.*" ". . . *L'imaginatif dit: 'Je veux illuminer les choses avec mon esprit et en projeter le reflet sur les autres esprits'* . . ." [11] But to the later symbolists it seemed that the artist had nothing to say of himself; he had only to decipher his visions, or if he could not, to manifest them for those who could. It was necessary, therefore, at the most to put oneself in a receptive posture. The rest went by itself.

A consequence of this attitude was the gradual abandonment of meaning in favor of form, with the consequence that poetry abdicated its intellectual eminence and strove to become a branch of painting or of music. Flaubert had dreamed of writing a novel without a subject. Mallarmé desired to write poetry as free from reference as a musical composition.[12] In pursuit of the Idea, Joyce eventually abandoned himself to a train of free association from which, as in *Finnegans Wake*, there was no probable issue. Thus after sustaining the fierce scrutiny of the impressionists for several decades, the subject little by little lost its fascination, and at last was abandoned altogether as the basis of art.

It was hardly possible to work, however, in the absence of a motif. A work of art, no matter how abstract, had to be about something if it was not to lapse into the merely decorative. Luckily, as far as poetry was concerned, the answer was at hand. In the *Corpus Hermeticum*, the *Tabula smaragdina*, and the works of Boehme, Swedenborg, Péladan, and Eliphas Lévi, the symbolists discovered the creative force of the word, the *logos*, and more especially the power of language to reveal through metaphor the correspondences between the world of appearances and the world which these appearances signified.

The theory of signatures was a commonplace of seventeenth-century thought. At that time, in similar circumstances, poets had suffered an analogous attack of mystical insight and, through a fine-spun web of metaphor and conceit, had thought to define the medieval universe in terms of the microcosm. The nineteenth-century symbolists, however, were products of the Enlightenment, and for them, the medieval cosmos was no longer altogether available for purposes of reference. Moreover, the precision of the allegorical method was found to be of no advantage to a poet who could not possibly be precise. Allegory was therefore repudiated in favor of the sort of symbol which suggests, evokes, implies, but does not signify. Villiers de l'Isle-Adam wrote: "To evoke the hidden object by allusive words, never directly, is the way of poetry and of magic."

The hidden object evoked in this manner was naturally never entirely definite, and the transcendental world that emerged from this process of allusion was barely habitable even by the imagination. At first this world appeared as pale and transparent as a painting by Puvis de Chavannes, though less intelligible. In time the colors of symbolism became stronger, the shapes more bold, but scarcely more meaningful than before. The world in question could not be represented, it had to be sensed; and, finally, also, perhaps it did not exist. In the absence of a reliable cosmos, the only recourse of the artist was to create for himself a provisional universe, a secondary reality; and since this was necessarily a private construction, a purely personal nature, the symbols by which the artist defined it were clear, if at all, chiefly to himself. Accordingly, the correspondences which formerly had served to signify God's work to man now served primarily to give coherence to the work of the artist. The next step was the reference of the artist's symbols to the artist's unconscious life, the unconscious in terms of Freud, or, more suitably, the universal unconscious of Jung.

"There are combinations of words," wrote Hofmannsthal, "from which, as the spark from the beaten flint, break forth the landscapes of the soul which, immeasurable as the starry heavens, stretch out into space and time." These psychic landscapes presumably would have a Swedenborgian or theosophical topography; it was in any case difficult, if not impossible, to convey the feeling of these *paysages* which become visible only under the most extraordinary psychic conditions. In order to explore the visions which certain words evoked, it was necessary for the poet to become a visionary. Rimbaud had written, how seriously it is impossible to say, but it was taken for Scripture:

The Poet makes himself a *seer* by a long, immense, and calculated *derangement* of *all the senses*. All the forms of love, of suffering, of madness; he himself seeks and exhausts in himself all the poisons, in order to retain only their quintessences. An ineffable torture in which he has need of all his faith, of all superhuman strength, in which he becomes among all men, the great invalid, the great criminal, the great accursed one—and the supreme Master! —For he reaches the *Unknown!* For he has cultivated his soul, already rich, more than anyone! He reaches the unknown, and even if he should end, in madness, by losing the meaning of his visions, he will have had them! [13]

Yet it was scarcely enough for the poet to reach the Unknown—his reader must also reach it, and preferably the same Unknown. In the interests of even the most exclusive poetry, it was necessary for the poet to have visions wide enough to accommodate at least two visitors. It thus became the goal of the symbolist to discover the magic words which would open a vista into the *au-delà* sufficiently accommodating to admit a certain proportion of his public as well as himself. Aside from drugs or drink, the chief possibility of arriving at words of such universality was a process of free association, in the course of which, it was hoped, the work of art would take shape without conscious purpose and without conscious direction, like a dream. This was the method, so far as one can judge, of Mallarmé.

The poem, from this viewpoint, would be not a communication, but an intimation. Its function would be not to convey a meaning, but to stimulate an experience. The poetic experience would be in the nature of an illumination, an insight not commensurate with, but in some measure analogous to, the Zennist *satori*, the sudden flash of comprehension which comes at the moment of despair.

The metaphysical basis for the alchemy of words and the poetic vision had been laid down long ago, and their possibilities had been thoroughly explored by such writers as Blake, Coleridge, De Quincey and, more recently, by Baudelaire; but Rimbaud, whose precocious excursion into the visionary world chiefly impressed the symbolists, was directly indebted for the new mysticism of language and the identification of poetry with hallucination to the *Dogme* of Eliphas Lévi. There were, besides, in Rimbaud's poetic theory, and in Mallarmé's preoccupation with nothingness and absence, striking analogies to the vein of Eastern mysticism which, since the time of Schopenhauer, had made its influence felt more and more strongly on the art and letters of Europe in this period.

In their zeal to find a world beyond life, the symbolists found it necessary to demolish the entire structure, and the basis, of realist art. Here the amateur philosophy of the symbolists was at a disadvantage. Professional philosophers had been over that ground many times, and material reality had successfully withstood every onslaught since the time of Parmenides and Zeno. In poetry, the Unconscious proved to be a less reliable source of inspiration than the Idea. In answer to Huret's questionnaire as to the future of literature, the naturalist Paul Alexis had hastened to wire: *"Naturalisme pas mort. Lettre suit."* He was quite right. Naturalism survived the school of Zola, and the school of Mallarmé, and for that matter, all other schools to the present day. For a time, the symbolist painting of Bresdin, Moreau, and Redon held the spotlight of fashion; Poe came once more strongly into vogue; then came a series of waves of quasi-symbolist art and quasi-symbolist literature. In the course of these movements, it became possible to relieve the art of the drama once for all from the weight of the actual, and the necessity for aping "nature" in the name of verisimilitude. Thus, under the guidance of Ibsen, Maeterlinck, Strindberg, and Yeats once more the dream found its way to the stage, and again drama drew close to poetry.

"I believe," Mallarmé wrote, "that literature, drawing once again upon its source, which is art and science, will give us a Theatre the productions of which will be the true modern cult . . ." [14] For Mallarmé, the prime subject of drama was the indviduality of the poet, and its goal was the expression of the Hymn which the hero has in himself and which in a lightning-like effusion he confronts dramatically with the Idea which is the Theatre.[15] Such a statement may not be at all times completely intelligible; but, whatever it may mean, Mallarmé discovered to his sorrow, in the course of the long years he spent on *Hérodiade*, it is no easy thing to formulate drama in such terms. The evolution of symbolism in the theatre took a less radical and much simpler course than this. The sort of symbolism which proved effective on the stage was cast, understandably, in the normal molds of nineteenth-century drama, and its beginnings were not far from impressionism.

Ghosts was published in 1881, the year after the publication of *Nana*. Since Ibsen made some mention in it of inherited disease, it was inevitably considered to be a work in the tradition of Zola, and the storm of critical vituperation that was directed against the naturalists also enveloped Ibsen, who acquired in this manner a reputation for blasphemy, obscenity, radicalism, and naturalism which served him admirably for the rest of his life. Ibsen, for his part, haughtily disclaimed any connection with the naturalist school: Zola was a democrat, he said; he himself, an aristocrat. In 1881, he was not averse to being cast in the role of social reformer. "Zola goes down into the sewer to take a bath," he is reported to have remarked. "I, in order to cleanse it." [16]

In fact, Ibsen's state of mind at the time of Ghosts, we have seen, had more to do with impressionism than with naturalism; if he was classed with the naturalists it was largely because of his obvious hostility to the idealist position with its fixed concepts, its optimism, and its academic conservatism. He had no idea, certainly, of representing carefully documented cross-sections of life objectively and scientifically for the sake of themselves alone. On the contrary, it was apparently his idea to study, impressionist-fashion, a single psychic landscape from various angles and under different conditions of atmosphere and light. As a dramatist he was far more interested in patterns than in problems; and in his long preoccupation with the plot-pattern of Brand in its various aspects he makes us think of Cézanne's preoccupation with Mont Saint-Victoire in its many moods: there is in each artist the same intensity of psychic identification with the object of contemplation.

Whether or not he actually read Zola very likely we shall never know; and, in any case, it hardly matters. As he said, in his crusty way, soon after the publication of Ghosts, he did not read books; he let his son and his wife do that.[17] Obviously, this too was part of his pose; but one did not have to be a naturalist in order to be aware of the role played by heredity and environment in the formation of character, nor was the idea that the sins of the father were visited upon the children the exclusive property of any school of literature.

In the latter half of the nineteenth century it was sensible to give one's ideas a scientific turn. It was sensible also to follow the example of the most successful dramatists of the time in directing attention to social and moral questions in the theatre. But Ibsen, as he himself said repeatedly, had no great interest in such matters:

it was as a poet that he viewed the facts of life. There was, accordingly, no contradiction in his mind between the impressionist's interest in the sensual aspects of the world and the symbolist's desire to see into the soul. His tendency toward symbolism had been perceptible even before the time of *Brand*, and with *Brand* he established a style which was useful to him all the rest of his career. In the drama, clearly, he was a symbolist some years before the symbolists.

In his essay, *Le Tragique quotidien* (1896), Maeterlinck recognized in *Ghosts*, as in Tolstoi's *The Power of Darkness*, that "anguish of the unintelligible" which distinguished the work of Verlaine and Mallarmé, and which was to become the distinguishing mark of the type of symbolist drama which he initiated. But a dozen years earlier, with the publication of *The Wild Duck* in 1884, and *The Lady from the Sea* in 1888, Ibsen's position as a symbolist had become clear to everyone, and, very likely, even to himself.[18] "Nobody has written symbolically for the theatre," Émile Faguet remarked some years later, "except M. Ibsen." For Maeterlinck, *The Master Builder* was the first masterpiece in the new genre he himself was promoting, and he praised it generously in a passage that recalls the terminology of Mallarmé somewhat more explicitly, perhaps, than Ibsen's work warrants:

Hilda and Solness are, I believe, the first characters in drama who feel, for an instant, that they are living in an atmosphere of the soul; and the discovery of this essential life that exists in them, beyond the life of every day, comes fraught with terror . . . Their conversation resembles nothing that we have ever heard, inasmuch as the poet has endeavored to blend in one expression both the inner and the outer dialogue. A new and indescribable power dominates this somnambulistic drama. All that is said therein at once hides and reveals the sources of an unknown life. And if we are bewildered at times, let us not forget that our soul often appears to our feeble eyes to be but the maddest of forces, and that there are in man many regions more fertile, more profound and more interesting than those of his reason and intelligence.[19]

It is not at all certain to what extent, if any, Ibsen was aware of the symbolist discussions which were finding their way into print in France, and elsewhere, in the late 1880's, but it is doubtful that he would have found them particularly edifying. As we have seen, *Brand* and *Peer Gynt* are nothing if not symbolic:

> L'homme y passe à travers de forêts de symboles
> Qui l'observent avec des regards familiers . . .

The symbolism of these early plays runs the full gamut from the simplest to the most complex sort of signification. Brand and Peer Gynt figure, each in his way, the man-who-is-himself, but these characters are by no means personifications, and they are too detailed to be called types. They might perhaps be called exemplars: each brings to mind a psychic pattern, an aspect of human personality; to be precise, of the author's personality. At the other extreme from these, is the Button Molder, obviously an abstraction. Yet as a symbol he lacks precision, and his very lack of reference gives him the mystery of a figure in a dream. The Button Molder is not Death, nor Annihilation. He is a presentiment of death and annihilation, personified in terms of a child's toy—the casting-ladle which is auctioned off with the other debris of the life of Peer Gynt.[20] He is, that is to say, that particular casting-ladle, embodied, living, and capable of speech. This type of symbol is essentially dramatic, a commonplace of the fairy tale, and the modern equivalent of the personifications of medieval drama.

In *Brand*, the Ice Church with its black finger pointing to heaven has, in its blend of conscious and unconscious allusion, a more complex character than the Button Molder, who is, after all, merely a figure of speech; but it is still entirely intelligible. The Boyg in *Peer Gynt*, on the other hand, defies analysis. The figure cannot be visualized. We can only feel vaguely what it represents —an unlocalized neurotic terror, the fear of darkness, the stuff of madness. Yet, while it is indefinable, it is not incomprehensible. It is only when we come to the hawk in *Brand* that we encounter a complexity of signification so extreme that the symbol eludes intellectual apprehension. The hawk is evil: it is said to be the spirit of compromise. It is good: it is *deus caritatis*. It is also a sun-symbol. Ibsen employs it as such; and in this guise it is well known to us. Obviously, too, it has phallic character, and its successive transformations, when it is shot, first into a white dove, then into a shower of white feathers, lastly into the overwhelming avalanche of snow, sufficiently suggest the erotic nature of Brand's encounter with the God of Love. In general, the symbols in *Brand* are intended to suggest states of mind, just as Brand suggests a state of mind, and, except perhaps for the hawk, they do not seriously resist interpretation. But when they are interpreted, the explanation adds curiously little to the efficacy of the metaphor, which operates poetically, quite apart from reason, and thus demonstrates its affinity with the type of symbolism which is characteristic of the nineteenth century rather than with the symbolism of the Renaissance.

The symbolism of *The Wild Duck*, more widely imitated than that of any other of Ibsen's plays, comes somewhat closer to the method of the medieval allegories, but it is not the same. The elusiveness of the Wild Duck as a symbol is different from that of the Pearl in the poem of that name, or of the Eagle of the *Paradiso*. The forest in the attic resembles only superficially the forests of error or of illusion in which it is customary for knights to lose themselves in Renaissance *romanzi*. What distinguishes the modern from the medieval symbol is not merely its ambiguity, but its capaciousness, its amplitude.

The Eagle of the *Paradiso* yields to no symbol in point of ambiguity; no one has succeeded in fixing its meaning. But the possible limits of interpretation are more or less fixed, and the symbol challenges the reason as an enigma which is entirely amenable to rational interpretation. The Wild Duck, on the other hand, like the White Horses of *Rosmersholm*, or the Rat-Wife of *Little Eyolf*, completely eludes this sort of approach: it prefers not to be defined. As a metaphor, the wounded bird serves to characterize the lives and souls of almost all the characters in the play from Old Ekdal to Gregers Werle; it refers to Hedvig in still another way; and it is used emblematically to describe in general the therapeutic role of illusion in life. In the end, the Wild Duck serves to unify in a single figure the entire action of the play: so much meaning radiates from this symbol that anything that serves to define it, serves also to restrict its efficacy. From Chekhov's *The Seagull* to Graham Greene's *The Living Room*, no device has been found more useful in searching out the poetic core of a dramatic action than a metaphor of this sort. One might imagine that in using it as he did, Ibsen had in mind the prescription of Mallarmé, published, however, some seven years later, in 1891:

> C'est le parfait usage de ce mystère qui constitue
> le symbole: évoquer petit à petit un objet pour
> montrer un état d'âme, ou, inversement, choisir
> un objet et en dégager un état d'âme par une
> série de déchiffrements.[21]

The Master Builder is usually considered Ibsen's masterpiece in the symbolic style; but it is not so much through symbol as through suggestion that this play makes its strangely mystical effect. What chiefly moved the enthusiasm of Maeterlinck was the way in which, behind the scenes of the human drama, there takes form, step by step, a drama of which the significance can only be surmised, which parallels the tragedy of Solness. The suggestion of invisible forces co-operating in the Master Builder's rise and fall, his reported colloquies with God on the rooftops, the sound of invisible harps at the end, the sudden reappearance of the girl whom he saw when he first defied the Almighty from the church steeple at Lysanger, his sense of laboring under the curse he then incurred—these seem to be merely the visible signs of a retributive operation which takes place not only in the feverish imagination of Solness, but perhaps also in the mysterious world which is the larger setting of the play.

The mythological groundwork on which Ibsen founded *The Master Builder* was, in fact, minimal—some odds and ends of

Swedenborg, perhaps; nothing more: the play is itself a castle in the air. There is nothing underlying it like the complex philosophic system that supports *To Damascus*, which also involves a struggle with God. With Strindberg, as with Maeterlinck, the Beyond is a constant presence, of which we are continually aware. In Ibsen's play, it is no more than the most tactful intimation—it may be beyond, it may be within, the characters. From this delicacy of suggestion, *The Master Builder* derives a sense of immediacy which we do not feel in such naturalistic fairy tales as *Pelléas et Mélisande*, or in such *tours de force* as *L'Intruse*. In evoking this equivocal mood, Ibsen came closer to Mallarmé than any playwright who attempted this style, save perhaps Chekhov.

It was almost certainly through Ibsen, his "favorite writer," that Chekhov arrived at the extraordinarily effective symbolism of *The Cherry Orchard*; but Chekhov was able to carry Ibsen's technique a step further than Ibsen. There is the transparent symbolism of the orchard, useless now, but still beautiful, and the obvious significance of its destruction; and parallel to this motive is the destruction of the family which is identified with the orchard. But the full power of the play is derived from yet another analogy, the manner in which the quiet dissolution of a country family symbolizes the economic cataclysm of Russia.

This is symbolism of correspondence; but not the sort of correspondence which was congenial to the metaphysical poets. The macrocosm which is mirrored in the modest action of *The Cherry Orchard* is neither moral nor intelligible. What is symbolized in the tragic inconsequentiality of Madame Ranyevsky is the helplessness of the individual in the face of the irresistible surge of a cosmic force. Her expropriation is a consequence of the dialectic which brings about the destruction of an entire social class and the birth of another. Her inability to come reasonably abreast of her situation indicates the extent to which her soul's sickness reflects the decay of a dying culture—and of all this, almost nothing is said. Trofimov touches lightly upon the subject in the course of a rambling harangue to which nobody listens; and that is all.

Nevertheless, the symbolism of the play is perfectly precise. Apart from the sound of the breaking string in the sky, there is nothing mysterious about *The Cherry Orchard*. It is purely through suggestion that we are made aware, in the course of the trifling action, of a force which is as enigmatic in its nature, and as ruthless, as Greek *ananké*. *The Master Builder* belongs, however, to another category. *The Cherry Orchard* illustrates and extends the technique, and in some measure, the subject matter also, of *Rosmersholm*.

Maeterlinck felt it was necessary to free his characters from reality in order to reveal their essential life; accordingly, he invented for them a drama of old, unhappy, far-off things where horrors might take place that did not have to be believed. In this respect, he was at the extreme pole from the naturalists. But this sort of abstraction, while it tends to put in universal terms what we are accustomed to view in the particular, ultimately reveals nothing of which we were not previously aware. These bloody deeds in an unknown land are, after all, no more than bloody deeds. They would be no different if they were set in Rome or New York; and in this respect, Maeterlinck seems closer to naturalism than at first appears. It is mainly in such quasi-realistic plays as *L'Intruse* and *Intérieur* that the lines of communication with the unknown seem to open, so that we have for a moment the illusion of dark powers moving silently among us.

In general, Maeterlinck went barely beyond Poe as a symbolist. *Pelléas et Mélisande* is in essence a conventional story of love and jealousy told in a mannered style; in putting the old story into his shadow-box, Maeterlinck hardly deepened its mystery—he merely obscured it. Ibsen, on the other hand, rarely parts company with the actual; at the most he gives it perspective by introducing a character from another world. *The Lady from the Sea, Little Eyolf, The Master Builder, When We Dead Awaken* are all quietly realistic plays, and it is out of their very actuality that their mysterious quality arises. What is ambiguous in them is fundamentally ambiguous; their poetry, their mystery, is not a matter of an artificially induced atmosphere: it is the poetry, the mystery, of life itself.

After Baudelaire, the line between prose and poetry wore thin; but it was some time before the poetic quality of Ibsen's plays became clear to anyone.[22] His readers, accustomed to the drama of the Second Empire, looked to Ibsen not for a poetic experience but for a message or an argument, and even the plays he composed in verse elicited discussions chiefly of their doctrine and its relation to the ideals which were considered indispensable to poetry. By the time *The Wild Duck* was played in England, Shaw had no doubt a better idea of Ibsen's quality than he manifested in *The Quintessence of Ibsenism*; but by this time the damage was done, and Ibsen's reputation as primarily a social dramatist was too firmly established to permit of any change of viewpoint. It is probable, besides, that, even at this late date, Shaw was unable to appreciate Ibsen at his true worth. Shaw was a brilliant rhetorician and a wit; Ibsen, an artist. The two species could hardly be further apart.

With the decline of naturalism in the 1880's, realistic drama became largely impressionist, and so it remains to this day. The shifting of interest from the actual to the poetic which accompanied the extension of the symbolist mode in the last years of the century merely interrupted the development of the impressionist style. It was, nevertheless, a serious interruption. Almost all the important dramatists who were writing at the close of the nineteenth century began as naturalists and ended as symbolists—Ibsen, Strindberg, Hauptmann, Chekhov, Schnitzler, Sudermann, Hofmannsthal, Claudel. But symbolism changed as rapidly in the theatre as it did in the other arts. By 1912, Guillaume Apollinaire understood that the technique of the symbolists was no longer a vital influence in poetry, and that it was necessary to return to Rimbaud and Mallarmé for a fresh start. By this time the symbolism of Maeterlinck had lost its impetus in the theatre. The *avant-garde* writers turned now to Strindberg.

Although Ibsen had many times intimated that his plays were primarily poems of self-revelation, nobody appears to have taken these suggestions seriously until after the publication of *When We Dead Awaken*. Strindberg, however, understood; and it was very likely in emulation of Ibsen that, in his hands, drama became for the first time consciously and explicitly a medium for the expression of the inmost subjectivity of the writer.

To miss the poetic depth of Ibsen's plays is simply to underestimate their value as works of art, but to judge the drama of Strindberg's naturalistic period simply as naturalistic drama is to misconstrue him completely. Viewed from this standpoint, the plays of 1887–1889 seem excessive and extravagant to the point of mania, whereas in fact they embody a technique of exaggeration and distortion which rapidly became a commonplace of modern painting and sculpture.

Strindberg had no idea of representing nature as it seemed to others, still less of conforming to academic standards of dramatic art. He saw life from a highly individualistic point of view, which was precious to him. He saw it in unusual shapes and colors, peopled with strange beings, ruled by occult forces, vibrant with such terrors as most people never feel; and he reported not only what he saw, but what he felt, dreamed, surmised, and imagined, without bothering to distinguish the one from the other, since for him the external and the internal life were equally valid, and equally useful. Nevertheless, he solemnly presented the plays of this period as examples of naturalistic technique. They were read therefore, and are read to this day, in connection with the Author's Foreword to *Miss Julie*, a superb summation of the naturalist position, and it apparently escaped the attention of many that these prodigious characters, playing a wholly improbable action in a thoroughly improbable way, belong to a world that is as unreal, and as sensational, as the world of Van Gogh; and therefore live with a life that is so intense that it can be expressed only through hyperbole.

In writing *The Father*, Strindberg had it in mind to present not a slice of life, but a modern tragedy, specifically, a modern version of the *Agamemnon*. *The Father* partakes accordingly of the nature of myth; its action is simplified in the manner of tragedy, and the characters are individualized concepts, heroically exaggerated so as to represent, without nuance or accidental detail, Man as Hercules, and Woman as Omphale.[23] Most of Strindberg's plays of this period were conceived in a manner equally remote from the methods of naturalism. The exception is *Miss Julie*. But even the characters of *Miss Julie* betray the hand of the artist. They are not drawn from life; they are composites assembled in accordance with the author's theoretical preconceptions, formulated, as if by a chemist, out of pre-established elements in carefully calculated proportions. They represent, if we may believe his words, something between a compound and a *collage*:

My souls [characters] are conglomerates of various stages of culture, past and present, bits out of books and newspapers, scraps of humanity, strips torn from old Sunday clothes which have become rags, all patched together as is the human soul. And I have added a little evolutionary history into the bargain, for I let the weaker steal and repeat the stronger's words, and I let these souls pick up ideas from each other by what is called suggestion.[24]

This is evidently not the method of naturalism. It describes a style of characterization which is from one viewpoint extremely old-fashioned, from another, so advanced for the theatre that not even Strindberg practiced it with any consistency. There is, furthermore, in this play of the man, the woman, and the cook something which presages not the expressionistic method of *A Dream Play*, but the surrealistic technique of his very last plays, an intimation of the last scene, for example, of *The Ghost Sonata*.

Strindberg's characters, on the whole, are the figments of a nightmare: they appear to have inspired the author himself with surprise and terror. But unlike Ibsen, Strindberg cultivated his neurosis as an important literary property; he made a career of it. His plays reach us, therefore, in all the vigor of their madness, making only the barest concessions to the amenities of the stage. Harriet Bosse tells us that, as a painter, Strindberg had no patience with a brush, and laid on his color *impasto* with great strokes of the palette knife. His plays make the impression of having been put together in much the same way. Upon one who is accustomed to the discipline and order of the tradition of Corneille, Strindberg's style makes an uncomfortable impression of wildness and hyperbole. It seems to exhibit neither the control nor the practical good sense of the craftsman. It has the frightening energy of genius, without the restraint that makes genius endurable.

In fact, as *Miss Julie* indicates, Strindberg was entirely capable of controlling his material. He could have written, doubtless, had he chosen to do so, in the tradition of Ibsen and Björnson. This was not his idea. For his purpose, the style of *Miss Julie* was a step beyond the style of *Marauders*; but he was aiming, whether consciously or not, at a different style of drama, at the style of *To Damascus*, toward which *The Father* was yet another step.

Miss Julie is drawn in a proper perspective, with a careful regard for the disposition of the stage properties and the development of the dramatic illusion. At this point in his career, Strindberg evidently believed that one had to ape reality in order to hypnotize the audience into the necessary subservience to the dramatist's will. He soon discovered that the inner recesses of the soul are accessible not through the way of reality but through the paths of dreams. In *The Father*, accordingly, Strindberg did something analogous to Cézanne's deliberate negation of perspective in the representation of nature. He was interested now, less in how the characters appear, than in what they are, and therefore approached his material not impressionistically but conceptually, in the manner of the medieval artist, borrowing from nature only what was necessary to his purpose. The characters of *The Father* are drawn, in consequence, entirely out of perspective, with an almost complete disregard for conventional proportion or verisimilitude, with an eye to their essential, not their accidental relationships. The play has very little external realism. Since it is the inner, not the outer reality, which it is intended to represent, its realism is not superficial, but essential.

Realism, obviously, is never realistic in the sense that it brings about an exact reproduction of nature—neither the camera nor the tape recorder are capable of that, much less the artist. Between the outer world, whatever its truth may be, and its artistic representation there stands always the mediating personality of the observer. No matter how objective or how neutral the dramatist may wish to be, or to appear, his selection of a subject, and the arrangement of the details which compose it, necessarily reflect and express his personality: in this respect every work of art is a work of self-revelation. "The artist," says Nietzsche, "paints ultimately solely that which pleases him, and that pleases him which he is capable of painting." 25

Realism has to do, therefore, in the first instance, with what is perceived in nature out of the totality of the visible world. Since every visual grouping, and every dramatic situation, is in some measure an expression of the artist's temperament, the difference between realism and expressionism is seen to be a matter of degree, a question of what happens in the mind to the recollected image before it is transmitted to the canvas, or reconstructed publicly on the stage. It is a question, in short, of the degree of conformity of the work of art with the inner or the outer nature. An artist who lives principally in terms of a psychic conflict is likely to perceive reality principally in terms of this conflict; one who wishes to prove something through his art will find that everything in the world springs forward with corroborating evidence. The difference between Miss Julie and The Father is thus largely a matter of the type of experience which Strindberg chose to reproduce in these plays. The former is ostensibly an interpretation of the life of the outer world; the latter interprets the inner life. Both are, in their fashion, realistic: they differ principally in the order of reality which they are intended to transmit, and the order of illusion they are intended to produce. Miss Julie betrays the constant supervision of the conscious craftsman. In *The Father* the unconscious is in command.

As Ibsen's purpose as an artist was different from Strindberg's, his perceptions were different, and entailed a different order of control. Ibsen was the greatest master of caricature the modern theatre has known, and in order to attain his ends, it was necessary for him to base his plays very solidly on the norms of conventional reality and conventional behavior. It is not necessary to believe Strindberg in order to feel his pressure; but Ibsen requires us to have complete faith in the situations his plays develop. Ibsen speaks to us mainly through the intellect, therefore all his characters are believable; and all of them, even the noblest and best, are ridiculed in some degree. The same may be said of his plots —it is clear that all of them, even the most sombre, at some point made him smile. Behind this smile we feel a vast reserve of melancholy, an unexpressed bitterness, as well as the deep cynicism which constitutes an essential element of the face which, through his plays, Ibsen presents to the world. Strindberg has no such reticence. He bustles immediately to the forefront of his action, and it takes place directly under his hand, like a play of marionettes. It is a completely different order of self-characterization. The two authors, in some ways so closely related, foreshadow therefore, in what is called their naturalistic manner, the two main styles of twentieth-century representational art, as well as the two main styles of twentieth-century artist. Ibsen stands somewhere near Daumier and Cézanne; but Strindberg belongs with Lautrec and Van Gogh.

From the calculated hysteria of Strindberg's naturalistic period to the mysticism of the post-Inferno plays is actually no more than a step. The visionary qualities of these plays were related, of course, to the nervous crisis through which he passed after his marriage in 1893, and the psychic disturbances he suffered in consequence are clearly reflected in his work. It was, however, precisely in these years that he came most strongly under French influence.

Strindberg was in Paris from August, 1894, until the summer of

1896. He returned to Paris at the end of 1897, and for some time thereafter he felt himself to be part of the French literary scene. At this time his sufferings, like his plays and novels, take on a distinctly symbolist cast. There is no question, of course, of the reality of his anguish. Strindberg suffered deeply. But suffering in itself is inchoate and inarticulate. Like everything else that emerges into consciousness, it must be given a certain form, and the giving of form on any level is, in some measure, a poetic process. Nothing is more rare than originality. There are, accordingly, patterns for suffering, set by sufferers of note, and it is demonstrable that pain has its modes and fashions of expression, like other aesthetic experiences which are capable of sublimation.

In the 1860's the high style of suffering was set by Baudelaire, and in the following generation his manner was carefully studied by those who desired to suffer with distinction. An exceptionally gifted group of eccentrics took up the style of Baudelaire, especially in Paris,

> Da schirmten held und sänger das Geheimniss:
> VILLIERS sich hoch genug für einen thron
> VERLAINE in fall und busse fromm und kindlich
> Und für sein denkbild blutend: MALLARMÉ.[26]

Besides the school of Paris, Strindberg had before his eyes in these years the fascinating example of Nietzsche, of whose work he became fully aware after 1888. Nietzsche, who in fact suffered from epilepsy, had carefully recorded his innermost experiences in the course of the spiritual upheavals that marked his troubled life; and his complete breakdown at the beginning of 1889 anticipated Strindberg's Inferno by only a few years.[27] Whether or not Strindberg was conscious of these influences is not clear. In Inferno he wrote, not without a certain complacency:

. . . all my sufferings I found described in Swedenborg . . . all exactly correspond, and these elements, taken together, constitute the spiritual catharsis (purgation) which was already known to Saint Paul.[28]

He says nothing of his relation to Baudelaire, or Baudelaire's gifted masochistic predecessor, Nerval.

In the 1890's, it was good to be a poet and accursed. The prime subject of poetry was the agony of life; a life without agony, as Baudelaire had indicated, had no distinction. The influence of Dostoievski on European thought was as yet not great—although *Crime and Punishment* had been published in 1866, it was not until the turn of the century that the French came under the spell of this master; but the idea of the tragic hero as a man tortured by an inscrutable power which is perhaps himself was certainly current before Strindberg dramatized it in *To Damascus*.

The pleasure of self-torture was the great discovery of the age. Ibsen, sturdy individualist, contented himself, after 1885, with passing his heroes through the fire; until his last period, so far as we know, he declined to take an active share in their discomfort. Strindberg, however, threw himself into the current agony with reckless abandon, and like Baudelaire and Mallarmé, descended repeatedly into hell in order to rise again into the consoling presence. His Inferno of 1897 may therefore be fairly considered in relation to Baudelaire's "spleen" of 1857, Mallarmé's torments of 1869, and Rimbaud's season in hell of 1873. Like these poets, he also was a "decipherer of analogies," and he savored as keenly as they *"le goût du néant."* Strindberg kept abreast of the times. In the time of the mages, he was a mage. In the time of lovers distasted with love, he too felt that his love gravitated always to a single object encountered in many forms, always deceptive and ever the same; and this inconstant lady spoke to him in much the same accents as Notre Dame de la Lune to Jules Laforgue:

> Et tu iras, levant encore bien plus de dupes,
> Vers le Zaïmph de la Joconde, vers la Jupe!
> Il se pourra même que j'en sois.[29]

So far as Strindberg was concerned, the obvious point of departure for the drama of symbolism was the magic of dreams and visions. There was also the question of words, colors, odors, and the symbolism of plants and animals. In his essay on Théophile Gautier, Baudelaire had written of that meticulous poet's "immense innate understanding of *correspondence* and universal symbolism, that repertory of all metaphor," which explained how it was that he could

without fatigue and without fault, define the mysterious attitude which the objects of creation assume under the gaze of man. There is in the word, in the *Word*, something *sacred* which forbids us to make of it a game of chance. To handle a language skillfully is to practice a kind of evocatory magic. It is then that color speaks, like a deep and vibrant voice; that monuments rise up and push forward into the depths of space; that animals and plants, the representatives of ugliness and evil, make their not equivocal grimace; that perfume provokes its corresponding thought and memory; that passion murmurs or roars its eternally recurrent language.[30]

It was precisely Strindberg's ambition in these years to attain the degree of skill in the sorcery of evocation which Baudelaire imputed to Gautier, but it was not the mystique of the *mot juste* which interested him. It was the wonder-world of symbolism and correspondence to which poetry was the key, the ambiguous world of the *voyant*. Baudelaire, in his essay on Victor Hugo, had indicated clearly the function of the poet in its largest aspect:

Swedenborg . . . has already taught us that *heaven is a very great man;* that everything, form, movement, number, color, perfume, in the *spiritual* as in the *natural*, is significant, reciprocal, converse, *correspondent.* . . . We arrive at this truth, that all is hieroglyphic, and we know that symbols are obscure only in a relative manner, that is to say according to the purity, the good will, or the native clairvoyance of the soul. Thus, what is a poet (I take the word in its widest sense) if not a translator, a decipherer? [31]

It was very much along these lines that Strindberg developed his art in the post-Inferno years. The action of *To Damascus* is set on the shadowy frontier from which the inner and the outer worlds are equally visible, and equally indistinct. Baudelaire had spoken in "Théophile Gautier" of the sort of novel which would retrace the course *"des drames silencieux qui se jouent dans un seul cerveau."* [32] It was in this mode precisely that *To Damascus* was conceived, and, later, *A Dream Play*, and *The Great Highway*. These were among the first plays that depended for their force on something other than character and action, and belonged pre-eminently to that genre

où le mystère scintille, où le mystère invite la rêverie curieuse, d'où le mystère repousse la pensée découragée. [33]

But it is not only in dreams that the hidden life is manifested. As Freud was soon to show, it is the unconscious that shapes the profile of a lifetime, so that a life may be considered as the allegory of the soul's struggle, its outward semblance. From this stand-point, correspondence takes on a new meaning. It becomes the key not to the world beyond, but to the world within; and thus it opens the way for a new sort of drama, of intense significance, in which the motivation, being unconscious, cannot be rationalized at all.

It was through their extraordinary intuition of the role of the unconscious as the shaping principle of life that Ibsen and Strind-berg—and, for that matter, Tolstoi and Chekhov—were able to give such astonishing dimension to their plays. The evocative power of these plays has not much to do with the alchemy of words, nor do they really show us another world. They show us our world. Their power depends on a poetic of action; and the consequence, in each case uncanny, is not so much a vision of supernatural forces as a revelation of the nature of human beings.

In Ibsen and Strindberg, as in Tolstoi, the intimation is that the supernatural world is not outside the individual soul but within it. When *Axël* was published in 1890, it identified symbolist drama with romantic settings, medieval castles, Christian ritual, and a longing for death, and it was along such lines that Maeterlinck at first directed the course of the symbolist theatre of the next decade. This style was necessarily short-lived. It was not in the romantic otherworld that the destiny of the drama lay in modern times, but in the present and the actual. Even before he brought out *Pelléas et Mélisande* in 1892, Maeterlinck foresaw the end of the gothic style he had developed and, in 1886, *Le Tragique quotidien* reawakened the world to the poetry of everyday life which Wordsworth and Coleridge had introduced to the wary English almost a century before. Under symbolist auspices, this poetry now bore splendid fruit in the theatre. The drama of the strangeness of familiar things passed from Belgium to Germany, thence to England, where eventually, in the hands of Yeats and Synge, it became an Irish specialty and resulted in Irish masterpieces, among which are some of the finest plays of our time.

Apart from the stimulating effect of a new technique, and of a renewed conception of drama as poetry, what was essentially significant in the symbolist drama was this recognition of the importance of the irrational faculty as the creative element in art. From classical times the matrix of art had been held to be the intellect: traditionally, the work of art was conceived along rational lines, and directed primarily to the understanding. The identification of the unconscious as the chief source of artistic creativity, and also its ultimate object, involved something like an aesthetic revolution, the full consequences of which could not possibly have been foreseen by those who helped to bring it about. In the meantime, the development of the drama of the irrational did more than naturalism to bring the well-made play into disrepute. The Scribean play, with its ingenious turns and planned surprises, was based firmly on the principle of logical sequence. Once it was realized that the role of logic as a motive for human behavior is largely ornamental, the drama of cause and consequence was seen to be a pleasant, but artificial genre, a game which, however satisfying, rarely touched the deepest human concerns, and therefore could not by itself attain the level of high art.

At the same time, realism, toward which the drama had been moving since the time of the Renaissance, was felt in many quarters to be a clog on the creative faculty. Among the first consequences of this reaction was the German expressionist movement of the 1920's, a short-lived, but extremely influential development associated with the type of post-impressionist drama that Strindberg had inaugurated twenty years before. This movement had many consequences. Once the dramatist felt free of the necessity for preserving the illusion of actuality, it became possible to treat a play as a play, to take direct account of the presence of the audience, and to control, rather than to be controlled by the illusion.

In the light of these developments, verisimilitude took on a deeper meaning—it became a question of accordance with what was felt to be essential truth or purpose, rather than conformity with the conventional modes of experience. The symbolist movement in the theatre, of no great importance, perhaps, in itself, thus opened three important lines of development which more or less define the ramifications of twentieth-century drama—the line which led to Pirandello, the line which led to Giraudoux, and the line which led to Brecht—while the surrealism of Strindberg's last plays became the basis of an entirely new concept of dramatic art, which has, after fifty years, barely developed beyond the point where Strindberg left it.

Once it was demonstrated that the drama could operate effectively beyond the sphere of the mimesis of nature, in areas comparatively free from intellectual control, the door was left open for every type of vagary. After the expressionism of the 1920's came the drama of the Ubuists and the Dadaists, then the fantasies of the Kafkaists, then the vogue of the Absurdists. By the middle of the century a refreshing breath of madness could be felt blowing across the stages of the world, sweeping away cheerfully much of the accumulated rubbish of a thousand years of dramatic history, and leaving in its wake new rubbish to be swept away.

From all this we may conclude that the influence of Ibsen and Strindberg on the drama of the last half-century is incalculable, and for that very reason indefinable. It is a simple matter to show the dependence of Chekhov, Shaw, or Galsworthy upon Ibsen, or the relation of Strindberg to Shaw, Wedekind, Kaiser, O'Neill,

Ionesco, or Genet. It is obvious that Gorki's *The Lower Depths* and O'Neill's *The Iceman Cometh* rest substantially upon *The Wild Duck*; [34] that Mr. Williams's *Camino Real* bears a certain formal similarity to *The Great Highway*; that Mr. Miller's *Death of a Salesman* and Jean Giraudoux's *Madwoman of Chaillot* include surrealistic effects which were unknown before they were demonstrated in *A Dream Play*; and it is in the highest degree probable that Pirandello found the theme of *Vestire gli ignudi* in a passage in the Author's Foreword to *Miss Julie*. But such trivialities, while interesting, are entirely inadequate to convey an idea of the importance of the Scandinavian masters for the drama of our time. Their influence was, and continues to be, a formative one. It is not so much that in our day we consciously imitate them, but rather that it is all but impossible at the moment to write for the stage without imitating them.[35]

In the nature of their influence, of course, they differ greatly. Ibsen summed up an era; Strindberg opened a new one. The play of ideas had been developed long before their time. None of the subjects with which Ibsen dealt was new, and his method also was an adaptation of pre-existent practice. Like Björnson, he—and Strindberg also—levied systematically on the French dramatists for his material. But both Ibsen and Strindberg brought to the drama an imaginative vigor that was wholly fresh and original, which radically transformed the tradition they transmitted, so that they were able to express the individualistic temper of the age in ways which make us think of the contemporary writings of Nietzsche, the poetry of Mallarmé, the painting of Van Gogh, Cézanne, and Matisse, the music-drama of Wagner, and the music of Richard Strauss and Debussy. Before Ibsen, the moral foundations of society had not been seriously questioned in the theatre. The traditional basis of tragedy had been the nonconformity of the individual with social law expressed as fate, necessity, or God. Ibsen was the first modern playwright to demonstrate systematically the tragedy of conformity; and through his example, the social drama took on a new excitement, a new importance, and a higher seriousness. The dramatist ceased to be a policeman, and became a critic of society. Moreover, in dramatizing the correspondence between the agony of the individual and the agony of mankind, Ibsen was able to create a genre, somewhere between the drama of ideas and classic tragedy, which complemented the intellectual interest of the one with the poetic depth of the other.

In this manner, Ibsen developed a modern concept of tragedy which was entirely worthy of comparison with the antique mode. Classic tragedy depended on the confrontation of the tragic hero with an unquestionable necessity which outraged the sense of justice. The Greek tragedies are from this standpoint always defiant, a series of hard cases involving a barely concealed protest against the unreasonableness of the gods. Apollo is inscrutable; but one does not argue with him. In tragic circumstances, the wise man bows the head, and the bitterness of the gesture gives classic tragedy its characteristic poignancy.

In the course of the Renaissance, which superposed these traditions on the romantic attitudes of the Middle Ages, the emphasis shifted gradually from the mind to the heart, and the hero became a man of sensibility. The tragic choice then generally involved the sacrifice of a desire—usually love—upon which it was assumed happiness depended, to a higher imperative, the sense of duty or social obligation. But, from the viewpoint of logic, a situation of this nature could be formulated acceptably only in a world of tolerably rigid moral outlines. In the absence of some fixed point in the flux of being, it becomes impossible to define the sense of duty clearly enough to justify any exceptional act of self-sacrifice. Heroism, in these circumstances, tends to become confused with masochism which, since it involves an element of pleasure, is not much to the purpose as a tragic motive. When the moral basis of existence is no longer certain, it is very arguable that the paramount duty of the hero is to himself, and presumably this obligation involves its own reward, and is completely self-justified.

Thus in the comedy of *Androcles and the Lion* Shaw could

find no better basis than the desire for self-realization with which to support his heroine's noble determination to be eaten alive. In *The Devil's Disciple,* no better motive is advanced for the hero's willingness to be hanged in the place of another than his need to be himself. In his *Antigone,* Anouilh assigns no other motive than self-respect for Antigone's insistence on being punished. These romantic attitudes would very likely have caused an ancient Athenian some bewilderment, and it cannot be said that they carry complete conviction in our time either. What is clear is the emphasis which such attitudes place on the idiosyncrasy of the individual in a world which presumably has no other reliable standard of value.

After the end of the nineteenth century, however, the romantic hero who insisted on dying out of sheer self-respect was felt to be too frivolous a character for the purposes of serious drama. In our time, such characters are chiefly useful in comedy. Anouilh, who has made a specialty of the absurd, in the end shrugs off the meaningless self-sacrifice of his Antigone, but not before he affords us a glimpse of a deeper motive in the girl's suicide. Driven to the wall by Creon's relentless logic, his heroine suddenly bursts out in a speech which unexpectedly reveals her as an idealist of the type of Villiers' Axël:

ANTIGONE: . . . I want to be sure of everything this very day; sure that everything will be as beautiful as it was when I was a little girl. If not, I want to die! [36]

Antigone thus makes us once more aware of the undercurrent of disappointment which motivates all of Anouilh's protagonists, reflecting the attitude of those who, in the absence of the ideal, view the world as a farce which is capable of exciting either laughter or nausea, but not respect.

The suggestion that anyone might be unable, or unwilling, to survive in a world of purely relative values is, however, not cogent in a theatre which has become increasingly skeptical of heroic postures. Since in our day nobody dies for such abstract reasons, one is driven to conclude that Anouilh's Antigone is seeking through pain a voluptuous experience which she is incapable of rationalizing, and which, in fact, defies rationalization. Before the time of Ibsen nobody looked for other than heroic motives in the behavior of heroic characters. Since such characters had height and breadth, it seemed unnecessary to insist that they have depth as well. It is the addition of this dimension, very likely, that is felt as the essential difference between Second Empire realism and the realism of our day; the consequence is that a considerable proportion of the drama that was useful in the days of Coquelin and Sarah Bernhardt is no longer playable. With all its faults, the modern audience gives every evidence of an immensely heightened sensitivity to psychological nuances which formerly played no part in the theatre, and which before Strindberg's time could not, in any event, have been suggested on the stage.

Twenty-five years ago, a situation such as Sartre describes in *Les Mains sales* would have been conceived either as a study in cowardice or as a political satire. But by indicating that it is because of a homosexual attachment of which he is not aware that his hero becomes an assassin, and that it is in order to rationalize his motive in heroic terms that he invites a gratuitous death, Sartre is able to unite in a profoundly convincing characterization the conventional motives that form the basis of the play. It is not likely that Strindberg intended in any but a mystical sense his suggestion that a man lives several lives simultaneously, and that the feeling of guilt in one life may be ascribed to actions performed in another. The psychological import of such an intuition could not be made intelligible until after Freud had brought to light the workings of the life of which we are not aware, and their relation to our consciousness. Sartre, obviously, understood. But without understanding in the least, Strindberg—and in a measure, Ibsen—were able to illustrate these workings in some detail. In *Miss Julie*, as in *The Master Builder*, both of which are ostensibly in the naturalistic tradition, we are aware of an added dimension which surrounds the actor, so to speak, with an atmosphere of reality. This is achieved not by showing the audience the backs of the characters, but by affording it a glimpse of their souls. It is possible that such things had been done before; but it is safe to say that had they not been done in this way, and at this time, such a play as *Les Mains sales*—whatever its value may be as art —would have been completely inconceivable.

The naturalists had sought a basis for tragedy in the inexorable workings of heredity, but scientific determinism could not take the place of the moral system it was intended to supplant. After the initial shock of positivism and its consequences was absorbed, the idea of a Godless universe and a pointless existence seemed improbable to many, and unbearable to some; and the ancient concepts reasserted themselves in renewed perceptions of the supernatural, and a renewed belief in its mysterious powers and purposes. Strindberg's experience was by no means unique. Like many other romantics of his day, it was in his inferno that he found his faith, and this faith was an intimation born of despair, beyond logic and beyond question—and perhaps not altogether firm. All of his later works reflect the conflict which accompanied this conversion, as well as the doubt that tormented him even to the last, and in this he thoroughly reflected the experience of his age, which is ours.

For Strindberg, tragedy was a condition inherent in the cycle of life, a necessary attribute of the impulse of all material creation to resolve itself into spirit. From this idea flowed philosophic consequences which Strindberg did not develop; but which Shaw developed fully in *Man and Superman,* and which formed the basis of his philosophic system. In this life, so it seemed to Strindberg, all things turn to evil, all things fade; only the untiring Will measures out endlessly the pain of existence—but this pain, though unavoidable, is not without its purpose, and this Will, in the end, is not in vain. As for the meaning of life, such questions had best be deferred, since the truth lies elsewhere, and reality must be viewed from a longer perspective than our world affords. "The only consolation given me," Strindberg wrote toward the end of his life, "I receive from Buddha, who tells me quite frankly that life is a phantasm, an illusion, which we will see in its proper perspective only in another life. My hope and my future lie on the other side—that is why I find life so hard to bear. Everything crumbles; every effort is spurned, and all is turned into a mockery. Everything has to be viewed from afar. This morning I gazed at the vista from my writing-desk . . . You know what unearthly beauty it takes on in the sunlight . . . I was in ecstasy. When I went down to have a closer look from the field—the view disappeared from the hilltops; and as I went toward it all its beauty vanished." [37]

For Strindberg, the view from The Great Highway did not, and could not, improve. Neither religion nor philosophy availed to rescue this unfortunate man from his agony of mind; and the pessimism which his works express is in some measure characteristic also of all the major drama of our time. For Strindberg, the only hope of this life is in art, which alone has power to transform pain into beauty: it is not through the perversion, but through the sublimation of nature that the troubled spirit gains its victory.

For Ibsen, there was no victory. For him, the greatness of the artist is measured by the height of the tower from which he falls, or the force of the avalanche that engulfs him. But for Strindberg, the agony of the laboring spirit is not pointless. The spirit is imprisoned, it is true, all its days in the dark castle; but the castle grows as the spirit impels it, until at last it bursts into flame.

Then blooms the golden flower.

Notes

Introduction

1. Barbey d'Aurevilly, *Le Roman contemporain* (Paris, 1902), p. 278.
2. J. P. Eckermann, *Gespräche mit Goethe* (Leipzig, 1909), Wednesday, February 27, 1827. James Huneker, *Iconoclasts* (London, n.d.) (1908). Bernhard Diebold, *Anarchie im Drama* (Frankfurt, 1925). Joseph Wood Krutch, *Modernism in Modern Drama* (Ithaca, New York, 1953), pp. 22, 42, 131. F. L. Lucas, *The Drama of Ibsen and Strindberg* (London, 1962), *passim*.
3. Cf. T. S. Eliot, "Hamlet and His Problems" in *The Sacred Wood* (London, 1920), pp. 87 ff.
4. Quoted by Baudelaire in "Théophile Gautier," *L'Art romantique*. In *Œuvres complètes de Baudelaire* (Paris, La Pléiade, 1954), p. 1035.

Tragedy and Comedy

1. "In works of genius there are clearly marked differences of subject and shades of style. . . . A subject for comedy refuses to be handled in tragic verse; the banquet of Thyestes disdains to be rehearsed in lines suited to daily life." Horace, *Ars poetica*, 86. Cf. Erich Auerbach, *Mimesis* (New York, 1957), pp. 316 ff.
2. Aristotle, *Poetics*, 1449a31; 1454a16; 1454b8 ff. (Bywater's translation). Cf. Trissino, *Poetica* (1529), in *Opere* (Verona, 1729), VI, 120, 127, transl. in Gilbert, *Literary Criticism: Plato to Dryden*

405

(New York, 1940), pp. 227 f.; Castelvetro, *Poetica* (Basel, 1576), ch. V, p. 97, in Gilbert, *op. cit.*, p. 313; Tasso, *Discorsi del poema eroico*, Bk. I, in *Opere* (Pisa, 1823), vol. XII, p. 9; Bk. VI, *Opere*, vol. XII, p. 168, translated in Gilbert, *op. cit.*, pp. 502 ff.; Guarini, *Il Pastor fido e il compendio della poesia tragicomica* (1601) (Bari, 1914), 15a; Heywood, *Apology for Actors* (1612), III, 3; III, 10; III, 13, in Gilbert, *op. cit.*, pp. 552 ff.

3. B. Weinberg, *A History of Literary Criticism in the Italian Renaissance* (Chicago, 1961), II, 953. Cf. Gregory Smith, *Elizabethan Critical Essays* (Oxford, 1904), vol. I, pp. lxxiii ff.

4. Minturno, *De poeta* (Venice, 1559), I, p. 38: "*Sed tamen docendus erat populus, et ad virtutem informandus, non praeceptis philosophorum, sed exemplis, quae non historici, sed poetae protullisent.*" Cf. Cicero, *De oratore*, II, 58 f.; Trissino, *Opere*, II, 127; Sidney, *An Apology for Poetry:* "Comedy is an imitation of the common errors of our life, which he representeth in the most ridiculous and scornefull sort that may be; so that it is impossible that any beholder can be content to be such a one." In Smith, *op. cit.*, vol. I, p. 176, l. 30; see also *ibid.*, I, 163, 10 ff. Cf. Castelvetro, *Poetica* (1576), ch. V, p. 93; Minturno, *Arte poetica* (1563), extract in Clark, *European Theories of the Drama* (New York, 1929), p. 59; Jonson, Dedication to *Volpone* (1607); Prologue to *Everyman in His Humour*; Prologue to *Everyman Out of His Humour*; Boileau, *L'Art poétique* (1674), extract in Clark, *op. cit.*, p. 161; Molière, Preface to *Tartuffe* (1669); *Critique de l'École des femmes* (1663), scenes VI, VII.

5. See Marvin T. Herrick, *Italian Comedy in the Renaissance* (Urbana, 1960), chap. III, IV; pp. 60 ff.

6. B. Croce, *Saggi sulla letteratura italiana del '600* (Bari, 1924), pp. 304 ff. See also C. Dejob, *L'Influence du Concile de Trente sur la littérature et les beaux-arts* (Paris, 1884), A. Lisoni, *Imitatori del teatro spagnuolo in Italia* (Parma, 1895).

7. Donatus, *De comœdia et tragœdia*, translated in Clark, *op. cit.*, p. 44. See H. Keil, *Grammatici Latini*, vol. IV (Leipzig, 1870–1880).

8. In connection with this period, I am indebted in more than one respect to Louise G. Clubb's excellent study, "The Theatre of Giambattista Della Porta" (unpublished dissertation, Columbia University, 1962).

9. Corneille, *Examen d'Andromède* in *Œuvres de Pierre de Corneille*, ed. Marty-Laveaux (Paris, 1862–1868), V, 307 f.

10. *Poetics*, 1450b21; 1451b33 to 1452b13.

11. E.g., see Corneille, *Troisième discours, Œuvres,* I, 104; d'Aubignac, *La Pratique du théâtre,* Bk. III, ch. 5, ed. Pierre Martino (Alger, Paris, 1927), pp. 226, 227.

12. Ernest Legouvé, *Eugene Scribe,* translated in Brander Matthews, *Papers on Playmaking* (New York, 1957), pp. 285 ff.

13. *Poetics,* 1453a21. See Giraldi, *Discorsi* (1554), p. 220, transl. in Gilbert, *op. cit.,* p. 256.

14. Riccoboni, *Histoire du théâtre italien depuis la décadence de la comédie latine* (Paris, 1728), p. 262.

15. See, e.g., Tasso, *Discorso primo dell'arte poetica,* in *Opere* (1823), XII, 207, transl. (in part) in Gilbert, *op. cit.,* p. 483.

16. *Poetics,* 1452a30. Preface to *Altile* in G. B. Giraldi Cinthio, *Tragedie* (Venezia, 1583), II, 9. Cf. *Discorsi intorno al comporre de i romanzi, delle comedie, e delle tragedie, e di altre maniere di poesie* (Vinegia, 1554), pp. 219 ff., 224, translated in part in Gilbert, *op cit.,* pp. 255 ff. On the role of Fortune as a tragic motive, see Minturno, *L'Arte poetica* (1564), Bk. II, in the Naples ed. of 1725, p. 76. Note the date, with relation to the Council of Trent.

17. Guarini, *Il Pastor fido, tragicommedia pastorale . . . con un compendio di poesia* (Venezia, 1602), pp. 13 ff.; *Il Verrato, ovvero difesa di quanto ha scritto M. Giason Denores contra la tragicomedia et le pastorali in uno suo discorso di poesia* (Ferrara, 1588): see especially p. 26. Cf. Jules Marsan, *La Pastorale dramatique en France* (Paris, 1905), pp. 58 ff., for a concise account of this controversy.

18. Marsan, *op. cit.,* pp. 256, 357 f.

19. Jean de la Taille, *Art de la tragédie,* prefaced to *Saül le furieux* (Paris, 1572), partly translated in Clark, *op. cit.,* p. 77.

La Taille also hints here at the necessity for observing the rule of unity of place. The rule of the three unities was first formulated by Castelvetro in 1570: *"La mutatione tragica non puo tirar con esso seco se non una giornata ed un luogo"* (*Poetica,* 1576), p. 534. The three unities were discussed separately in the preface to Mairet's *Silvanire.* It was Jules Chapelain who first codified the "rule of unities" in France (*Demonstration de la Règle des vingt-quatre heures*) in 1630.

20. L'Abbé d'Aubignac, *La Pratique du théâtre,* Bk. III, ch. 5, ed. Martino, p. 225.

The static character of regular tragedy is inherent in the classic conception of drama as an art closely related to painting, in which the figures have a limited freedom of motion as well as the capacity to speak. Ideally, such a "speaking picture" would remain within its frame, and changes of place or of time would necessitate a confusing disorientation. The idea of drama as audible painting was already a commonplace in the days of Sidney. It was, very likely, derived from Horace, *Ars poetica*, 361 (cf. Plutarch, *De aud. poetis*, 3). In speaking of comedy, Vives writes: ". . . *ut merito Plutarchus de his dixerit poema esse picturam loquentem, et picturam poema tacens, ita magister est populi, et pictor, et poeta*" (*De causis corruptione artium*) (1555), p. 367. See Smith, *op. cit.*, I, 386.

21. *Poetics*, 1453a7. Bywater's translation.

22. *Ibid.*, 1453b13.

23. *Ibid.*, 1453b1.

24. Francisque Sarcey, *Essai d'une esthétique de théâtre* (Paris, 1876), translated by Hatcher Hughes as *A Theory of the Theatre by Francisque Sarcey* (New York, 1916), reprinted in Clark, *op. cit.*, pp. 392 ff. On the dramatic action, see Corneille, *Œuvres* (Marty-Laveaux), I, 43; I, 104–6; I, 394. On climax, *ibid.*, IV, 421. On the denouement, *ibid.*, I, 26; III, 279. Cf. A. Dumas *fils*, *Préface, La Princesse Georges*, in *Théâtre complet* (Paris, 1890), vol. V, pp. 75 ff.

25. Dryden, Preface, *An Evening's Love* (1668), in *Essays of John Dryden*, ed. Ker (Oxford, 1926), I, 14. Cf. Dryden, *Essay of Dramatic Poesy*, in *Essays*, I, 88.

26. Quoted in Giorgio Santangelo, *Il Secentismo* (Palermo, 1958), pp. 43–44: [*La lirica*] ". . . *che puo chiamarsi un sogno, che si fa in presenza della ragione ed ella vi sta sopra con gli occhi aperti a rimirarlo e averne cura.*"

27. *Poetics*, 1450b21. Cf. Tasso, *Dell'arte poetica discorso secondo*, in *Opere* (1823), XII, 213.

28. La Mesnardière, *La Poétique* (Paris, 1639).

29. D'Aubignac, *La Pratique du théâtre*, Bk. II, ch. 3; ed. Martino, p. 88. Cf. Tasso, *Del poema eroico discorso terzo*, in *Opere* (1823), vol. XII, p. 90.

30. *Poetics* (tr. Bywater), 1452a2 ff.; 1452b30; 1460a11. The question of the marvellous and of the excitement of admiration as one of the principal ends of poetry was much discussed by Renaissance critics. To the Horatian functions of instruction and delight, Minturno added the power to excite emotion, and since Aristotle had said nothing about that, but had spoken of astonishment and admiration in laudatory terms, admiration sometimes came to be confused with the power to evoke compassion. In *De poeta* (1559), pp. 179 f., Minturno writes that it is the business of the tragic poet "to demonstrate, to delight, and to move" ("*ut probet, ut delectat, ut moveat*"), and the poet

"moves vehemently when he excites admiration." Admiration nevertheless was considered, in certain quarters, an aim unworthy of the efforts
of a serious poet. Thus, J. C. Scaliger says: ". . . nor should the
poet give his attention merely to causing the spectators to admire
or to be astounded, as the critics say Aeschylus did, but he should
think of teaching, moving, and delighting" (*Poetice* [1561], III, 96,
p. 145). Boileau apparently disapproved of the practice of Corneille:
"*Il n'a point songé comme les poëtes de l'ancienne tragédie à émouvoir
la pitié et la terreur, mais à exciter dans l'âme des spectateurs, par la
sublimité des pensées et par la beauté des sentiments, une certaine
admiration, dont plusieurs personnes . . . s'accomodent souvent beau-
coup mieux que des véritables passions tragiques*" (*Lettre à Charles
Perrault*, 1700). Cf. Spingarn, *History of Literary Criticism in the
Renaissance* (New York, 1930), pp. 110–17; Castelvetro, *Poetica*
(Basel, 1576), pp. 221, 228, 229; Minturno, *L'arte poetica* (1564)
(Naples, 1725), III, 76; Tasso, *Del poema eroico, discorso primo*, in
Opere (1823), vol. XII, pp. 19, 30, 46.

31. Cf. G. Santangelo, *op. cit.*, pp. 130 ff.; Giovanni Getto, "La
polemica sul Barocco," in *Letteratura e critica* (Milano, 1954); René
Rapin, *Réflexions sur la poétique d'Aristote* (1672) in *Œuvres de
Rapin* (Amsterdam, 1709), pp. 125 ff.; Boileau, *Art poétique* (1674),
ed. Brunetière, 7th ed. (Paris, 1907), I, 45 ff.; Dominique Bouhours,
Manière de bien penser dans les œuvres d'esprit (1687) (Paris, 1743),
pp. 353 ff.

32. Racine, *Cantique III*, ll. 17 f. (1694), in *Œuvres*, ed. Paul
Mesnard (Paris, 1865–1873), vol. IV, p. 157.

33. B. Croce, *Storia della età barocca in Italia*. 2nd ed. (Bari,
1946); see pp. 76 ff. for a discussion of the *ragion di stato* in the Italian
drama of the previous century.

34. Racine, Preface to *Bérénice* in *Œuvres*, ed. Mesnard, vol. II
p. 367.

35. Corneille, *Premier discours sur le poème dramatique*, in *Œuvres
complètes* (Paris, 1835), vol. II, p. 547. Transl. in Clark, *op. cit.*, p.
141.

36. See Farquhar, *The Beaux' Stratagem*, Act 5, sc. 4; Vanbrugh,
The Relapse, Act 5, sc. 4.

37. Diderot, *Les Bijoux indiscrets* (1748), in *Œuvres de Diderot*,
ed. André Billy (Paris, La Pléiade, 1957), p. 172; *Entretiens sur Le
Fils naturel* (1757), in *Œuvres* (1957), pp. 1274 ff.

38. Beaumarchais, *Essai sur le genre dramatique sérieux* (1767), in

Œuvres complètes de Beaumarchais, ed. Saint-Marc Girardin (Paris, 1861), p. 3, translated in Clark, *op. cit.,* p. 304.

39. *Ibid.* In Clark, p. 305.

The New Drama

1. G. d'Avénel, *Les Revenus d'un intellectuel de 1200 à 1913* (Paris, 1922), p. 231.

2. Cf. Maurice Albert, *Les Théâtres des boulevards 1789–1848* (Paris, 1902).

3. Cf. W. G. Hartog, *Guilbert de Pixerécourt* (Paris, 1912), pp. 51 ff.

4. Paul Ginisty, *Le Mélodrame* (Paris, 1910), pp. 14 ff.; Alexander Lacey, *Pixerécourt and the French Romantic Drama* (Toronto, 1928); Edmond Estève, "Guilbert de Pixerécourt," in *Études de littérature pré-romantique* (Paris, 1923).

5. *Hamlet,* I, 4, 3–4.

6. Cf. Dryden, *Essays,* ed. Ker, I, 192; I, 147.

7. Cf. Corneille, ed. Marty-Laveaux, vol. I, p. 43. See also vol. I, pp. 105–6; I, 394; XII, 474. Cf. Jacques Scherer, *La Dramaturgie classique en France* (Paris, 1955), pp. 101 ff.

8. Cf. d'Aubignac, *La Pratique du théâtre,* ed. Martino (Paris, 1927), Bk. III, ch. 5, p. 229; Bk. III, ch. 7, pp. 246 ff.

9. A. Thibaudet, *Histoire de la littérature française de 1789 à nos jours* (Paris, 1936), pp. 295 ff.

10. Francisque Sarcey, *Quarante ans de théâtre,* Vol. I (Paris, 1900), pp. 120 ff.; vol. V (1901), pp. 284 ff.

11. Cf. Croce, *Storia della età barocca in Italia.* 2nd ed. (Bari, 1946), p. 77; *Nuovi saggi sulla letteratura italiana del seicento* (Bari, 1931), p. 53.

12. See Hebbel, *Mein Wort über das Drama* (1843), transl. (in part) in T. M. Campbell, *Hebbel, Ibsen, and the Analytic Exposition* (Heidelberg, 1922); Preface to *Maria Magdalene* (1844), in the same, pp. 79–95. Cf. Julius Bab, *Das Wort Friedrich Hebbels* (München, 1923); Kurt Küchler, *Fr. Hebbel, sein Leben und sein Werk* (Jena, 1910).

13. Cf. Mario Praz, *The Romantic Agony,* 2nd ed. (New York, 1956), p. 75. Professor Praz seems to have been under the impression that Antony stabbed his mistress out of jealousy.

14. A. Dumas *fils*, Preface to *La Princesse Georges*, in *Théâtre complet d'Alexandre Dumas fils* (Paris, 1890–1918), vol. V (1890), p. 79.

15. *Les Idées de Madame Aubray*, Act II, sc. 4, *Théâtre* (Paris, 1890), vol. IV, p. 265.

16. Dumas *fils*, *Francillon*, Act III, sc. 6, *Théâtre* (Paris, 1892), vol. VII, p. 393. See also Act II, sc. 7, pp. 347 f.; Act III, sc. 3, pp. 379 f.

17. *Les Idées de Madame Aubray*, Act I, sc. 2, *Théâtre* (1890), vol. IV, p. 236.

18. The *raisonneur* was re-established in the theatre by Théodore Barrière in *Les Filles de marbre*, in the character Desgenais, whose name became a byword for this role. See René Doumic in Petit de Julleville, *Histoire de la langue et la littérature française*, (Paris, 1899), VIII, 107 ff.

19. Preface to *Le Fils naturel* in *Théâtre d'Alexandre Dumas fils* (Paris, 1890), vol. III. See F. A. Taylor, *The Theater of Alexandre Dumas fils* (Oxford, 1937).

20. L. G. Vapereau, *Année littéraire et dramatique*, 1859 (Paris, 1860).

21. On the *dubbio*, see Pio Rajna, in *Romania* XXXI, 28 ff.; J. M. Manly in *Lorenz Morsbach Festschrift* (Halle, 1913), pp. 282 ff.; Boccaccio, *Filocolo*, Bk. IV, in *Opere volgari*, ed. Moutier (Firenze, 1831), VIII, 27 ff.

22. *L'Art romantique*, X: "*Les Drames et les romans honnêtes*," in *Œuvres complètes de Baudelaire* (Paris, La Pléiade, 1954), p. 971.

Realism

1. For example, J. Champfleury, *Le Réalisme* (Paris, 1857); G. Merlet, *Réalisme et fantaisie dans la littérature* (Paris, 1861).

2. *Le Feuilleton d'Aristophane*, by Philippe Boyer and Théodore de Banville (Paris, 1852).

3. A. David-Sauvageot in Petit de Julleville, *Histoire de la littérature française*, VIII, 3.

4. On the question, in general, see the excellent account in A. David-Sauvageot, *Le Réalisme et le naturalisme dans la littérature et dans l'art* (Paris, 1889). See also Émile Zola, *Le Roman expérimental* (Paris, 1880), *Le Naturalisme au théâtre* (Paris, 1881); Louis Desprez,

L'Évolution naturaliste (Paris, 1884); F. Brunetière, *Le Roman naturaliste* (Paris, 1883); and especially Jean Jullien, *Le Théâtre vivant*, 2 vols. (Paris, 1892–1896). Cf. Claude Bernard, *Introduction à l'étude de la médicine expérimentale* (Paris, 1865), briefly summarized in Zola, *Le Roman expérimental*, pp. 2–23.

5. Preface to *Thérèse Raquin* (Paris, 1873), in *Œuvres complètes d'Émile Zola* (Paris, 1927–1929), vol. 38; translated in Clark, *European Theories of the Drama*, p. 401.

6. Preface to the *Lyrical Ballads* (1802).

7. P.-J. Proudhon, *Du Principe de l'art et de sa destination sociale* (Paris, 1861), p. 287.

8. Zola, *Le Roman expérimental*, p. 128. Translated in *The Experimental Novel and Other Essays* by Belle M. Sherman (New York, 1894).

9. "*Tout notre théâtre est monstrueux parce qu'il est bâti en l'air*:" *Le Naturalisme au théâtre*, p. 45. Cf. Zola's critique of Sardou in the essay, "Naturalism on the Stage" in Sherman, *The Experimental Novel*, pp. 131 ff.

10. Zola, *Le Naturalisme au théâtre* (Paris, 1881), p. 23.

11. *Le Naturalisme au théâtre*, *Œuvres*, ed. Maurice le Blond (Paris, 1927–1929), XLII, 24 f.; *Nos auteurs dramatiques*, *Œuvres*, XLIII, 28 f.; *Le Roman expérimental*, (1928), p. 38, transl. Sherman, p. 17.

12. "In practical life men but make experiments upon one another." Attributed by Zola to Claude Bernard in *Le Roman expérimental*, transl. Sherman, p. 10. Cf. Pierre Martino, *Le Naturalisme français* (Paris, 1923), pp. 38 ff.; Harry Levin, *The Gates of Horn* (New York, 1963), pp. 307 ff.

13. "*Le roman expérimental est une conséquence de l'évolution scientifique du siècle; il continue et complète la physiologie . . . il est la littérature de notre âge scientifique comme la littérature classique et romantique a correspondu à un âge de scolastique et de théologie. . . .*" *Le Roman expérimental* (Paris, 1880), p. 22. To the same effect, see *Le Naturalisme au théâtre*, pp. 14 ff. But cf. Desprez's criticism of *Thérèse Raquin* in *L'Évolution naturaliste* (Paris, 1884), pp. 32 ff.

14. In *Le Naturalisme au théâtre*.

15. "*Ce n'est pas du théâtre*": Zola used the phrase over and over in the course of his campaign for naturalism in the theatre. "*Ce qu'il appelle le théâtre, c'est un théâtre, rien de plus*" (*Le Naturalisme au théâtre* [1881], p. 134).

16. The family is appropriately called Reynaud. The analogy—doubtless purely co-incidental—to Miss Hellman's *The Little Foxes* (1948) is interesting.

17. See S. M. Waxman, *Antoine and the Théâtre Libre* (Cambridge, Massachusetts, 1926).

Ibsen

1. The bookselling season in Scandinavian countries was November and December. See Ibsen, Letter to Edvard Fallesen, 3 October 1877. In *Letters of Henrik Ibsen*, translated by Laurvik and Morison (New York, 1905).

2. Letter to Björnson, 4 March 1866. In the same collection.

3. Letter to Björnson, 9 December 1867; Letter to Hegel, 14 December 1869, and 25 January 1870; to J. H. Thoresen, 27 December 1872 ("People who permit Jaabaek and Björnson to be at large ought to be shut up themselves."); to Olof Sklavan, 24 January 1882.

4. Letter to Peter Hansen, 28 October 1870. To the same effect, see Letter to Edmund Gosse, 20 February 1873; to Ludwig Daae, 23 February 1873; to Ludwig Passarge, 16 June 1880.

5. Cf. O. P. Monrad, *Sören Kierkegaard, sein Leben und seine Werke* (Jena, 1909), pp. 56 ff. See Ibsen, Letter to Hegel, 8 March 1867, in Laurvik and Morison, *op. cit.*, p. 136.

6.   *"At ej du kan, dig visst forlades,—*
              men aldrig at du ikke vil."

Brand, Act 3. In *Samlede digterverker*, ed. Seip (Kristiania, 1922), vol. II, p. 174.

7. *Brand*, Act 3. *Samlede digterverker*, II, 174.

8. *Ibid.*, p. 177.

9. *Ibid.*, p. 176. The term *quantum satis* evidently reflects the pharmaceutical Latin of Ibsen's apprenticeship in the pharmacy at Grimstad. The same may be said of the doctor's idea of God as an accountant. Cf. Letter to Michael Birkeland, 4 May 1866.

10. *Ibid.*, p. 180.

11. *Ibid.*, p. 285.

12. *Ibid.*, p. 286.

13. Letter to Laura Kieler, 11 June 1870; to Peter Hansen, 28 October 1870; to Georg Brandes, 26 June 1869. All in *Letters of*

Henrik Ibsen (1905). See also Letter to Hegel, 9 June 1866, *op. cit.*, p. 119.

14. *Brand*, Act 2. In *Samlede digterverker* (1923), II, 170.

15. Peter Christian Asbjörnsen, *Norske folke- og huldre- eventyr* (1866), 3rd ed. (Christiania, 1870), transl. as *Norwegian Fairy Tales* by Helen and John Gade (New York, 1924). See Ibsen's letter to Frederik Hegel, 8 August 1867.

16. Letter to Magdalene Thoresen, 15 October 1867.

17. Letter to Hegel, 8 August 1867.

18. *Peer Gynt*, Act 5. *Samlede digterverker* (1923), II, 439.

19. Halvdan Koht, *The Life of Ibsen* (New York, 1931), II, 28.

20. Letter to Edmund Gosse, 14 October 1872. Cf. Wilhelm Hans, *Ibsens Selbstporträt in seinem Drama* (München, 1911).

21. Letter to Björnson, 9 December 1867.

22. Letter of 16 December 1864; letter to Georg Brandes, 23 July 1872. In a letter to Edmund Gosse, written shortly before the completion of the second part of *Emperor and Galilean*, Ibsen wrote: "It is a part of my own spiritual life which I am putting into this book; what I depict, I have, under different conditions, gone through myself" (14 October 1872). Six months later, he assured Gosse once again: "There is a good deal of self-analysis in this book" (20 February 1873). About the same time, he wrote as much to Ludvig Daae: "In the character of Julian, however, as in most of what I have written in my riper years, there is much more of my own inner life than I care to acknowledge to the public" (23 February 1873). He had long ago assured his publisher that this book would be his chief work (Letter to Hegel, 12 July 1871). On the eve of its publication, he told Daae, "It will be my *Hauptwerk*" (4 February 1873). All five letters are in *Letters of Henrik Ibsen*, translated by J. N. Laurvik and Mary Morison (New York, 1905).

23. But see Koht, *Life of Ibsen*, II, 97. Cf. Letter to Hegel, 10 June 1869 and 12 July 1871; letter to Roman Woerner, 7 July 1899; letter to Ludvig Daae, 23 February 1873. Besides Listov's articles, the chief sources of his material appear to have been Ammianus, Neander, and Eunapius's *Life of Maximus*.

24. Letter to Julius Hoffory, 26 February 1888.

25. "Verse is doomed." Letter to Lucie Wolf, 25 May 1883.

26. Letter to Björnson, 28 December 1867; to J. H. Thoresen, 27 December 1872.

27. Letter of 29 December 1884.

28. Letter to Hegel, 14 December 1869, and 25 January 1870.

29. Cf. Letter to J. H. Thoresen, 21 December 1870; letter to Magdalene Thoresen, 5 June 1870; letter to Hans Braekstad, —August 1890.

30. Letter to Hegel, 23 October 1875.

31. Letter to Georg Brandes, 4 April 1872.

32. "To Alexandre Dumas I owe nothing as regards dramatic form—except that I have learned from his plays to avoid several very awkward faults and blunders, of which he is not infrequently guilty." (Letter to Georg Brandes, 11 October 1896.) Jules Lemaître had written of Ibsen's dependence on Dumas.

33. Cf. Weigand, *The Modern Ibsen* (London, n.d., 1925), pp. 74 f. Weigand came to a similar conclusion as to Ibsen's method, but for very different reasons. This process of composition is doubtless in some relation to the idea of "romantic irony" and its literary consequences in the later nineteenth century. Cf. Baudelaire, "De l'essence du rire," *Œuvres* (La Pléiade), pp. 727 f.; Pirandello, *L'Umorismo* (Milano, Mondadori, 1923); Preface to *Erma bifronte* (Milano, Treves, 1906).

34. Ibsen himself provided, *supra protest*, an altered version of the ending for use in Germany. In this version, Torvald drags Nora to the door of the children's bedroom. There she collapses. This ending he called a "barbaric violence" to the play. See "Letter to The Editor," *National-tidende*, 17 February 1880, and letter to H. Laube, 18 February 1880.

35. Letter of 6 January 1882.

36. *Le Naturalisme au théâtre* (Paris, 1881), p. 10.

37. Letter to Hegel, 25 October 1880. This and the following letters may all be found in the Laurvik and Morison collection.

38. Letter to Sophus Schandorf, 6 January 1882; to Olof Sklavan, 24 January 1882.

39. Letter to Hegel, 9 September 1882.

40. Letter to Georg Brandes, 4 April 1872.

41. Letter to Markus Grönvold, 22 January 1879.

42. Letter to Georg Brandes, 17 February 1871.

43. Letter to Georg Brandes, 3 January 1882.

44. Letter to Georg Brandes, 20 December 1870; 4 April 1872.

45. Letter to Jonas Collin, 31 July 1895.

46. Letter to Georg Brandes, 12 June 1883.

47. Letter of 27 June 1884.

48. Letter to Hegel, 2 September 1884.

49. Letter to Björnson, 2 March 1885.

50. Edmund Gosse, "Ibsen's Social Dramas," *Fortnightly Review*, January, 1889; G. B. Shaw, in *Saturday Review*, 10 May 1897 reprinted in *Our Theatres in the Nineties*, 3 vols. (London, 1948), vol. III, p. 138. Cf. William Archer in *The Theatrical World*, 1894 (London, 1895), p. 139.

51. Letter of 10 November 1886.

52. To Björnson's young nephew, Björn Kristensen.

53. Letter to Björn Kristensen, 13 February 1887.

54. Cf. Praz, *The Romantic Agony*, p. 243.

55. B. Croce, *Storia d'Europa* (Bari, 1932), p. 53.

56. Cf. Praz, *op. cit.*, ch. III, *passim*.

57. Koht, *Life of Ibsen*, II, 248.

58. Speech of 24 December 1887.

59. Act 5.

60. Letter to Emilie Bardach, 13 March 1898. In Georg Brandes, *Die Literatur* (Berlin, 1907), vol. 32.

61. *The Critic* (London), August, 1947, p. 82.

62. *Tilskueren*, August, 1916, p. 100.

63. Alfred Ahlberg, *Det ondas problem* (Stockholm, 1923), p. 82, draws interesting metaphysical conclusions from Strindberg's theory of vampirism as the spiritual hunger of an empty soul.

64. *Le Plaidoyer d'un fou, revision française de Georges Loiseau* (Paris, 1895), p. 383. This work had an interesting history. The first recorded publication is the German version, *Die Beichte eines Toren*, 2e Auflage (Budapest, 1894), the first German edition having been suppressed as immoral by the Berlin authorities. It was then published in French with two prefaces (one dated 1888, the other 1895). It was subsequently translated from the French by John Landquist as *En dåres försvarstal*. The first English version, *Confession of a Fool*, is by Ellie Schleussner (New York, 1925). Cf. R. Zetterlund, *Bibliografiska anteckningar om August Strindberg* (Stockholm, 1913); Hedén, *Strindberg*, p. 219.

65. Author's Preface to *Miss Julie* (1888). *Skrifter av August Strindberg* (Stockholm, 1951), XII, 82. Also in *Fröken Julie, etc.* (Stockholm, 1957), p. 11.

66. *Hedda Gabler*, Act 2, *Samlede digterverker* (1922), V, 354. In *Henrik Ibsen's Prose Dramas*, ed. William Archer (London and New York, 1902), V, 309 (*Collected Works of Henrik Ibsen*, ed. Archer [London, 1906 ff.], vol. 10).

67. *Prose Dramas*, V, 309.

68. *Op. cit.*, Act IV. *Prose Dramas*, V, 358.

69. Letter of 3 June 1897.

70. Letter to Georg Brandes, 6 March 1870.

71. Koht, *Life of Ibsen*, II, 301. Francis Bull, *Ibsen: The man and the dramatist*, Taylorian Lecture (Oxford, 1954).

72. Cf. G. Leneveu, *Ibsen et Maeterlinck*, 2nd ed. (Paris, 1902).

73. This incident has been amply documented. See Basil King, "Ibsen and Emily Bardach" in *The Century Magazine*, New York, 1923, October, pp. 803 ff., and November, pp. 83 ff.; A. E. Zucker, *Ibsen, The Master Builder* (New York, 1929), pp. 225 ff.; Emilie Bardach, "Meine Freundschaft mit Ibsen," *Neue Freie Presse*, March 31, 1907. Georg Brandes, *Die Litteratur*, vol. 32: *Henrik Ibsen* (Berlin, 1907), reprints all the Bardach letters Ibsen wrote. Michael Meyer, Introduction to *The Master Builder* in *When We Dead Awaken and Three Other Plays* (New York, 1960), pp. 115 ff.

74. Letter to Emilie Bardach, 15 October 1889.

75. Weigand, *The Modern Ibsen*, p. 291.

76. *The Master Builder*, Act 3. In Michael Meyer, *When We Dead Awaken and Three Other Plays*, p. 200. His translation.

77. *The Master Builder*, Act 3. *Op. cit.*, p. 208.

78. *Ibid.*

79. *Ibid.*, p. 209.

80. *From Ibsen's Workshop*, in *Collected Works of Henrik Ibsen*, ed. Archer, vol. XII, pp. 479 ff.

81. For a quite different view of Allmers see Roman Woerner, *Henrik Ibsen* (München, 1912), II, 28. Cf. Weigand's excellent discussion, *The Modern Ibsen*, p. 322.

82. G. B. Shaw, Review of *John Gabriel Borkman*, *Saturday Review*, 3 May 1897. In *Our Theatres in the Nineties*, 3 vols. (London, 1948), vol. III, p. 122.

83. Koht, *Life of Ibsen*, II, 293. Mohr reproduces the portrait in *Henrik Ibsen som Maler* (Oslo, 1953).

84. Letter to Georg Brandes, 26 June 1869.

85. *When We Dead Awaken*, Act 1. In Meyer, *When We Dead Awaken*, p. 321.

86. *Ibid.*

87. *Ibid.*, Act 2. My translation. Cf. Meyer, *op. cit.*, p. 348.

88. *Ibid.*, Act 2. *Op. cit.*, p. 362.

89. *Ibid.*, Act 2. *Op. cit.*, p. 356.

90. Letter of 11 February 1895.

91. *From Ibsen's Workshop*, Introduction, p. 19. In Archer, *Collected Works*, XII.

92. Lines written by Ibsen in Emilie Bardach's album, 20 September 1889.

93. *John Gabriel Borkman*, Act 2. In Meyer, *When We Dead Awaken*, etc., p. 268.

94. *When We Dead Awaken*, Act 2. *Op. cit.*, p. 353.

95. *Ibid.*, Act 2. *Op. cit.*, p. 360.

96. Letter of 5 March 1900.

Strindberg

1. *Till Damaskus III*, in *Samlade skrifter*, ed. John Landquist (Stockholm, 1912–1921), 55 vols., vol. XXIX. In *Skrifter av August Strindberg* (Stockholm, 1955), XI, 213. *The Road to Damascus*, transl. Rawson (New York, 1960), p. 220.

2. *En Själs utvecklingshistoria* in *Samlade skrifter*, ed. Landquist, XVIII.

3. A. Jolivet, *Le Théâtre de Strindberg* (Paris, 1931), p. 4.

4. Author's Foreword to *Miss Julie*, *Skrifter* (1951), XII, 59; *Fröken Julie och andra skådespel* (Stockholm, 1957), p. 7; *Six Plays of Strindberg*, translated by Elizabeth Sprigge (New York, 1955), p. 61.

5. *The Son of a Servant: Tjänstekvinnans son*, *Samlade skrifter*, XVIII, 330; *Skrifter* (1945–1952), vol. VII.

6. *Samlade skrifter*, XVIII, 163. For a standard psychiatric interpretation of Strindberg's mental conflict, see K. Bachler, *August Strindberg, eine psychoanalytische Studie* (Wien, 1931). See also Torsten Eklund, *Tjänstekvinnans son, en psykologisk studie* (Stockholm, 1948).

7. Martin Lamm, *Strindbergs dramer* (Stockholm, 1924), I, 47.

8. *Samlade skrifter*, XVIII, 386 f.

9. Cf. Lamm, *Strindbergs dramer*, I, 98; Jolivet, *Strindberg*, p. 55; *Samlade skrifter*, L, 123; 238. Text in *Fröken Julie*, etc., pp. 65 ff.

10. *Samlade skrifter*, XIX, 40. Cf. Tocqueville, *La Démocratie en Amérique, Deuxième Partie*, I, ch. 1, 2; IV, ch. 6, 7.

11. *Samlade skrifter*, XIX, 130. Cf. Eduard von Hartmann, *Die Philosophie des Unbewussten* (1869) (Leipzig, 1923), 3 vols., English translation, *The Philosophy of the Unconscious*, by W. C. Coupland (London, 1884). See R. Köber, *Das philosophische System Eduard v. Hauptmanns* (Breslau, 1884); A. Drews, *Eduard v. Haupt-*

manns philosophisches System im Grundriss (Heidelberg, 1902). Cf. the chapter on Hartmann in G. Stanley Hall, *Founders of Modern Psychology* (New York and London, 1912).

12. *Samlade skrifter,* XIX, 61.

13. *Mäster Olof, Samlade skrifter,* II, 260; II, 301.

14. *Samlade skrifter,* II, 130.

15. *Ibid.,* II, 305.

16. *Ibid.,* XXII, 62.

17. Cf. Karin Smirnoff, *Strindbergs förste hustru* (Stockholm, 1925), p. 143.

18. Cf. Boccaccio, *Decameron,* Prologue, Bk. 4 (Tale of Balducci); Wagner, *Der fliegende Holländer; Siegfried;* Voltaire, *Candide;* Ibsen, *Peer Gynt.* See also Lamm, *Strindbergs dramer,* I, 201.

19. *Samlade skrifter,* IX, 376.

20. *The Wife of Sir Bengt,* Epilogue, sc. 3. *Samlade skrifter,* IX. *Skrifter* (1955), XI, 106.

21. *Le Plaidoyer d'un fou* (Paris, 1895), p. 329.

22. Karin Smirnoff, *op. cit.,* pp. 210 f.

23. *Le Plaidoyer d'un fou,* pp. 383 ff.

24. *Samlade skrifter,* IX, 376. Cf. Lamm, *Strindbergs dramer,* I, 220 f.

25. Cf. Erik Hedén, *Strindberg,* transl. Julia Koppel (München, 1926), pp. 152 ff.

26. Jolivet, *Strindberg,* p. 105.

27. *Samlade skrifter,* XIX, 164.

28. *Ibid.,* XVII, 195, 212, 234, 246.

29. Letter to Carl Larssen, 22 April 1884. In *August Strindbergs Brev, utg. av Torsten Eklund* (Stockholm, 1948–1961), vol. IV, p. 127.

30. Cf. Helene Welinder's excellent account of the summer of 1884 in the periodical *Ord och bild,* 1912, fasc. 9. Cf. Hedén, *Strindberg,* pp. 120, 157.

31. *L'Affaire Clemenceau* (Paris, 1882), pp. 298 f.

32. Louis Desprez, *L'Évolution naturaliste,* (Paris, 1884), p. 102.

33. Paul Lafargue's article "Le Matriarcat" in *La Nouvelle revue,* 15 March 1886, evidently made a deep impression on Strindberg. Lafargue expressed the fear, which Strindberg amply shared, that the matriarchy was extending its power. See Strindberg's letters of March, April, 1886, to Edvard Brandes. In *Georg og Edvard Brandes Brevveksling* (København, 1939), VI, 77, 79.

34. *Samlade skrifter,* XXXIII, 374.

35. The play is called *Fadren*. Perhaps, in English, *Father*, without the article, would best convey Strindberg's meaning. In *Skrifter* (1951), vol. XII, p. 32.

36. Cf. Karl Strecker, *Nietzsche und Strindberg. Mit ihrem Briefwechsel* (München, 1921); Hedén, *Strindberg*, pp. 182 ff.; Henri Albert, "Nietzsche et Strindberg," *Mercure de France*, 16 April 1923, p. 780.

37. A collection of essays, entitled *Vivisections*, written toward the end of 1887, reflects Strindberg's keen interest in the psychological researches which were currently attracting attention in France. Most important of these are the essays "The Battle of the Brains," and "Psychic Murder." In *Samlade skrifter*, XXII, 123 ff.; 192 ff. See also Hans Lindström, *Hjärnornas kamp: Psykologiska idéer och motiv i Strindbergs åttiotalsdiktning* (Uppsala, 1952).

38. "*Själamord*," "Soul-murder," in *Samlade skrifter*, XXII, 188 ff.

39. *Samlade skrifter*, XVII, 285.

40. Desprez, *op. cit.*, pp. 313, 322.

41. In Eklund, *Strindbergs Brev*, vol. VI (1958), p. 154.

42. Cf. the discussion of possible sources in Lamm, *August Strindberg*, 2nd ed. (Stockholm, 1948), p. 158, note, and in Jolivet, *Strindberg*, p. 157. See also the discussion in Dumas' *L'homme-femme* (1872). A. Dumas fils, *L'homme-femme* (Paris, 1875), p. 127.

43. 15 March 1886, cited above.

44. *The Father*, Act 3, sc. 7. In *Skrifter* (1951), XII, 54. In *Fröken Julie*, etc. (1957), p. 218. In *Six Plays by Strindberg*, tr. Sprigge, p. 54.

45. *The Father*, Act 2, sc. 5. In *Skrifter* (1951), XII, 48. In *Fröken Julie*, p. 203. In *Six Plays*, p. 41.

46. *Ibid.*, Act 2, sc. 5.

47. *Ibid.*, Act 3, sc. 8. In *Skrifter* (1951) XII, 56. In *Fröken Julie*, etc., p. 221.

48. Cf. Dahlström, *Strindberg's Dramatic Expressionism* (Ann Arbor, 1930), pp. 92 ff. On Strindberg's naturalism, and his relation to Zola, see the excellent discussion in B. G. Madsen, *Strindberg's Naturalistic Theatre: Its Relation to French Naturalism* (Seattle, 1962).

49. Axel Lundegård, *Några Strindbergsminnen knutna till en handfull brev* (Stockholm, 1920), is the best account of Strindberg in the 1880's. Letter of 12 November 1887. Hedén, *Strindberg*, pp. 156 ff. Cf. Praz, *The Romantic Agony*, chap. IV, *passim*.

50. *Miss Julie*. In *Skrifter* (1951), XII, 80; in *Fröken Julie*, etc., p. 54; in *Six Plays*, p. 107.

51. Letter to K. O. Bonnier, 21 August 1888. In *August Strindbergs Brev*, ed. Torsten Eklund (Stockholm, 1948–1961), vol. VII, p. 105.

52. *Creditors*, in *Skrifter* (1951), XII, 93. In *Six Plays* (Sprigge), p. 22.

53. *Ibid.*, *Skrifter* (1951), XII, 106. Cf. Zola's suggestion in *Le Roman expérimental:* "In practical life, men but make experiments upon one another."

54. Letter to Gustav von Geijerstam, 1 December 1888.

55. Letter to Ola Hansson, 3 January 1888, in *Strindberg och Ola Hanssons Brevväxling*, 1888–1892 (Stockholm, 1938). In Eklund, *Strindbergs Brev*, vol. VII, pp. 217 f.

56. The interpretation is confirmed by a letter which Strindberg wrote Siri von Essen, during her administration at the Experimental Theatre, concerning the casting of the play. Strindberg said X is the stronger, and consequently the softer type. See Karin Smirnoff, *Strindbergs förste hustru*, p. 276. Cf. Lamm, *August Strindberg*, p. 176.

57. Cf. Rimbaud, Lettre à Paul Demeny, 15 Mai 1871. *Arthur Rimbaud. Œuvres complètes* (Paris, La Pléiade, 1954), p. 270.

58. Quoted in André Barre, *Le Symbolisme* (Paris, 1911), p. 56. Cf. Baudelaire, "Victor Hugo" in *L'Art romantique. Œuvres*, p. 1085: *"D'ailleurs Swedenborg, etc."*

59. Baudelaire, "Mon cœur mis a nu," XCIV, in *Œuvres* (Paris, La Pléiade, 1956), p. 1236.

60. *Ibid.*, LXXXVII, *Œuvres*, p. 1253.

61. Baudelaire, *Fusées*, III, in *Œuvres*, p. 1191. Cf. "Choix de maximes consolantes sur l'amour," in *Œuvres*, pp. 265 ff.

62. *Inferno*, 2nd ed. (Paris, 1898), p. 257. English translation: *The Inferno*, tr. by Claud Field (New York and London, 1913).

63. Adolf Paul, *Min Strindbergs bok* (Stockholm, 1930), is the source of some interesting but generally unreliable anecdotes regarding Strindberg's relations in this period. Also, *Strindberg-Erinnerungen und-Briefe* (München, 1914), by the same author.

64. Frida Strindberg, *Strindberg och hans andra hustru* (Stockholm, 1934); Frida Uhl, *Strindberg, Leid, Liebe, und Zeit* (Hamburg-Leipzig, 1936). An excellent account of this period in Strindberg's life is to be found in Hedén, *Strindberg*, pp. 222 ff., 236 ff.

65. *Antibarbarus* (1894); *Sylva sylvarum* (1896); *Jardin des plantes* (1896); *Typen och prototypen* (1898), in *Samlade skrifter*, XXIX. Cf. H. P. Blavatsky, *The Secret Doctrine* (New York, 1888).

66. Letter of 8 March 1898. *Samlade skrifter*, XXIX, 367.

67. See Lamm's excellent summary in *August Strindberg*, p. 234. Cf. Hedén, *Strindberg*, pp. 251 ff., 304 f.

68. In *Legends*, chap. 11, Strindberg recalls how he was kept awake one night by the ticking of a death-watch beetle in the wall. The pun in the text is not translatable: Swedish *timma* means hour; *timmer* is lumber; a *timmerman* is a lumberman or a builder, and also the name for the beetle which makes the ticking sound. I translate "carpenter-ant," *faute de mieux*.

69. E.g., *To Damascus II*, Act 1, "Outside the House." In *Skrifter* (1955), XI, 177. Translated (Rawson) as *The Road to Damascus* (New York, 1960), p. 121

70. Hedén, *Strindberg* (tr. Koppel), p. 229. When Delius met him in Paris in the early 1890's, Strindberg was living at No. 2, Rue de la Grande Chaumière, in Montparnasse, in the heart of the artists' quarter. Gauguin was one of the habitués of the *crémerie* of La Mère Charlotte where Strindberg took his meals. The Strindberg-Gauguin correspondence has been published. See F. Delius, "Recollections of Strindberg," *The Sackbut*, London, Vol. I, no. 8, December, 1920, pp. 353 f. I am indebted to Professor William Randel for this reference.

71. Of this nature are such figures as the identification of the Beggar and the Unknown in I, sc. 1; the identification of the Beggar and the Confessor in the last scene of II; the setting of II, sc. 4, which is both winter and summer; the banquet of II, sc. 3; the assemblage of phantoms in I, sc. 9; the transformation of wife into mother in III, sc. 3; as well as the more familiar metaphorical devices of the monastery in the clouds beyond the river in III, and the symbolic mill and forge of I, sc. 6. This technique is further elaborated in *The Great Highway*.

72. *To Damascus III*, sc. 3 (*Terrace on the Mountain*), *Skrifter* (1955), XI, 219 (FRESTAREN: *Da sköt jag henne*, etc.). In Rawson's translation, p. 235.

73. The *Studien über Hysteria* which Freud published with Breuer came out in 1895, but the *Traumdeutung* was not published until 1900, and the *Drei Abhandlungen zur Sexual-Theorie* not until 1905.

74. Letter of 2 April 1899.

75. *Briefe an Emil Schering* (München, 1924), p. 81. In Schering's German edition of Strindberg's works.

76. In a letter to Richard Bergh (20 January 1901), Strindberg wrote that Eleanora is "*lite släkt med Swedenborgs nièce Seraphita, härligt framställd av Balzac*." Cf. Lamm, *Strindbergs dramer*, II,

210 f.; *Strindbergs brev till Harriet Bosse* (Stockholm, 1932), translated by A. Paulson, *Letters of Strindberg to Harriet Bosse* (New York, 1959), letter of 8 February 1901, p. 19.
77. Letter written in December 1904. In Paulson, *Letters to Harriet Bosse*, p. 117.
78. Paulson, *op. cit.*, p. 24.
79. Paulson, *op. cit.*, p. 26.
80. See Letter to Schering, 18 January 1902. The title is *Ett Drömspel*, literally *A Dream Play*.
81. See Paulson, *op. cit.*, pp. 48 ff.
82. Letter to Schering, 17 April 1907. Strindberg speaks of *A Dream Play* as "*mitt mest älskade drama, min största smärtas barn*" —"my best-loved drama, the child of my greatest pain."
83. Quoted by Lamm, *August Strindberg* (2nd ed., 1948), p. 289.
84. Cf. E. H. Short, *The Painter in History* (London, 1948), p. 361; M. J. Friedländer, *On Art and Connoisseurship*, 3rd edition (London, 1944), pp. 75 ff.
85. Cf. E. Loran, *Cézanne's Composition* (Berkeley and Los Angeles, 1946), pp. 31 ff.
86. Eric Newton, *European Painting and Sculpture* (Harmondsworth, England, Pelican, 1941), p. 122.
87. Alfred Soergel, *Dichtung und Dichter der Zeit* (Leipzig, 1926); cf. Walter Muschg, *Von Trakl zu Brecht, Dichter des Expressionismus* (München, 1962), particularly the title-essay.
88. Cf. C. Dahlström, *Strindberg's Dramatic Expressionism*, pp. 117 ff.; Diebold, *Anarchie im Drama*, 3rd ed. (Frankfurt am Main, 1925), pp. 165 ff.
89. Author's Foreword, *A Dream Play*, *Skrifter* (1955), XI, 348. In *Fröken Julie*, etc., p. 225. In *Six Plays* (tr. Sprigge), p. 193.
90. E.g., Elizabeth Sprigge, *Six Plays by Strindberg* (New York, 1955), p. 188.
91. Cf. Lamm, *Strindbergs dramer*, II, 303–336; H. Taub, *Strindbergs Traumspiel, eine metaphysische Studie* (München, 1917); V. Börge, *Strindbergs mystiske Teater* (København, 1942), on *Till Damaskus*, pp. 77 ff.; on *Drömspelet*, pp. 179 ff.; Dahlström, *op. cit.*, pp. 175 ff.
92. *A Dream Play*, last scene. *Samlade skrifter*, XXXVI, 327; *Skrifter* (1955), XI, 377; *Fröken Julie*, etc., pp. 294 f.; *Six Plays*, p. 258. Cf. W. A. Berendsohn, *The Oriental Studies of August Strindberg, 1849–1912*, transl. by Rudolf Loewenthal (Washington, 1960).
93. These ideas were by no means new to Western thought in

Strindberg's day. It was more than a half-century since Friedrich Schlegel first brought Brahmanism within reach of Western readers (*Über die Sprache und Weisheit der Indier* [1808]). See: *Rigveda*, ed. Max Müller, 2nd ed., (London, 1890-1892), X, 90 ff.; *Brihadāranyaka Upanishad*, tr. F. M. Müller, *Sacred Books of the East*, Vol. XV, I, 4.5; IV, 2.4; *Chāndogya Upanishad*, VIII, 3.12. On the general subject see A. B. Keith, *The Religion and Philosophy of the Veda and Upanishads* (Cambridge, Mass., 1925).

94. The word *brahman* has the root *brih*, to grow.

95. Some of the people Strindberg had in mind in characterizing the dream-figures have been more or less confidently identified. For a list of such identifications, see Lamm, *August Strindberg*, pp. 292 ff., or the corresponding section in Lamm, *Strindbergs dramer*, vol. II.

96. This aspect of the Poet is emphasized particularly in the second Fingal's Cave episode, *Samlade skrifter*, XXXVI, 301. *Skrifter* (1955), XI, 371. In *Fröken Julie*, etc., p. 280; *Six Plays*, p. 245. See also the last scene: *Six Plays*, p. 257; *Samlade skrifter*, XXXVI, 324. *Skrifter* (1955), XI, 377.

97. *Samlade skrifter*, XXXVI, 327; *Skrifter* (1955), XI, 377; *Fröken Julie*, etc., p. 295; *Six Plays*, p. 258. Cf. Dante, *Purgatorio* 31, 115 ff.

98. *Le verrier* would mean, of course, the glass-maker, not the glazier. Cf. Baudelaire, *Œuvres*, p. 290, for *Le Mauvais Vitrier*. The Swedish glasscutter, a kind of Lorraine cross surmounted by the diamond cutting-point, resembles a skeleton key. The symbol is by no means abstruse.

99. Paulson, *Letters to Harriet Bosse*, p. 41; Lamm, *August Strindberg*, p. 292.

100. Letter of 4 September 1901, Paulson, op. cit., p. 61.

101. Hedén's dating. *Strindberg*, tr. Koppel, pp. 262-272.

102. *Samlade skrifter*, L, 12.

103. Letter to Schering, 29 March 1907.

104. Letter of 2 April 1907.

105. *En blå bok* (Stockholm, 1907), p. 62.

106. Ollén says that a Japanese screen which Strindberg saw in his sister's apartment was associated in his mind with a description he had heard of hospital procedure attending a death. See Gunnar Ollén, *Strindbergs dramatik*, 2nd ed. (Stockholm, 1961), p. 469.

107. *The Ghost Sonata*, sc. 3. In Evert Sprinchorn's excellent translation, *The Chamber Plays* (New York, 1962), pp. 105 ff.

108. The hyacinth, in Strindberg's opinion, was perfectly beau-

tiful; perhaps it was even sentient, and could feel pain and pleasure, but it was incapable of developing a soul: "Without self-consciousness, reason, and free will there is no possibility for a soul to develop, and to be without a soul is virtually to be dead—at least to those of us who are alive" (*En blå bok III, Samlade skrifter,* XLVIII, 84).

109. Hedén, *Strindberg,* tr. Koppel, pp. 364 ff. See also Sprinchorn, *op. cit.,* pp. 205 ff.

110. Fanny Falkner, *Strindberg i blå tornet* (Stockholm, 1921).

111. *Stora landsvägen,* sc. 1, in *Skrifter* (1955), XI, p. 400.

112. *The Great Highway,* sc. 7, *op. cit.,* p. 419.

113. *Ibid.,* sc. 7, *op. cit.,* p. 422.

The Flower and the Castle

1. Cf. "Memoirs of Dadaism," by Tristan Tzara, reprinted in Edmund Wilson, *Axel's Castle,* Appendix II (New York, 1931), pp. 304 ff.; Tzara, *Sept manifestes dada* (Paris, 1920).

2. See R. H. Wilenski, *The Modern Movement in Art* (London, 1937), pp. 115 ff., 158 ff., 221 ff.; J. Meier-Graefe, *Der moderne Impressionismus* (Berlin, 1903), pp. 10 ff.; Richard Hamann, *Der Impressionismus in Leben und Kunst* (Köln, 1907); Arnold Hauser, *The Social History of Art* (New York, 1952), vol. II, pp. 907 ff. Cf. Desprez, *"De l'impressionisme"* in *L'Évolution naturaliste* (Paris, 1884), pp. 77 ff.

3. Letter to Jens Halvorsen, 18 June 1889. See Otto Lous Mohr, *Henrik Ibsen som Maler* (Oslo, 1953), for reproductions of Ibsen's paintings and drawings. At least 60 examples are extant and traceable.

4. The Author's Foreword to *Miss Julie* includes an interesting summary of the impressionist position with regard to characterization, but Strindberg's description of his own practice is unduly "scientific" for impressionism. He is evidently thinking in this passage in terms of the experimental novel. It appears to reflect, moreover, the discussion of the multiple nature of the human personality in Theodore Ribot's *Les Maladies de la personnalité,* 4th ed., (Paris, 1891), p. 75. The book was found in Strindberg's library after his death.

5. E. Newton, *European Painting and Sculpture* (Harmondsworth, England, Pelican, 1941), p. 112.

6. Jules Huret, *Enquête sur l'évolution littéraire* (Paris, 1891).

7. See Baudelaire, *Salon de 1859,* III, IV, in *Œuvres* (ed. La Pléiade), pp. 722 ff., 776 ff.

8. In *Le Figaro*, 18 September 1886.

9. *Salon de 1859*, IV, in *Œuvres*, p. 779.

10. Mallarmé, *Enquête de Jules Huret*, in *Œuvres de Mallarmé* (Paris, La Pléiade, 1956), p. 871

11. *Salon de 1859*, III, "La Reine des facultés," *Œuvres*, p. 774; IV, "Le Gouvernement de l'imagination," *Œuvres*, p. 780.

12. Cf. Henri Brémond, *La Poésie pure* (Paris, 1926), pp. 16 ff. Cf. A. Thibaudet, *Histoire de la littérature française* (Paris, 1936), pp. 485 ff.; Mallarmé, "La Musique et les lettres" in *Œuvres*, pp. 648, 649; "Variations sur un sujet," in *Œuvres*, p. 367, pp. 382 ff.

13. Rimbaud, Letter to Paul Demeny, 15 May 1871, in *Œuvres complètes* (Paris, La Pléiade, 1954), p. 270. See also E. Lévi, *Dogme de la haute magie* (Paris, 1855).

14. Mallarmé, "Sur le théâtre," *Proses diverses*, in *Œuvres*, p. 875.

15. Mallarmé, "Igitur," in *Œuvres*, p. 427.

16. Koht, *Life of Ibsen*, II, 172.

17. *Ibid.*

18. Cf. Letter to Hegel, 2 September 1884.

19. "Le Tragique quotidien," in *Le Trésor des humbles*, 66th ed. (Paris, 1911), transl. by Alfred Sutro as *The Treasure of the Humble* (New York, 1916). Extracts in Clark, *European Theories of the Drama*, p. 412.

20. *Peer Gynt*, Act 5, sc. 2.

21. Huret, *Enquête*, in *Œuvres de Mallarmé* (ed. La Pléiade), p. 869.

22. Cf. Baudelaire, *Le Spleen de Paris*, 1869, letter of dedication to Arsène Houssaye, *Œuvres de Baudelaire*, p. 281.

23. Cf. the Captain's last speeches in Act 3; cf. Lamm, *August Strindberg*, p. 159.

24. Author's Foreword, *Miss Julie*. In *Skrifter* (1951), XII, 61. In *Fröken Julie*, etc. (Stockholm, 1957), p. 11.

25. Quoted in M. J. Friedländer, *On Art and Connoisseurship* (London, 1944), p. 21.

26. Stefan George, "Franken," in *Der siebente Ring* (1907): seems appropriate. Cf. Praz, *The Romantic Agony*, chapters IV and V for citations of analogous material.

27. See Henri Albert, "Nietzsche et Strindberg," *Mercure de France*, 16 April 1923, pp. 780 ff.

28. *Inferno*, p. 120. Strindberg was certainly aware of the relation of his psychic crises to his poetic inspiration: "It comes when it wants

to come. But most frequently and with greatest force after the major catastrophes of my life." *Samlade skrifter*, LIV, 472.

29. Jules Laforgue, "Pierrots (On a des principes)," in *L'Imitation de Notre Dame de la Lune* (1886).

30. Baudelaire, "Théophile Gautier," in *L'Art romantique*. In *Œuvres*, p. 1035.

31. "Victor Hugo," in *Œuvres de Baudelaire*, p. 1085.

32. "Théophile Gautier," in *Œuvres*, p. 1036.

33. "Victor Hugo," in *Œuvres*, p. 1090.

34. *The Iceman Cometh* depends equally, it is true, on the piece in *Le Spleen de Paris* called "Portraits des maîtresses," *Œuvres de Baudelaire*, p. 348. The last story furnished O'Neill's plot, as *The Wild Duck*, his theme; and *The Lower Depths* his method. The local color and the *longueurs*, O'Neill supplied.

35. For a useful study of Strindberg's influence in Germany, see Maurice Gravier, *Strindberg et le théâtre moderne, I: L'Allemagne* (Lyon-Paris, n.d., 1942).

36. Anouilh, *Antigone* (Paris, 1946), transl. by L. Galantière as *Antigone* (New York, 1946).

37. Letter of 4 October 1905, to Harriet Bosse. In Paulsen, *op. cit.*, p. 130.

A Selected Bibliography

Tragedy and Comedy

Apollonio, Mario, *Storia del teatro italiano*. 2nd ed., 3 vols., Firenze, 1943–1951.

Aristotle, *Poetics*, translated by Ingram Bywater, *in Basic Works of Aristotle*, ed. R. McKeon. New York, 1941.

Aubignac, L'abbé de, *Pratique du théâtre*, ed. René Martino. Paris, 1927.

Auerbach, Erich, *Mimesis*, translated by W. Trask. Princeton, 1953.

Bernbaum, Ernest, *The Drama of Sensibility*. Boston and New York, 1915.

Bertana, Emilio, *La Tragedia*. Milano, 1905.

Beaumarchais, Pierre Augustin Caron, "Essai sur le genre dramatique sérieux" in *Œuvres complètes*, ed. Saint-Marc Girardin. Paris, 1861.

Biancale, Michele, *La tragedia italiana nel cinquecento*. Roma, 1901.

Bieber, M., *The History of Greek and Roman Theater*. Princeton, 1939.

Boileau-Despréaux, Nicolas, *L'Art poétique* (1674), ed. F. Brunetière. 7th ed., Paris, 1911.

Bouhours, Dominique, *Manière de bien penser dans les œuvres d'esprit* (1687). Paris, 1743.

Bowra, C. M., *Sophoclean Tragedy*. Oxford, 1944.

Castelvetro, Lodovico, *La Poetica d'Aristotele vulgarizzata e sposta*. Basel, 1576.

Cesareo, E., *La Tragedia di Seneca*. Palermo, 1932.

Chasles, E., *La Comédie en France au seizième siècle*. Paris, 1862.

Clark, Barrett H., *European Theories of the Drama*. Cincinnati, 1918.

Clubb, Louise G., "The Theatre of Giambattista della Porta." Unpublished dissertation, Columbia University, 1962.

Coppola, G., *Il teatro tragico in Roma repubblicana*. Bologna, 1940.

Corneille, Pierre de, *Œuvres*, ed. Marty-Laveaux. 12 vols. Paris, 1862–1868.

Croce, Benedetto, *Nuovi saggi sulla letteratura italiana del seicento*. Bari, 1931.

——, *Saggi sulla letteratura italiana del '600*. Bari, 1924.

——, *Storia d'Europa*. Bari, 1932.

——. *Storia della età barocca in Italia*. 2nd ed., Bari, 1946.

Cunliffe, J., *The Influence of Seneca on Elizabethan Tragedy*. London, 1893.

D'Amico, Silvio, *Storia del teatro italiano*. 4 vols. Vols. I and II. Milano, 1936.

D'Avénel, Georges, *Les Revenus d'un intellectuel de 1200 à 1913*. Paris, 1922.

Dejob, Charles, *De L'influence du Concile de Trente sur la littérature et les beaux-arts chez les peuples Catholiques*. Paris, 1884.

Diderot, Denis, *Œuvres*, ed. André Billy. Paris, La Pléiade, 1957.

Diomedes, *Ars grammatica*, Bk. III. In H. Keil, *Grammatici Latini*, Leipzig, 1870–1880. Vol. I, pp. 488 ff.

Donatus, Aelius, *Ars grammatica* in H. Keil, *Grammatici Latini*, Leipzig, 1870–1880, Vol. IV.

——, *Publii Terentii Comœdiae sex, post optimas editiones emendatae, Accedunt Aelii Donatus commentarius integer*. Lugd. Batav. et Roterod., 1699.

Dryden, John, *Essays*, ed. by W. P. Ker. 2 vols. Oxford, 1926.

Duckworth, G. E., *The Nature of Roman Comedy*. Princeton, 1952.

Dunkin, P. S., *Post-Aristophanic Comedy*. Urbana, 1946.

Eckermann, J. P., *Gespräche mit Goethe*. Leipzig, 1909.

Eggli, Edmond, *Le Débat romantique en France 1813–1830*. 2 vols. Paris, 1933.

Eliot, T. S., *The Sacred Wood*. London, 1920.

Eloesser, Arthur, *Das bürgerlicher Drama*. Berlin, 1898.

Estève, Edmond, *Études de littérature pré-romantique*. Paris, 1923.

Farquhar, George, *Works*, ed. by W. Archer. London, 1907.

Fasso, Luigi, *Il teatro del seicento*. Milan, 1956.

Gaiffe, F., *Le Drame en France au XVIIIe siècle*. Paris, 1910.

Gilbert, A. H., *Literary Criticism: Plato to Dryden*. New York, 1940.

Giraldi Cinthio, Giovan Battista, *Le Tragedie*. 2 vols. Venetia, 1583.

——, *Discorsi intorno al comporre dei romanzi, delle comedie, e delle tragedie* . . . Vinegia, 1554.

Guarini, Giovanni Battista, *Il Pastor fido e il compendio della poesia tragicomica* (1601). Bari, 1914.

——, *Il Verrato, ovvero difesa di quanto ha scritto M. Giason Denores contra la tragicomedia*. Ferrara, 1588.

Herrick, Marvin T., *Italian Comedy in the Renaissance*. Urbana, 1960.

——, *Tragicomedy*. Urbana, 1955.

Herrmann, Léon, *Le Théâtre de Senèque*. Paris, 1924.

Heywood, Thomas, *An Apology for Actors. In Three Books*. London, 1841.

Jonson, Ben, *Works*, ed. C. H. Herford and P. Simpson. Oxford, 1925–1952. Vols. 3 and 5.

Kennard, Joseph S., *The Italian Theatre from Its Beginning to the Close of the Seventeenth Century*. New York, 1932.

Kernodle, G. R., *From Art to Theatre: Form and Convention in the Renaissance*. Chicago, 1946.

Klein, J. L., *Geschichte des Dramas*. 13 vols. Lipsia, 1866–1868. Vols. IV, V, VI.

La Mesnardière, H. J. Pilet de, *La Poétique*. Paris, 1640.

La Taille, Jean de, *Art de la tragédie* in *Saül furieux*. Paris, 1572.

Lancaster, H. C., *French Tragedy in the Time of Louis XV and Voltaire, 1715–74*. 2 vols. Baltimore, 1950.

——, *French Tragedy in the Reign of Louis XVI and the Early Years of the French Revolution, 1774–92*. Baltimore, 1953.

——, *A History of French Dramatic Literature in the Seventeenth Century*. 9 vols. Part II: *The Period of Corneille, 1635–51*. 2 vols. Part III: *The Period of Moliere, 1652–72*. 2 vols. Baltimore, 1932, 1936.

Lanson, Gustave, *Esquisse d'une histoire de la tragédie française*. Paris, 1927.

——, *Nivelle de la Chaussée et la comédie larmoyante*. 2nd ed. Paris, 1903.

Lawton, H. W., *Handbook of French Renaissance Dramatic Theory*. Manchester, 1949.

Lemonnier, L., *Corneille*. Paris, 1945.

Lintilhac, E., *Histoire générale du théâtre en France*. 5 vols. Paris, 1904–1909.

Lisoni, Alberto, *Imitatori del teatro spagnuolo in Italia*. Parma, 1895.

Mairet, Jean de, Preface to *Silvanire*, ed. Otto. Paris, 1890.

Marsan, Jules, *La Pastorale dramatique en France*. Paris, 1906.

Menéndez y Pelayo, M., *Historia de las ideas estéticas en España*. Vol. II. Madrid, 1885.

Meozzi, Antero, *La Drammatica della Rinascità italiana en Europa secolo XVI–XVII*. Pisa, 1940.

Mercier, Sebastien, *Du Théâtre ou nouvel essai sur l'art dramatique*. Amsterdam, 1773.

Minturno, Antonio Sebastiano, *L'Arte poetica* (1563). Napoli, 1725.

————, *Antonii Sebastianii Minturni de Poeta*. Venetiis, 1559.

Molière, J. B. Poquelin de, *Œuvres*, ed. Despois et Mesnard. Paris, 1881–1883.

Momigliano, Attilio, *Storia della letteratura italiana*. 8th ed. Milano, 1960.

Morel-Fatio, A., *La Comédie espagnole du XVIIe siècle*. 2nd ed. Paris, 1923.

Neri, Ferdinando, *La Tragedia italiana del cinquecento*. Firenze, 1904.

Nolte, F. O., *The Early Middle-Class Drama*. Lancaster, Pa., 1935.

Norwood, G., *Plautus and Terence*. New York, 1932.

Picard, R., *La Carrière de Jean Racine*. Paris, 1956.

Racine, Jean, *Œuvres complètes*, ed. Mesnard. Paris, 1865–1873.

Rapin, René, *Reflexions sur l'art poétique d'Aristote*. Paris, 1672.

Riccoboni, Louis, *Histoire du théâtre italien depuis la décadence de la comédie latine*. Paris, 1728.

Rigal, Eugène, *Alexandre Hardy et le théâtre français*. Paris, 1889.

————, *De Jodelle à Molière*. Paris, 1911.

Sanesi, I., *La Commedia*. 2 vols. 2nd ed. Milano, 1954.

Santangelo, Giorgio, *Il Secentismo*. Palermo, 1958.

Scaliger, J. C., *Poetices libri septem* (1561), *editio secunda*. Leiden, 1581.

————, *Select translations* by F. M. Padelford. New York, 1905.

Scherer, Jacques, *La Dramaturgie classique en France*. Paris, 1955.

Scherillo, Michele, *La Commedia dell'arte, studi e profili*. Torino, 1884.

Sidney, Philip, *The Defence of Poesie*. In *The Complete Works*. 4 vols. Cambridge, 1912–1926. Vol. III.

Smith, Gregory, *Elizabethan Critical Essays*. 2 vols. Oxford, 1904.

Spingarn, Joel E., *Critical Essays of the Seventeenth Century*. 3 vols. Oxford, 1907.

————, *A History of Literary Criticism in the Renaissance*. 2nd ed. New York, 1908.

Staël, A. L. G. N., Madame de, Œuvres complètes. 17 vols. Paris, 1820–1821.

Stendhal (Pierre Beyle), Racine et Shakespeare (1822), ed. Pierre Martino. 2 vols. Paris, 1925.

Tasso, Torquato, Discorsi del poema eroico (1595) in Opere. 33 vols. Pisa, Rosini, 1823. Vol. XII.

——, Prose, ed. Cesare Guasti. 2 vols. Firenze, Le Monnier, 1875.

Thomson, George, Aeschylus and Athens. London, 1941.

Thorndike, A. H., Tragedy. Boston and New York, 1908.

Trissino, Giangiorgio, Poetica (1529) in Tutte le opere. 2 vols. Verona, 1729.

Vanbrugh, John, Complete Works, ed. B. Dobrée and G. Webb. 4 vols. Bloomsbury, 1927–1928.

Vaughan, C. E., Types of Tragic Drama. London, 1908.

Vigny, Alfred de, Preface to Chatterton. Paris, 1835.

Voltaire, Commentaires sur Corneille (1761). In Œuvres complètes, ed. Louis Moland. 52 vols. Paris, Garnier, 1886.

——, Preface to Œdipe. Paris, 1730.

Weber, Gottfried, Herder und das Drama. Weimar, 1922.

Webster, T. B. L., Studies in Later Greek Comedy. Manchester, 1953.

Weinberg, Bernard, A History of Literary Criticism in the Italian Renaissance. 2 vols. Chicago, 1961.

Wilamowitz-Moellendorf, Tycho von, Die dramatische Technik des Sophokles. Berlin, 1917.

The New Drama

Albert, Maurice, Les Théâtres des boulevards 1789–1848. Paris, 1902.

Allard, L., La Comédie de mœurs en France au XIXᵉ siècle. 2 vols. Paris, 1922–1923.

Arvin, N. C., Eugène Scribe and the French theatre 1815–1860. Cambridge, Mass., 1924.

Bab, Julius, Das Wort Friedrich Hebbels. München, 1923.

Doumic, René, De Scribe à Ibsen. Paris, 1893.

Dumas fils, Alexandre, Théâtre complet. Vols. 3, 4, 5, 7. Paris, 1890–1918.

Filon, Augustin, De Dumas à Rostand. Paris, 1898.

Gaillard, H., Émile Augier et la comédie sociale. Paris, 1910.

Ginisty, Paul, Le Mélodrame. Paris, 1910.

Hartog, W. G., Guilbert de Pixerécourt. Paris, 1913.

Hebbel, Friedrich, Maria Magdalene, ein bürgerliches Trauerspiel in drei Aufzügen mit Vorwort. Leipzig, 1894.

——, Mein Wort über das Drama. Hamburg, 1843.

——, Sämtliche Werke, besorgt von R. M. Werner. 24 vols. Berlin, 1901 ff.

Hugo, Victor, Préface de Cromwell (1827), ed. M. Souriau. Paris, 1897.

Küchler, Kurt, Friedrich Hebbel, sein Leben und sein Werk. Jena, 1910.

Lacy, Alexander, Pixerécourt and the French Romantic Drama. Toronto, 1928.

Legouvé, Émile, Eugène Scribe. Paris, 1874.

Lenient, Charles, La Comédie en France au XIXᵉ siècle. 2 vols. Paris, 1898.

Morillat, P., Émile Augier (1820–1889). Grenoble, 1901.

Mouly, G., La Vie prodigeuse de Victorien Sardou. Paris, 1931.

Nebout, Pierre, Le Drame romantique. Paris, 1895.

Noël, C. M., Les Idées sociales dans le théâtre d'Alexandre Dumas fils. Paris, 1912.

Parigot, Hippolyte, Émile Augier. Paris, 1890.

——, Le Drame d'Alexandre Dumas. Paris, 1898.

Taylor, F. A., The Theatre of Alexandre Dumas fils. Oxford, 1937.

Vapereau, L. G., Année littéraire et dramatique 1859. Paris, 1860.

Walzel, O., Friedrich Hebbel und seine Dramen. 3rd ed. Leipzig and Berlin, 1927.

Wellek, René, A History of Modern Criticism 1750–1950. 2 vols. New Haven, 1955.

Realism

Antoine, André, Mes Souvenirs sur le Théâtre-Libre. Paris, 1921.

Archer, William, The Old Drama and the New. London, 1922.

Bahr, Hermann, Studien zur Kritik der Moderne. Frankfurt am Main, 1894.

Bernard, Claude, Introduction à l'étude de la médecine expérimentale. Paris, 1865.

Beuchat, Charles, Histoire du naturalisme français. 2 vols. Paris, 1949.

Brunetière, F., Le Roman naturaliste. Paris, 1883.

Champfleury, Jules, *Le Réalisme*. Paris, 1857.

Darzens, R., *Le Théâtre-Libre illustré*. 2 vols. Paris, 1889–1890.

David-Sauvageot, A., *Le Réalisme et le naturalisme dans la littérature et dans l'art*. Paris, 1889.

Desprez, Louis, *L'Évolution naturaliste*. Paris, 1884.

Doumic, René, "Le Théâtre" in Petit de Julleville, *Histoire de la langue et la littérature française*. Vol. VIII. Paris, 1899.

Dumesnil, René, *L'Époque réaliste et naturaliste*. Paris, 1945.

Got, A., *Henri Becque*. Paris, 1923.

Jullien, Jean, *Le Théâtre vivant*. 2 vols. Paris, 1892–1896.

Kerr, Alfred, *Das neue Drama*. Berlin, 1905.

Levin, Harry, *The Gates of Horn*. New York, 1963.

Martino, Pierre, *Le Naturalisme français*. Paris, 1923.

Proudhon, P. J., *Du Principe de l'art et de sa destination sociale*. Paris, 1861.

Sarcey, Francisque, *Essai d'une esthétique de théâtre*. Paris, 1876.

————, *Quarante ans de théâtre*. 5 vols. Paris, 1900–1902. (Vol. I: *Les Lois du théâtre*.)

Scheifley, W. H., *Brieux and Contemporary French Society*. New York, 1917.

Sondel, B. S., *Zola's Naturalistic Theory with Particular Reference to the Drama*. Chicago, 1939.

Stuart, D. C., *The Development of Dramatic Art*. New York, 1928.

Thalasso, Adolphe, *Le Théâtre-Libre*. 3rd ed. Paris, 1909.

Waxman, S. M., *Antoine and the Théâtre-Libre*. Cambridge, Mass., 1926.

Zola, Émile, *Le Naturalisme au théâtre*. Paris, 1881.

————, *Le Roman expérimental*, Paris, 1883.

————, Preface to *Thérèse Raquin*. Paris, 1873.

————, *Œuvres complètes*, ed. Maurice Le Blond. 50 vols. Paris, 1927–1929.

Ibsen

Archer, William, *Collected Works of Henrik Ibsen*. 12 vols. New York, 1912. (Vol. XII: *From Ibsen's Workshop*.)

Asbjörnsen, Peter Christian, *Norske folke- og huldre- eventyr*. 3rd ed. Christiania, 1870. Translated by Helen and John Gade as *Norwegian Fairy Tales*. New York, 1924.

Björnson, B., *Brev, Förste Samling*. Ed. by H. Koht. Christiania, 1912.

Brandes, Georg, *Die Literatur*. Vol. 32: *Henrik Ibsen*. Berlin, 1907.

————, *Main Currents in Nineteenth Century Literature*, 6 vols. New York, 1901–1906.

————, *Das Ibsenbuch*. Dresden, 1923.

Buckle, H. T., *History of Civilization in England*. Vol. I, London, 1857. Vol. II, London, 1861.

Bull, Francis, *Ibsen: The Man and the Dramatist*. Taylorian Lecture. Oxford, 1954.

Campbell, T. M., *Hebbel, Ibsen and the Analytic Exposition*. Heidelberg, 1922.

Chesterton, G. K., *A Handful of Authors*. London, 1953.

Collin, C., *Björnsterne Björnson*. 2 vols. Kristiania, 1902–1907 and 1924.

Croce, B., *European Literature in the Nineteenth Century*. London, 1924.

Downs, B. W., *A Study of Six Plays by Ibsen*. Cambridge, 1950.

Edel, Leon, *Henry James: les années dramatiques*. Paris, 1931.

Fergusson, Francis, *The Idea of a Theater*. Princeton, 1949.

Hans, Wilhelm, *Ibsens Selbstporträt in seinem Drama*. München, 1911.

Halvorsen, J. B., *Norsk Forfatter-Lexikon 1814–1880*. Vol. III. Kristiania, 1892.

Huneker, J., *Egoists: A Book of Supermen*. London, 1909.

————, *Iconoclasts: A Book of Dramatists*. London, 1905.

Ibsen, Bergliot, *The Three Ibsens: Memories of Henrik, Suzannah and Sigurd Ibsen*. transl. by G. Schjelderup. London, 1951.

Ibsen, Henrik, *The Collected Works*, ed. by W. Archer. 12 vols. London, 1906–1912, New York, 1912.

————, *Brev*. 2 vols. ed. H. Koht and J. Elias. Kristiania, 1904.

————, *Letters of Henrik Ibsen*, transl. by J. N. Laurvik and M. Morison. New York, 1905.

————, *Nachgelassene Schriften, in vier Banden*, ed. J. Elias and H. Koht. Berlin, 1909.

————, *Samlede Digterverker, standardutgave ved Didrik Arup Seip*. Kristiania, 1922.

————, *Speeches and New Letters*. Transl. by A. Kildal. Boston, 1910.

————, (*Works*), *Volume VI. An Enemy of the People, The Wild Duck, Rosmersholm*, translated by J. W. McFarlane. Oxford, 1960.

Jacobs, M., *Ibsens Bühnentechnik*. Dresden, 1922.

Jaeger, H., *The Life of Henrik Ibsen*, tr. C. Bell. London, 1890.

Koht, Halvdan, *Ibsen, eet Diktarliv*. 2 vols. Oslo, 1928–1929.

————, *Henrik Ibsen*. London, 1931.

Lavrin, Janko, *Ibsen and His Creation: A Psycho-critical Study*. London, 1921.

————, *Ibsen: An Approach*. London, 1950.

Lee, Jeannette, *The Ibsen Secret*. New York, 1907.

Leneveu, G., *Ibsen et Maeterlinck*. Paris, 1902.

McFarlane, J. W., *Ibsen and the Temper of Norwegian Literature*. London, 1960.

Meyer, Michael, *When We Dead Awaken and Three Other Plays by Ibsen*. New York, 1960.

Mohr, Otto Lous, *Henrik Ibsen som Maler*. Oslo, 1953.

Monrad, O. P., *Sören Kierkegaard, sein Leben und seine Werke*. Jena, 1909.

Northam, John, *Ibsen's Dramatic Method: A Study of the Prose Dramas*. London, 1953.

Paulsen, John, *Erinnerungen an Henrik Ibsen*. Berlin, 1907.

Pettersen, Hjalmar, *Henrik Ibsen, 1828–1928, bedømt af Samtid og Eftertid*. Oslo, 1928.

Pirandello, Luigi, *L'Umorismo*. Milano, Mondadori, 1923.

————, *Erma bifronte*. Milano, Treves, 1906.

Scandinavian Plays of the Twentieth Century. 2 vols. Princeton, 1944.

Shaw, G. B., *Our Theatres in the Nineties*. 3 vols. London, 1932.

————, *The Quintessence of Ibsenism*. 2nd ed. London, 1913.

Woerner, Roman, *Henrik Ibsen*. 3rd ed. 2 vols. Monaco, 1923.

Weigand, Hermann J., *The Modern Ibsen: A Reconsideration*. New York, 1925.

Zucker, Adolf E., *Ibsen, The Master Builder*. London, 1929.

Strindberg

Ahlberg, Alfred, *Det ondas problem*. Stockholm, 1923.

Ahlström, Stellan, *Strindbergs ërovring av Paris: Strindberg och Franrike 1884–1895*. Stockholm, 1956.

Albert, Henri, "Nietzsche et Strindberg" in *Mercure de France*, Paris, 16 April 1923.

Bachler, K., *August Strindberg, eine psychoanalytische Studie*. Wien, 1931.

Balzac, Honoré de, *Séraphita* in *Œuvres*, ed. A. Houssiaux. Paris, 1885–1863. Vol. XVI.

Bentley, E., *The Playwright as Thinker*. New York, 1946.

Berendsohn, W. A., *The Oriental Studies of August Strindberg 1849–1912*, transl. by R. Loewenthal. Washington, 1960.

Börge, Vagn, *Strindbergs mystiske teater*. København, 1942.

Brandes, Georg og Edvard, *Brevveksling med nordiske forfattere og videnskabsmaend*. Utgivet af Morten Borup, etc. 8 vols. København, 1939–1942.

Dahlström, Carl, *Strindberg's Dramatic Expressionism*. Ann Arbor, 1930.

Delius, Frederick, "Recollections of Strindberg," in *The Sackbut*, London, Vol. I, no. 8, December, 1920, pp. 353 f.

Diebold, Bernhard, *Anarchie im Drama*. Frankfurt am Main, 1925.

Drews, A., *Eduard von Hartmanns philosophisches System im Grundriss*. Heidelberg, 1902.

Dumas fils, Alexandre, *L'Affaire Clemenceau, roman*. Paris, 1882.

———, *L'Homme-femme*. Paris, 1875.

Eklund, Torsten, *Tjänstekvinnans son, en psykologisk studie*. Stockholm, 1948.

———, *August Strindbergs Brev, utg. av T. Eklund*. 7 vols. Stockholm, 1948–1961.

Erdmann, Nils, *August Strindberg*. 2 vols. Stockholm, 1920. (German translation by H. Goebel, Leipzig, 1924.)

Esswein, Hermann, *August Strindberg im Lichte seines Lebens und seine Werke*. München, 1909.

Falkner, Fanny, *Strindberg i blå tornet*. Stockholm, 1921.

Goncourt, Edmond Louis de, *Charles Demailly. Nouvelle édition*. Paris, 1876.

———, *Manette Salomon, roman. Édition définitive*. Paris, 1929.

Gravier, Maurice, *Strindberg et le théâtre moderne, I: L'Allemagne*. Paris-Lyon, 1942.

Gustafson, Alrik, *A History of Swedish Literature*. Minneapolis, 1961.

Hansson, Ola, *Strindberg och Ola Hanssons Brevväxling, 1888–92*. Stockholm, 1938.

Hartmann, Eduard v., *Die Philosophie des Unbewussten*. 3 vols. Leipzig, 1869. English transl. by W. C. Coupland. London, 1884.

Hedén, Erik, *August Strindberg. En ledtråd vid studiet av hans verk*. Stockholm, 1921. (Translated as *Strindberg, Leben und Dichtung*, by J. Koppel. München, 1926.)

Jaspers, Karl, *Strindberg und van Gogh. 2ᵉ Auflage*. Berlin, 1926.

Jolivet, A., *Le Théâtre de Strindberg*. Paris, 1931.

Keith, A. B., *The Religion and Philosophy of the Veda and Upani-shads*. Cambridge, Mass., 1925.

Kierkegaard, Søren, *Enten-Eller, et livs-fragment*. Utg. af Victor Ere-mita. København, 1950.

————, *Either-Or, A Fragment of Life*. Transl. by D. L. Swenson. Princeton, 1944.

Krutch, J. W., *The Modern Temper*, New York, 1929.

————, "*Modernism*" in *Modern Drama*. Ithaca, 1953.

Lafargue, Paul, "Le Matriarcat." In *La Nouvelle revue*. Paris, 15 March 1886.

Lamm, Martin, *August Strindberg*. Stockholm, 1928.

————, *Strindbergs dramer*. 2 vols. Stockholm, 1924.

Lévi, Eliphas, *Dogme de la haute magie*. Paris, 1855.

Liebert, Arthur, *August Strindberg, seine Weltanschauung und seine Kunst*. 3e Auflage. Berlin, 1925.

Lindblad, Göran, *Strindberg som berättere*. Stockholm, 1924.

Lindström, Hans, *Hjärnornas kamp: Psykologiska idéer och motiv i Strindbergs åttiotalsdiktning*. Uppsala, 1952.

Lundegård, Axel, *Några Strindbergsminnen knutna till en handfull brev*. Stockholm, 1920.

Madsen, Børge G., *Strindberg's Naturalistic Theatre: Its Relation to French Naturalism*. Seattle, 1962.

Marcus, Carl David, *Strindbergs dramatik*. München, 1918.

Molander, Olof, *Harriet Bosse*. Stockholm, 1920.

Mörner, Birger, *Den Strindberg jag känt*. Stockholm, 1924.

Mortensen, B. M. E. and Downs, B. W., *Strindberg: An Introduction to His Life and Works*. Cambridge, 1949.

Nietzsche, Friedrich, *Die Geburt der Tragödie*. Basilea, 1871.

Ollén, Gunnar, *Strindbergs dramatik*. 2nd ed. Stockholm, 1961.

Paul, Adolf, *Min Strindbergs bok*. Stockholm, 1931.

————, *Strindberg-Erinnerungen und -Briefe*. München, 1914.

Paulson, Arvid, *Letters of Strindberg to Harriet Bosse*. New York, 1959.

Péladan, Josephin, *Le Prince de Byzance, drame romanesque en 5 actes*. Paris, 1896.

Réja, Marcel, *Avant-propos, l'Inferno d'Auguste Strindberg*. Paris, 1898.

Ribot, Théodore, *Les Maladies de la personnalité*. 4th ed. Paris, 1891.

Smirnoff, Karin, *Strindbergs förste hustru—Siri von Essen*. Stockholm, 1925.

Strecker, Karl, *Nietzsche und Strindberg. Mit ihrem Briefwechsel*. München, 1921.

Strindberg, August, *Brev*, utg. *av Torsten Eklund*. 7 vols. Stockholm, 1948–1961.

———, *Briefe an Emil Schering*, München, 1924.

———, *The Chamber Plays*. Transl. by E. Sprinchorn and S. Quinn. New York, 1962.

———, *Dramaturgie*. Transl. by Emil Schering. München, 1911.

———, *En blå bok*. Stockholm, 1907.

———, *Fagervik och Skamsund*. Stockholm, 1902

———, *Five Plays of Strindberg*. Transl. by Elizabeth Sprigge. New York, 1960.

———, *Fröken Julie och andra skådespel*. Stockholm, 1957.

———, *Inferno*. Paris, 1897.

———, *Le Plaidoyer d'un fou. Revision française de Georges Loiseau*. Paris, 1895.

———, *Notes to the Members of the Intimate Theatre*. Transl. by E. Sprinchorn in *The Chamber Plays*. New York, 1962.

———, *Samlade skrifter*. Anmärkingar *av John Landquist*. 55 vols. Stockholm, 1912 ff.

———, *Six Plays of Strindberg*, Transl. by Elizabeth Sprigge. New York, 1955.

———, *Skrifter av August Strindberg*. Ed. by Gunnar Brandell. 14 vols. Stockholm, 1955.

———, *Strindberg och Ola Hanssons Brevväxling 1888–92*. Stockholm, 1938.

———, *Strindbergs brev till Harriet Bosse, med kommentarer av Harriet Bosse*. Stockholm, 1932. Transl. by Arvid Paulson, *vide supra*.

———, *To Damascus*. Transl. by G. Rawson as *The Road to Damascus*. New York, 1960.

———, *Werke. Deutsche Gesamtausgabe, unter Mitwirkung von Emil Schering*. 49 vols. München, 1908 ff.

Strindberg, Frida, *Strindberg och hans andra hustru*. Stockholm, 1934.

Swedenborg, Emanuel, *De caelo et ejus mirabilibus et de inferno ex auditis et visis*. Ed. by S. H. Worcester. New York, 1890.

———, *Heaven and its wonders, and hell, from things seen and heard*. New York, 1952.

Taub, H., *Strindbergs Traumspiel. Eine metaphysische Studie*. München, 1917.

Tocqueville, Alexis de, *De la Démocratie en Amérique*. 3rd ed. Paris, 1868.

Uhl, Frida, *Strindberg, Leid, Liebe und Zeit.* Hamburg-Leipzig, 1936.
Zetterlund, Rune, *Bibliografiska anteckningar om August Strindberg.* Stockholm, 1913.

The Flower and the Castle

Anouilh, Jean, *Antigone*, Paris, 1946.
Arnold, R. F., *Das deutsche Drama.* München, 1925.
Barbey d'Aurevilly, J.-A., *Le Théâtre contemporain.* 5 vols. Paris, 1887–1896.
———, *Le Roman contemporain.* Paris, 1902.
Balmforth, Ramsden, *The Problem Play and Its Influence on Modern Life and Thought.* New York, 1928.
Barre, André, *Le Symbolisme.* Paris, 1911.
Baudelaire, Charles, *Œuvres.* Paris, La Pléiade, 1954.
Bithell, Jethro, *The Life and Writings of Maurice Maeterlinck.* London, 1913.
Brémond, Henri, *La Poésie pure.* Paris, 1926.
Brooks, Van Wyck, *The Opinions of Oliver Allston.* New York, 1941.
Cassirer, Else, *Künstler-Briefe aus dem 19 Jahrhundert.* Berlin, 1919.
Edschmid, Kasimir, *Über den Expressionismus in der Literatur und die neue Dichtung.* Berlin, 1919.
Esslin, Martin, *The Theatre of the Absurd.* New York, 1961.
Evreinov, Nicolas, *The Theater in Life.* New York, 1927.
Fechter, Paul, *Das europäische Drama.* 3 vols. Mannheim, 1956–1958.
Friedell, Egon, *A Cultural History of the Modern Age.* 3 vols. New York, 1932.
Friedländer, M. J., *On Art and Connoisseurship.* 3rd ed. London, 1944.
Gassner, John, *Form and Idea in the Modern Theatre.* New York, 1956.
George, Stefan, *Gesamtausgabe der Werke.* Berlin, 1927–1934. *Band 6, 7: Der siebente Ring* (1931).
Grumman, P. H., *Ibsen's Symbolism in the Master Builder and When We Dead Awaken.* Lincoln, Neb., 1910.
Hamann, Richard, *Der Impressionismus in Leben und Kunst.* Köln, 1907.
Hauser, Arnold, *The Social History of Art.* 2 vols. New York, 1952.

Huret, Jules, Enquête sur l'évolution littéraire. Paris, 1891.

Huysmans, J. K., Œuvres complètes. Paris, 1928–1934. Vol. XII: Là-bas; Vol. XIII: En route.

James, Henry, Essays in London and Elsewhere. New York, 1897.

———, The Scenic Art, ed. Allan Wade. London, 1949.

Kerr, Alfred, Die Welt im Drama. In one volume. Köln-Berlin, 1954.

Laforgue, Jules, L'Imitation de Notre Dame de la Lune in Œuvres complètes. Paris, 1919. Vol. I.

Lamm, Martin, Modern Drama. Transl. by Karin Elliott. Oxford, 1952.

Linge, Tore, La Conception de l'amour dans le drame de Dumas fils et d'Ibsen. Paris, 1935.

Lewisohn, Ludwig, The Modern Drama. New York, 1915.

Loran, E., Cézanne's Composition. Berkeley and Los Angeles, 1946.

Lucas, F. L., The Drama of Ibsen and Strindberg. London, 1962.

Maeterlinck, Maurice, Le Trésor des humbles. 66th ed. Paris, 1911. (Transl. by Alfred Sutro as The Treasure of the Humble. New York, 1916.)

Mallarmé, Stéphane, Œuvres. Paris, La Pléiade, 1956.

Meier-Graefe, J., Der moderne Impressionismus. Berlin, 1903.

Merlet, G., Réalisme et fantaisie dans la littérature. Paris, 1861.

Muschg, Walter, Von Trakl zu Brecht, Dichter der Expressionismus. München, 1962.

Newton, Eric, European Painting and Sculpture. Harmondsworth, Middlesex (Penguin), 1941. 4th ed. revised, 1956.

Nicoll, Allardyce, The Theory of the Drama. London, 1931.

Picard, Max, Das Ende des Impressionismus. 2nd ed. Zurich, 1920.

Praz, Mario, La Carne, la morte e il diavolo nella letteratura romantica, transl. by Angus Davidson as The Romantic Agony. London and New York, 1954. 2nd ed. New York, 1956.

Rimbaud, Arthur, Œuvres complètes. Paris, La Pléiade, 1954.

Samuel, R. and Thomas, R. H., Expressionism in German Life, Literature and the Theater 1910–1924. Cambridge, 1939.

Sayler, O. M., Revolt in the Arts. New York, 1930.

Schlaf, Johannes, Maurice Maeterlinck. Berlin, 1906.

Short, E. H., The Painter in History. London, 1948.

Soergel, Albert, Dichtung und Dichter der Zeit. Neue folge. Leipzig, 1926.

Steiner, George, The Death of Tragedy. New York, 1961.

Thibaudet, Albert, Histoire de la littérature française de 1789 à nos jours. Paris, 1936.

Villiers de l'Isle-Adam, J. M., *Œuvres complètes*. 9 vols. Paris, 1922–1938. Vol. I: *L'Éve future;* Vol. IV: *Axël.*

Wedekind, Frank, *Schauspielkunst.* München, 1910.

Wiese, Benno von (ed.), *Das deutsche Drama.* Düsseldorf, 1958.

Wilde, Oscar, "The Soul of Man Under Socialism" in *Intentions and Other Writings.* New York, 1961.

Wilenski, R. H., *The Modern Movement in Art.* London, 1927.

Wilson, Edmund, *Axel's Castle.* New York, 1931.

Yeats, W. B., "The Tragic Theatre" in *The Cutting of an Agate.* London, 1919.

Index

445

Comedians, depictions of ancient, 13
Comédie-Française, 47, 49, 57, 59, 61, 83
La Comédie humaine (Balzac), 50
Comédie rosse, 108, 113, 133
Comédie-vaudeville, 62–68
Comedy, ancient, 11–13; classic, 15; development of, 16–18, 27; English Restoration, 19; French, Italian, and Spanish influence on, 18; influence of Church on, 17; influence of troubadour love system on, 17; Italian, 19; Latin, 19; learned, 19; medieval, 15; modern social, 28; narrative intricacy in, 19–20; of Renaissance, 15–16; Romanesque, 18, 20; Romantic, 18; Spanish influence on Italian comedy, 18; Terentian, 19
Comici dell'arte, 15–16
Commedia erudita, 15–16
Comment on devient mage (Péladan), 291
Comrades (Strindberg), 254; discussed, 259–260, 261
Congreve, William, 52
The Conscious Lovers (Steele), 53
La Converzione del peccatore a Dio (1591) (Leoni), 28
Copenhagen Dagmar Theatre, 281
Coquelin, Ernest, 401
Les Corbeaux (Becque), 105–107, 108, 133, 159, 371
Coriolanus (Shakespeare), 247
Corneille, Pierre, 5, 31, 41, 43, 46, 53, 66, 108, 262; on action of Andromède, 20; baroque style of, 42; critical writings and methods of, 39–40; discusses Horace, 39; influence of, 32, 34; insistence on truth, 42; and Le Cid, 34–38, 39–40; quoted on comic and tragic poetry, 51; quoted on Le Cid, 32; and Racine, 43, 44, 45
Corpus Hermeticum, 375
Contile, Luca, 17
Council of Trent, 17, 27
Courbet, Gustave, 97
La Course au flambeau (Hervieu), 114
Courteline, Georges, 110

Cousin, Victor, 78
La Couvée (Brieux), 114
Crébillon, Prosper Jolyot, 59
Creditors (Strindberg), 254, 262, 264, 274, 309, 319; discussed, 278–281
Crime and Crime (Strindberg), 213, 308; discussed, 308–311
Crime and Punishment (Dostoievski), 393
La Critique de l'École des femmes (Molière), quoted, 51
Croce, Benedetto, quoted on mal du siècle, 182
The Crown Bride (Strindberg), 342; discussed, 321–342
Cubism, 364
Curel, Françoise de, 110, 115
Cusanus, Nicolas, 15

Dadaism, 8, 364, 397
Dalila (Feuillet), 309
Damaged Goods (Brieux), 162
La Dame aux camélias (1852) (Dumas), 80
The Dance of Death (Strindberg), 293, 348; discussed, 315–319
Dante Alighieri, 12, 34, 52, 287, 304
Darwin, Charles, 262
The Day of Ressurection (Ibsen) (see also When We Dead Awaken), 222
Death of a Salesman (Miller), 5, 88, 398
Debussy, Claude, 398
De l'Allemagne (1813) (De Staël), 48
Della Porta, G. B., 20, 42
Demetrius, and epic style, 26
Le Demi-monde (1854) (Dumas), 71, 79, 80
De Quincey, Thomas, 287, 377
The Descent of Man (Darwin), 262
Design for Living (Coward), 77
Desprez, Louis, 255, 263
De sma (Strindberg), 261
De stora (Strindberg), 261
Determinism, and naturalism, 402
The Devil's Disciple (Shaw), 400
Dickens, Charles, effect on Strindberg, 254

A SELECTED LIST OF *Universal Library* TITLES

HISTORY AND POLITICAL SCIENCE

LITERARY CRITICISM, DRAMA, AND POETRY

TITLES OF GENERAL INTEREST